SLAVE REVOLT ON SCREEN

CARIBBEAN
STUDIES
SERIES

Anton L. Allahar and Natasha Barnes
Series Editors

SLAVE REVOLT ON SCREEN

The Haitian Revolution in Film and Video Games

ALYSSA GOLDSTEIN SEPINWALL

University Press of Mississippi / Jackson

The University Press of Mississippi is the scholarly publishing agency of the Mississippi Institutions of Higher Learning: Alcorn State University, Delta State University, Jackson State University, Mississippi State University, Mississippi University for Women, Mississippi Valley State University, University of Mississippi, and University of Southern Mississippi.

www.upress.state.ms.us

The University Press of Mississippi is a member of the Association of University Presses.

First printing 2021
∞

Library of Congress Cataloging-in-Publication Data

Names: Sepinwall, Alyssa Goldstein, 1970– author.
Title: Slave revolt on screen : the Haitian revolution in film and video games / Alyssa Goldstein Sepinwall.
Other titles: Caribbean studies series (Jackson, Miss.)
Description: Jackson : University Press of Mississippi, 2021. | Series: Caribbean studies series | Includes bibliographical references and index.
Identifiers: LCCN 2021006498 (print) | LCCN 2021006499 (ebook) | ISBN 9781496833105 (hardback) | ISBN 9781496833112 (trade paperback) | ISBN 9781496833129 (epub) | ISBN 9781496833136 (epub) | ISBN 9781496833143 (pdf) | ISBN 9781496833150 (pdf)
Subjects: LCSH: Revolutions in motion pictures. | Blacks in motion pictures. | Haiti—History—Revolution, 1791–1804.
Classification: LCC F1923 .S47 2021 (print) | LCC F1923 (ebook) | DDC 972.94/03—dc23
LC record available at https://lccn.loc.gov/2021006498
LC ebook record available at https://lccn.loc.gov/2021006499

British Library Cataloging-in-Publication Data available

CONTENTS

Part III: Video Games on Slavery and the Haitian Revolution

SLAVE REVOLT ON SCREEN

INTRODUCTION

In 2016, comedian Chris Rock hosted the eighty-eighth Academy Awards. The dearth of Black nominees that year had sparked an outcry, symbolized by the hashtag #OscarsSoWhite. Rock addressed this controversy in a provocative opening monologue, highlighting racism in Hollywood and beyond. He joked that the Oscars should be called the "White People's Choice Awards." And, interspersed with jokes on topics like Rihanna's panties, Rock invoked painful parts of the past such as lynchings. Prior to 2016, he noted, there had been equally few Black nominees, but not the same protests: "Why? Because we had real things to protest [back then], you know? . . . When your grandmother's swinging from a tree, it's really hard to care about best documentary foreign short."[1]

Some commentators interpreted Rock as belittling the #OscarsSoWhite movement. However, Rock was engaging in a bit of mischief in suggesting that protests about Hollywood racism were new. Rock himself had long complained about the industry's hostility to serious films about Black History. In 2014, his independently produced film *Top Five* (which he wrote, directed, and starred in) told the story of a Black actor/director named André Allen, who decides to make a film about slave revolt, centered on the Haitian Revolution. Allen enthusiastically tells others about the significance of that revolution, and he urges them to see his film. However, *Top Five*'s white characters have never heard of the Haitian Revolution, and they are hostile to a film about slave revolt, because it chronicles Black violence against whites. Allen's film within a film becomes a catastrophic flop. *Top Five* subtly pointed to Hollywood's avoidance of subjects like the Haitian Revolution and its near-total disinterest in portraying Black revolutionaries sympathetically. However, film critics largely overlooked this message, focusing on other themes in Rock's film.

This book presents the first-ever overview of the Haitian Revolution in film, providing serious analysis to complement Rock's humor. As a historian of Haiti,[2] I interrogate the relative invisibility of this event in cinema, especially compared to other revolutions. I ask what it is about Haiti's revolution—and slave revolt more generally—that has seemed so radioactive to film funders. I also explore how the economic legacies of slavery and colonialism warp cinematic portrayals of the past, leaving audiences with distorted understandings of history.

The Haitian Revolution (1791–1804), long forgotten outside of Haiti, was one of the major events of modern world history. Taking place in what was then a French colony called Saint-Domingue, the Revolution was the first uprising of enslaved Africans in the New World to succeed in creating an independent state. This revolution sent shockwaves throughout the Atlantic world. For slaveowners in the US, Europe, and Latin America, it conjured up a terrifying alternative universe in which whites could lose their property and even their lives. For enslaved peoples, the Haitian Revolution served as a beacon of hope.

The twists and turns of this event, in which enslaved Haitians and their allies defeated French revolutionary forces and then Napoleon, have inspired hundreds of epic histories and novels.[3] Some of them have brought to life the Revolution's iconic generals; others have portrayed the ordinary men and women who suffered through enslavement before attaining freedom. Fictional accounts of the Revolution have been penned by giants in world literature from Victor Hugo to C. L. R. James, as well as Haitian writers such as Évelyne Trouillot and Marie-Vieux Chauvet. In addition to novels, many plays, operas, and paintings on the Revolution have been created, including by iconic Harlem Renaissance figures like Langston Hughes and Jacob Lawrence.[4]

Despite so many literary and artistic treatments, far fewer films on the Revolution exist. As Robert Toplin has noted, revolutions and wars are staples of big-budget epics.[5] Numerous films have been made on the American, French, Russian and Chinese Revolutions. However, though scholars increasingly recognize the importance of Haiti's revolution in creating modern ideas of freedom, there has been no true epic on the topic. Charles Forsdick and Christian Høgsbjerg have called the lack of such a film centered on the revolutionary general Toussaint Louverture "a particularly surprising omission given the epic treatment regularly granted to Louverture's contemporary, Napoleon Bonaparte, who has now been portrayed, with varying emphases, by over 200 different actors," from Marlon Brando to Danny DeVito.[6]

In providing the first comprehensive analysis of Haitian Revolution cinema, I examine both how films portray this event and why more films on the subject do not exist.[7] While there has never been a big-budget epic on the Revolution, films in other genres do exist. I also present a host of planned feature films that were never made, real-life illustrations of the points Rock made in *Top Five*. Surprisingly, although many scholars have analyzed novels and plays on the event,[8] the subject of Haitian Revolution film has attracted scant attention.[9]

In tracing the conceptual problems of films on the Revolution, I draw on Michel-Rolph Trouillot's ideas about the event's "unthinkability" for non-Haitians (explained in greater detail in chapter 1); I explain how the Revolution's significance has often been minimized even when it is shown on screen. The best-known films related to the Revolution—*The Emperor Jones*, *Burn!*, and the French *Toussaint Louverture* miniseries—have been made by non-Haitians. I argue that, even when they are well intentioned, foreign filmmakers often distort the Revolution's history, resorting to stereotypes about Haitians and people of African descent in general. Even as I highlight the flaws of foreign films on the Revolution, I also uncover a neglected corpus of Revolution-related films by Haitians.

Given the "failures of narration" (to borrow a phrase from Trouillot) in most foreign Haitian Revolution films—and the limited viewership for films by Haitians—I turn also to an overlooked set of multimedia representations of the Revolution: video games. I note that depictions of slave revolt in Haiti in games like *Assassin's Creed: Freedom Cry*, which are quite cinematic in appearance, have reached millions more viewers than Revolution-related films. Yet these games—and others on Atlantic slavery—have been ignored by historians. *Slave Revolt on Screen* therefore is not only the first book on Haitian Revolution film, but also the first on video games about the Revolution, the first on slavery games by a historian, and one of the very first about video games on any topic by a historian.[10]

In analyzing Revolution-related films and games, I seek to contribute to multiple scholarly fields and public discussions. In addition to conversations about how Hollywood depicts Black History, these fields include slavery and memory, Haitian Studies, French and French colonial history, Film and History, Cinema and Media Studies, Caribbean literature, African American history, Atlantic world history, historical methodology, and Game Studies. I draw inspiration from multiple theorists, from the anthropologist Trouillot and the Haitian social historian Carolyn Fick to the pioneering film historian Robert Rosenstone.

First, this book intervenes in discussions about how slavery (and Black History more generally) have been remembered and how they have been portrayed on screen. I argue that the Revolution's presences and absences in cinema offer unparalleled insight into these topics. As Natalie Zemon Davis noted in *Slaves on Screen: Film and Historical Vision* (2000), "slavery has been a subject of films since the early days of cinema." Davis pointed to a 1913 film about Roman slave revolt leader Spartacus, as well as to D. W. Griffith's *The Birth of a Nation* (1915).[11] The former film, it should be noted, centered on an uprising by white slaves, while the latter glorified the Ku Klux Klan while portraying Blacks viciously. As Brenda Stevenson has noted recently, early Hollywood films occasionally noted the brutality of slavery, but more commonly portrayed enslaved people "as happy, devoted, passive simpletons."[12] The patterns set by *The Birth of a Nation* and 1939's *Gone with the Wind* in erasing the brutality of slavery have only begun to be broken recently. In the last two decades, Hollywood has sought to offer more accurate portrayals of slavery in the Americas, which lead audiences to sympathize with enslaved people. Such efforts have accelerated since the #OscarsSoWhite controversy.

Nevertheless, even with increased attention to slavery, producers have generally shied away from slave revolt story lines in favor of those involving friendly whites helping enslaved people. *Amistad* (1997, dir. Steven Spielberg), *Amazing Grace* (2006, dir. Michael Apted), and *12 Years a Slave* (2013, dir. Steve McQueen) fit this pattern, as did *Free State of Jones* (2016, dir. Gary Ross).[13] Like *Amistad*, the latter film starred Matthew McConaughey as a white protagonist who wins freedom for enslaved people (in court in the former, and on the battlefield in the latter).

These treatments of slavery fit larger cinematic patterns. The controversial Oscar victory of *Green Book* (Best Picture, 2019, dir. Peter Farrelly) highlighted the prevalence of films on Black History that actually emphasize the benevolence of whites. As Hernan Vera and Andrew Gordon argue in *Screen Saviors: Hollywood Fictions of Whiteness*, the idea of "white messiahs who lead people of another color" is nearly inevitable in Hollywood films on Black History. Vera and Gordon see the white-messiah trope as a "powerful cultural myth because it presents whites with pleasing images of themselves as saviors rather than oppressors of those of other races." In describing the "white savior film" genre, Matthew Hughey has similarly explained that, in "an unsettled and racially charged time," the figure of the white savior comforts audiences by seeming to deal with difficult histories while simultaneously reinforcing "ideas of white supremacy and paternalism."[14] As the eminent sociologist Joe R. Feagin has explained, this portrayal of whites has structural roots:

> Who are the members of the U.S. moviemaking elite? Today, just a few dozen people, almost all of them white men, run the movie business. . . . Women and people of color have, at best, a marginal presence in the shaping of moviemaking and most other media enterprises. Many of the white male moviemakers are relatively liberal in their personal politics; yet when it comes to racial

> matters . . . they still offer up a mostly sanitized and whitewashed view of the . . . history of the United States.[15]

Such analyses help explain why funders greenlight films on slavery only when they include a friendly white in whose shoes audiences—and the executives—can imagine themselves. Hollywood films in which African-descended slaves are liberated peacefully with the help of a white hero have thus predominated over those that would show enslaved Africans rising up to obtain their freedom by any means necessary.

Some exceptions to these patterns exist. John Berry's 1958 *Tamango*, starring Dorothy Dandridge, featured an unsuccessful slave-ship rebellion. Med Hondo's 1979 epic musical *West Indies: Les nègres marrons de la liberté* (The Fugitive Slaves of Liberty) focused on continuities between slave resistance and post-abolition activism in the French Caribbean, while skewering the hypocrisy of French colonizers. Haile Gerima's powerful 1993 film *Sankofa* presented a brutal look at slavery, while celebrating efforts by Africans to liberate themselves. Of course, all three films were made outside of the Hollywood studio system. Berry had been blacklisted and had difficulty distributing *Tamango*.[16] *Sankofa*, as Robert Weems has noted, became a cult classic among Black audiences in urban centers but was ignored by "mainstream distributors"; as Clarence Munford has stated, "white movie-goers stayed away" from the film in "droves." And though *West Indies* was the most expensive African film ever made at the time, according to Françoise Pfaff, it was seen by limited audiences, mostly on the festival circuit.[17]

Quentin Tarantino's *Django Unchained* (2012) might also seem to be an exception, as a high-grossing major-studio picture on slave revolt. However, *Django* drew criticism for being a Blaxploitation version of slave revolt, as well as for relying on a white hero, Dr. King Schultz, who had what Joseph Vogel has called an "instructor to pupil" relationship with the slave Django. The writer Roxane Gay called *Django* a "white man's slavery revenge fantasy, . . . one in which white people figure heavily and where Black people are, largely, incidental."[18] Spike Lee famously denounced Tarantino's film on Twitter: "American Slavery Was Not [a] Sergio Leone Spaghetti Western. It Was [a] Holocaust."[19]

Adding the Haitian Revolution to conversations about slavery on screen will help us understand structures that have favored certain story lines over others. Unlike *Django*'s story, the Revolution was planned by African-descended peoples without direction from whites. Unlike the Nat Turner insurrection (the subject of Nate Parker's 2016 *The Birth of a Nation*), the Haitian Revolution was successful in overthrowing white rule and forcing slavery's end. The Revolution thus does not fit into the kinds of Black History plotlines that Hollywood prefers. In exploring failed attempts to immortalize the Revolution on screen—and highlighting the flaws of existing films and games—I illustrate how unequal divisions of film capital (between whites and Blacks in Hollywood, between filmmakers in formerly colonizing and formerly colonized countries, and between filmmakers in Haiti and elsewhere) distort cinematic depictions of slavery.

Slave Revolt on Screen also contributes to the historiographies of France and Haiti. It extends the colonial and Haitian "turns" in French history, which have examined France's imperial history outside Europe. It also adds to scholarship on the limits of French universalism, as well as on the illusions of decolonization, whereby formal control of one country by another may end, but without altering power differentials. As a function of where film capital is concentrated and because Haiti was once part of France, a sizable fraction of existing films on the Haitian Revolution have been made by French directors or in French coproductions. In analyzing these films, I highlight the difficulties that the French have had in grappling with their colonial past, as well as the economic imbalances that give French filmmakers greater power to recount Haiti's history on screen than Haitians themselves. I also illustrate that, even when French whites acknowledge slavery, they often discuss it in problematic ways. This book thus adds to recent studies of what Nicola Frith and Kate Hodgson have called the "limits of memory" in France, as well as what Crystal Fleming highlights as the persistence of racist ways of thinking underlying ostensibly color-blind commemorations.[20] I examine how French films on Haiti's revolution often emphasize the benevolence of white abolitionists—and the liberating force of French ideals—rather than the agency of enslaved people. However, rather than only analyzing metropolitan representations of colonized peoples, as a previous wave of French colonial history did, I seek to uncover Haitians' own perspectives on their history.

I also aim in this book to deepen our awareness of competing approaches to the Haitian Revolution. I seek not only to amplify Haitian accounts of their own history, but also to compare how they and non-Haitians often explain it. Though scholarly attention to Haiti's revolution has exploded in recent decades in North America and parts of Europe, scholars outside of Haiti frequently stop their analyses of the Revolution with independence in 1804.[21] However, as historians and filmmakers within Haiti recognize, the Revolution would have consequences for Haitian history far into the future, without which the event cannot be fully understood. In identifying films by Haitians, I call attention to how they view connections between the revolutionary past and the Haitian present.

In addition, I hope in this book to open up the field of Haitian cinema more generally. Rather than focus only on the content of their films, I explore the logistical challenges that Haitian filmmakers have faced since the early twentieth century. Indeed, the limited size of the Haitian film industry—especially compared to Haiti's Caribbean and Latin American neighbors—is a fascinating and little-understood subject.

In noting the absence of a high-quality feature film on the Revolution, this book also joins the efforts by Gina Ulysse, Millery Polyné, and others to interrogate dominant narratives about Haiti. I also add to conversations in Haitian Literature about how the Revolution has been represented in fiction, as well as the effects of these representations today. I argue that the Revolution's relative absence on screen has reinforced other forms of silencing this event.[22] Given that the public often learns history more from Hollywood than from historiography,[23] this absence helps the Revolution remain obscure. Unaware of Haiti's role in the birth of modern universalism, general audiences in the US and Europe imagine the country only as a place of poverty, "voodoo," and dictatorship.

In addition to contributing to Haitian Studies, I hope to add to theoretical scholarship on Film and History. Where historians once viewed films as error-filled simplifications that were irrelevant to their scholarship, new paradigms suggest that films need not get every detail right to portray the past meaningfully. Robert Rosenstone, the leading figure in these new approaches, has explained, "By academic standards, all historical films are . . . laced with fiction. Dramatic works depend upon invention to create incident, plot and character." Rosenstone notes that putting complex histories into commercial-length films often compels directors to compress characters, turning multiple individuals into composites. He and others have suggested that historical feature films should not be evaluated on whether they invent characters or details, but on whether they build historical understanding in ways that written works cannot.[24]

Nonspecialists may assume that documentaries are naturally superior to feature films in portraying the past. However, a large literature has noted that documentaries are also selective constructions, even when appearing only to present facts.[25] Dramatic films can reach broader audiences than even the most successful documentaries, and they have the potential to affect them more deeply. As Richard Francaviglia and Jerry Rodnitzky have noted, dramatic historical films can help recreate the emotions (whether "elation, anger, despair, grief, [or] fear") that historical subjects may have felt.[26] In comparing dramatic film to historical text, Rosenstone has argued that "film lets us see landscapes; hear sounds; witness strong emotions as they are expressed with body and face, or physical conflict between individuals and groups." Building on Rosenstone to analyze feature films on the Holocaust, Lawrence Baron has argued that they can be "an alternative version of history capable of imparting a more tangible sense of how past events were experienced than most academic histories can achieve. . . . Movies should not be judged by whether they are historically, politically, or theoretically 'correct' but by whether they . . . evoke a sense of the collective and individual choices and historical circumstances" of past events.[27]

Inspired by this work, I fuse multiple modes of analyzing film. I combine my expertise in Haitian and French history with that of other scholarly approaches, including cultural history analysis of representations, postcolonial studies, reception history, and memory studies. I am certainly concerned with distortions of Saint-Domingue's slave system and the Revolution, and I assess films in light of the excellent scholarship produced in recent decades. However, I do not catalog each factual error.

Indeed, building on the ideas of Trouillot, Rosenstone, and Baron, I am less interested in mistakes like incorrectly dating the Bois Caïman ceremony (a key moment in launching the Revolution) than in larger failures of narration that dehumanize the revolutionaries or sanitize colonialism. For instance, given research on resistance among enslaved peoples in Haiti long before 1789, I am more critical of films that overemphasize the role of French ideas in the Haitian Revolution—or which fixate on retributive Black violence instead of the brutality by white slaveowners that prompted it—than I am of films that err on more minor points.[28]

Still, I remain interested in films with flawed analytical frameworks from the standpoint of memory studies. Using a concept popularized by Pierre Nora, Claudy Delné has referred to foreign novels on the Haitian Revolution as *lieux de mémoire*, sites of memory, illustrating how the Revolution has been remembered.[29] Similarly, I consider films on the Revolution from around the world as revealing diverse ideas about this event, thus serving as a kind of popular historiography. Finally, I draw upon Robert Toplin's notion of three levels of historical film analysis. The first two (analyzing a finished film for its content and tracing its reception history) are relatively common among historians who study film. But Toplin noted in 2003 that "only a few historians" had performed what he calls a "third and deeper level" of historical film analysis: excavating debates behind the production of films. I deploy all three levels, in varying degrees depending on the film. I look at production particularly for *Lydia Bailey*, as well as for failed efforts to make Revolution films and for films and games whose creators I have been able to interview.[30]

My including video games alongside films also seeks to forge new paths within the discipline of History. Though Game Studies and its subfield Historical Game Studies have exploded since the early 2000s in fields such as Literature and Sociology, the same has not been true in History. Whereas the Popular Culture Association and the Society for Cinema and Media Studies routinely feature multiple panels on historical video games, the American Historical Association's annual meetings have not paid the same attention to the field.[31] Historians have traditionally ignored video games, on the assumption that they trivialize the past. This attitude has begun to change slightly.[32]

However, as Game Studies scholars have noted, historical video games can reach millions more players than an independent film; titles like *Assassin's Creed: Freedom Cry* are not only cinematic in appearance but have budgets larger than most feature films. Adam Chapman has noted that digital history games often surpass movies among younger generations in how they learn about the past. He adds that, whether or not players buy such games intending to learn history, they are "exposed to . . . the historical representations that these games entail." As Soraya Murray has argued, scholars must analyze these representations: "The faulty idea that video games are unimportant galvanizes their power. This allows them to proceed unchecked in the world . . . , without the same modicum of accountability and critical analysis that even films and theatre bear."[33]

Though historians are not accustomed to thinking of cinema and video games as analogous, a large literature in Cinema and New Media Studies has examined similarities between these forms. As Mark J. P. Wolf declared in *The Medium of the Video Game* (2001), "many of the same issues and concepts in film theory can also be applied to video games." Stephen Keane noted that the "figure of the screen" is common to both forms, as well as television. In addition, movies increasingly have taken the form of video games—whether adapting well-known game franchises into screenplays or using computer-generated game aesthetics in action movies. Meanwhile, many video games use cinematic techniques and have cinematic-style cutscenes (short film interludes between tasks), or are spin-offs of movie franchises. As Keane notes, "The most cinematic games are very much presented like films with title sequences, closing credits, 'realistic' sound effects, and an overall musical soundtrack that provides narrative- and character-based themes."[34]

Rosenstone has recognized this commonality and endorsed a digital turn by historians. In a 2017 update to his classic book *History on Film/Film on*

History, Rosenstone noted that the approaches he and others called for in the late 1980s legitimized the field of Film and History. But he insisted that historians' efforts to rethink audiovisual representations of the past should "not apply only to motion pictures or television." He added that new approaches to film were "but a first step towards investigating all the forms of historical representation and thought that currently flash across our computer screens, or appear in video games."[35]

Given games' popularity and the ideas of theorists like Rosenstone, I see video game depictions of slave revolt in Saint-Domingue as just as important to study as cinematic ones. As I note in chapter 9, there are debates about whether something as horrific as slavery can be treated respectfully in a game. Nevertheless, some of these "interactive fictions" or "interactive films"[36] present subaltern perspectives better—and make the Haitian Revolution more "thinkable"—than most existing films. Such games, as I explain, have been created not only by North American gaming companies but also by descendants of enslaved peoples in the Caribbean. I argue that the best games force identification with African-descended characters; they show Black revolutionary violence as a rational response to white enslavers' cruelty. Indeed, the techniques historically used in cinema to make slavery palatable to white audiences (white heroes and happy slaves) are absent from these games. Because I am comparing games to cinema, I focus on the narrative aspects of games (cutscenes and other in-game text) that are most analogous to films.[37]

More generally, I aim to help historians rethink the kinds of sources we can use in our research. I was trained as an eighteenth-century intellectual historian, studying revolutions by mining manuscript correspondence and political pamphlets. While I focus in this book on popular culture, I have used many traditional kinds of sources. Chapter 3 is based on multiarchival research in the papers of several individuals involved in *Lydia Bailey*. Chapter 4 uses unpublished correspondence to uncover never-completed film projects. In addition to manuscript sources like letters and script drafts, I draw on print forms customarily used to trace reception history, from box office statistics to published reviews by critics. In addition, I have used bibliographic and filmographic databases to identify overlooked films.

Beyond these traditional sources, I draw on others that historians do not normally use. Inspired by Trouillot and others, I recognize that official archives privilege the ideas and experiences of elites.[38] To overcome these limits, I have looked in nontraditional places for information on film/game reception and sought to generate my own archive on films and games. These nontraditional sources range from tweets showing popular reception of multimedia forms, to game code, to YouTube videos posted by filmmakers with limited access to formal distribution channels. I have also sought to bypass the absences in formal press circuits by conducting my own interviews with independent filmmakers and game developers. In highlighting these sources, I hope to suggest new means for understanding popular memories of slavery and for accessing the views of those not included in official archives. My work intersects with the Decolonize Media movement in Cinema Studies and social media,[39] as well as with scholarship that has focused on digital film and new modes of distribution.[40] I focus not only on images created by Hollywood (or only on expensive feature films) but also on digital films made by those with lesser access to traditional distribution channels. In addition, my effort to uncover Haitian perspectives aims to decolonize our understanding of the Age of Revolutions more generally.

Before beginning my analysis, I want to present a general time line of the Revolution; I offer it not only to nonspecialists but also to readers familiar with the Revolution who want to understand the historiographical lens that I bring to my analysis.[41] Historians now consider the Revolution a unique event in world history, one that helped birth modern egalitarian ideals.[42] The Revolution took place in the western part of Hispaniola, which the French had seized in the seventeenth century and called Saint-Domingue. Saint-Domingue became the New World's richest colony. However, that prosperity came at a price: the colony's wealth depended on the labor of kidnapped Africans transported across the Atlantic to work on plantations. Saint-Domingue's slaveowners were among the most brutal in the Americas. By forcing enslaved people to do backbreaking labor, they gained enormous profits; Saint-Domingue was the Atlantic world's largest producer of coffee and sugar.[43] As Carolyn Fick has noted, slave resistance had long taken diverse forms in the colony, from *marronage* (running away) to suicide, since the chances of armed rebellion were slight and attempts at open resistance were met with unspeakable brutality.[44] François Makandal, a Vodou priest accused of leading a conspiracy to poison slaveowners, was burned at the stake in Cap Français in 1758; others suspected of planning revolt were subjected to other inhumane tortures.[45]

The French Revolution of 1789 changed the situation in the colony. Following Carolyn Fick, I view the French Revolution's impact not in terms of its ideology; enslaved people did not need to learn about France's Declaration of the Rights of Man to know that they wanted to be freed from slavery. However, France's revolution presented a window of opportunity for the colony's enslaved people, during which they realized that armed resistance might for the first time succeed. Indeed, as John Thornton has indicated, many newly arrived slaves in Saint-Domingue were veterans of African conflicts, with military training they were eager to use once they had an opportunity. Thornton argues further that the French Revolution likely did not provide enslaved people with their notions of liberty, but that they drew instead on African political theory, particularly from the Kingdom of Kongo.[46]

As Parisian conflicts spread to the colony in 1789–91, French whites began fighting with each other as well as with free people of color. Whites loyal to the king fought others who wanted more autonomy, as in the fights in North America between those loyal to the Crown and those who wanted independence. Meanwhile, Vincent Ogé and other free people of color (derisively termed "mulattoes" at the time)[47] used the French Revolution as an occasion to contest the discriminatory laws—somewhat akin to Jim Crow—that colonial whites had been passing since the 1760s.

To colonists' horror, amid this conflict between (and among) whites and free people of color, enslaved people launched their own freedom struggle. This revolution began in the north of the colony in August 1791, reportedly after a Vodou ceremony in the Bois Caïman forest organized by a Jamaican-born enslaved person named Boukman Dutty and a priestess named Cécile Fatiman.[48] Soon, this movement spread to the rest of Saint-Domingue. After Boukman's death, several generals continued the Revolution, including Georges Biassou and Jean-François Papillon. Ultimately, Toussaint Louverture, an aide to Biassou, took over the Revolution's direction. The formerly enslaved Toussaint (figure 0.1), who is often referred to by his first name à la Napoleon, had been free even before the Revolution's start, but his wife Suzanne and his children seem to have still been enslaved. After being manumitted himself, Toussaint had operated his own small plantation, renting enslaved people to support himself and to try to buy loved ones out of slavery.[49] Once the Revolution started, Louverture chose to fight on the side of enslaved people rather than free people of color. He strategically leveraged the rivalry between different European powers over the course of the 1790s, fighting for Spain before the French agreed to abolish slavery (1794), and switching afterward to the French army.

From 1794, slavery was officially abolished in Saint-Domingue. An earlier scholarship celebrated abolition as the result of a magnanimous decree that year by French revolutionaries in Paris. More recently, some scholars have emphasized the role of commissioners sent from Paris (Sonthonax and Polverel) in abolishing slavery in the colony in 1793. Others have contended that slavery was not abolished by French beneficence, but achieved by enslaved people themselves after successfully overthrowing their enslavers, a perspective that I share.[50]

Figure 0.1. Portrait of Toussaint Louverture, ca. 1800. Wikimedia Commons. Original at the John Carter Brown Library.

With abolition in place, Saint-Domingue remained a French colony in the late 1790s. As France battled Spain and Great Britain in the French Revolutionary Wars, Toussaint Louverture and other Haitian revolutionaries became generals in the French army; they were particularly eager that the colony not be conquered by an empire maintaining slavery. In 1796–1800, General Toussaint Louverture became the colony's most powerful figure. While envisioning that Saint-Domingue remain part of France, he eventually declared himself the colony's governor-general and authored a constitution for it in 1801. After Napoleon's armies attempted to remove him from power and reimpose slavery in 1802 (led first by Napoleon's brother-in-law General Charles Leclerc and later by other generals), the former slaves of Saint-Domingue fought back. Louverture himself was captured and sent to prison in France, where he died in 1803. However, he was correct in predicting that the "tree of liberty of the blacks" would continue growing without him.

On New Year's Day in 1804, Jean-Jacques Dessalines, who had been one of Toussaint's generals, declared Haitian independence. Dessalines was crowned emperor of Haiti later that year, but was assassinated in 1806 amid struggles between Toussaint's former lieutenants. After Dessalines's death, Haiti split into two regimes, each helmed by a rival revolutionary general. Henri Christophe, who had been enslaved before the Revolution, led the North, which became a monarchy in 1811 after Christophe declared himself King Henry I. Alexandre Pétion, who had been a wealthy free person of color before the Revolution, led a military republic in the South. The leaders of Christophe's regime tended to be *nouveaux libres* (enslaved people freed by the Revolution), while *anciens libres* (those who had been free even before the Revolution) predominated in Pétion's government. Pétion was succeeded after his death in 1818 by Jean-Pierre Boyer, another *ancien libre* who had fought in the Revolution.

In 1820, Christophe, who had forced his people to build a massive fortress called the Citadelle, committed suicide rather than be overthrown. Following Christophe's death, Boyer reunited both states into one Republic of Haiti. France had refused to recognize the country's independence after 1804, and other major powers (including the United States) had followed suit. In 1825, France agreed to recognize Haiti in exchange for an indemnity of 150 million francs. Boyer's decision to pay this amount in order to be integrated into the community of nations remains controversial in Haiti; the young nation did not have sufficient funds, and the interest on this debt remained a crushing obligation for Haiti into the twentieth century.

As this overview makes clear, the Revolution had many key figures. Novels and plays on the Revolution feature different protagonists, from Makandal,

Toussaint, and Christophe, to fictional characters; the same is true for films. Toussaint reigns in the twenty-first century as the most famous revolutionary; several recent projects were planned as biopics of him. However, in the mid-twentieth century, Henri Christophe was more famous in the US; films and unmade projects of that era focused on him.[51] Some films and games about slave resistance have featured Boukman or Makandal; a few mention women revolutionaries alongside Dessalines and other men.[52] Films and games examining the ripple effects of the Revolution elsewhere—from Cuba to Curaçao to New Orleans—also feature fictional characters inspired by Haitian icons.

Slave Revolt on Screen thus looks at a variety of Revolution-related story lines, in films and games from around the world. Part I centers on foreign (non-Haitian) films on the Revolution. Chapter 1 details Trouillot's ideas about the Revolution's unthinkability to foreigners, before analyzing the small corpus of feature films related to the Revolution. I look at the comparatively well-known films *The Emperor Jones* (1933), *Burn!* (1969), and the *Toussaint Louverture* miniseries (2012), as well as the lesser-known drama *Royal Bonbon* (2002); I consider how each of them distorts the history of the Revolution. I turn in chapter 2 to lesser-known films from the Caribbean that invoke the Revolution's influence or legacy. A few better acknowledge the Revolution's historical significance, but they are not without flaws.

Chapter 3 continues my analysis of foreign features, focusing on *Lydia Bailey* (1952, 20th Century Fox), Hollywood's only film set during the Revolution.[53] Because of its uniqueness and available archives, I analyze *Lydia Bailey* in greater detail than the films in chapters 1 and 2. I place the film within the histories of Cold War and decolonization cinema as well as that of race in postwar Hollywood film. I explore how *Lydia Bailey* treated Haitian leaders sympathetically, while deploying stereotypes about Haiti and Blacks in general. I note that the producers did not set out to make a film on the Revolution; they deliberately focused on white characters while keeping the Revolution in the background. Finally, I discuss reactions to this film in the US, Haiti, and Europe, and why it has fallen into obscurity.

Chapter 4 chronicles a host of planned epics on the Revolution, across the twentieth and twenty-first centuries, which were never made. I show that such films have been proposed by several Hollywood legends and world cinema giants. Because the Revolution's story line features violence by African-descended people, with no "white heroes" (unless producers wanted to credit the Revolution's success to Sonthonax, the French abolitionist abbé Grégoire, or more minor figures[54]), these projects failed to obtain funding. I situate the problem of making a Haitian Revolution epic within the larger challenge of funding serious stories about Black History. Chapter 5 revisits the topic of failed films on the Revolution by focusing on Chris Rock's *Top Five*. I explore how Rock used the Revolution to make a larger critique about white disinterest in the value of Black lives, whether in the past or present.

After examining the limits of existing feature films, I turn in chapter 6 to other genres of film by non-Haitians about the Revolution. I discuss feature-length documentaries from France and the US, live-action shorts, and the groundbreaking animated short *Black Dawn* (1978). I note that documentaries and short films reach more limited audiences than dramas, but remain important for what they reveal about the memory of the Revolution in France and North America. In this chapter, I also introduce another layer in the story of how structural inequalities influence screen representations of the Revolution; I show how, even as independent filmmakers everywhere struggle for resources, non-Haitians have many more opportunities for funding than do Haitians.

Part II turns from foreign representations of the Revolution to Haitians' visions of their own history. I explain that, even though Haitians have not yet produced an epic on their Revolution, they have presented their perspectives in other kinds of film. The films treated in part II come from Haiti's leading directors as well as emerging ones. Given how funding and other obstacles have limited the number of films by Haitians, I also consider a handful of films made by foreign directors in Haiti with heavy Haitian participation and narrative content. Chapter 7 begins by exploring the history of Haitian cinema and the challenges that have prevented it from attaining the size of other national cinemas. Next, I present Revolution-related films by Haitians. Chapter 7 focuses on documentaries and dramas (made either in Haiti or the diaspora) concerning the Revolution's legacy as refracted through the Duvalier era, the 2004 Bicentennial of the Revolution, or the 2010 earthquake. While these films generally offer better treatments of the Revolution than those discussed in earlier chapters, they are not epics and have been seen by fewer people.

Like chapter 7, chapter 8 focuses on films by Haitians, and it notes differences between their approaches to the Revolution and those of many non-Haitian films. It differs from chapter 7 in two ways. First, it shifts from established filmmakers like Arnold Antonin or Raoul Peck (who have their own production companies or nonprofits) to younger filmmakers without access to such capital. Secondly, it moves from films treating the Revolution indirectly to films centered on it. I look at a trio of documentaries on Toussaint Louverture from a new generation of Haitian filmmakers. Rather than only analyze the content of their films, I also discuss how funding impacts their ability to make films. Finally, I show that non-Haitian filmmakers are not the only ones who have tried in vain to make epics on the Revolution. I examine how Raoul Peck and others have been thwarted in their attempts to make such films—films that had the potential to be better than any by non-Haitians.

After describing the limitations of foreign films on the Revolution and the smaller audiences for films by Haitians, I turn in part III to video games concerning slave revolt in Saint-Domingue. I show that, unlike their counterparts in Hollywood, video game funders have not shied away from depicting violence by enslaved peoples. Because historians have largely ignored video games, I begin chapter 9 with a theoretical discussion of whether they are worth studying and how to approach them. To contextualize games invoking slave revolt in Haiti, I examine earlier games on slavery and slave revolt from the US and Europe. In the chapter's final section, I analyze games made in North America that invoke or center on slave revolt in Saint-Domingue. I focus on the widely played game *Assassin's Creed: Freedom Cry*, which I consider the best of the North American games.

Chapter 10 turns to games related to slave revolt in Haiti that were created in the French Caribbean. These titles, predating those discussed in chapter 9, seem to have been the earliest games ever made on Atlantic slavery. They were created by Caribbean intellectuals who used interactive fiction to honor their ancestors and preserve the memory of slavery. Though scholarship on his work has not mentioned this fact, I reveal that the creators of such games include Patrick Chamoiseau, one of the Caribbean's most eminent novelists and theorists. Indeed, Chamoiseau (working with the groundbreaking game developer Muriel Tramis) created two games in the late 1980s. I offer detailed analyses of their games, made by French game company Coktel Vision, considering how they differ from North American games.

Finally, in the conclusion, I move from Haitian Revolution films to *Planet of the Apes*, *The Birth of a Nation*, and *Black Panther*, to examine what they suggest about the future of the patterns I have traced. I hope that this book will demonstrate that popular-culture representations of the Haitian Revolution—and of slavery more generally—require historians' attention. In an age of controversies over Confederate monuments and ongoing demonization of Black responses to white violence, how slavery is depicted in cinema, games, and other forms of popular memory demands increased scrutiny. As Vincent Brown has noted, "because slaveholders wrote the first draft of history, subsequent historiography has strained to escape from their point of view."[55] The same pattern exists in visual media; centuries after the Age of Abolition, descendants of slaveowners and of enslaved peoples have unequal resources—and thus asymmetrical access to defining slavery in global public culture. Until we recognize and rectify these inequities, the public's knowledge of the past will remain distorted.

Part I

FOREIGN VIEWS OF THE REVOLUTION

1

AN UNTHINKABLE PLOT?

The Haitian Revolution in US and European Feature Films

Haiti's revolution is a subject well suited for an epic film—a grand struggle, with a cast of thousands, during a time of war. However, there has never been a true epic on the Revolution. This chapter and the next two therefore treat the small corpus of feature films from around the world (full-length dramas if not epics) related to the Haitian Revolution. Some of them have been epic in theme and scope, even without the lavish sets and costumes typically associated with the genre.[1] Still, I argue, none of them does justice to the Revolution. The makers of these films either could not conceive of people of African descent designing their own revolution, or they could not imagine them carrying it out in a dignified fashion. The conceptual failure of these features, I suggest, bolsters Michel-Rolph Trouillot's arguments about the Revolution having been "unthinkable" to European and US whites. The weaknesses of these films are especially unfortunate given funding structures that have enabled US and European directors to represent the Revolution on screen more easily than Haitians themselves.[2]

This chapter begins by considering the earliest cinematic depictions of Haiti, in US zombie horror films. I then consider how three films from different periods and places (*The Emperor Jones* [1933, US], *Burn!* [also called *Queimada*, 1969, Italy], and *Toussaint Louverture* [2012, France]) improved on these images but still fell short in representing the Revolution. These films are among the most epic in style of any Revolution-related films; however, only *Toussaint Louverture* centers on the Revolution, while the other two use it as inspiration for a fictional story. Both *The Emperor Jones* and *Burn!* depict struggles between an African-descended leader, modeled after Toussaint or Christophe, and a manipulative white man seeking to control him. I also examine a Christophe-related feature film (*Royal Bonbon*, 2002) from a French director.

My analysis here and in subsequent chapters is inspired by Trouillot's idea of the Revolution's "unthinkability" to non-Haitian whites. Trouillot's 1995 *Silencing the Past: Power and the Production of History* has been one of the most important books in the humanities and social sciences of the last twenty-five years. In its chapter "An Unthinkable History: The Haitian Revolution as a Non-Event," Trouillot argued that whites in the eighteenth century, imbued with racism, found the idea of slaves deciding to revolt to be unthinkable. Because they could not process the Revolution once it happened, Trouillot contended, they sought to ignore it. Trouillot argued further that colonists' attempts to erase the Revolution from their consciousness was continued by generations of whites, including many modern historians.[3]

In examining this suppression, Trouillot divided most foreign writing on Haiti's revolution into two categories: "formulas of erasure" and "formulas of banalization." Where the first ignored the Revolution, the second acknowledged it while dismissing its significance. Banalizers, he argued, "empty a number of singular events of their revolutionary content so that the entire string of facts . . . becomes trivialized." Either they suggested that enslaved people could not have led the Revolution ("the uprising must have been 'prompted,' 'provoked,' or 'suggested' by some higher being than the slaves themselves: royalists, mulattoes, or other external agents") or they assumed that Africans could not have had independent ideas about freedom and must have been awakened by French ideals. Trouillot continued, "Many historians are more willing to accept the idea that slaves could have been influenced by whites and free mulattoes, with whom we know they had limited contacts, than . . . to accept the idea that slaves could have convinced other slaves that they had the right to revolt."[4]

While critiquing foreign scholarship on the Revolution, Trouillot acknowledged that Haitian scholarship itself was not perfect. Haitian scholars, he noted, have lesser access to archives than scholars in France or the US. In addition, he argued, their work was sometimes "too respect[ful]" of the Revolution's leaders. Trouillot also conceded that specialists outside Haiti were creating work that is "increasingly sophisticated and rich empirically." Nevertheless, he argued, the "vocabulary [of this foreign scholarship] and often its entire discursive framework recall frighteningly those of the eighteenth century. Papers and monographs take the tone of plantation records." Trouillot further contended that, even if foreign historians did not intend to be racist, they often could not help themselves, for "the narrative structures of Western historiography" were rooted in an "ontology" that saw non-Europeans as subhuman.[5]

A number of studies have appeared challenging Trouillot's ideas, and questioning the extent to which the Revolution was in fact unthinkable to foreigners. Certainly, the silencing of the Revolution was not total, as David Geggus, Ada Ferrer, Sybille Fischer, and Yun Kyoung Kwon have shown. Moreover, as I have argued elsewhere, the Revolution has become progressively less unthinkable for non-Haitians.[6]

Nevertheless, even as foreign scholars increasingly study the Haitian Revolution, they have tended to view it differently from Haitians. Though discourses of erasure have declined since the publication of *Silencing the Past*, at least in North American academia, discourses of banalization have continued. Mirroring the famous French revolutionary images showing an African man and woman declaring "Moi libre aussi" (Me free too) (figure 1.1), one strain of scholarship has depicted enslaved people in Saint-Domingue as mimics of French ideals. Such analysis implies that they were not intelligent enough to conceive of rebelling themselves, but did so only after overhearing talk from white Frenchmen about "liberty, equality, and fraternity." This mode of thought overlooks the many ways in which enslaved people in Saint-Domingue had resisted slavery long before 1789.[7] It also reflects certain assumptions of Eurocentric thinking more generally, by portraying non-Westerners as passive objects who act only when awakened by European ideas.

In cinema, in contrast, both types of silencing endure. The most dominant cinematic treatment of the Revolution has been erasure: the topic rarely appears on screen. As Claudy Delné has written, though "films on the French and American Revolutions are legion," filmmakers seem to be uncomfortable with "the victory of the blacks . . . and the defeat of whites being immortalized visually."[8] The cinematic silencing of the Revolution fits a larger pattern of Western directors' discomfort with slavery, two centuries after the Age of Abolition.

When the Revolution does appear on screen, discourses of banalization are common. As I illustrate in this and subsequent chapters, non-Haitian filmmakers who treat the Revolution generally render it an intellectual byproduct of France's revolution. They have struggled to conceive of the Haitian Revolution as an autonomous movement in which enslaved Africans masterminded their own struggle while profiting from infighting among the French. Where films do acknowledge African influences on enslaved people's decisions to revolt (for example, in invoking Vodou), they generally do not portray African culture positively, from the gaze of Africans themselves; instead, they use

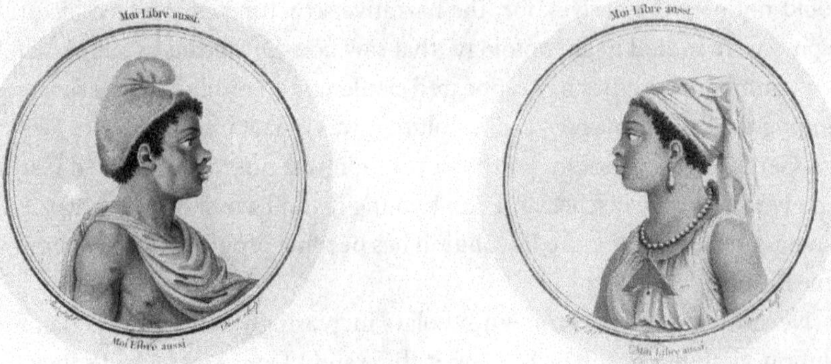

Figure 1.1. *Moi libre aussi* (Me Free Too) images. J.-Louis Darcis and Simon-Louis Boizot, ca. 1795. Wikimedia Commons.

it as a marker of primitivism and backwardness. While some foreign feature films are better in this regard than others, they tend either to suggest that the Haitian Revolution's leaders were savages who revolted under the influence of drunk "voodoo" priests, or that Haitians learned about freedom from white Frenchmen and wanted to copy it.

An Early Hollywood Feature: *The Emperor Jones* and the US Occupation of Haiti

Hollywood interest in Haiti began early in the twentieth century, prompted by US intervention in the country. Though Haiti should have been able to enjoy full sovereignty after its independence, the US and other foreign governments sought to prevent Haiti's success long after 1804. In addition to the indemnity Haiti was pressured to pay to France, the country was isolated in numerous other ways.[9] The US (which remained a slaveholding country) continued to treat Haiti as a den of criminality from which Africans might export revolution. In the 1850s, amid expansionist fervor following the US-Mexico War, some Americans called for annexing Haiti to the US. The *New York Herald* pushed for Haitian emperor Faustin Soulouque (whom it called a "baboon") to be punished for purported mistreatment of US businessmen, and for the "n*** population of Hayti" to be "licked into good behavior."[10] Though the US finally recognized Haiti in 1862 during its Civil War, calls for occupying Haiti continued. These plans came to fruition in 1915, when the US invaded the country on pretext of ensuring stability (but in fact to help US business interests). Haitians resisted this invasion bitterly. Charlemagne Péralte, a Haitian military officer, led this resistance; after the Marines killed him, he became a national icon. Though the occupation was challenged not only by Haitians but also some Americans (especially African Americans and white peace activists), the US retained control of the country until 1934. The occupation forced Haitians to do compulsory labor; it was presided over by Marines such as Colonel Littleton Waller, who declared that he "knew the n*** and how to handle him."[11]

Popular culture in the US during this era reflected these prejudices; negative images of Haiti permeated the film industry sprouting in Hollywood. "Zombie" pictures were one way in which anxieties about Haiti—and Blacks in general—manifested themselves. Toni Pressley-Sanon has written that the "'birth' of the zombie as a popular phenomenon in the American imagination [was] part and parcel" of the occupation. After Griffith's *The Birth of a Nation* exacerbated US whites' racial anxieties, a nearby country—run by Blacks who practiced "voodoo"—became a monstrous specter. Indeed, Jude Ulysse has pointed to several zombie films from this era as embodying US whites' fears about Haiti and race.[12]

If US films of the early twentieth century offered negative stereotypes about Haiti, other artistic genres provided more varied portrayals. The occupation prompted a flood of histories, novels, paintings, and drama on the Haitian Revolution. US whites were eager to understand the history of this country that the Marines were occupying, with a past too fantastic to believe: former slaves who had defeated Napoleon's armies, a slave-turned-king who built a massive stone fortress rivaling other wonders of the world, etc.[13] Many African Americans already knew about Haiti's revolution; as Maurice Jackson and Jacqueline Bacon have explained, the event had had "a profound influence on the development of African American history, culture, and political thought" since the 1790s. The occupation coincided with the Harlem Renaissance; during this period, African Americans produced many works extolling Haiti's revolution. Along with left-leaning whites, they highlighted the heroism of the Revolution's generals.[14]

The Emperor Jones, the earliest feature film with a Haitian Revolution–inspired theme, arose from this context. The film was released by the Hollywood studio United Artists (founded by D. W. Griffith and others) near the end of the occupation in 1933. Directed by Dudley Murphy, *The Emperor Jones* was based on a 1920 play of the same name by Eugene O'Neill.[15] It starred legendary actor Paul Robeson as Brutus Jones, an African American gambler who becomes a Caribbean emperor before being felled by gunshot in the jungle near his palace (figure 1.2). Lindsay Twa has noted that, although

Figure 1.2. *Emperor Jones* lobby card. © United Artists, 1933. Author's personal collection.

the film is set on a fictional Caribbean island, it is full of "thinly veiled allusions to Haiti's history." As VèVè Clark has explained, O'Neill's protagonist was inspired by three Haitian leaders: Toussaint Louverture, Henri Christophe, and Vilbrun Guillaume Sam (the Haitian president toppled by the Marines at the start of the occupation). Jones most closely parallels Christophe, in rising from poverty to royalty before suffering a tragic death (though his pretentions to being an emperor rather than a king, Clark notes, reference Dessalines).[16]

The Emperor Jones improved over zombie films yet still banalized the Revolution. The play on which it was based, in the spirit of works celebrating Haiti's revolutionary generals, departed from some pejorative depictions of Blacks. As Twa has noted, the play had been groundbreaking in placing an African American actor in a serious role alongside white actors. Thomas Cripps has argued that, in the film version, Robeson elevated Jones's character further, imbuing it with "heroic dimensions." Mary Renda notes that Jones embodied the masculinity normally reserved for white men; he was a "strong black lead [who] . . . could put whites in their place."[17] Indeed, Brutus Jones does what African Americans of the era could not, speaking impertinently to whites. At many points in the film, Jones also outwits them. Smithers, a British merchant, thinks that Jones will be a useful puppet in his effort to overthrow the island's previous ruler. But once their plot succeeds, Jones pushes Smithers aside. Declaring that "I'm the boss here now" (40:17) and that his own cleverness caused their success, Jones treats Smithers like a flunky. This aspect of the film, a self-sure Black man dominating whites, sparked cheers among African American audiences.[18]

Still, even if *The Emperor Jones* featured a strong Black protagonist, it drew heavily on negative stereotypes about people of African descent. Though Brutus Jones succeeds in becoming a head of state, he is not a laudable one. He begins the film as a Pullman porter who drinks and chases women, before murdering a man over dice. He is forced to join a chain gang and uses violence to escape. Working on a steamer, he jumps overboard, swims to an island, and becomes its emperor through trickery. Once head of state, he taxes the people heavily to pay for custom finery. As Roland L. Williams Jr. has described the film's plot, "Savage compulsions drive Jones." Such stereotypes led many African Americans to condemn the film. Gerald Horne cites one review calling O'Neill's play a "travesty on the Negro race," while another said that the film made him "feel like making a dive for the garbage can." Robeson reportedly felt constrained by the role, but thought he had little choice in an era without better roles for Black actors.[19] While depicting Blacks negatively, *The Emperor Jones* took a particularly dim view of Haiti. For Jerry Philogene, the film made the country "a place of mysterious black magic, zombies, and barbarous Vodou ceremonies," including "carved 'voodoo' dolls and 'zombified' Haitians burying their dead." Philogene argues that "all of this reinforced the nonhuman quality of Haitians."[20]

The film's Christophe-inspired protagonist also incarnated the idea of the Haitian Revolution as unthinkable. Certainly, Henri Christophe was a complex character, and plays and novels centered on him have explored his cruelty alongside his efforts to defend his country from invasion. Mariana Past explains that Christophe has been a particularly popular protagonist because he "outlives the other revolutionary leaders, and his time in power spans both the Haitian Revolution and its difficult aftermath." Moreover, she notes, "Christophe ends up performing the most complex tasks involved in founding the new nation, and is forced to deal with the realities of the outside world in a way that Toussaint and Dessalines avoided."[21] Yet, despite the dramatic potential of Christophe's story and Robeson's efforts to humanize the role, the Christophe-inspired character in *The Emperor Jones* is a caricature of a Black leader. A Haiti-inspired monarch was not imagined in the film as a flawed statesman—who earned the right to lead his people after a valiant liberation struggle, only to make crucial errors—but as a crook eager to enrich himself. Jones contrasts Smithers's "little stealin'" with the "big stealin'" that will put him "in the hall of fame when [I] croak" (45:11). In the film's fictionalized Haiti, Black heads of state rise to power through criminality. And the people are gullible enough to follow them—until their volatility leads them to make another revolution.

Ultimately, *The Emperor Jones* did not do justice to Christophe's story or the Revolution's. Instead, it reinforced the occupation's racist premises. By portraying African-descended people as unfit to lead themselves, the film highlighted the inability of many whites to take seriously the idea of an autonomous Black state. Despite Haiti's more than a century of self-rule, the spectacle of a Black man acting as head of state was made to seem ridiculous.[22]

Benevolent Banalizations from European Leftists: *Burn!* and *Royal Bonbon*

Other than *Lydia Bailey* (discussed in chapter 3), the next major film to be inspired by the Haitian Revolution would be made in 1969: Gillo Pontecorvo's *Burn!* (*Queimada*). Ostensibly set in the 1840s in a fictional Portuguese colony called Queimada, this action-adventure epic has been widely interpreted as modeled on the Haitian Revolution.[23] *Burn!* starred Marlon Brando as a duplicitous British agent (Sir William Walker) and Evaristo Márquez as the dock porter (José Dolores) he tricks into leading a slave rebellion. The character of Dolores has often been seen as inspired by Toussaint Louverture. Indeed, Walker invokes Dolores and Toussaint together in one scene, as the same type of African whom a European might manipulate into starting a rebellion (31:27).

Pontecorvo had previously made the Academy Award–nominated *Battle of Algiers* (1966), widely considered—and rightly so—as one of the greatest anticolonial films of all time. For that film, Pontecorvo worked with the new leaders of Algeria, who provided a substantial portion of its funding. The film cost approximately $800,000—a large sum for the Algerian government but a small budget for an epic. Because of this unprecedented partnership, *The Battle of Algiers* was groundbreaking in highlighting the agency of colonized peoples, and in showing anticolonial battles from their perspective (even as Pontecorvo also sought to humanize French colonizers).[24]

Burn!, in contrast, came about when an Italian producer asked Pontecorvo to build on his success with *The Battle of Algiers* by making a "commercial film" that could appeal to a "mass audience." Pontecorvo eventually agreed to make "an adventure story . . . in the style of a nineteenth-century novel," while adding an anticolonial angle. *Burn!* had a much larger budget ($3 million) than *The Battle of Algiers*, with financing from Italian and French companies and a distribution deal with United Artists, the studio that released *The Emperor Jones*. The film, I would argue, was funded more as a decolonization film (a genre discussed in chapter 3) than as a slave revolt film. This funding enabled Pontecorvo not just to cast a Hollywood star, but also to have, in Danny Peary's words, "beautiful color cinematography [and] great attention to costumes and pageantry." Brando played Walker, the adventurer sent to foment a rebellion so that Britain could capture Queimada's sugar trade. For José Dolores, Pontecorvo selected Márquez, a nonactor with the "right face" whom he had spotted riding horseback in a Colombian forest.[25]

Burn! features Walker exploiting the grievances of enslaved peoples for his own ends. When he first arrives in Queimada, an enslaved rebel named Santiago is being executed. Walker wants rebellion to continue so he can overthrow the Portuguese; he identifies Dolores as the best candidate to direct it. Walker convinces Dolores to lead a group in stealing gold, then betrays them. Once they are faced with execution, Walker arms them with rifles, teaches them to shoot, and encourages them to kill soldiers (figure 1.3). Meanwhile, he persuades Creole plantation owners in Queimada's capital to assassinate the

Figure 1.3. William Walker (Marlon Brando) teaches enslaved people to revolt. *Burn!* publicity photo. © United Artists, 1970. Author's personal collection.

colony's governor so that they can assume power. Walker aims to shift Queimada from a slave economy in which Portugal monopolizes sugar profits, to a capitalist model in which England will have an exclusive lease on sugar production, using poorly paid laborers. Both the slaves and Creoles succeed in their tasks; they abolish slavery and eject the overseas Portuguese.

Conflict ensues when Dolores realizes that he has limited power, despite his military victory. Walker has constituted the Creoles into a provisional government that expects former slaves to disarm. Dolores (who commands a stronger force) is ready to arrest them and assume control. However, Walker warns him that his men will be incapable of ruling on their own. "Who will govern your island, José?" he asks. "Who will run your industries? . . . Who will cure the sick? Teach in your schools? This man? Or that man? [dismissively pointing to former slaves] . . . Civilization is not a simple matter, José. You cannot learn its secrets overnight" (49:38).

Frustrated and wanting the best for his people, Dolores concedes to Walker; his men return to the plantations, now as paid laborers. Walker leaves Queimada for his next assignment, placed symbolically (for the 1960s) in Indochina. Soon, however, the Royal Antilles Sugar Company (a British charter company) has assumed control not only of the island's sugar industry, but also its governance; both the Creoles and former slaves see that their independence has been stolen. Within five years, Dolores and the sugar cutters rise anew. The RASC uses British soldiers and local mercenaries to crush them, and Walker returns. More amoral than ever after Indochina, Walker insists that the island—and its population—be burned to the ground if necessary. Even if Queimada's sugar industry is decimated with its population, he cautions, it is necessary to prevent other Caribbean people from wanting to emulate Dolores.

Walker seems to get the upper hand; he captures José Dolores and kills his lieutenants. Walker is alarmed, though, by his protégé's evolution. Dolores now spits at Walker's idea of "civilization." Walker tries to induce Dolores to escape so that he will not become a martyr (he tells his European colleagues, "A martyr immediately becomes a myth. A myth is more dangerous than a man because you can't kill a myth. . . . Think of his ghost running through the Antilles!" [1:44:17]). But Dolores refuses to remain alive just because Walker prefers it. José gives a monologue reminiscent of Toussaint's famous "tree of liberty" speech. He predicts that others will pursue liberty after him, and the white man will be "pursued and hunted all over the island, till he falls into one of the great fires that he himself has made. And the groans from this dying beast will become a first cry of freedom, one that will be heard far, far beyond this island" (1:35:28). After Dolores's execution, Walker gets ready to return to England. But he is stabbed at the dock by a porter offering assistance, as the film's cycle of betrayal and violence comes full circle.

Like *The Battle of Algiers*, *Burn!* exposes how Europeans exploited those they colonized. In many ways it dramatizes resistance by enslaved people effectively and improves over *The Emperor Jones*. *Burn!* shows the difficulties endured by both enslaved peoples and freedmen, and the way resistance was channeled into religion and dance even when not apparent on the surface. It also shows the complicated choices faced by individuals, such as former slaves who worked for the RASC because they needed an income. Moreover,

Pontecorvo treats Brando's character unsympathetically. Walker is vicious, racist, and self-interested; after capturing Dolores, Walker even calls him a "black ape" (1:40:12).

The film is not as successful as *Battle of Algiers*, however, in showing the agency of colonized peoples. This may be because Pontecorvo did not have the same partnership with Haitians as he did with Algerians, or because the "unthinkability" Trouillot spoke of has persisted among certain European leftists. While not erasing the Haitian Revolution from history, Pontecorvo could only imagine a revolt by enslaved people as a conspiracy organized by whites. Where other scholarship on *Burn!* has focused on the film's anticolonialism, the eminent historian Brenda Stevenson has criticized the film on this front. She compared *Burn!* unfavorably to Spielberg's *Amistad*, since in Pontecorvo's film the "slave revolutionaries have to be duped into revolting." Similarly, Alan Stone (a Harvard law and psychiatry professor) has asked, "Why is the slave of Pontecorvo's political parable unable to conceive his own rebellion as did Toussaint L'Ouverture in what was then Santo Domingo . . . ? There is a patronizing psychological assumption in *Queimada* that did not appear in *The Battle of Algiers*." Jude Ulysse adds, "*Burn*! turns the historical enemy of the Revolution—white European bourgeois intellectuals—into heroes while turning the historical heroes into supporting actors taking orders and instructions."[26]

Indeed, standing in for Toussaint, José Dolores is not a heroic figure capable of plotting his own uprising, but a pawn manipulated (at least initially) by Walker. Scholars have noted that Pontecorvo, referencing Vietnam, was commenting on how Western powers manipulate colonized peoples.[27] Certainly, Pontecorvo was less concerned with depicting Caribbean slave revolts accurately than in using them to criticize the world of the 1960s. However, his treatment of the film's Africans was exoticizing. Dolores was the only African whom the viewer got to know, and frenzied dance scenes made the enslaved masses seem Other (for instance 10:23, 26:12, and 33:04) without exploring what the rituals meant to them. Moreover, though Pontecorvo made clear that Walker was manipulative, he found the African population easy marks (though eventually Dolores stops obeying). Pontecorvo's portrayal of mixed-race women in the colony as prostitutes was also problematic, typifying stereotypes popularized by the French colonist Moreau de Saint-Méry and what Marlene Daut has called the "tropical temptress" trope.[28] Commentators have pointed to still other dimensions of the film in which Pontecorvo "unwittingly and repetitively displayed his own racism."[29] *Burn*! hardly erased the Haitian Revolution from history, but put at its allegorical center a European mastermind. In my view, the film works better as an allegory about Western manipulation of colonized peoples—and a critique of US conduct in Vietnam—than as a serious cinematic depiction of the agency of enslaved Africans in the Caribbean.

Despite United Artists giving *Burn!* a sizable budget for a slave revolt film, the film ultimately did not meet the studio's expectations. Production troubles, including fights between Pontecorvo and Brando, led to a lack of enthusiasm by the producers and the star by the time filming wrapped. Postproduction, the studio edited *Burn!* down considerably and did not release it widely. Whereas *The Battle of Algiers* had earned nearly double its initial budget, United Artists reportedly decided to take a loss on *Burn!* rather than spend more money promoting it.[30]

Not until 2002 would another European filmmaker make a Haitian Revolution–related drama. French filmmaker Charles Najman's film *Royal Bonbon* shows a fascination with Henri Christophe, revolutionary general turned monarch. Najman would later make an excellent documentary about the Revolution's bicentennial (*Haïti, la fin des chimères?* [2004], discussed in chapter 7). However, *Royal Bonbon* repeats many of the same banalizing tropes as *The Emperor Jones*.[31] Najman made the film in Kreyòl, to add authenticity to a film shot in Haiti using local actors; the film was released with French and English subtitles for audiences abroad.

Royal Bonbon's scope is narrower than *Burn!*; it offers not a sweeping historical tale, but a parable about the present imitating the past. Set in the twenty-first century, *Royal Bonbon* focuses on a delusional resident of Cap Haïtien who decides that he is Henri Christophe reborn. He goes around the city with his wheelbarrow, telling residents to obey him. Paralleling Christophe's journey from slave to king, one who forced other former slaves to build the Citadelle, the man calls out, "I am Henri [Christophe]. . . . I was a slave like you. I suffered like you. . . . Don't stop working!" (2:10). Wherever he goes (except for a brothel, where he can buy respect for a pittance), he is ridiculed; children and adults alike mock him as the "caca king." Despite his delusion, the "king" eventually finds a band of elderly followers eager for a savior, followed by a court of pretty young women willing to be his mistresses. They sing the Haitian national anthem, "La Dessalinienne," and he grants them titles of nobility. He seems poised to fulfill his subjects' wishes and to reverse injustices.

However, trouble is afoot in his "kingdom"; his rule is being threatened. A masked man (played by Haitian actor-singer Erol Josué) claims to have communicated with Makandal while underwater with the *lwa* (spirits in Haitian Vodou); he suggests that he is reincarnating the spirit of eighteenth-century Haitian slave revolt. He finds a group of modern-day maroons in the hills and teaches them about Haitian slave resistance. He reports that Makandal told him that "we chased the white man from this country a long time ago. We sent him flying across the border. But since that day blacks have been fighting blacks. Makandal asked for change" (45:29). He tells the men that "the whites tried to stop Makandal. They tied him to the stake and set fire to it. But he would not die. He became a butterfly and was liberated from the flames. Ever since, every generation awaits his return" (46:14).[32] The men promise to carry on Makandal's struggle and to liberate Haitians from this despot; bearing torches, they set out to find him.

Meanwhile, the king has betrayed the hopes of his people, and is incompetent and despotic. He tries forcing them to work on large building projects and whips them when they do not work quickly enough. Fearing that rebellious spirits are encroaching on him, he yells, "Makandal! I'm the king here, not you!" (1:06:01). As his followers abandon him, he becomes unhinged. After calling them a "miserable lot! Worms!" (1:11:16), he decides that his dream of kingship was delusional. After what is either a real or imagined gunshot kills him, the king's reign ends, just as in *The Emperor Jones*.

Though *Royal Bonbon* was filmed on location in the North of Haiti, it is a weaker reimagining of Christophe's story than Raoul Peck's *Moloch Tropical* (discussed in chapter 7), which was also filmed in the area. In an extra on *Royal Bonbon*'s DVD, Najman declared that he made the film because he was fascinated by the Haitian people. He called their history "singular" and "fantastical," and said his "main motivation was to make the Haitian Revolution better known" worldwide.[33] Though these comments express good intentions, *Royal Bonbon*'s effect was the same as that of *The Emperor Jones*. An unhinged Black man appoints himself leader of the Haitians and becomes a tyrant. It left non-Haitian whites to wonder: What kind of delusional Black man would think he is a king, and what kind of people would follow him?

Sugarcoating French Slavery: The *Toussaint Louverture* Miniseries

With so few features related to the Revolution, expectations were high when a French television channel announced in 2012 that it would air a two-part miniseries on the Haitian Revolution. The film would be a biopic of Toussaint Louverture, the first ever completed after numerous failed efforts (see chapter 4). Unlike *The Emperor Jones* or *Burn!*, France 2's miniseries would not be a fictional story modeled on Haitian revolutionary history, but one about the

Revolution itself. *Toussaint Louverture* (2012, dir. Philippe Niang) garnered a great deal of publicity and was watched by three million viewers on its first airing.[34] Though not an epic released in theaters, it had a far larger audience than nearly any other Revolution-related film.

Unfortunately, *Toussaint Louverture* was deeply problematic.[35] Though it had some positive features, the miniseries distorted slavery and the Revolution. It implicitly shifted blame away from French whites and toward people of mixed race, the Spanish, and even Blacks themselves. The violence of slaveowners was almost entirely absent, while that of enslaved insurgents was shown in vivid detail. In its shortcomings, the movie exemplified French amnesia about Haiti's revolution as well as denial of the realities of slavery and colonialism.

On the one hand, it is remarkable that the miniseries was even made. As Yves Benot and others have shown, there has long been amnesia in France regarding Haiti and slavery in general. So little known are these histories that Jacques Chirac insisted in 2000 that Haiti had never actually been a French colony. French ignorance on these topics has begun to lift to some extent, following activism by French citizens of Antillean descent and a 2001 law, named for legislator Christiane Taubira, that mandated teaching about French slavery.[36] Like its predecessor, *Tropiques Amers* (2007), France 3's miniseries about the era of slavery in Martinique,[37] *Toussaint Louverture* fit into these larger efforts to acknowledge France's slaveholding past. Haitian-born actor Jimmy Jean-Louis, selected to play Toussaint, was elated to play the role of a lifetime for a Haitian: "I have heard for a long time about scripts [on Toussaint] in Los Angeles. . . . I would never have imagined getting the lead role! . . . Through this work of fiction, I am very happy to be able to educate certain people who are unaware of this completely forgotten part of French history."[38] The millions of viewers who watched episode 2 were able to see a roundtable about slavery and race following the episode, which raised issues rarely discussed on French television.

Aside from the fact that *Toussaint Louverture* addressed this history at all, the miniseries had other virtues. Jean-Louis imbued Toussaint with dignity. Such a portrayal was significant considering longtime debates about Louverture. For many years, foreigners portrayed him in racist ways. In scholarly literature, as Madison Smartt Bell has noted, Toussaint was rendered as either a "devil" or a "saint."[39] Recent scholarship by Haitian and foreign scholars has depicted the general in more nuanced terms. It has recognized his virtues and flaws, but also the difficult circumstances in which he operated as he tried to protect the island from foreigners eager to reimpose slavery.

The *Toussaint Louverture* miniseries paralleled this new scholarship in offering a principled, but imperfect, Louverture. Jean-Louis's Toussaint has human flaws such as stubbornness, but fights ardently for the freedom of Saint-Domingue's enslaved. While there are certainly inaccuracies in the film's portrayal of Toussaint, simply representing the leader of a slave revolt positively in a French film was noteworthy. Indeed, as several scholars have underscored, while French attention to slavery has increased, commemorations generally focus on white abolitionists rather than on the enslaved people who fought for their own liberation.[40]

Aïssa Maïga's turn as Toussaint's wife Suzanne was also remarkable, considering that Saint-Domingue's women of color have often been depicted as sex-obsessed temptresses. Maïga's Suzanne is a pious and feisty market woman and single mother. She knows how to read, and at first rebuffs Toussaint's attentions. While some aspects of this portrayal may have been anachronistic, the film's Suzanne represented an unusual case among portrayals of Black women in European or US film.

Nevertheless, despite the film's virtues, its depictions of the Haitian Revolution—and of the slave system that preceded it—are deeply problematic. Historical dramas invariably have some factual errors; as critics pointed out here, though, the film departed from the truth so often that one lost count. Inaccuracies ranged from depicting Suzanne as skinny, though sources say she was not, to inventing characters who never existed (such as the Napoleonic officer Pasquier, who drives the film's narration), to killing off characters who survived until years later (such as Biassou, Mars Plaisir, and Toussaint's father). Such criticism led to a last-minute change in the film's description from a history to a "work of fiction." It also occasioned a lively debate: How far can a filmmaker stretch historical truth? Director Philippe Niang, who is not Haitian but a Frenchman of mixed French and Senegalese heritage, professed more interest in depicting the general injustices faced by Toussaint and his family than in adhering to the historical record: "I would have produced a documentary if I wanted to make something faithful to history." Critics worried that viewers would remember the film's inventions rather than real facts.[41]

The film's portrayal of history had still more flaws. The miniseries made Blacks and people of mixed race absolute enemies even though they often fought together against French atrocities. Furthermore, the Spanish are portrayed as inherently deceitful in contrast to the French; the film has Spanish general Hermona try to kill Louverture's family, even though the real Hermona liked Toussaint.[42] The miniseries also hinted that Louverture was personally responsible for the disasters that befell him, from his proposing to

Suzanne at a funeral (which she warned could only bring unhappiness) to his insistence on authoring a separate constitution for the island in 1801 rather than simply following Napoleon's French constitution.

These factual errors (and a soapy style) were hardly the worst aspects of the film. *Toussaint Louverture* papered over the brutality of slavery; violence against slaves in the film is rare. Even in isolated instances (such as an invented scene where Toussaint's chained father drowns, another where his invented sister reports being raped, and another in which a mob of angry colonists chases Toussaint), the film was quick to contrast bad whites with kindly slaveowners.[43] Whippings were absent, and work on the plantation looked peaceful and bucolic. While Bayon de Libertat, who managed the Bréda plantation, was reportedly kind, the miniseries did not show other plantations to provide a more realistic view of slavery in Saint-Domingue.

Overall, the film, which purported to educate French audiences about slavery in Haiti, offered a revisionist history of this past. Certainly, the film suggested, the notion of a human owning another violated *les droits de l'homme* (human rights). On the other hand, it implied, slavery was not that bad. Parties on Bayon's plantation featured happy Black servants serving smiling whites. Enslaved people like Toussaint went on pleasure rides to markets, where they flirted with attractive women and joked about their "melons." Slaveowners were like bosses who engaged in profit-sharing with slaves. Toussaint's master frees him as a birthday surprise after a bountiful sugar crop; Toussaint later repays him with ingratitude when he leaves to strike out on his own. The film offered a nostalgic view of slavery, with whites and Blacks coexisting peacefully. Though Suzanne was in fact enslaved when Toussaint met her, the film renders her free, so we can be told that she was liberated by a benevolent slaveowner who fathered her child and taught her to read. All that scholars know about torture on Saint-Domingue—reportedly the most brutal New World slave society because of its high ratio of slaves to slaveowners, and thus the greater danger of revolt—is missing from the film.[44]

The miniseries consequently negated the idea that enslaved people could have been unhappy about their fate; it suggested that they only felt that way once they learned from Enlightenment *philosophes* that slavery was wrong. The film thus embodied what Daut has called the "Enlightenment literacy" narrative of explaining the Revolution.[45] The film's Toussaint was pleased with life until he read the abbé Raynal's *Histoire des deux Indes*; as he recalls from prison, "That book opened my eyes. Back then, I thought of myself as happy. But I was only a slave who was slightly better off than the others" (ep. 1, 17:58). While the real Toussaint did claim in 1799 to have read Raynal and to have been influenced by him, Daniel Desormeaux and Deborah Jenson have called this a strategic move meant to make the general palatable to French audiences at a time when he was viewed as anti-French. More crucially, the text on which the scene was based did *not* suggest that Toussaint was happy until a book changed his mind; it said merely that he already saw slavery as an injustice, and deepened this view after hearing of Raynal.[46] The miniseries also has Toussaint declare in 1802, after Leclerc captures him, that "for the first time in my life I was no longer master of anything . . . not even my destiny" (ep. 2, 1:24:27). That the film places such words in the mouth of a formerly enslaved person is astonishing.

In addition to grossly understating colonists' violence before the Revolution, the miniseries distorted the Revolution so that its only violence appeared to be by enslaved people against their enslavers. Whenever corpses are shown, they are the work of savage rebels; the only lynched person in the film is a beautiful white woman whose blond ringlets dangle from a tree. In addition, Vodou is depicted pejoratively, as if it alone bore responsibility for slaves' murderous behavior. Its strange ceremonies—in which priests yell "Kill the whites!"—are contrasted with peaceful Catholic ones. The film's depiction of the 1791 Bois Caïman ceremony shows worshipers dancing frenetically, drinking pigs' blood, asking the *lwa* to possess them, and swearing an oath to exterminate whites, before overrunning plantations and hacking them to death (ep. 1, 30:31–37:01). In contrast, *Toussaint Louverture*'s white generals eschew violence, while racist "mulattoes" who hate Blacks urge the French to attack them savagely. As French soldiers scrupulously obey the laws of war, Black rebels ambush them and slash them to death with machetes (ep. 1, 01:02:35–01:04:40; 01:05:47–01:06:20).[47]

This omission of white colonists' violence forms a pattern in *Toussaint Louverture*. For every villain like the Napoleonic General Cafarelli (portrayed as murdering Toussaint's servant Mars Plaisir, though he did no such thing), the film highlighted several virtuous whites. Overall, the miniseries was far more sympathetic to colonists than to the revolutionaries, with the exception of Toussaint. The film's General Leclerc hardly resembled the deceitful, incompetent, massacring general chronicled in recent studies. In real life, Leclerc did not allow Louverture's sons (who had been studying in France) to disembark when his troops arrived in Saint-Domingue in 1802, angering Louverture and inviting conflict with him. This Leclerc, in contrast, is a handsome young general who is happy to let the Louverture boys go ashore.[48]

Another way in which the film made the Haitian Revolution seem unnecessary is that it does not even mention Napoleon's 1802 reestablishment of slavery elsewhere in the empire. After this brutal decree was implemented on Guadeloupe, news traveled quickly to Saint-Domingue; former slaves there justifiably feared that Leclerc would force the same fate on them. Yet instead of portraying the battle against Leclerc as one for their lives and freedom, the film depicts the war as resulting exclusively from Toussaint's decision to issue a constitution for the island, despite the kindly white general Laveaux telling him it is unwise. Other than one massacre by Rochambeau, mentioned in passing, no French atrocities of the War of Independence are acknowledged. Nowhere does the miniseries suggest that Napoleon or Leclerc would have reenslaved anyone. The film even has Napoleon voice his commitment to Black freedom. Leclerc battles Toussaint here, not because Toussaint and the others are ready to die to preserve their freedom, but only because Toussaint is dangerously insubordinate. Leclerc laments that, because the rebels do not observe honored principles of war, he will have to depart from his cherished revolutionary values and engage in sneakier tactics (ep. 2, 1:17:33).[49]

Because the film's whites are mostly kind, and slavery not so terrible, the Haitian Revolution becomes in the film a capricious war of choice. Suzanne, transformed from an enslaved person into a free one, opposes Toussaint's desire to take up arms, seeing it as a vengeful inability to forgive slights. She begs him to leave "politics" alone and to "stop meddling in whites' affairs" (ep. 1, 30:20). Acting as if overturning slavery is unnecessary, she complains, "I know your father was thrown in the water . . . [and] your sister was raped and assassinated, but. . . ." Struggling in vain to persuade Toussaint to return to growing sugar, she exclaims, "You have a wife and kids and land! Are you even thinking of us?" (ep. 1, 43:54).

Interestingly, even with its whitewashing of slavery, some French intellectuals thought *Toussaint Louverture* was too hard on whites. Far from complaining that the miniseries sanitized the colonists, these critics thought it made them appear too racist. Gérard de Cortanze, an editor at Gallimard, complained that *Toussaint Louverture* "distorted historical truth so that whites appear to be supporters of slavery and *négrophobes*." He suggested that French youth of color would riot after watching it. Alain Foix, the writer of a popular biography of Toussaint, insisted that the miniseries should have included the French abolitionist priest abbé Henri Grégoire to show that whites were not all bad. Foix alleged that *Toussaint Louverture* distorted history in its very suggestion that Haitians had fought against the French, and that whites had fought against Blacks.[50] In the roundtable aired after episode 2, scholars Marcel Dorigny and Françoise Vergès struggled to present a more accurate view of slavery, resistance, and colonial racism. Dorigny emphasized the long history of slave revolt in the colony, and Vergès pointed out that "the first abolitionists were the slaves themselves." However, the moderator was less interested in their comments than in asking the panel's members of color how it felt to go through life with black skin.[51]

The *Toussaint Louverture* miniseries thus represented an extreme example of banalizing the Revolution. It did more to reveal contemporary French ignorance about slavery and Saint-Domingue than to bring Haiti's history to life. Nowhere did audiences learn about resistance in the colony before 1789, let alone African ideas of liberty that enslaved people brought to the New World. And the Revolution figured not as a righteous struggle for liberation by brutalized slaves, but a set of unprovoked attacks on peace-loving French men and women.

In this chapter, I have considered the most famous epic-style films related to the Haitian Revolution, all made by European and US filmmakers. I have argued that these films, to different degrees, distort the Revolution. The *Toussaint Louverture* miniseries, the only one centered on the Revolution, has the most serious flaws. These films corroborate Michel-Rolph Trouillot's arguments about the Revolution's unthinkability to many white Americans and Europeans (the same people with the greatest access to film funding). Still, as I will discuss in the next two chapters, these are not the only feature films related to the Revolution. In chapter 2, we turn to less well-known features from the Caribbean that treat the Revolution as a subplot or otherwise reference it; we consider whether they have done any better at introducing the Revolution's historical significance to film audiences.

2

INVOKING THE REVOLUTION IN CARIBBEAN FEATURE FILMS

This chapter analyzes films from the Caribbean (outside of Haiti itself) related to the Haitian Revolution. Only a handful of such films exist, coming either from Cuba or Curaçao. I examine the Cuban film *The Last Supper* (1976), the Cuban-French coproduction *El siglo de las luces/Le siècle des lumières* (1992), and two films from Curaçao, *Almacita de Desolato* (1986) and *Tula: The Revolt* (2013). I note that, where US and European films have had difficulty discussing the Revolution without banalizing it, some of these films have done a better job of acknowledging the Revolution's importance. Cuban directors have tended to invoke the Revolution as a metaphor, to comment on Cuban society; films from Curaçao have taken more seriously the Revolution's impact around the Caribbean. Still, all of these films (even *Tula*, which stars Danny Glover) have had limited distribution. In addition, like the films discussed in chapter 1 but to different degrees, each has flaws in its depiction of the Revolution or of slave revolt in general.

Submerging Haiti's Past in Cuba's Present

Humberto Solás's 1992 *El siglo de las luces/Le siècle des lumières* (The Century of Enlightenment) is the weakest of the Caribbean films. It sets some scenes amid the Revolution, while minimizing its importance. Solás was a leading Cuban director who had previously made a short film on Haitian history, *Simparele* (1974). That film, as I argue in chapter 7, offers a far better depiction of the Revolution than *El siglo de las luces* because of its deep collaboration with Haitian artists. *El siglo*, in contrast, is closer to European films in its treatment of Haiti's revolution. The film was coproduced with a French agency, the Société française de production; it aired on French television as a miniseries, with three episodes of approximately eighty-six minutes each. There was also a 120-minute version of the film that screened at festivals in Latin America.[1] *El siglo de las luces* aimed to offer a sweeping panorama of the Age of Revolutions; however, its form was that of a soap opera, focused on enslavers' perspectives rather than those of the enslaved.

El siglo de las luces was based on Alejo Carpentier's 1962 historical novel of the same name (translated into English as *Explosion in a Cathedral*).[2] Part telenovela, part epic, and part philosophical treatise on revolution, *El siglo de las luces* teemed with melodramatic music, battle scenes, and sex. While focusing on the French Revolution, the miniseries introduced Haiti's revolution in its first episode. *El siglo de las luces* has been described as the director's veiled commentary on the state of Cuba's revolution in the 1990s, via its discussion of the French Revolution; the film has interested commentators chiefly in this respect.[3] In depicting the Haitian and French Revolutions themselves, the miniseries is far less compelling. It treats historical fact loosely; it depicts the Haitian Revolution negatively and without the perspective of enslaved Haitians.

The miniseries follows three attractive Spanish-descended Cubans, a brother and sister (Carlos and Sofia) and their cousin Esteban, from 1788 through 1808. The young Havanans live idyllically on their family's estate; their tutor manages their late father's business so they can read, play music, and have masquerade parties. One day an outsider appears: Victor Hugues, a colonist and merchant from Port-au-Prince. A real historical figure, Hugues has received more attention in recent years as part of rising interest in the history of slavery in France; he is most famous for implementing the 1794 abolition decree in Guadeloupe, over the objections of other colonists. When Carpentier wrote his novel, Hugues was an obscure historical figure; the author freely fictionalized his life.[4]

In the first episode of the miniseries, "The Fires of the Revolution," Hugues introduces the cousins to Freemasonry and the political ideals sweeping the Atlantic. He spouts platitudes about "living in the century of Enlightenment" (ep. 1, 20:59). When Esteban falls ill, Hugues summons a friend from Saint-Domingue who is visiting Havana, a Doctor Ogé. We later learn that Doctor Ogé is the older brother of the famous Vincent Ogé, the mixed-race planter who helped spark the Haitian Revolution by insisting on equal rights for *gens de couleur*.[5] The cousins, who are slaveowners, are at first shocked that Hugues would bring a "Negro" to treat them. But Hugues instructs them that "all men are equal" (ep. 1, 26:09). He assures them that Ogé received his medical training in Paris and belongs to a Masonic lodge in Cap Français. With Ogé's help, Esteban recovers; Ogé joins the cousins and Hugues in their decadent parties. Later, after Hugues discovers that the cousins' tutor is siphoning money from their business, the tutor seeks revenge and tells the authorities that Hugues and Ogé are Freemasons, which would mark them as seditious. Sofia and Esteban bring the Saint-Dominguans to their plantation outside Havana, where Ogé and Hugues continue to awaken the cousins' political consciousness (even as loyal slaves cater to their needs). Ogé and Hugues tell Sofia and Esteban that revolution is spreading around the world and that racial equality is being decreed in France (ep. 1, 50:14).[6]

The film introduces the Haitian Revolution—rather confusingly—shortly afterward. To avoid being arrested for their beliefs, Hugues, Ogé, Esteban, and Sofia depart for Santiago de Cuba, leaving Carlos in Havana to bring the tutor to justice. Upon arrival, they hear rumors about a disturbance in Saint-Domingue—variously, an earthquake or a revolution (ep. 1, 58:20). While visiting a brothel, Ogé and Esteban learn that there has been a "catastrophe"—a "nightmare"—in Saint-Domingue that all Freemasons must fight against. It is surprising to have heard Ogé and Hugues declare that a revolution for equality is necessary—but then seem to want to save colonists fighting against it.

El siglo de las luces portrays the Haitian Revolution as full of violence, rape, and chaos. The group plans to leave for Port-au-Prince, but Sofia is told that she should not come because women are "being raped there," presumably by the enslaved revolutionaries (ep. 1, 1:00:23). While she remains in Santiago, the others sail to Port-au-Prince to help survivors of this "catastrophe" (chiefly white colonist refugees) escape the island. The four go ashore in Port-au-Prince as flames engulf the city, which would place the scene in November 1791. Amid general chaos, whites and Blacks alike run around shrieking; Hugues is shocked to discover his own properties burned to the ground. Ogé surprises the others by saying that Hugues deserved to have them destroyed, since he has learned that his own brother was burned at the stake by French colonists. No longer calling Hugues his brother in Freemasonry, Ogé now addresses Hugues as "you, the French" who did this to Vincent Ogé (ep. 1, 1:09:22). Doctor Ogé declares that "there's a lot more [that should] be burned" (ep. 1, 1:09:46).[7] But he does not explain why he feels that way, and he still wants to send Hugues and the cousins to safety.

Later episodes refer to the Haitian Revolution indirectly, but not any more meaningfully. In episode 2 ("The Blood of the People"), Esteban accompanies Hugues to Paris and becomes involved in the French Revolution. As he sees the Revolution depart from its principles, he grows disgusted. Yet Esteban remains in Hugues's service even as the latter becomes a ruthless opportunist. Hugues announces the abolition of slavery in Guadeloupe, as liberated slaves dance in gratitude (ep. 2, 37:35–38:59). But he also orders the mass guillotining of revolutionaries whose loyalty he suspects.

The film's attempt to show Esteban overcoming his racism is particularly dubious. To demonstrate that he has become an egalitarian, *El siglo de las luces* shows him evolve from disgust at being treated by a Black doctor to happily having sex with multiple women of color. When he sails with privateers tasked by Hugues with liberating slaves from a foreign slave ship, and each greedily grabs a woman, Esteban does too. In *El siglo*, this is not presented as rape; rather, the freed woman is overjoyed to be carried off. She and Esteban have romantic sex on the beach as waves crash over them (ep. 2, 54:30). Esteban is later crushed to learn that Hugues has abandoned his revolutionary principles. The woman and her fellow slaves will not be emancipated; Hugues has decreed that they be sold, notwithstanding abolition, as enemy property confiscated for the benefit of French forces. In episode 3 ("Explosion in a Cathedral"), the chameleonlike Hugues moves even further from universalistic ideals. In service to Napoleon as governor of Guiana, he reinstates slavery with as much energy as he had earlier abolished it, which would place this scene in 1802 (ep. 3, 54:08). This nineteenth-century Hugues is eager to crush maroon revolt everywhere, from Haiti to Venezuela (ep. 3, 01:08:47).

Overall, *El siglo de las luces* treats the Haitian Revolution disconcertingly. The Port-au-Prince scenes communicate nothing about the Revolution but disorder. We do not learn who has revolted against whom, only that whites and Blacks alike are distraught. And the Revolution is described as having brought "rape" to the colony—a shocking assertion given the prevalence of rape by white colonists against enslaved women in French colonial Saint-Domingue.[8] *El siglo de las luces* never introduces us to enslaved revolutionaries and never shows or discusses oppression by slaveowners; the only detail we learn about the Revolution—other than its "rapes"—is the execution of Vincent Ogé. Other parts of the film do no better at showing the perspective of enslaved Haitians or other people of color. Like *Burn!*, the miniseries categorizes women of color as hungry for sex (for instance, ep. 1, 30:56; ep. 2, 50:45, 54:30). More importantly, we do not get to know any enslaved people by name except for the cousins' loyal domestics. The only sighting of slave revolt on screen in *El siglo* is when Guianese maroons battle Victor's forces in episode 3.

A better—and more well-known—Cuban film related to the Haitian Revolution is Tomás Gutiérrez Alea's *The Last Supper* (*La Última Cena*, 1976).[9] This drama is set on an eighteenth-century Cuban sugar plantation; it takes more seriously than *El siglo* the Revolution's implications for Caribbean slavery. The Revolution is not the film's main focus; while *The Last Supper* is ostensibly about Cuban slavery, Jorge Camacho has argued that it is really a critique of the Cuban Catholic Church. Where Solás's miniseries critiqued Cuban revolutionary hypocrisy, Gutiérrez Alea's film sought to support Castro's campaigns against Catholic clergy. But, like *El siglo*, *The Last Supper* uses the Haitian Revolution instrumentally. According to Camacho, the film invoked colonial slavery to teach Cubans about the Church's complicity in that system and to suggest that Afro-Caribbean religions embodied the spirit of revolution better than Catholicism imported by Europeans.[10]

Haiti's revolution looms as background in *The Last Supper*. Action centers on the Count, a Cuban slaveowner who sees himself as pious but permits his overseer to brutalize his slaves. The Count finds himself caught between two men: his ruthless overseer Don Manuel, who maintains a frenetic pace of sugar production by dispensing wanton violence, and his priest, who urges the Count to be more devout (for instance by drinking less and "spending less time with" enslaved women). The plantation's sugar manager, Don Gaspar, is recently arrived from Saint-Domingue, having narrowly escaped after the Revolution broke out. Paralleling the changes Ada Ferrer has traced as the Caribbean sugar industry shifted to Cuba after the Haitian Revolution, Gaspar has brought new sugar-refining techniques from Saint-Domingue.[11] The Count is excited by these innovations and wants to purchase even more slaves to increase his profits. Gaspar, however, is terrified of how that will affect the plantation: if enslaved people outnumber whites too much, he will be in danger of a Saint-Domingue-style revolution. The Count urges him not to worry, since Don Manuel knows how to "control the blacks" (12:43).

As Easter approaches, the Count unwittingly prompts the very uprising that he is certain cannot happen. Trying to be more pious, he styles himself after Jesus and behaves bizarrely. First, he demonstrates his abjection by washing the feet of twelve enslaved men, then he hosts them at a dinner styled after the Last Supper. The Count's wining and dining his slaves, and telling stories with them, results in expectations of improved conditions. He promises manumission to one elderly man and assures the rest that, at the very least, they will get Easter off to attend church. But on Easter morning, when they see that Don Manuel still has free reign over them and believes neither in manumission nor days off, a revolt breaks out. Enslaved people torch the plantation, but many pay with their lives. As the Count screams, "This is not Saint-Domingue!" (1:38:28), he has them eaten by dogs or has their heads mounted on pikes. Only one enslaved person, longtime rebel Sebastián—who, unlike the other men, practices an Afro-Caribbean religion rather than Catholicism—escapes. Presumably he will carry the revolutionary spirit into the future.

Certainly, unlike *El siglo*, *The Last Supper* places slave revolt at its center and highlights colonial brutality. As Philip Kaisary has noted, the film "makes clear that the institution of slavery was founded on systematically orchestrated violence and terror." Kaisary identifies other ways in which the film references Haiti, particularly in the character of Sebastián, whom he sees as inspired by Makandal. Jude Ulysse, in contrast, sees Saint-Domingue serving mainly as a warning in the film, "not as a source of inspiration." He concludes that "even for progressive, Marxist-inspired Tomás Gutiérrez Alea . . . , the Haitian Revolution cannot figure as a paragon for freedom and equality, let alone the redefinition of a human. . . . The filmmaker sidelines the influence of Afro-Haitian culture and revolutionary ideas in Cuba. The crossing of ideas, as well as financial and military assistance, from Haiti is nowhere to be found."[12]

Haiti's Revolution as a Beacon of Freedom: Features from Curaçao

El Siglo and *The Last Supper* thus show how Cuban filmmakers have invoked Haiti's revolution to comment on their country's history, even while downplaying the agency of enslaved people. In the Dutch Caribbean, we find two different attempts to represent the Revolution's importance for Caribbean peoples. The first is Felix De Rooy's allegorical film *Almacita de Desolato* (1986). Set in rural Curaçao, the film has been described by Jean Antoine-Dunne as a "mythical retelling" of Caribbean history, one that foregrounds a female protagonist and examines "dominant ideas of masculinity" in the Caribbean.[13]

Almacita focuses on a mute priestess named Solem. As the movie opens, Solem and her helper, a boy named Lucio, find a wounded man lying on the ground. He wears a tattered military uniform; he says he has fled from "San Christophe" and that "they want to stone me" (3:24). Lucio wants to report the man's appearance to the authorities so he does not get in trouble, but Solem convinces him to keep quiet; she soothes the soldier's wounds and finds him a hiding place. Though *Almacita* does not announce when it is set, Gilberto Blasini has argued that it seems to take place after the end of slavery in Curaçao (1863). But Jean Antoine-Dunn has insisted that the film is more likely set at the end of the eighteenth century: "*Almacita* has its original focus on what appears at the onset to be a runaway from a place called San Christophe, a name that resonates with Haiti. . . . This, combined with costuming, hints that the film is loosely set at the time of the Haitian revolution." Certainly, Solem's caring for the "San Christophe" fugitive acknowledges the Haitian Revolution's serving as a beacon for Caribbean peoples, who wished to help even if they did not themselves engage in open revolt.[14]

A more direct examination of the Haitian Revolution's influence in the Caribbean appears in another film made in Curaçao, Jeroen Leinders's 2013 *Tula: The Revolt*. While involving some historical invention, this fascinating epic chronicles a real slave uprising in Curaçao in August 1795. It was led by an enslaved man named Tula, who may have lived previously in the French Caribbean. According to statements he made to a priest, Tula drew inspiration from Haiti. He adopted the surname Rigaud, after the Haitian revolutionary André Rigaud; one of Tula's comrades nicknamed himself Toussaint. Tula also decided to revolt after hearing about France's 1794 abolition; given that France had defeated the Dutch in the French Revolutionary Wars, Tula reasoned that the decree should apply in Curaçao. Tula's uprising was very large by the standards of early modern slave revolts; Gert Oostindie estimates that two thousand of the island's twelve thousand enslaved people participated.[15]

Leinders's film resulted from long-term interest in Tula's story in Curaçao combined with increased interest in slavery in contemporary Europe. Leinders, a Dutch filmmaker who grew up in Curaçao, made *Tula* as part of a revival of memory about slavery in the Netherlands. This revival culminated in a series of programs in 2013 commemorating the 150th anniversary of the Dutch abolition of slavery. According to Oostindie, Curaçaoans already commemorated slavery on the day Tula's revolt began, rather than on that of abolition. But his story was virtually unknown in the Netherlands. Leinders has noted that he sought to reach not only audiences in the Dutch Caribbean and mainland, but also internationally. Thus, though *Tula* was filmed in Curaçao, dialogue is in English.[16]

Leinders obtained $3.5 million for the film—a modest budget for an epic, but a princely sum compared to most other films discussed in this book. The film was coproduced by Dutch company Inspire Pictures, with further sponsorship from companies such as KLM and Coca-Cola Curaçao.[17] The European and corporate funding sources may have constrained how Tula's story was told. However, it also allowed Leinders to hire several well-known Dutch actors as well as an international star: Danny Glover. As I discuss in chapter 4, Glover had been trying to make his own Haitian Revolution epic for many years. But in the absence of funding, Glover eagerly participated in a different slave revolt film. The film's DVD begins with an extra featuring Glover, designed to precede the film at festivals. Glover declares that *Tula* is an "extraordinary movie" about an important topic. He explains that *Tula* shows what happened when "slaves heard about . . . the abolition of slavery in Haiti" and "decide[d] to go on strike." "Sometimes," Glover notes ruefully, "we live in denial of those slave revolts." He calls the film "important for so many reasons," as well as "an opportunity . . . to really begin the healing process . . . after such a tragic event" (Glover DVD extra, 1:19).

Unlike Philippe Niang of the *Toussaint Louverture* miniseries, Leinders sought to follow the historical record in his film, stating that he "made a great effort to build . . . this story with the help of local historians" in Curaçao. But many details of Tula's revolt remain unknown, including whether it was planned or erupted spontaneously.[18] Leinders thus needed to invent many details, including dialogue.

Leinders's film suggests that Tula began his revolt because he was frustrated by being made to work on Sunday (contrary to Dutch law) and because he was distraught by his brother's death from overwork. Tula is pushed to action after his girlfriend Speranza, a house slave, tells him she has overheard plantation whites describing the Haitian Revolution and the French abolition of slavery. Tula and Speranza are elated. The film shows Tula (played by Obi Abili) ask his master (Willem Van Uytrecht, played by Jeroen Willems) for freedom (figure 2.1) and insist on speaking to the colony's governor when Van Uytrecht will not grant it.[19] Whether or not these details are true, Tula's having been inspired by the Haitian Revolution does follow the historical record.

Tula also illustrates the reluctance that many enslaved people had regarding open resistance, even given the news from Haiti. Glover's character, Shinishi (figure 2.2), initially provides a counterpoint to Tula. Shinishi is a wizened elder who has learned to accommodate himself to the overseer's whims. His dynamic with Tula is much like that of Fiddler to Toby (Kunta Kinte) in *Roots*; Shinishi urges Tula to obey Van Uytrecht and remain calm. After the plantation owner orders Tula whipped early in the film, Shinishi applies a salve to Tula's back, while telling the younger generation that "the problem is . . . all of you have it too easy, you can't take a whipping. . . . None of you can make do and get through!" (13:35). Later, when Tula insists on talking to Van Uytrecht, because "we should be free, by rights" (16:55), Shinishi responds, "The master don't have to do nothing, except be white and eventually die" (17:22). Later, Shinishi overcomes his preservation instincts and joins the others; as Glover has explained, it takes Shinishi time to "make the leap" and realize that freedom may be possible.[20]

Especially given how few features exist on the Haitian Revolution or on slave revolt in general, *Tula* has many excellent qualities. The film inspires

Figure 2.1. Tula (Obi Abili) presses Willem Van Uytrecht (Jeroen Willems) for freedom, after hearing about the Haitian Revolution and France's abolishing slavery. *Tula: The Revolt*. © Fisheye Feature Films, 2013. Courtesy of Jeroen Leinders.

sympathy with Tula and his forces, and humanizes them. Tula is portrayed neither as an African savage nor as wanting to imitate the Dutch. He is calm and logical, and speaks the colonists' language eloquently, versus other characters' dialect-inflected speech. But rather than valorize him as a subaltern who is nearly European, as in the Raynal-reading Toussaint of the French miniseries, the film respectfully shows Tula's disdain for European culture. When the slavery-accommodating priest offers him communion, Tula replies that he is not "interested in anything your god has for me" (6:08).[21] Tula and his men are fully realized characters who exhibit a range of human emotions; they are not enslaved masses whom one observes from a distance dancing to strange African rituals, as in *Burn!* or *Toussaint Louverture*.

Another way that the film humanizes the revolutionaries is in making clear that it was the Dutch who were savage, not them. Leinders suggests that Tula's movement turned bloody only because of the machinations of Dutch forces, against whom they needed to defend themselves. Repeatedly, Tula restrains members of his group who (because of their experiences while enslaved) want to kill whites; he insists that they need to get freedom "the right way" (37:38). When Dutch forces triumph, Leinders details the real-life punishments meted out to Tula and his allies, including broken bones and burned faces—part of what Oostindie has called an "unprecedented orgy of state violence."[22] Though we are not forced to watch this violence reenacted, as in Nate Parker's *The Birth of a Nation*, Leinders makes clear that colonists could be monstrous.

While focused on the Revolution's meaning for enslaved people, *Tula* also does a good job signaling how whites feared the Revolution's potential impact. For instance, one member of Tula's movement has second thoughts as the

Figure 2.2. Danny Glover as Shinishi, working in the fields. *Tula: The Revolt.* © Fisheye Feature Films, 2013. Courtesy of Jeroen Leinders.

Dutch execute his comrades. He realizes that he can obtain manumission for himself (damn the others), if he tells the whites what they expect to hear. He claims that Tula and the others forced him to fight "at gunpoint," and that Tula wanted not freedom but dominance. In court, he tells the Dutch that Tula said, "We're going to take the island—like the Black folks took Haiti!" (1:27:07).

Certainly, *Tula: The Revolt* is not perfect.[23] Beyond compressing characters and imagining details, it has several anachronisms. This includes dialogue that does not sound credible for the eighteenth century. For instance, the film's African American screenwriter, Curtis Holt Hawkins, has Tula begin his revolt by using African American slang ("Hell no!") to tell Shinishi that he will not return to work (18:01). Another weakness is the film suggesting that Tula decided spontaneously to begin his movement—and yet somehow his supporters already had rifles. The film shows them using these firearms without any difficulty, even though they would previously have been kept far from such weapons. The film includes many battle scenes, with the enslaved forces nearly as well armed as the colonists, excepting the latter's cannons.

Tula also ends up underplaying the terror under which the enslaved lived. The film makes colonists hesitant about dealing with unrest, while making enslaved people seem too optimistic about swaying colonists through logic. Tula tells Van Uytrecht that work assignments are unreasonable: "We can't keep on like this. . . . If I can just explain . . ." (12:00)—to which Van Uytrecht responds, as if to educate twenty-first-century audiences about colonial realities, "Need I remind you of your place?" (12:07). Tula also thinks the governor will declare slaves free if only he can talk to him. Later, Tula speaks more impudently to Van Uytrecht: "I guess maybe I wasn't [clear before]. . . . We ain't putting one foot on them damned fields . . . until somebody can tell me how we still slaves when the French have done away with slavery. By law, we is all equal!" (18:36). Van Uytrecht scoffs, but he does not immediately punish Tula; he simply hopes that the governor will do so if Tula dares visit him.

Not surprisingly, given its metropolitan and corporate funding sources, the film also resorts to the white-hero trope; it adds a friendly white woman in whose place metropolitan Dutch viewers can imagine themselves.[24] Mrs. Lesire helps Tula; she tells him, "My home . . . is yours for as long as you need it" (31:38). She allows Tula to turn her plantation into base camp, and she lets him and Speranza move into a luxurious bedroom. She transitions quickly from owning human beings to shaking Tula's hand and shrugging that she supports his cause "because it's right" (32:02). Later, when the priest begs her to talk Tula out of his plans, Mrs. Lesire says that "he's a good man, with good intentions" (45:26)—an odd formulation in an era when enslavers routinely denied that enslaved people were men.

Still, despite these flaws, *Tula* is the best of the foreign features we have surveyed. It indicated how enslaved peoples in Haiti—and those they inspired elsewhere—were thinking human beings, with legitimate grievances. It went far beyond *Burn!* in suggesting that enslaved people were capable of formulating their own resistance plans. But *Tula* also made clear how difficult it was for enslaved peoples outside Haiti to emulate its success. *Tula*'s closing scroll indicates that Dutch slaves did not win abolition until 1863, when Tula's son with Speranza would have been sixty-eight.

Tula might have seemed to point the way toward a changing future for the Haitian Revolution—and the cinematic portrayal of slave revolt in general—in global cinema. Given increasing consciousness of slavery in Europe and the growing interest in slavery-related films in the US, Leinders's goal of reaching a wide global audience seemed attainable. However, *Tula* had a bifurcated reception, reflecting how the Haitian Revolution and slave revolt are seen more generally. In England, where slavery has received increased attention in public culture, *Tula* won a prize. The film also screened at film festivals around the world with themes such as the African diaspora or the Caribbean. Outside these venues, *Tula* did not garner the same attention; it was not distributed globally like Glover's other films. Even in the Netherlands, the film had very limited impact.[25] Elsewhere in the world, many people who would want to see an epic on slave revolt—including scholars—have never heard of the film. By 2018, the DVD (released only in the European DVD format PAL-2) was out of circulation.[26]

Tula and some of the other films in this chapter make the Revolution more thinkable than the films discussed in chapter 1. Still, the Revolution remains a subplot or a metaphor in these films, rather than their center. While *Tula* treats the Haitian Revolution far more meaningfully than *El Siglo*, it is not centered on Haiti's revolutionaries themselves. Finally, none of these Caribbean films has reached audiences as large as the films discussed in chapter 1.

The number of Haitian Revolution–related features remains limited; there is still no high-quality epic set during the Revolution itself. However, the story I have told so far is incomplete without one more entry: Hollywood's only feature film set amid the Haitian Revolution, 20th Century Fox's *Lydia Bailey*. We turn in the next chapter to this fascinating film.

3

HANDLING HAITI IN HUAC-ERA HOLLYWOOD

20th Century Fox's *Lydia Bailey*

If I were a native today whose liberty was threatened by Napoleon's cutthroats, I would kill every white man I could lay my hands on.
—Albion Hamlin, *Lydia Bailey*

In 1952, 20th Century Fox released *Lydia Bailey*, a love story set amid the Haitian Revolution. Unlike *The Emperor Jones* and *Burn!*, *Lydia Bailey* did not chronicle a Haiti-inspired fictional revolution; unlike the films discussed in chapter 2, *Lydia Bailey* is set in Haiti itself, with real characters such as Toussaint Louverture. Written by Philip Dunne and Michael Blankfort, and directed by Jean Negulesco, the film's story unfolds during the Leclerc expedition—which began in 1801, though the film places it in 1802. Adapted from a 1947 novel, the film focuses on a Baltimore lawyer, Albion Hamlin. Albion arrives in Haiti seeking a young American named Lydia Bailey; he needs her signature on some forms. As he searches, he befriends a fictional Haitian revolutionary named King Dick, is introduced to Toussaint, and becomes integral to their struggles against Leclerc (figure 3.1). Albion finds Lydia and they fall in love—while battling Lydia's fiancé (a French plantation owner) and Haitians opposed to Toussaint.

Lydia Bailey arrived in theaters with great expectations and a publicity blitz. It premiered in Port-au-Prince, in a gala event covered by newspapers across the US. Haiti's president, Paul Magloire, welcomed Fox executives, journalists, and the film's stars; he praised Fox for putting on screen "one of the most glorious episodes of our national life."[1]

Figure 3.1. Albion (Dale Robertson) carries a message from Toussaint Louverture to General Leclerc (Luis van Rooten), as Lydia (Anne Francis) and Gabriel d'Autremont (Charles Korvin) look on. *Lydia Bailey* publicity photo. © 20th Century Fox, 1952. Author's personal collection.

Why did a major studio make a film in the 1950s about the Haitian Revolution? How did its portrayal of that event and of Toussaint compare to other films? How was *Lydia Bailey* received in the US, Haiti, and elsewhere? And why has it fallen into obscurity? Unlike *Burn!* or *The Emperor Jones*, *Lydia Bailey* has been largely forgotten by the public and scholars.[2] The film was never issued in a home-viewing format in the US, and it has not been shown on television for decades; until recently, only one US library owned a copy.[3] The film was startlingly antiracist and ahead of its time in many ways. It made the Haitian Revolution far more thinkable than other foreign features, the result of a particular US postwar combination of antiracism and anticolonialism, with sources as diverse as 1930s Marxism and the policies of the Truman administration. It supported the aspirations of decolonizing peoples in particularly strong terms—and endorsed Black retributive violence against oppressive white rulers. Nevertheless, as I shall argue, the film contained stereotypes in other regards, as well as less focus on the Revolution than its writers had hoped.

The fascinating, never-told story of making *Lydia Bailey* could fill its own book. Archives from multiple individuals involved in the film, as well as press coverage, illustrate its evolution. While I can present only a snapshot here, I want to emphasize that the film's production was complicated by competing imperatives. *Lydia Bailey* was made during a perfect storm of economic, political, and social changes in Hollywood and the world, which led to conflicting ideas about what kind of film it should be. Finalizing the screenplay took years, and compromises left many of the cast and crew dissatisfied. *Lydia Bailey* was shaped not only by Cold War anxieties but also by postwar decolonization. I focus in this chapter on the film's development, before analyzing its final version and its reception.

Launching *Lydia* in a Changing Industry (1946–47)

In considering why *Lydia Bailey* came to exist—and why it was so quickly forgotten—it is important to recognize that Fox never set out to make a Haitian Revolution picture. In the 1940s, films adapted from bestselling novels were bankable propositions—and one of the era's top historical novelists was Kenneth Roberts. Two of his novels, 1934's *Captain Caution* (about the war of 1812) and 1937's *Northwest Passage* (on the French and Indian War), were adapted into successful movies in 1940, the former by United Artists and the latter by MGM.

Before the release of Roberts's novel *Lydia Bailey* in January 1947, studios competed for the rights. Eager not to lose another Roberts project, Fox offered a staggering bid in September 1946, the company's highest ever: $215,000 for a ten-year lease on the rights. As a Fox executive told the *New York Times*, "We saw nothing—no manuscript or outline when we negotiated for it." The *Times* commented that this winning bid, promised "sight unseen," illustrated how eager studios were for material from the era's leading authors.[4]

Once Fox saw the novel, it discovered several problems. One was its sprawling plot. Whereas *Captain Caution* and *Northwest Passage* took place in the US, *Lydia Bailey* spanned the globe, from early nineteenth-century New England to Haiti and North Africa. This, along with the novel's densely packed 488 pages, complicated adapting it into a feature-length timeframe.

Budget became another concern. After 1945, Hollywood revenues dropped. The growing number of televisions depressed ticket sales; so did the postwar baby boom. New parents stayed at home with their babies instead of visiting theaters, and ticket purchases competed with new spending categories such as home improvement. Fox's domestic revenues fell $10 million between 1945 and 1947; protectionist measures in Europe caused foreign revenues to fall from \$28 million in 1944 to \$17.7 million in 1947. In addition, a government antitrust action (culminating in a 1948 Supreme Court decision called the *Paramount* case) began to separate studios from theaters. No longer were studios guaranteed venues for their releases; they now had to pitch each film to independent theater owners.[5]

Even as revenues declined, technological changes and evolving audience preferences increased the costs of moviemaking. Audiences of the late 1940s, many of whom had traveled during the war, had become more sophisticated; they shunned movie-set versions of foreign countries. Shooting on location, far more expensive, became necessary. According to Aubrey Solomon, 1947 was Fox's year of "runaway production costs." And because theater bookings were no longer guaranteed, each film required an increased PR budget.[6]

All of this meant that, even though Roberts's novel became the success everyone expected (staying on bestseller lists for months), Fox realized it had overpaid for what would be smaller-than-projected box office revenues, with higher costs. Studio head Darryl F. Zanuck, who has been called "the most important and influential producer in the history of the American cinema,"[7] hired a succession of writers, each trying to wrestle the novel into a compelling film of minimal cost.

The studio's decision to set *Lydia Bailey* in Haiti thus resulted not from an express interest in the Revolution, but as a logistical solution for adapting Roberts's sprawling novel. Zanuck entrusted the project to producer Sol Siegel; in April 1947, Siegel sent Zanuck a film treatment, commissioned from writer Milton Krims. Siegel explained that he did not want to disappoint Roberts fans with too many plot changes. He and Krims had decided that the most feasible strategy would involve focusing on the novel's middle section. This would place the action entirely in Haiti.[8]

Message Picture or Adventure-Romance? White Lovers in Haiti (1947–48)

In offering this solution, Siegel identified what he considered a possible pitfall: the Haitian setting risked leading to a focus on Haitians, but the film needed to center on Roberts's white protagonists. "The all-important problem," he told Zanuck, "was to create a story in which the *white people were the principal characters* (emphasis added) and occupied the foreground of the picture. I believe we accomplished it . . . and at no sacrifice to the color and history of Haiti." Zanuck, once a scriptwriter himself, responded that he shared this concern. *Lydia Bailey* needed to be a romance-adventure film, about the white Americans Albion and Lydia. Zanuck complained of Krims's treatment that "the personal story has been smothered in the epic of historical events." Zanuck added that the film should be a romance and a suspenseful "mystery."[9]

Zanuck and his screenwriters retained different ideas about how to make *Lydia Bailey* compelling. Roberts's novels were historical fiction, not generic adventure-romances. And whereas Zanuck wanted a crowd-pleasing adventure with action scenes that foreign audiences would also enjoy, the writers were keen to keep a focus on history. Screenwriters of the era tended to be politically engaged, whether or not they were far enough to the left to be blacklisted.[10] Many had spent the war in the military or writing patriotic films for studios. And the country was in turmoil, as red-baiting swept through Hollywood and Americans debated the meaning of patriotism. The writers thus projected their own ideals onto Haiti's revolution.

Imbuing feature films with larger social messages was not inherently a problem for Zanuck. As Bernard Dick has noted, Zanuck "prized good screenwriting, regardless of the writer's politics." In addition, the 1940s were the golden age of the "message picture," a kind of film designed to call attention to racism and other injustices. In the 1930s, Hollywood had begun efforts to improve representations of African Americans; they were prodded by Walter White, executive secretary of the NAACP, who thought film could change white Americans' hearts and minds. World War II accelerated these efforts. Americans sought not to appear hypocritical as they fought Nazi racism, and the US Office of War Information released its own message films, encouraging whites and Blacks to feel united in the fight against racism in Europe and at home. As Thomas Cripps has written, in the period 1945–48, a new "liberal-Hollywood-black alliance" reshaped depictions of Blacks on screen.[11]

Fox was particularly engaged in these efforts. The studio's chairman, former Republican presidential nominee Wendell Willkie, also served on the NAACP board. And Zanuck was, in Cripps's words, a "genuine ally" of these initiatives. Certainly, some of his films trafficked in stereotypes about Blacks and Asians, as they had since his days as a writer in the 1920s; moreover, some of Fox's films had, in Ellen Scott's words, "strange racial messages." However, Zanuck sought in the postwar period to improve, showing scripts to the NAACP's Walter White for his input—though he did not always accept White's suggestions.[12] Fox's desire to combat racism also supported President Harry S. Truman's civil rights and foreign policy initiatives. Historians have questioned whether Truman's motives were sincere or politically minded. However, recognizing that discrimination harmed the US image and heightened Communism's appeal abroad (and hoping to capture African American votes in the 1948 election), Truman had begun a number of civil rights initiatives, including establishing a Committee on Civil Rights. In 1947, the committee issued a report calling for widespread desegregation. Cinema would be one prong in this effort, building on steps like Jackie Robinson's 1947 integration of baseball.[13]

The same year, Fox scored a huge success with one of the era's most impactful message films, *Gentleman's Agreement*. Produced by Zanuck, directed by Elia Kazan, and starring Gregory Peck, *Gentleman's Agreement* shone a harsh spotlight on US antisemitism—with a side of boy meets girl and raises her consciousness. Though many Jews were apprehensive about the film, fearing that it would only highlight their presence in the film industry, the non-Jewish Zanuck turned the film into one of 1947's biggest box office draws.[14] In 1948, *Gentleman's Agreement* won a flurry of Oscars, including Best Picture.

Thus, as they worked on *Lydia Bailey* (especially in 1948), Zanuck and his team were basking in the success of *Gentleman's Agreement*—and thinking of what to tackle next. Their works in progress included *Pinky*, a film about racial passing that became a huge commercial success while receiving mixed critical reviews. *Pinky*'s screenwriter, Philip Dunne, later recalled that Zanuck never "subscribed to the theory of some producers that 'messages should be left to Western Union'" but "wanted to . . . take a whack at racism as he had at anti-Semitism."[15] Fox's highest-grossing films of 1948 and 1949 were message pictures.[16]

It was not obvious to Zanuck, however, that *Lydia Bailey* should be this kind of film. For one thing, the message picture was beginning its decline after 1947. A major factor was the House Un-American Activities Committee (HUAC), which ramped up its red-baiting in 1947 with hearings in Hollywood. Films with leftist messages became suspect, as Judith E. Smith has noted, pushing studios away from such messages. A second factor came from audiences. Message pictures were not fail-safe propositions; challenging existing beliefs could sound preachy or cause offense.[17] In addition, Zanuck had purchased the rights to *Gentleman's Agreement* and *Pinky* intending to make message pictures; with *Lydia Bailey*, he had planned a more generic historical adventure romance.

Still, there was no clear path for making *Lydia Bailey* into a film that stayed true to the novel, with the elements Zanuck wanted and minimal costs. The film's screenwriters, fresh from other message pictures, felt that it would be most compelling if they blended adventure-romance with politics. They tried to sell Zanuck on scripts that included what he wanted, while rendering the Haitian Revolution relevant to viewers. Dunne and Blankfort in particular gave Albion and Toussaint Louverture impassioned speeches about freedom.

To turn *Lydia Bailey* at least partially into a message film, the screenwriters had to reshape the novel, since Roberts was hardly a progressive. As Leonard Dinnerstein and Jack Bales have noted, Roberts had been a leading anti-immigration voice; he portrayed Jews as "undesirable" and "Asiatic," and was xenophobic and racist in other ways. Roberts's novel improved in some ways over his earlier writings, but not in others. Roberts portrayed Toussaint as intelligent and thoughtful, but primarily because he was a good colonial who was kind to former enslavers, unlike other Haitians who wanted revenge against them. Roberts's main villains were not the French, but Jean-Jacques Dessalines, whom he portrayed as "the worst man in the world." Roberts also referred to the "dark-skinned thousands" Albion encountered in Haiti as having a "musky, animal smell," and he described Blacks as having their "own negroid ideas of logic." These aspects of the novel distressed the NAACP. As Walter White wrote to Haiti's ambassador to the US in 1947, "While [Roberts's novel] is not viciously anti-Haiti, nevertheless the scene it depicts of incredible barbarity by men like Dessalines has done irreparable harm to the country."[18] Though the novel featured Albion helping King Dick and Louverture, it did so not to highlight the Haitian cause but to portray Americans as natural world leaders in an era of French decline. Indeed, as Stacy Holden has argued, the novel "*Lydia Bailey* is a Cold War text encouraging readers to support an internationalist agenda in which the spreading of U.S. values in developing countries—even by military might—is recognized as a legitimate means of protecting the country's strategic interests."[19]

Roberts was furious that Zanuck and the writers did not consult him,[20] but their scripts departed from his novel in many ways. Krims was more progressive than Roberts, less so than his successors on the project. Krims had written both the anti-Nazi film *Confessions of a Nazi Spy* (1939) and the 1948 anti-Communist film *Iron Curtain*, which he, Siegel, and Zanuck worked on coterminously with *Lydia Bailey* in 1947. During the war, Krims had served as a combat correspondent and made patriotic films for the Army Air Corps. He later wrote that he had been a strong antifascist before the war and "spent some unpleasant years in the Pacific because I believed democracy was something to fight for." Krims's personal papers indicate that his anti-Communism led him to oppose both the Hollywood Ten and the Screen Writers Guild's opposition to HUAC, positions markedly different from Dunne's and Blankfort's.[21]

Krims's initial 1947 treatment shared some of Roberts's outlook, including viewing the 1800s from the vantage point of the late 1940s. In this decolonizing era, Krims expressed US sympathy for colonized peoples seeking independence from European rulers. His Albion—so different from the real-life

Americans who had invaded Haiti and robbed it of its independence in 1915—stood for Haitian self-determination, backing the freedom-fighting Toussaint against the racist French. Krims's treatment evinced postwar patriotism and anti-Gallic sentiment; it depicted young, virile Americans' superiority to old-fashioned Frenchmen. Krims portrayed the French as hypocrites; they claimed to stand for "liberty, equality, and fraternity" but had imposed "years of the most inhuman brutal slavery." (Certainly, the fact that they were French and not Southern made it possible to condemn their enslavement of Africans, without white US audiences feeling attacked). In some ways, Krims's descriptions of Blacks resembled Roberts's, with slight improvement; describing Toussaint as "very black," Krims added that the general "possess[ed] the most statesman-like brain yet produced in the Negro race." Like Roberts, Krims also portrayed Toussaint as atypically reasonable for a Haitian: "Only the wisdom and vision of Toussaint Louverture restrains [other Haitians] from exterminating the Whites."[22]

Still, because of his postwar anti-Gallicism and his general opposition to injustice, Krims depicted the Revolution very differently from the films discussed in chapter 1, as a movement led by Haitians themselves. He noted that the French had "thoughtlessly" enslaved "some of the best warriors in all of Africa . . . in the mistaken belief that they were human cattle." He described French plantation owners as "more savage than the most ignorant natives." Far from being inspired by French ideals (inconsistent at best), Haitians had simply "picked the most opportune time to revolt against the brutality of their French masters." Luckily, they did so just as a strapping young American arrived to help.[23]

As Krims continued to revise in 1947, Zanuck remained unsatisfied. By January 1948, with Hollywood revenues dropping and costs rising, Krims found himself at an impasse. He wrote Zanuck that he could eventually produce a script that would satisfy Zanuck's multiple needs. However, its epic scale would be much too expensive to produce in this changed industry: "Spectacle is inherent in Lydia Bailey; it requires difficult locations, masses of people, expensive sets." Krims had determined that it was pointless to put the film into production.[24]

Dunne's *Lydia Bailey*: Decolonization and Décolletage (1948)

As the *New York Times* reported, the issue of cost had also worried Zanuck. However, after shelving the project briefly, he charged ahead in April 1948.

To replace Krims, Zanuck brought in his go-to writer Philip Dunne. Dunne had spent the war making patriotic message films for the US Office of War Information; he was not only one of Hollywood's most acclaimed screenwriters but also one of its most politically active. Dunne stated that he had been "born and bred to liberal politics" as a New Deal Democrat whose father was close with Teddy Roosevelt. Before his thirty-first birthday (1939), as Dunne recalled in his autobiography, "I had become a rather prominent politician in California," including posts with several Democratic Party organizations and the Screen Writers Guild. Dunne explained, "I have always worn my political heart on my sleeve. . . . My opinions have always been lusty and unashamed." Though Dunne's politics differed from Zanuck's, their working relationship was close and productive.[25]

Where Krims did not oppose HUAC, Dunne had led a national fight against it; he saw *Lydia Bailey* as a useful tool in this battle. Though Dunne had never been a Communist, his membership in several prewar antifascist organizations made him one of the first Hollywood figures investigated for un-American activities in 1940, alongside his friends James Cagney and Humphrey Bogart. Reynold Humphries has argued that Dunne never faced real danger, since "his anti-Communism was known to all; he had publicly opposed Dalton Trumbo over the Nazi-Stalin pact." Still, the experience cemented for Dunne a belief that "no government official . . . has any right to inquire into the political beliefs or affiliations of any citizen." In 1947, Dunne had become a courageous ally to his Hollywood Ten colleagues facing the blacklist. As HUAC held its Hollywood hearings, with freshman congressman Richard Nixon an energetic new member, Dunne founded the Committee for the First Amendment with John Huston and William Wyler. They gathered hundreds of famous friends to speak out in favor of the Ten.[26]

Though Dunne hoped to imbue *Lydia Bailey* with anti-HUAC and antiracist messages, he knew that message pictures could be tricky. In a 1949 op-ed anticipating debates over *Pinky*, Dunne explained that "the production of a controversial film entails a very real financial risk," since a "boycott by any group . . . can turn a legitimately anticipated profit into a loss.'" He stated that issues of race were particularly challenging to treat in film, since "every American citizen, white or colored, has his own ideas on the subject." Still, Dunne stated, he avoided neutrality in his scripts, since he found it "as sterile dramatically as it is politically." Dunne declared that he did not aim to please every theatergoer, and that "no member of the Ku Klux Klan will find [*Pinky*] either entertaining or edifying." He concluded that, despite message films' risks, he felt obliged to use cinema in pursuit of social justice: "The experience of the war has taught us that the motion picture is a powerful and persuasive vehicle of propaganda. What we say and do on the screen . . . can affect the happiness, the living conditions, even the physical safety of millions of our fellow-citizens." He added that Zanuck supported him as long as his scripts did not simply lecture but told "an emotional human story."[27]

For *Lydia Bailey*, Dunne tried to balance Zanuck's requests for an audience-pleasing, sexy adventure film with the larger social messages important to him. Implicitly blasting HUAC, Dunne spoke passionately of US ideals of freedom. Though he had to excise much of Roberts's novel, Dunne kept a reference to the 1798 Alien and Sedition Acts. He used it to explain true American values—by which one should be free to disagree with the government—to a skeptical Frenchman. In this scene, Dunne championed the superiority of US ideals of freedom to French ones, while lambasting dangerous officials who distorted them.[28]

Dunne also treated Haitian culture more positively than Roberts and Krims. He changed their references to "voodoo" to the more respectful spelling *vodoun* (a French variant for Vodou), suggesting that he had read some of the sympathetic scholarship on Haiti that emerged from the US occupation. Still, Dunne left intact Roberts's portrayal of Dessalines as an evil man worse than French enslavers. Keeping Roberts's juxtaposition of Dessalines and Toussaint, Dunne wrote that Dessalines "suffers from race prejudice. He hates all whites. He was a bad slave and was whipped often." The idea that Dessalines had been tortured because he was "bad" was problematic, of course, since it erased the notion that slavery was inherently brutal.[29]

While building on Roberts's and Krims's patriotic anticolonialism, Dunne turned it into something more progressive. In a May 1948 version of the script, Dunne's Toussaint offered a universalistic account of the Haitian struggle. Toussaint explains to Albion that Haitians are at the forefront of the global fight for freedom: "[Liberty] is even dearer to us than it is to you—for you were never slaves." Toussaint expresses a desire for peace, but says that if Napoleon's troops threaten Haitians' freedom, "We will fight Bonaparte's divisions with weapons they have never faced . . . with the disease that lurks in our jungles. We will destroy every plantation, every field that's been bathed in our sweat. We will burn the cities, poison the wells and streams. . . . We will leave nothing on this island but freedom." Evoking those who stood idle against Nazi expansionism, Dunne's Toussaint warned that if Napoleon was not stopped in Haiti, he would next invade the US.[30]

In August, Dunne added something more radical to the script: the idea that colonized peoples should direct their own freedom struggles, without US meddling. Krims's Albion had played a key role in Toussaint's strategy, urging him to fight Leclerc.[31] Dunne altered this: when Albion discovers that Napoleon has sent Leclerc to reenslave Haitians and deport Toussaint, Toussaint thanks Albion—but adds that Haitians will fight without US help.

ALBION: I should like to help, Citizen.
TOUSSAINT: You can help us best by going home, telling our story to the American people.

In addition, Dunne offered a far more negative view of the French than in Roberts's novel. Where Roberts's main villain had been Dessalines, Dunne's was the French colonist d'Autremont (Lydia's employer in the novel and her fiancé in the film). Dunne's d'Autremont was an overt racist who called Americans gullible, and said they did not understand that "this black society is rotten to the core." This part of Dunne's script built on Krims, but also reflected Dunne's own keen interest in decolonization. Dunne closely watched national liberation struggles in Asia and elsewhere. As he would tell a Chinese correspondent in 1950, the US should stop new nations from adopting Communism not by military means, but by being an exemplar of freedom at home. Later, Dunne would blast US interference in Vietnam.[32]

Though Dunne's views were more progressive than many of his colleagues, he was not unique in making decolonization central in his film. As Jon Cowans has noted, a flurry of decolonization films were released in the postwar United States, Britain, and France. As national liberation movements erupted worldwide, films helped audiences process these changes. Paralleling US foreign policy, Hollywood decolonization films could have conflicting messages. The US did not want newly independent people to ally with the Soviets, so they pressured allies to decolonize peacefully. On the other hand, the US did not want to offend its allies. And since studio heads worked closely with the US government, both because of their wartime service and government pressure, films reflected this ambiguity. Even as films often supported the idea of national liberation, studio heads frequently restrained anticolonial content for commercial reasons—since, as Cowans notes, "The two largest European colonial powers were also Hollywood's two largest foreign markets." In Cowan's words, one could see "blended conservative and liberal viewpoints" on decolonization in a single film.[33]

Consequently, it is not surprising that Zanuck accepted Dunne's vision, but with two sets of reservations. First, though Dunne's script attacked racism and supported Haitian aspirations in many ways, Zanuck worried that parts of it, following Roberts's novel, reflected poorly on Blacks. Since Zanuck wanted to satisfy the NAACP, African American audiences, and the Truman administration, he wrote Dunne in October 1948, "please take out as much as possible the talk about Negroes double-crossing their own people."[34]

Second, Zanuck wanted greater balance in discussing decolonization. He endorsed Dunne's idea that the audience should root for Haitian freedom fighters. Moreover, linked to his worry about "double-crossers," he felt that Dunne, building from Roberts, was making the notion of Black government look bad. In August, Dunne had eliminated the character of Dessalines, turning him into a fictional Haitian villain named Mirabeau. Still, the character remained, and Zanuck feared that it offered a negative depiction of Black leaders:

> We want to be able to believe that the Haitian government is a good government. It is young, and it is growing. They have their trouble with the Mirabeaus and other extremists and radicals. . . . But we should feel that it is a pretty solid government or else we won't pull for them when the French try to take them over. We want to believe that they are substantial people who will govern well if left alone."

However, though Zanuck endorsed Dunne's wanting the audience to sympathize with Haitians, he was concerned that supporting them too strongly would offend the French. In November 1948, he asked Dunne to make Americans look neutral. He suggested that Albion say, "I undertook this mission for [Toussaint], as a neutral emissary. . . . I have always loved France. Every American has a warm spot in his heart for France. . . . But in these weeks when I have lived side by side with Toussaint's men I have also come to know and understand their side."[35]

Dunne took Zanuck's notes, but put his own spin on them; he used the suggestions to inject even more anticolonialism into the script. Dunne had Albion express gratitude to France, while declaring that Haitians better understood freedom:

> Every American acknowledges a debt to France. You saved our Revolution. We have had the same ideals of liberty. But in these weeks I have spent with Toussaint's men, I have come to learn that *they are the ones who stand for these ideals here in Haiti. I have learned about liberty, equality and fraternity from the blacks* [emphasis added].[36]

For a studio film written when Jim Crow reigned and the Haitian Revolution was not widely acknowledged, such words were striking; Dunne showed that the Revolution was *not* necessarily unthinkable for a progressive postwar American.

Dunne also included something unprecedented in Hollywood film: a full-throated justification of Black violence against oppressive white colonizers. As Albion realizes how cruel the French have been, he tells Lydia: "If I were a native—here today—I'd kill any white man I could get my hands on." This powerful line justified not only anticolonial revolt but also killing whites en route to freedom. Dunne closed his final November script with a quote (which Zanuck did not keep in the film) seemingly aimed at HUAC. A closing title card would read, "'WE SHALL KNOW HOW TO DEFEND OUR LIBERTY OR PERISH . . .' TOUSSAINT L'OUVERTURE."[37]

Lydia Stalls Again (1948–50)

In spring and fall 1948, Fox had seemed optimistic that *Lydia Bailey* would be made. In June, the studio had announced that Linda Darnell would play Lydia, and that it would solve the cost problem by filming in England. Postwar currency restrictions, aimed at helping European economies rebuild, required that profits made in Europe remain there. Fox could thus put its immobile pounds sterling to good use on the film.[38]

By November 1948, the studio was almost ready to begin production. But first, Dunne and Zanuck had to submit the script to the Production Code Administration (PCA), which had to approve films. To fulfill Zanuck's desire that *Lydia Bailey* combine history and sex appeal, Dunne had included plenty of innuendo—and French and Haitian characters wearing low-cut dresses. Joseph Breen, the PCA censor, often objected to sexual content; however, *Lydia Bailey*'s references to interracial sex had him particularly perturbed. Breen declared the script "unacceptable." He was particularly concerned with references to "loose sex between the white men and the Negro [women]." Following Roberts, who had drawn heavily on Moreau de Saint-Méry's descriptions of Saint-Domingue, Dunne's Haiti teemed with mixed-race prostitutes; Breen insisted that they be removed. Even more problematic for Breen was the suggestively named King Dick, so hypermasculine that he had eight wives. Breen's objections ranged from their costumes (he feared they would reveal too much cleavage) to a moment when King Dick tells his wives smirkingly that they should give Albion "anything he wants. Anything."[39]

On another film, the writers could have simply revised, eliminating the content troubling the censor. But *Lydia Bailey*'s balance between history, adventure, and sex was already precarious—and Fox's financial challenges remained. Thus, by late November, Dunne found himself, as Krims had, at a creative standstill. He and Zanuck turned to more promising projects.

Fox continued to proclaim that the film would be made. In December 1948, *Variety* said it would be one of 1949's biggest-budget films, at a cost of $3 million. By autumn 1949, with the cast not set, Zanuck reaffirmed that the film would be headquartered in England and shot mostly in Haiti. By February 1950, reports circulated that Tyrone Power would play Albion.[40] However, no new work was being done on the script.

In late June 1950, Siegel returned to *Lydia Bailey*, this time with screenwriter Charles O'Neal. O'Neal was more conservative than Dunne; his versions lacked stirring defenses of the Haitian cause. Though O'Neal referred to a "dark era of the white man's domination of the black," he also described the Revolution from white colonists' perspective, as having produced "suffering" and slaughter. And seeming, literally, not to have gotten Breen's memo on eliminating sexual innuendo, O'Neal seasoned his script outlines with lines designed to elicit "dirty laughs" from the actors. As Albion first approached Haiti by ship, sailors debated whether to have some fun with Haitian "women [who] are as black as the [coffee] they brew—and twice as hot!" or to try to get "a bit o' cream in my coffee."[41] Siegel does not seem to have liked O'Neal's draft, and no record exists of his working on the film after July.

In November 1950, Fox encountered yet another setback. Though they had planned to shoot in Haiti, "disturbances in that part of the world" (the military coup against Dumarsais Estimé and the uncertainty about who would replace him) gave them cold feet. Once again, Zanuck reset his plans; they would film in California.[42]

Now, a new screenwriter took over: Harry Brown, fresh off an Oscar nod for the John Wayne picture *Sands of Iwo Jima* (1949). Brown eliminated Dunne's message-film language and streamlined the script. His Albion criticized slavery, but also pointed out, "I have nothing against the French." Brown also sought to retain the sexed-up adventure content for Zanuck, but in a way that might pass Breen's red pen (like a seductive "mulatto" café singer who distracts Albion while others rob him).[43] Ultimately, Brown's script does not seem to have pleased the studio any more than O'Neal's. He disappeared from the project after December 1950—though this turned out well for him, since he was able to write and win an Oscar for 1951's *A Place in the Sun*.

Blankfort Enters from Stage Left, HUAC from the Right (1951)

By January 1951, Zanuck had a new *Lydia* team: Jules Schermer as producer, Michael Blankfort as screenwriter, and Jean Negulesco as director—with the latter being the least influential.[44] If Zanuck had been trying to make the film *less* political with O'Neal and Brown, Blankfort was a curious choice; he had been a prominent Marxist writer in New York in the 1930s. But Blankfort was one of Hollywood's hottest screenwriters, having just written Fox's Western/message film *Broken Arrow*, for which he would win a Screen Writers Guild Award. Actually, Blankfort had been credited in place of the real author, his blacklisted friend Albert Maltz. But Blankfort did *Broken Arrow*'s final rewrites while Maltz was imprisoned.[45] Zanuck and Schermer (himself an Oscar-nominated writer) thought the talented Blankfort, finally, might produce a crowd-pleasing *Lydia* that would still have meaningful content.

Unfortunately for Zanuck, HUAC now became a real threat to *Lydia Bailey*. The months January–March 1951 were marked by feverish script revisions, while Blankfort fought to stay off the blacklist and out of jail. Multiarchival research offers a glimpse into this chaotic time. The Fox archives at USC and Blankfort's papers at Boston University show only script battles, while Blankfort's papers at the Academy of Motion Pictures Arts and Sciences detail the HUAC prosecution and his anger at having to fight for his career while struggling with the script.

Blankfort used Dunne's scripts as the basis for his revisions, rather than those of O'Neal and Brown. Though Blankfort was further to the left than Dunne, the men were friends who had each spent World War II making patriotic films (Blankfort as a captain in the Marine Corps). Both were also active in the Screen Writers Guild. Blankfort admired Dunne's courage in decrying HUAC, and he later called Dunne a "first-rate . . . mensch."[46] Blankfort built on the political aspects of Dunne's script, while making the dialogue lively and sexy enough for Zanuck. His first script draft began conversationally, as Albion recalled his arrival in Haiti:

> On that January day back in 1802 . . . , I was [little] prepared for a great and exciting moment of its history. . . . I didn't know as I heard the distant drums that ahead of me was a world of terror—and also of great men. All I wanted was to do the task I was paid to do with as little inconvenience as possible, and . . . [have] rum and wenches. . . . I was a man without meaning to my life—but deep down . . . , I wanted to find a meaning."[47]

Blankfort's Albion evolved from a man wanting drink, sex, and money to realizing his life must be about bigger things, like helping the Haitian cause.

Blankfort's angle—with Albion as a salt-of-the-earth macho type having his consciousness raised—would not have surprised anyone who had known him before his Hollywood days.[48] While a University of Pennsylvania student (class of 1929), Blankfort led classmates in defending a professor who was fired for comments on the Soviet education system. Blankfort himself became interested in socialism, alongside his friend I. F. Stone. After graduation, Blankfort visited the Soviet Union, writing in his diary that "this trip changed much of my life because it made a radical out of a liberal" and that "Karl Marx has as yet not been refuted." After stints teaching psychology at Bowdoin and Princeton (where he declared, "This place is beautiful . . . [but] I would rather be a half-baked, third rate playwright than a looked up to academic"),[49] Blankfort became active in New York Marxist circles. He criticized the "bourgeois press" as an associate editor at the leftist magazine *Modern Monthly*. But he left with others when its chief editor, V. F. Calverton, quarreled with the Communist Party.[50]

Blankfort's commitment to racial equality grew out of his Marxism. In 1934, he had directed the play *Stevedore* for the Theatre Union. The play has been called seminal in suggesting that racism was not a mere byproduct of class oppression, which would disappear if capitalism did, but needed to be combated separately among white workers. Blankfort publicly criticized leftists who assumed that Black actors were lazy, and he declared that his production differed from those of "bourgeois theater": it had "no stock 'mammies' . . . or comic butlers, or any of the other false characters which colored actors and actresses are called on to play." Blankfort declared that his art was based on going "to the workers." Elsewhere, he argued that "revolutionary theater" must not only appeal to the "class-conscious vanguard" but also "attract the mass of less advanced workers. Our plays must . . . organize them." Among Blankfort's works in this period was 1936's *Battle Hymn*, an abolitionist play about John Brown mounted at the WPA Federal Theater, written with his friend Michael Gold. Blankfort also wrote about theater for *New Masses* and the *Daily Worker*, the newspaper of the Communist Party of the United States (CPUSA).[51]

After moving to Hollywood, Blankfort still hoped to extinguish racism; he brought this desire to his *Lydia Bailey* scripts. Blankfort would find himself needing to battle on two fronts while writing: against Negulesco and HUAC. Blankfort had enlivened Dunne's draft while deepening its Revolution focus, whereas the Romanian-born director wanted adventure and the white characters to dominate. After reading Blankfort's first draft, Negulesco complained to Schermer: "About whom are we telling this story? . . . All of a sudden . . . our principals are completely secondary to a crowd of [Haitian] generals." Negulesco insisted, "Our basic story, if we are going to seek the most box-office appeal here, is <u>love</u> and <u>adventure</u>." Negulesco also objected to Blankfort's effort to have Albion evolve, which he felt made Albion look "weak." He argued that Blankfort had made Dunne's versions worse. Zanuck (who had not yet read Blankfort's revision) panicked, writing Schermer:

> It took practically a year and a lot of effort on Phil Dunne's part to boil the novel down to at least the framework of an adventure story . . . , and if the story of the revolt and political aspects have been pushed into the foreground then there has certainly been a mistake or a big misunderstanding.
>
> To me LYDIA BAILEY offered a great chance for an adventurous story loaded with sex, romance, off-beat characterizations and excitement. I am not for a split second interested in the "cause" of the political incidents connected with the revolution in Haiti except as we use them as the background of our personal story.

Fortunately for Blankfort, Schermer took his side. He told Zanuck that Blankfort's script had "better motion picture in it" than Dunne's, and that "Negulesco has alarmed you unnecessarily." Schermer added that Dunne and Blankfort had talked, and that "Dunne feels that we have made a great improvement over his script." After a mediated sit-down with Negulesco, Blankfort delivered a revised screenplay on January 22.[52]

Unfortunately for Blankfort, the same week he was battling Negulesco, letters calling him a Communist reached the studio. The newsletter *Alert* had called Blankfort a "notorious [participant] in Communist fronts and causes" and suggested that patriotic citizens boycott his new film *Halls of Montezuma*. Readers then wrote Fox. After Zanuck forwarded these letters to his writer, Blankfort replied, "I'm hot as hell about this damn sniping and I'm seeing an attorney as soon as I can about my civil rights in these matters." However, since he needed more than anger to defend himself, Blankfort shared with Zanuck the more measured replies he was sending, explaining that he was a Marine veteran whose film had been approved by the military, and that *Halls of Montezuma* aimed to inspire patriotism and "faith in God." Zanuck praised Blankfort's responses; Blankfort assured him that he was not a Communist, and that "LYDIA BAILEY moves ahead. I am working double-time . . . since I am aware of the nearness to the shooting date."[53]

In February, Blankfort continued to argue with Negulesco—and to work to clear his name. Blankfort's marginalia on Negulesco's critiques offer a glimpse into his mood. On one, Blankfort wrote, "Shit! Over my dead body," "Fuck!" and "VOMITOUS" (but in one case, "possible!"). At the same time, Blankfort gathered documents for his attorneys, hoping to show that he had been a left-leaning idealist, but never a Communist.[54]

On February 21, Blankfort got what he dreaded: a HUAC subpoena. He agreed to testify on April 4, and kept working in the meanwhile. He retained Dunne's defenses of the Haitian Revolution, while trying to make them less pedantic and more conversational, for instance in punching up Dunne's line empathizing with Blacks wanting to kill whites.[55] More of the cast was set, including Anne Francis as Lydia (replacing Darnell and others whose names had been floated) and Dale Robertson as Albion, replacing Power. The film's new African American star, William Marshall, would earn a larger salary than the lesser-known white leads. A giant (both literally and metaphorically) of the New York theater scene, Marshall had been the studio's dream pick for King Dick (figure 3.2).[56] Blankfort wrote some powerful speeches for Marshall, articulating the Haitian cause. Marshall's King Dick would be an educated anticolonial, a far cry from the dialect-speaker of Roberts's novel. By the end of March, the new script went to the PCA. Breen was happier with Blankfort's version, though he asked that Fox reduce its "killing and bloodshed," as well as some "sex-suggestive" scenes.[57]

On April 4, 1951, Blankfort gave his HUAC testimony, in closed session. The nature of his testimony then and in January 1952 has been hotly debated in scholarship on the period. However, it is important to note that only Blankfort's 1952 statement was public—and Blankfort's personal papers make several things clear. One is that Blankfort appeared as a "friendly" witness in 1951, though he was irate, because he was terrified of being blacklisted and unable to support his daughters. Second, he engaged in serious spin, portraying himself as a naive person who never knew that organizations he joined were Communist fronts. He even suggested that he had written for *New Masses* and the *Daily Worker* not because of Marxism, but because he heard that play reviewers could get "free tickets." This belied the fact that Blankfort was then hardly a starving unknown, but a prominent Marxist dramatist whose plays and lectures were covered in the *New York Times*. Blankfort also denounced Communism and suggested that, because he sent his daughters to Hebrew school and belonged to the American Jewish Congress (which formally opposed Communism), he could not have been a Communist. As Blankfort would admit later, however, "For me, in . . . the late twenties and early thirties, God was superstition and Judaism was a backward religion."[58] It remains unclear whether Blankfort was ever a CPUSA member, as opposed to an unaffiliated Marxist traveling in CPUSA circles. But he seems to have distanced himself from Stalinism long before the Nazi-Soviet pact that was the breaking point for other Jewish leftists, possibly as early as Stalin's 1935 pact with Franco.[59] By the early 1950s, following the

Figure 3.2. King Dick (William Marshall, center) helps Albion maneuver past Haitian villain Mirabeau (Roy Glenn, facing Marshall). *Lydia Bailey*. © 20th Century Fox, 1952. Ex-libris William Marshall, author's personal collection.

Holocaust, Blankfort had reembraced his Jewish identity, becoming both a sincere anti-Communist and a strong supporter of Israel. Indeed, while working on *Lydia Bailey*, he had begun his novel *The Juggler* (later a film with Kirk Douglas), one of the earliest works about Holocaust survivors and the state of Israel.[60]

While Blankfort creatively described his past in April 1951 to save his career, it is also clear that he sought to avoid identifying friends as party members. Several weeks after this testimony, Blankfort learned that he had received a "clean bill of health."[61] His strategy, thanking HUAC for allowing him to appear and criticizing Communism, enabled him to keep working. But it lost him dear friends such as Maltz, who thought he had betrayed them. Though testifying in 1951 temporarily cleared him, Blankfort lived in fear that he would be called again. Not only would that happen in January 1952, but his earlier beliefs continued to cause him trouble, notably when the State Department denied him a passport in 1954 to travel to Israel for *The Juggler*'s filming.[62]

HUAC was not yet finished with *Lydia Bailey*. Though Blankfort had moved on to other work by the time he was called again before HUAC in 1952, other members of the *Lydia Bailey* team fell under suspicion. As the studio waited in April to hear if Blankfort was cleared, Zanuck drafted Dunne for final revisions. Dunne then learned that he himself was in danger of becoming a blacklist target, since his work on the Committee for the First Amendment was now labeled pro-Communist. On May 7, Dunne sent Zanuck a detailed letter documenting that he had always been both antifascist and anti-Communist. He then produced a "Revised Shooting Final," credited to "Philip Dunne and Michael Blankfort" (the name reversal that placed Blankfort first in the final credits would be one of many disappointments for Dunne on *Lydia Bailey*).[63] In June 1952, even Zanuck would be accused of Communism, despite being considerably farther to the right than his writers.[64]

Toward "Action!" and Release (Summer 1951–Spring 1952)

Press coverage intensified in summer 1951, as the film neared its shooting date. Encouraged by Fox's team, an Associated Negro Press film columnist marveled at how many "sepian" actors had been hired (188, more than the number of African Americans with guild cards). Marshall told the *New York Amsterdam News* that it was an honor for him to play King Dick: "We have had the Negro pictured so often as a stereotyped character, usually a buffoon, . . . but this time the Negro is drawn from history, from a period when he was resisting a tyranny that had engulfed most of Europe."[65]

Once filming began in June in Los Angeles, behind-the-scenes tribulations continued. Anne Francis would have many calamities in her role as Lydia, including being thrown from a horse as she learned to ride. In September the studio did some final post-shooting rewrites, with Richard Murphy, another Oscar-nominated writer, stepping in for Dunne.[66]

As 1952 arrived, with the film wrapped and general release set for June, the studio wanted to make sure people had not forgotten Roberts's novel. *Lydia Bailey*, as Judith Smith has pointed out, was Fox's first release after the *Paramount* antitrust case.[67] Since theaters now had to be persuaded to book the film, an unparalleled press campaign began. Fox's Exhibitor's Campaign Book offered posters that theaters could use in advertisements, with slogans such as "Now the world of Lydia Bailey comes savagely, passionately alive!" (figure 3.3). In addition, the studio pressed Black publications to write about the film. In August 1951, the studio had signed Marshall to a multipicture contract, which prompted the *Los Angeles Sentinel* to declare, "At long last it has happened! A Negro actor has been signed to star in dramatic roles under an

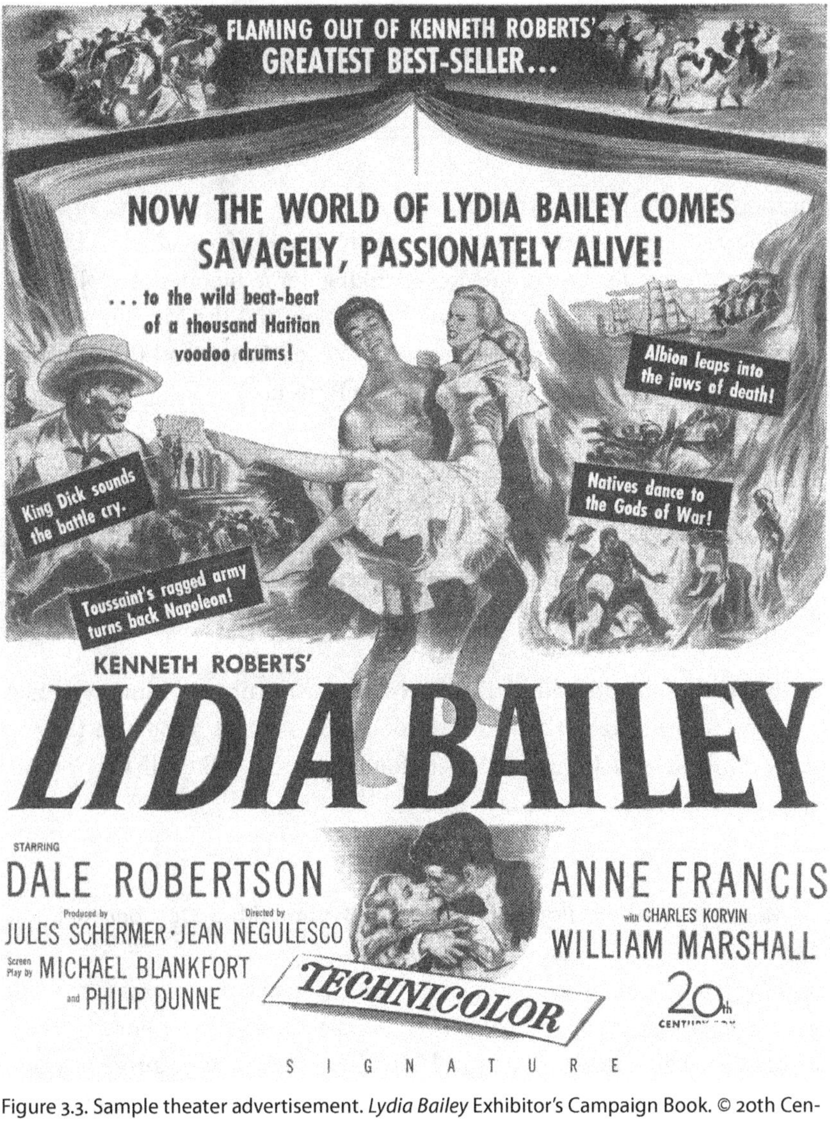

Figure 3.3. Sample theater advertisement. *Lydia Bailey* Exhibitor's Campaign Book. © 20th Century Fox, 1952. Author's personal collection.

iron-bound and lucrative contract in a major Hollywood studio. . . . On an equal footing with John Wayne and other Fox stars of the Caucasian race, Marshall will be starred in two pictures a year, of vast importance to the race[;] these films are to be built around important figures in Negro history." And in January 1952, *Ebony* gushed: "Negro history will be glorified in a major Hollywood movie for the first time when Twentieth Century-Fox releases its excellent production of *Lydia Bailey*." Another *Ebony* article exclaimed, "*Lydia*

Bailey marks a milestone for Hollywood. For the first time a motion picture has been built around a black country with great leaders. . . . Never has a picture carried such a tremendous indictment of slavery."[68]

Beyond these elements of its press campaign, Fox added something truly unprecedented: the film would have its gala world premiere in Haiti, with journalists flown in from across the United States.[69] This premiere, on May 4, 1952, merged three factors: Fox's desire to publicize *Lydia Bailey* (and to gain foreign audiences to compensate for shrinking domestic ones), the NAACP's desire to help Haiti become a tourist destination, and the Magloire government's hopes for attracting foreign capital. Walter White had been pushing this idea to Zanuck since 1949, writing from Port-au-Prince:

> Dear Darryl: I have an idea. . . . [It] is that you hold the world premiere of 'Lydia Bailey' here in the 3,000 seat open air theater in the incredibly beautiful exposition grounds where beginning next December there will be celebrated the 200th anniversary of the founding of Port-au-Prince. The public relations aspect could be like nothing done before.

White successfully pressed Magloire to consider the premiere an investment in Haiti's future. Fox got a relatively good deal: it spent $5,000 on the premiere, while the Magloire government footed the rest of the bill: $25,000 (the equivalent of $228,000 in today's money).[70]

Releasing *Lydia* in Port-au-Prince and Beyond (May–October 1952)

On May 3, fifty-two top journalists from the US—what the Kansas City *Plaindealer* called "newsmen and women of all races, creeds and colors"—set out for an all-expenses-paid junket to Haiti. They flew to Port-au-Prince on a brand-new Pan Am plane christened the *Lydia Bailey* (figure 3.4). Accompanying them were Fox executives and the film's stars Francis and Marshall. The group received a gala tour of Haiti, including a reception at the Presidential Palace, lavish banquets with top Haitian musicians, and plenty of Barbancourt rum. Francis was the life of the party, dancing with Marshall, Magloire, and others until the wee hours of the morning. It was widely reported that she charmed her hosts with her openhearted attitude and her efforts to speak French. On May 4, President Magloire proclaimed Lydia Bailey Day. African American journalists found their visit particularly moving; as Constance Curtis of the *New York Amsterdam News* noted, "the majority of us were

Figure 3.4. Journalists, Fox executives, and film stars arrive in Haiti for the *Lydia Bailey* world premiere on Pan Am's new flagship, the *Lydia Bailey*, May 3, 1952. Ex-libris William Marshall, author's personal collection.

seeing our first Negro leader of government." After a parade (figure 3.5) and fireworks, the film was shown at a black-tie event.[71]

Haitian and US newspapers covered the premiere enthusiastically. *Haiti Sun* hoped it would give the US visitors a view of Haiti's "attributes as a vacation paradise." Magloire expressed a hope that the premiere would spur greater US assistance for Haitian development, and that foreign capital would "flow abundantly to Haiti." American journalists wrote enthusiastically of their trip, even if some complained of torrential rains during their climb to the Citadelle.[72]

A few weeks later, *Lydia Bailey* opened in Los Angeles and then nationwide. Zanuck's team had finally completed the film, overcoming HUAC, the PCA, script battles, and cost problems. The publicity campaign generated strong initial box office receipts, though word of mouth did not power as many subsequent viewers. The final film had cost approximately $1.775 million, and it earned $1.75 million domestically. That placed it in the upper half of Fox films from 1952 for its gross, and fifty-seventh among all Hollywood films for the year.[73]

How did the completed film treat the Revolution? How did it compare to other features we have examined? And what did audiences make of it? Though Blankfort and Dunne were credited as the film's authors, it bore the

Figure 3.5. William Marshall and Anne Francis in motorcade before *Lydia Bailey* world premiere, Port-au-Prince, May 4, 1952. Ex-libris William Marshall, author's personal collection.

mark of the entire team. As one might guess, *Lydia Bailey* was a hodgepodge of the disparate elements that its creators, especially Zanuck, wanted from it. The film began with adventure, suspense, and romance, before turning more to the Revolution. It depicted the Haitian Revolution as analogous to other Atlantic Revolutions, even as its anti-French content was markedly toned down. In many ways, *Lydia Bailey* was better than *Toussaint Louverture* or *Burn!*, though it also had inaccuracies in chronology and included fictional details alongside real ones.

As in its earlier scripts, *Lydia Bailey* did not glorify the French; it also did not suggest that enslaved Haitians borrowed their ideals of freedom. French figures like Leclerc were portrayed as liars and racists rather than models to imitate. Pauline Leclerc (Napoleon's sister) mocks her husband's successes in destroying some "stinking black villages" (1:06:55). And after Leclerc describes Napoleon's orders to befriend Toussaint and trick him into being captured—and Lydia asks, "But . . . is that fair?" (1:08:25)—Pauline archly dismisses Toussaint as someone "whose father was a cannibal somewhere in Africa" and does not deserve fairness (1:09:39). The film contrasted Albion and Lydia, standing for decency, with the Leclercs, who epitomized French hypocrisy. Despite this portrayal, the film did not explore the brutality of slavery, and d'Autremont was not presented as a racist. The final film thus invited postwar viewers to disdain the French, but to a far lesser extent than in Krims's and Dunne's original plans.[74]

Together, Dunne, Blankfort, and Zanuck also succeeded in portraying Haitian leaders as principled and dignified. The film's King Dick is eloquent and daring, though he often has to hide these abilities in front of whites and speak performatively in dialect. Most importantly, the film retained Dunne's vision of Albion. Though he is a "white hero" friend of Dick and Toussaint, he neither ignites the Revolution (in the style of William Walker in *Burn!*) nor teaches Haitian leaders how to wage war (as in the *Toussaint Louverture* miniseries). While initially focused on Lydia, Albion later gets plenty of speeches defending the Haitian cause. After King Dick talks about "we Black men who were slaves but yesterday," Albion says he understands what they have been fighting for, and that "it is no different than what men in my country fought for" (1:10:21–1:11:41). After meeting Toussaint, Albion comments, "Now I know why you think of him as your George Washington" (1:13:34).

The final film also portrayed Toussaint positively, even while retaining the villainous Mirabeau. Louverture, played by Ken Renard, was a model anticolonial leader for the postwar era—a Gandhi type who responded to European violence with a desire for peaceful self-determination. "Only through peace," he declares, "can we rebuild our country" (1:12:14). Toussaint instructs Albion to tell Leclerc how eager he is "to put a stop to this senseless war" (1:16:00). Certainly, the film's Louverture was more anodyne than the real one; however, the portrayal of Haitians as forced into fighting by the French differed sharply from depictions that have fixated on Haitians' violence alone.

Preserving Dunne's initiatives, the film also gave Vodou a more respectful treatment than most foreign depictions. While the film showed Haitians on d'Autremont's plantation engaging in a Vodou ceremony, the religion appeared not as one of pig-blood-drinking, but of deeply spiritual singing and dancing (32:35–38:40). Though the scene reflected a 1940s tourist view of Vodou dance, it is still remarkable that the filmmakers did not imagine the religion in an entirely savage way. The dancers, including the future dance legend Carmen de Lavallade, were both beautiful and graceful.[75]

In many ways, then, *Lydia Bailey* depicted the Revolution atypically. It emphasized Haitian agency in organizing against Leclerc. The film's Haitian revolutionaries were hardly copying the French, but engaging in a well-thought-out campaign to prevent reenslavement.

Despite its strengths, *Lydia Bailey* still reflected the biases of Roberts's novel, as well as others introduced by the filmmakers. Notwithstanding moments when Vodou is shown positively, others (part of making *Lydia Bailey* suspenseful) render it scary and irrational. The opening credits, departing from Blankfort's plan, explain that the "tiny nation" was "keyed to hysteria by the constant beat of jungle drums" (1:38). The film also had some moments akin to the *Toussaint* miniseries. As Leclerc's ships arrive, Vodou drums beat out warnings, backed by menacing horns; Haitians armed with torches and machetes take off, as Mirabeau yells, "KILL, KILL, KILL, KILL, KILL!" (46:38). Indeed, because Zanuck seems to have worried about offending the French more than African Americans, Mirabeau ended up a greater villain than d'Autremont. In addition, in keeping with Zanuck's desire for danger, Haiti is presented as a perilous place, a den of thieves. When Albion first meets King Dick, the latter warns him of "our fine Haitian flesh-eating ants" ready to devour his eyes (12:39).

Other portions of the film played to disturbing stereotypes about Black sexuality. Chief among them were the idea that King Dick had eight wives, and the phallic connotations of his name. No less offensive were scenes preserved from Roberts's novel where Albion and Lydia, under instructions from their Haitian friends, disguise themselves with brown camouflage (a kind of blackface) to hide from Mirabeau and d'Autremont. In these troubling scenes, Lydia lets go of her inhibitions and falls in love with Albion only when dressed "as a Haitian girl" (figure 3.6). The scenes imply that "becoming Black" sexualizes her and makes her more licentious.[76]

Though some of the film's troubling aspects stemmed from Roberts, others came from the Fox team. The writers attacked racism in many ways, but their scripts were not wholly free of it. Krims had used animal imagery for Haitians, saying that Lydia's maid Marie Jeanne "moved silently as a jungle animal," and that "black boys" in Haiti "sang and cavorted like puppies, seemingly indifferent to the loads they carried." An early Dunne draft had Toussaint declaring, "The fault of my race is that we are gullible." The final film featured dogs, trained to attack disobedient Blacks, realizing that Albion is white, even when blacked up, but that King Dick is not. Penned by Blankfort, the scene suggested that dogs could smell the difference between whites and Blacks (23:53, 30:35).[77] Another scene, written by Blankfort, described "black doctors" as treating patients by rubbing them "with goat vomit" (8:47). The Exhibitor's Campaign Book included posters with taglines such as "Into this pagan land—into this half-jungle world . . . he came to claim its most dazzling jewel! . . . Voodoo Drums . . . King Dick . . . Toussaint . . . Magic and Terror!"[78]

Finally, some of the African American actors were disturbed to discover that Negulesco wanted them to wear blackface makeup, presumably to look

Figure 3.6. Albion and Lydia dressed as Haitians. *Lydia Bailey* publicity photo. © 20th Century Fox, 1952. Author's personal collection.

like "real" Haitians. The light-skinned Carmen de Lavallade reported that she and others had to wear a ridiculous makeup called "Negro Number Two." Ironically, since it was designed to make pale skin look black, she thought it looked the least preposterous on the film's white choreographer Jack Cole (figure 3.7), who was dancing in place of Alvin Ailey (who would have been making his film debut in the Vodou dance scene but had fallen ill).[79]

Critics had varying reactions to the film. Among the first to see *Lydia Bailey* were the Haitians at the world premiere. There, the Revolution angle was of greatest interest—and viewers noticed how much the film departed from the historical record. *Haiti Sun* critiqued *Lydia Bailey* for dumbing the Revolution down and for having "'Cops and Robbers' chases" fill its story line. It also pointed to the strange "stylized ballet quality" of the Vodou dance scene. One letter to the editor laughed at Marshall's "faux pas of the epoch": telling Haitians how proud he was to play "King Dick, a great Haitian hero!" as if Dick were a real person. Notwithstanding such criticisms, the *Sun* insisted that the film had "genuine warmth and sympathy for the Haitian cause," and that it would "transmit that emotion to millions of movie goers throughout the world."[80]

Figure 3.7. Vodou dance scene, featuring Carmen de Lavallade and white choreographer Jack Cole (in blackface). *Lydia Bailey.* © 20th Century Fox, 1952. Ex-libris William Marshall, author's personal collection.

The Haitian newspaper *Le Nouvelliste* also pointed to historically questionable parts of *Lydia Bailey*. It found the imposition of an American in Toussaint's camp to be especially bizarre. Nevertheless, the paper praised Fox's "merit and courage, in making such a film." They were particularly impressed by Blankfort's and Dunne's "audacity, in putting in the mouth of a white American . . . this sentence sure to provoke controversy among American viewers" (referring to the final version of Albion's line, "If I were a native today whose liberty was threatened by Napoleon's cutthroats, I would kill every white man I could lay my hands on" [55:35]).[81]

In the US, Black critics similarly emphasized the film's Revolution dimension. Some stressed its failings. Writing before the film's release, with rumors of a previous version of the dog scene, the *California Eagle*'s theatrical editor noted that "millions [will rise] in anger at 20th Century-Fox unless they drop [this scene] from the picture. *Lydia Bailey* may be giving employment to 180 Negro actors but this episode turns my stomach." Pointing to the film's all-white creative team, the editor asked indignantly, "How can an industry that doesn't employ blacks as writers" or crew members "direct or produce a sincere and sensitive picture relating to Negro life?" The writer raised an essential point: though the white filmmakers intended to be progressive and asked White for input, they included not a single African American—let alone a Haitian—on their creative team.[82]

Other African American critics praised *Lydia Bailey* while acknowledging its flaws. In his syndicated column, the NAACP's White told readers, "I beg you not to miss it," and that "the action is terrific." Still, White (who had strongly opposed the US occupation of Haiti) could not resist mentioning the flaws of the Vodou dance scene—and the startling imposition of a white Baltimorean in Toussaint's circle. The *Chicago Defender*'s Marion Campfield joked about the film's "disdain for historical authenticity," but urged viewers to support it with repeat visits. Most important, she argued, was "that 20th Century Fox has treated Haiti's valiant fight to live proudly with sensitivity and dignity." She called it "potent and provocative" that the script had Haitians exemplifying liberty and equality, rather than the French.[83]

Given the film's novelty in treating the Haitian Revolution sympathetically, and the flaws of so many Hollywood films on Black History, many African American reviewers were inclined to overlook its weaknesses. *Jet* called *Lydia Bailey* the "first picture to truly depict the bravery of Negroes whose love for freedom did not melt in the face of guns." The *Los Angeles Sentinel*'s Hazel Lamarre declared, "It is an undisputed fact that Hollywood . . . has left itself open to criticism when making films dealing with colored people." But she added that, "in our opinion 'Lydia Bailey' is out of this class." Lamarre called the film "inspiring" and said that it "gives us great hope that someday in the immediate future, 20th Century Fox or some other movie company will go many steps further in utilizing the dramatic incidents that fill the lives of non-white people." And despite the critique by one *California Eagle* writer, another declared that "the flick shows off Negro talent at its best." The writer continued, "We doubt if southerners will take to it. However it is rated the best to come out of Hollywood."[84]

Though Haitian and African American writers emphasized the film's Revolution content, white critics focused on the parts pushed by Zanuck. Several found the film compelling. *Film Daily* called *Lydia Bailey* a "rousing historical adventure romance . . . [with] plenty to hold attention [and] feed imagination." Edwin Schallert of the *Los Angeles Times* praised the film's "solid performances" and said it had "real glow as an adventure picture." *Library Journal* thought it was a strong adaptation of the novel: "As in *The Emperor Jones*, the beat of ominous drums points up the exciting action. . . . Nobody but nobody is likely to be bored by *this* picture." *Newsweek* lauded the sex angle and the camera work, which it thought had been done on location: "Negulesco builds up his tensions with voodoo drumming; he has pleasant sport with such scenes as a review of King Dick's eight wives. But it is the luxuriant island of Haiti itself, richly caught by the color camera, which is the film's most striking feature."[85]

Other white critics highlighted the film's identity crisis; they found it mediocre or worse. The *Cedar Rapids Gazette* wrote, "The bigwigs of Hollywood have taken a perfectly good historical novel and turned it into an imperfect adventure movie." The *Dallas Morning News* said, "'Lydia Bailey' doesn't exactly jell," and that it "makes a transplanted horse opera out of a historical romance." In the *Saturday Review*, Hollis Alpert referred to the film's Haitian Revolution content more than other white critics. Yet he noted that, with the "fine talk about freedom" jumbled up with things like "voodoo," "I couldn't quite unravel it all." A number of publications called Marshall's performance the film's best part.[86]

The *Daily Worker* was an exception among white US publications, in focusing on Toussaint and the Revolution. The paper's Ben Levine generally enjoyed the film; he appreciated that Blankfort and Dunne depicted Toussaint as perfectly capable of leading the Revolution without Albion. However, critic David Platt appraised *Lydia Bailey* more harshly: "When a film corporation, economically based on white supremacy, produces a movie that appears to be defending the revolutionary rights of colored peoples, there's a catch." Platt felt that *Lydia Bailey* neutralized Toussaint as a revolutionary leader by making him forgiving toward colonists, while demonizing the more militant Mirabeau.[87]

Foreign audiences, who Zanuck had hoped would make up for US ones, were no more enthusiastic. In Canada, the *Globe and Mail* called the film's historical story line "pretty confusing." In England, *Picturegoer*'s Derek Walker felt that the film's notorious cost issues had doomed it: "*Lydia Bailey* lost much of its . . . grandeur. The romance between Anne Francis and Dale Robertson was played up at the expense of the sweeping theme." In France, *Lydia Bailey* was slammed by critics of all political persuasions. *Libération*'s critic hated Albion, called Lydia a poor woman's Scarlett O'Hara, and complained that Hollywood had turned Napoleon into a "villainous European petty tyrant." *Le Figaro* criticized the film for emphasizing a "happy ending" for Albion and Lydia without caring what happened subsequently in Haiti, and for making Toussaint into a "precursor of the fight against fascism." Paule Sengissen of *Radio cinéma télévision* complained that the French people Albion meets "are for him no more than lying oppressors from whom one can steal a fiancée." She also criticized the film's displacement of racism onto the French: "This anti-French [film] wants us to believe that our country has a monopoly on antiblack racism?" Even critics who would have welcomed a good film on the Haitian Revolution found *Lydia Bailey* wanting. Pierre Kast complained that the Hollywood machine had ruined a promising story: "a beautiful subject, the liberation of Saint-Domingue by slaves in revolt. . . . And at the end of the [Hollywood] machine, out comes *Lydia Bailey*."[88]

Despite their best efforts, the celebrated team received no award nominations for *Lydia*, let alone box office glory; the film had tried to be too many things to too many people. Blankfort and Dunne had tried to stress the Revolution and its contemporary implications. But Zanuck's "intimate personal story" and adventure had predominated, while the Revolution remained in the background. Though *Le Nouvelliste* predicted that Albion's line about killing white men would cause great controversy in the US, it seems to have gotten lost in the jumble of King Dick's wives and "voodoo" drums.

After 1952, Fox would let *Lydia Bailey* quietly fall into obscurity. The middling grosses corresponded to a feeling that the film had not been the studio's best work. Negulesco was not proud of it; he called it a "so-so costume action film" and criticized Schermer for having pushed the studio to proceed despite the budget limits. As for Dunne, though he scrupulously preserved other records, he saved almost nothing from *Lydia*. He later told an interviewer that he "should have walked off" the film. Calling Roberts "sort of a Tory," he deemed the novel "dull" and "ponderous." He recalled, "I just had a lot of trouble with the script. Finally I said, 'Look, I just don't know how to do it.' This was a bad [assignment] for me. . . . I just couldn't lick it." Dunne admitted that he never even went to see the film.[89]

Within Haiti, *Lydia Bailey*'s legacy would also be short-term. The premiere did inspire Haiti's government to partner with Hollywood on one more film, Abner Biberman's *The Golden Mistress* (1954). Hoping that movies could bolster tourism, the Magloire government supported *The Golden Mistress*'s filming on location in Haiti in fall 1953. Like *Lydia Bailey*, the film featured two US whites exploring Haiti with local help—this time as a romance-adventure-scuba-diving-voodoo-horror-travelogue.[90] Aside from its American leads (John Agar and Rosemarie Bowe), *The Golden Mistress* had an almost entirely Haitian cast. This included La Troupe folklorique nationale (which had performed at the *Lydia Bailey* premiere) and choreographer André Narcisse. They staged Vodou dance performances that were far more authentic than those in *Lydia Bailey*. Following *Lydia*, *The Golden Mistress* would also hold its world premiere in Port-au-Prince, in October 1954, under President Magloire's auspices. Despite Haitian expectations, however, *The Golden Mistress* ended up portraying Vodou and Haitian culture far worse than Blankfort's and Dunne's film; the shocked Magloire government banned it two days after the premiere. While the film had some positive depictions of Haitians, and beautiful shots of the Citadelle and of Haiti's underground coral reefs, its villains were savage Afro-Haitians ("the Untamed") who had lived apart from civilization since the Revolution. *The Golden Mistress* drew derision from critics (who nevertheless liked seeing the beauty of Haiti) and relatively few viewers, though it was released in several European countries following its run in the US.[91] Any effect it and *Lydia Bailey* may have had in increasing tourism was, however, short-lived; the dawn of the brutal Duvalier dictatorship in 1957 ended Haiti's dreams of becoming a leading Caribbean vacation destination.[92]

Despite being forgotten for decades, *Lydia Bailey* remains significant for its representation of the Haitian Revolution. It showed that foreign filmmakers could imagine Haitians conceiving of their own freedom, while depicting the French—and slavery itself—as unjust. Because of its origins in the late 1940s (when support for peoples seeking decolonization was higher than it would be after the Cold War prompted proxy conflicts in Korea and Vietnam), the film had a more radical anticolonial bent than most others of its era. *Lydia Bailey* is also remarkable for having depicted the Revolution as akin to—and more radical than—other Atlantic Revolutions in its vision of liberty. Even the addition of the Mirabeau character, problematic as it was, illustrated the reality that Haitian leaders disagreed passionately about how to deal with former enslavers. Still, despite these virtues, the fact that Zanuck had not wanted to make a Haitian Revolution film in the first place—and had sought to avoid offending the French—left the film's message muddled.

Unfortunately, *Lydia Bailey* was the twentieth century's best chance for a high-quality, well-funded film on the Revolution. The interest in antiracist message pictures had temporarily displaced Hollywood fears about glorifying Black violence. Soon, however, in large part thanks to HUAC, studios' appetite for message pictures would decline. And in the 1950s and 1960s, the idea of Blacks responding to oppression by killing whites became more fraught. *Lydia Bailey* receded from popular consciousness; when filmmakers talked about making a new Haitian Revolution movie, they almost always referred back to *The Emperor Jones*. Marshall himself, despite the raves that earned him a high-profile contract, would fall victim to the blacklist in 1954.[93] *Lydia Bailey* became an obscure memory.

4

NO WHITE HERO, NO FUNDING?

Unmade Revolution Epics

So far, we have looked at Haitian Revolution–related feature films, from 1933's *The Emperor Jones* to the 2013 film *Tula: The Revolt*. These were not, however, the only dramas that filmmakers have imagined on the Revolution. Since the 1930s, numerous filmmakers have attempted to improve on films like *The Emperor Jones*. Such projects have come from African American filmmakers, white Hollywood legends, and directors from around the world. These artists have all seen the Revolution as worthy of an epic treatment. However, nearly all such projects have remained unfunded and unfilmed. This chapter surveys an array of never-completed feature films on the Haitian Revolution proposed by non-Haitian directors (chapter 8 discusses Haitian attempts). John Vandercook's 1928 bestseller *Black Majesty* led many artists to imagine epics about Christophe, while others (especially more recently) have hoped to make films focused on Toussaint Louverture or Jean-Jacques Dessalines. No matter the protagonist, filmmakers have had difficulty persuading funders to see the value in a Haitian Revolution epic.

The problem of funding such an epic relates to Hollywood's more general difficulty depicting African-descended people. Donald Bogle, Thomas Cripps, and others have highlighted Hollywood's reduction of African Americans to racist archetypes, summed up by Bogle in the title of his classic study *Toms, Coons, Mulattoes, Mammies, and Bucks*. Bogle notes that these archetypes entertained whites "by stressing Negro inferiority. Fun was poked at the American Negro by presenting him as either a nitwit or a childlike lackey." As Cripps has explained, from Hollywood's earliest days, films were made "to fit current American values and tastes. This whole expensive and complex structure allowed little role for blacks . . . , [who] were tolerated only as long as they accepted their inferior status." Decades after Griffith's *The Birth of a Nation*, that film still had an outsize influence in Hollywood; according to Valerie Smith, the images established in *Birth* were "reproduced throughout the history of U.S. cinema—types that run the gamut from indolent, subservient, buffoonish men and women to vicious black male rapists."[1]

In recent decades, some Hollywood filmmakers have moved away from these archetypes; they have sought to make more serious stories about Black History, in which multidimensional Black characters battling oppression are presented sympathetically. However, such films have appealed to funders chiefly when they include friendly whites, who make white filmgoers feel as if they too would have fought against racism. *Amistad*, *12 Years a Slave*, and *Green Book* all fit this pattern. The latter film sparked bitter controversy over its white-savior trope; Ty Burr of the *Boston Globe* noted that its Oscar victory over movies by Spike Lee and Barry Jenkins suggested that "a film about the black American experience still has to be filtered through a white lens to be fully embraced by a white audience."[2]

The Haitian Revolution's story line, however, does not fit the mold of a white hero winning justice for oppressed Blacks. In contrast to the based-on-a-true-story plot of *12 Years a Slave*, where Chiwetel Ejiofor's Solomon Northup suffers quietly until Brad Pitt's character arrives to help, the Haitian Revolution involved enslaved Africans taking up arms to emancipate themselves. Moreover, unlike the historical cases invoked in *Amistad* (featuring McConaughey's white lawyer) or *The Free State of Jones* (featuring McConaughey's white rebel leader), the Revolution was not directed by a white protagonist who led enslaved people to freedom. The topic of slavery has been controversial enough in Hollywood even with white heroes mitigating its stark realities. A story line showing enslaved African protagonists killing brutal white colonists, without being guided by other whites—and gaining independence in the process—has not appealed to those capable of funding epics.

Funding has been a particular challenge for African American artists envisioning Haitian Revolution films. As noted in chapter 1, the Revolution has long had special meaning to African Americans; their view of the Revolution differed from most white Americans, seeing it not as frightening or unthinkable but as inspirational. Consequently, African American actors and directors have seen in the Revolution a powerful source of alternate images of African-descended people on screen—as generals and statesmen rather than criminals or clowns. Repeatedly, African Americans have sought to make better Revolution dramas than *The Emperor Jones* or *Lydia Bailey*, centered on heroic Black protagonists. Yet even if African American writers have found the Revolution's story appealing, funders have not; imagining that audiences would avoid such films, they have resisted bankrolling dramas about this event.[3]

From a Soviet Toussaint to a New *Emperor Jones*?

After the US occupation of Haiti as well as *The Emperor Jones*, filmmakers in different parts of the world sought to make epics on the Haitian Revolution. In the 1930s, the legendary Soviet director Sergei Eisenstein tried to make a film about Louverture, starring Paul Robeson. The film would not have shied away from Black revolutionary violence but celebrated it, in order to highlight Blacks' potential within the international history of revolution. Robeson was eager to make the film, expecting his role to be richer and more humanized than in *The Emperor Jones*. However, Eisenstein's project eventually fizzled, as part of what Charles Forsdick and Christian Høgsbjerg have called the "degeneration of the Russian Revolution into Stalinist counter-revolution." In the mid-twentieth century, several African-descended writers also sought, in vain, to make films on the Revolution. In the 1950s, the African American novelist Richard Wright tried to make a film about Toussaint, in collaboration with Haitians, in which he would star. And C. L. R. James sought unsuccessfully to interest British studios in adapting *The Black Jacobins*.[4]

During the mid-twentieth century, a handful of white Hollywood legends also attempted epics on the Haitian Revolution. These projects, building on interest in Haiti that had developed during the occupation, focused mainly on Christophe. In 1948, Darryl Zanuck had tried to convince Gregory Peck to play Albion in *Lydia Bailey*. Peck, who was educated at Berkeley and had visited Haiti with his wife, felt that Roberts's novel treated the Revolution too superficially. Fresh off his role combating antisemitism in *Gentleman's Agreement*, Peck responded that a film on the Revolution was an excellent idea. However, he told Zanuck that it should tackle weighty topics such as poverty and racism, not be "just another historical adventure romance," as he anticipated *Lydia Bailey* would be.[5]

In declining the role of Albion, Peck pitched an alternative to Zanuck: he would star in a different kind of Haitian Revolution film. He explained, "I have been to Haiti and have studied enough of its history to feel a great conviction about the possibilities of a terrific drama centered around Henri Christophe." Christophe, Peck continued, "is the part that I would really like to play." While portraying Christophe personally would have required Peck to appear in blackface, Peck's other comments on the Revolution were more sophisticated than one might expect from a mid-century white actor:

> The popular conception of [Christophe] as a ruthless despot has some basis in fact, but to Haitians he is as great and revered a national hero as George Washington is to us. He carried on the democratic ideals of Toussaint L'Ouverture and maintained the newly established Haitian Republic against all the efforts of the French to retake the island and continue the exploitation of the people, their former slaves. He built the Citadel (a tremendous engineering feat) as a symbol of Haitian independence and as an impregnable stronghold.[6]

Zanuck, however, showed no interest in Peck's proposal, especially given that he had not wanted to make a Haitian Revolution epic in the first place.

Soon after Peck, another white Academy Award winner became fascinated by Christophe. Director John Huston had cofounded the Committee for the First Amendment with Philip Dunne in 1947, speaking out against anti-Communist witch hunts long before others. In 1954, *Jet* reported that Huston had purchased the rights to adapt *Black Majesty* into a screenplay. Huston tapped Trinidadian singer Edric Connor to play Christophe. Michaëlle Lafontant-Médard has found that President Magloire appointed a commission of leading historians in Haiti to help Huston, and filming commenced. Like Eisenstein, though, Huston never was able to complete his Christophe epic. In 1956, the director instead made *Moby Dick*—a film with the singular distinction of featuring two failed Christophes, Gregory Peck and Edric Connor.[7]

As African Americans began to gain more power in Hollywood, hope arose for a new Revolution-related film that might replace *The Emperor Jones* and *Lydia Bailey*. In 1955, *Jet* reported that producers were planning a remake of *The Emperor Jones*; in 1956, Harry Belafonte was announced as the star. If he was to participate in the film, Belafonte insisted that it not demean African Americans.[8]

Belafonte hoped that this project could help change images of Blacks on screen. He asked his friend John Killens, a Black novelist, to write a revised script. Killens was initially reluctant to get involved, based on the "crap-shooting, razor-toting, [and other] tired stereotypes" in the 1933 original. Belafonte assured Killens that the studio would make any changes they wanted; Killens turned Jones from a train porter into an enslaved person. Rather than a criminal who murdered another Black man while gambling, this Brutus was an enslaved person who killed "his white whipping boss" after suffering too much. He then escaped to an island identified more clearly as Haiti, so the audience could learn how equality reigned there far more than in the antebellum US.[9]

With encouragement from Sidney Poitier, both Belafonte and Killens tried to convince the studio "to tell the real story of Henri Christophe." As Killens later recalled, "Belafonte talked to them as if he had just stepped out of Haitian history. We would make a movie that would include not only Christophe, but Toussaint L'Ouverture and all the other Haitian heroes." Killens and Belafonte imagined a wildly successful film, including "all of the major Negro actors as well as white ones." Killens wanted the studio to understand that a film on Black History—with Black leads—could be extremely profitable. He reported that "I could almost hear the sound of the cash register clanking in the producer's head." After initially agreeing, producers had second thoughts. They told Belafonte that if he refused to play Jones as written by O'Neill, "we will get a Negro star who will." British television did run a televised version of O'Neill's play in 1958 on Armchair Theatre, featuring actor Kenneth Spencer, but it is unclear whether this teleplay was a scaled-back version of the project intended for Belafonte. In 1959, Poitier considered starring in a different Christophe epic, this time written by African American actor Herb Jeffries. Like other such projects, however, Jeffries's film never came to fruition.[10]

Who Needs a White Hero When You Have a White Christophe?

In 1972, another white Oscar winner had the same dream as Gregory Peck—to make and star in an epic about Christophe. Anthony Quinn, best known as Zorba the Greek, reportedly spent $150,000 developing a Christophe script to "bring to life the great hero of Black people." By the early 1970s, African Americans—especially those who had been trying to make their own films on the Revolution—were shocked that a white actor would intend to play Christophe. A successful white actor not only had more power to make a Haitian Revolution drama—but also planned to star in blackface. For his part, Quinn, who maintained that he was not white but "Irish-Mexican," refused to fund a film in which he did not play the lead.[11]

Debate raged in several places, including the Arts and Leisure section of the *New York Times*. In a much-discussed essay there entitled "Black History Does Not Need Tony Quinn," the celebrated actress Ellen Holly bravely challenged Quinn. She noted that it was ironic that Hollywood refused to give African American actors roles seen as "white," while whites did not object to Quinn's playing a Haitian. Holly called Quinn's declaration that he wished to play Christophe distressing, "because Christophe was, quite possibly, the most remarkable single figure in all of black history," and because "a generation of black children searching so earnestly to define their racial identity would learn of [Christophe] for the first time from a screen image that presents him as a white man in makeup." "Must we live through Alec Guinness as Toussaint L'Ouverture," Holly asked, "and Charlton Heston as a prince of Benin?"[12]

Holly disputed Quinn's assertion that African American artists were not interested in making a film on Haiti. She herself, she explained, had long tried to make a Christophe film. In 1971, she had written in the *New York Times* about her project, which was inspired by *Black Majesty*. Holly had been working in the 1960s on a script linking the Revolution to contemporary struggles, but had not obtained funding:

> The next step was to take [the completed script] to the dream factory. I didn't want to. The film industry is run by the white male who is, understandably, involved with manufacturing his own fantasies rather than any that are quintessentially black and female. Instead, I left the script on the shelf and projected it in my imagination, finished, produced by a mythological black film company emotionally equipped to enter into the obsession.

Holly noted that she was continuing her efforts, but was not optimistic: "The reception [the script] gets is often intrigued, always respectful, but the chances of getting it done are virtually nonexistent." In her 1972 response to Quinn, Holly stated that several other African Americans were trying to make Haitian Revolution films. These included Yaphet Kotto on Dessalines, Poitier and Belafonte on Christophe, and others on Louverture. She insisted that Quinn "show a decent regard for the . . . black community and relinquish the title role to a black actor."[13]

As the controversy raged, Quinn responded to Holly with an article entitled "Can I Not Play a Black?" Seemingly unaware of funding inequities and his own privilege, Quinn declared that if African American actors had wanted to play Christophe, a film on him would already exist. He told Holly that Christophe was a "hero of mine long before you ever heard of him." He declared that preventing him from playing Christophe was as unjust as banning James Earl Jones from "white" roles.[14]

The Holly-Quinn debate occasioned a torrent of letters to the editor. A few supported Quinn. R. J. Thompson, a reader self-presenting as Black, said that "it would not be offensive to my sensibilities . . . to have an artist of this caliber play Christophe." He added, "If Anthony Quinn wants to play Henri Christophe, I say 'Right on!'" Another reader, N. Morton Fybish, dismissed Holly. Embodying a long tradition of whites blaming Haitian slaves for violence but ignoring that of their enslavers, Fybish argued that he would rather see a film about Martin Luther King than "the Haitian revolters who committed inhuman atrocities against the wives, daughters and infants of the French colonists."[15]

Most letter writers, however, blasted Quinn's plan. The novelist Louise Meriwether declared: "If we appear sensitive about our history, it is because it has been aborted and distorted . . . and its existence denied for centuries by white historians." A Brooklyn reader, Rick Haynes, asserted that Quinn's dressing up as Christophe would be "insultingly reminiscent of the ridicule we blacks suffered all too silently in the heyday of the minstrel show when your kind blackened your faces to laugh at my kind." The acting legend Ossie Davis, who had appeared in Langston Hughes's play *Emperor of Haiti*, also raised his voice. He wrote to the *Times*, "Tony is a great actor and I am happy to count him as a friend. . . . But more than art is at issue here." Davis stated that he agreed with those "who feel it would be absolutely wrong for Tony Quinn to try to portray Henry Christophe on film, especially at this time when we black folks and other Third World people are fighting so hard to establish control over our identities."[16]

A few Haitians also joined the debate. The *Times* printed a letter from two living in Boston: Alix Mathieu and Pierre-Michel Fontaine. The men expressed satisfaction that Christophe was inspiring so much interest in the US. However, they noted that neither Holly nor Quinn had acknowledged "the obvious fact that Christophe was a Haitian, that his story took place in Haiti and that, consequently talented Haitians should have an opportunity to make a contribution to the movie." Mathieu and Fontaine stated that there were many qualified artists in Haiti, from actors to cameramen, but that "we know of no attempt on the part of either Miss Holly or Mr. Quinn to use their services, though we are sure that some Haitians will be hired on location as porters and messenger boys." Without meaningful Haitian participation, the project would be another instance where "enterprising Americans," white or Black, were "exploiting Haitian history, culture, or natural beauty, with little benefit accruing to the Haitians." This debate was not confined to the *Times*. *Jet* reported that Haitians in Haiti were critical of Quinn's "audacity." Nevertheless, it reported, Jean-Claude Duvalier's government (hungry for foreign capital) had given Quinn a "full endorsement."[17]

King Dick No More: William Marshall and "Christophe of Haiti"

In the midst of this controversy, William Marshall, who had played King Dick so powerfully in *Lydia Bailey*, stepped forward to challenge Quinn.

Marshall's career had stalled after he was blacklisted in 1954; only two years after receiving his groundbreaking contract, Fox released him from it after a right-wing publication called him a Communist. Hollywood's leading African American actor following *Lydia Bailey*, Marshall was then surpassed by his former friends Poitier and Belafonte.[18] By the late 1960s, with starring movie roles going to them, Marshall made a living from less glamorous television work, playing characters such as an African in *Tarzan*. However, he continued to act in the kinds of serious stage roles that first brought him to Hollywood's attention. In 1972, he gained new prominence in the Blaxploitation horror film *Blacula*. For that film, Marshall insisted on removing stereotypes from the script, and turned his character into an African prince seeking to end the slave trade.[19]

Like Holly, Marshall was frustrated that Quinn could fund himself playing a Black man, when African American filmmakers were unable to bring serious Black History to the screen. Shocked that Quinn would propose to incarnate Christophe, Marshall wrote a series of open letters in 1972. Marshall told Quinn, "What you can bring to this production is immeasurable." However, he continued, "the Black king must be Black." Marshall disputed Quinn's assertion that "Black actors are either not interested in playing the role of Christophe or do not consider themselves qualified." "What has been lacking," Marshall wrote, "is financing. Thus far, producers and distributors have in no way demonstrated any interest in backing a Black actor who wishes to play a Black king in a story of successful slave revolt and independent Black nation-building."[20]

At the time Marshall made *Lydia Bailey*, he had known little about Haitian history. His chief goal in playing King Dick, he had told the *New York Amsterdam News*, was to bring "human dignity" to a Black character on screen. He also told *Ebony* that King Dick was "the finest role I ever read or had the pleasure to portray." After completing *Lydia Bailey*, Marshall had become more knowledgeable and wanted to make a better film about the Revolution. According to one report, despite having been blacklisted, Marshall was initially considered for the 1957 *Emperor Jones* remake to which Belafonte had been attached. Just like Belafonte, Marshall likely doomed his chance after insisting on script changes.[21]

Throughout the 1960s and early 1970s, as Marshall learned more about the Revolution, he had planned his own Christophe epic. Unlike others with Christophe projects, Marshall did not seek to adapt *Black Majesty*. Instead, he and Sylvia Gussin (his companion and the former wife of blacklisted writer Paul Jarrico) planned to use the legendary Martinican writer Aimé Césaire's play *The Tragedy of King Christophe*. In 1964, Césaire gave his blessing for their adapting his play into English. In May 1970, the pair mounted a stage production of their *Tragedy of King Christophe* at San Fernando Valley State College in Los Angeles.[22]

Marshall and Gussin then worked to convert their adaptation into a screenplay. However, after determining that Césaire's play could not become the kind of action-adventure film that they thought suitable for Christophe ("there's too much talk, beautiful or not, and there's too little movement"), Marshall and Gussin hired Julian Mayfield to write a new script. Mayfield, a prominent African American writer, actor, and anticolonial activist, was working for the newly independent government of Guyana. With input from Africana Studies pioneer John Henrik Clarke, Mayfield, Marshall, and Gussin drew on Hubert Cole's *Christophe, King of Haiti* (1967) and other scholarship, as well as Césaire's play.[23]

Marshall and Mayfield had an ambitious plan for their project, "Christophe of Haiti." Marshall named his production company Black Heritage Films; he intended "Christophe of Haiti" as the first in a series of "Black heritage genre" pictures. Marshall hoped that the series could bring Black History to "the largest possible world audience" and inaugurate new ways of depicting Black History on screen. The film "must be what the black community has been waiting for." To ensure that such stories be told properly, Marshall sought to persuade Ousmane Sembène, the world's leading African filmmaker, to direct his film.[24]

Marshall wanted "Christophe of Haiti," the first film in this series, to take a completely different approach to the Revolution than *Lydia Bailey*. In contrast to his earlier enthusiasm about that film, Marshall now offered a fundamental critique of its focus on Lydia and Albion instead of on Haitians. As he told the *Los Angeles Sentinel* in 1975, "The successful revolt of the African people in Haiti, unique in history, was used in 'Lydia Bailey' as a backdrop for the love story of two white Americans. My objective is to bring the backdrop to the forefront."[25]

Both Marshall and Mayfield insisted that, unlike previous US films on Black History, "Christophe of Haiti" would not feature a white hero. Clarke had suggested that the script include the English abolitionist Thomas Clarkson's efforts to mentor Christophe. But Mayfield told Clarke that this made him "uneasy": "I do not doubt the historical accuracy of what you wrote but in this film the Black leader must be seen to be his own man." Mayfield noted that, in a script for a previous film, he had been persuaded to add in a friendly white working alongside the film's Black revolutionary protagonists—but that "in 1974, we have moved far beyond that."[26]

When they began the project, Mayfield was not initially convinced that Christophe should anchor a Haitian Revolution film. He preferred that it focus on Toussaint or Dessalines. Marshall tried to convince him that Christophe's nation-building represented the "payoff" on what Louverture and Dessalines had started. Marshall and Mayfield also had different visions of Christophe's importance. They eventually agreed on treating Christophe as a revolutionary proud of his African heritage and eager to advance his nation. Indeed, rather than highlight white fellow travelers, their scripts valorized Christophe for opposing accommodation with whites. Mayfield juxtaposed a Francophile Toussaint, more willing to compromise with colonists, against a Christophe who was hostile to them. In the script's first draft, after Toussaint tells Dessalines and Christophe that Bonaparte and Leclerc have considered him an equal and that they should treat colonists with kindness, Christophe exclaims: "As an equal! . . . Those slave mongers have killed thousands of our brothers and sisters. . . . I am drenched in blood up to my knees, but I would wade in a river of it, and drown, rather than take any chance that they will ever return us to slavery!" Similarly, when Toussaint insists that he is just as French as those in France, Christophe responds, "I am not French. I am black. I am African."[27]

The script's Christophe also served as a precursor of twentieth-century anticolonialism. He denounced what he had been taught growing up: that Europe was the center of civilization. In language reminiscent of King Henri's spokesman the Baron de Vastey as well as twentieth-century anticolonial activists, the script's Christophe declared:

> Brothers and sisters, what do they mean when they say "civilization"[?] They mean "white," and they don't even mean all whites . . . only those who live off the sweat of our backs. They eat well, they drink well, while we work! With this money they learn to talk the best talk . . . to read books . . . while you and I bring their food and rum to the tables. . . . Now give your ears to me, brothers and sisters. . . . You are better than they are because everything they have told you is a lie. . . . Because you cannot be a good slave if you remember that you were once of a great people.

Mayfield saw the epic's potential for success as assured by anticolonial victories worldwide. In material aimed at investors, he declared that the film would be a surefire winner in a climate of decolonization and Black Power.[28]

Mayfield saw the film as especially relevant because of the contemporary challenges of postcolonial nation-building. From his post in Guyanese premier Forbes Burnham's Ministry of Information, Mayfield argued that the lessons of Christophe's life could be a cautionary tale for newly independent peoples. They could help grassroots revolutionaries appreciate the challenges now facing their leaders: "Ex-slaves and former colonial peoples have a distressing tendency to think the good life is at hand and hard work is over. Their leaders . . . know that the hard work has just begun. . . . So 'CHRISTOPHE' has a relevancy bound to grow over the years."[29]

While Mayfield was right that the world had changed a great deal since the 1950s, he was too optimistic. Raising money for a Black-authored anticolonial message epic proved no easy feat. Marshall and Gussin were creative; long before the age of crowdfunding, the couple sought money outside the studio system. Gussin told Mayfield in 1973 that she and Marshall had "organized a group of people . . . [interested] in helping our movie come successfully into existence. We have regularly weekly meetings . . . , and people report on what they've done." Marshall wrote personally to Black executives and elsewhere asking for help. In addition, *Jet* reported that a "Friends of Christophe" committee had formed and that Marshall was traveling the country raising funds. Marshall also sought help from the Haitian government.[30]

Marshall and Mayfield did receive some interest from Hollywood producers and filmmakers who could see the value in a Black-penned epic of this kind. In 1975, Marshall told the *Los Angeles Sentinel* that he was "completing production plans." But, ultimately, he was unable to raise sufficient resources for a film with a slave revolt theme. Those who declined to fund the project were not only whites; Poitier also refused to help his old friend, seeing such a film as an unwise investment.[31] Without the $3.5 to 4 million needed, "King Christophe of Haiti" joined the list of unfilmed Haitian Revolution screenplays.

Ellen Holly's Christophe-related project would meet the same fate. She gave more details about it in 2013, explaining how the script would have offered more complex representations of Black women on screen. Her film would have centered on a classically trained pianist who arrives in Duvalierist Haiti to give a concert, but is swept back into the era of slavery. Holly noted that the project had drawn interest from some of the world's leading directors, including Louis Malle (who "was fascinated by it") and Robert Altman (who "agreed to do it on a handshake but later . . . changed his mind").[32] Without funding, Holly eventually abandoned the project.[33]

We might not be surprised that Marshall's and Holly's films never were made, given the difficulty that African Americans have had in bringing Black History to the screen from their own point of view. However, it is important to note that Quinn's project also failed to materialize. Despite his financial resources, he later told an interviewer that he had received no encouragement in Hollywood except from Belafonte. "My life was threatened if I [went ahead and played Christophe]. I got scared. I lost $500,000 on that venture."[34] Quinn might have expected that he would have more success than others who had attempted such projects, given growing interest in Black History in the 1970s and his track record at the box office. However, even if African Americans were unable to get their own Revolution projects funded, their activism at least thwarted a blackface Christophe.

Recent Unmade Toussaint Epics

While the unfilmed projects I have discussed are little known today, another from the early twenty-first century has become legendary: the Toussaint biopic planned by African American actor/director Danny Glover. Glover explained that he became interested in the Revolution after reading *The Black Jacobins* and realizing others did not know this story:

> Bringing Toussaint and the Haitian Revolution to the screen is a dream that I've been working on for the last 20 years. Toussaint led the only successful slave rebellion in history and in the process defeated Napoleon's army. . . . It's an amazing story. . . . [After the US and French Revolutions], the Haitian Revolution represents the third leg: universalizing these principles to all men—not just privileged, landed, wealthy men of European ancestry. In terms of world historical movements and revolutions, it was actually the most important of the three. . . .
>
> A critically important question for African Americans is, "Why has this monumental achievement been so erased from our history and from our consciousness?"

Glover emphasized the Revolution's effect in inspiring enslaved peoples throughout the New World to dream of freedom; he suggested that the subject could inspire oppressed peoples worldwide to believe that change is possible. Glover and his partners wrote a screenplay, and he set up a company called Louverture Films. He was determined that his film "have the epic scale these events require." He and his partners recruited high-profile actors: reportedly, Wesley Snipes, Don Cheadle, Angela Bassett, Chiwetel Ejiofor, and Mos Def.[35]

However, the project ran into multiple roadblocks. Most significantly, Glover reported, what prevented him from getting sufficient funding was the lack of a white hero. As he told Agence France Presse in 2008:

> Producers said "It's a nice project, a great project . . . where are the white heroes?" . . . I couldn't get the money here [in Paris], I couldn't get the money in Britain. I went to everybody. You wouldn't believe the number of producers based in Europe, and in the States, that I went to. . . . The first question you get, is "Is it a black film?" All of them agree, it's not going to do good in Europe, it's not going to do good in Japan.

"Somebody," Glover insisted, "has to prove that to be a lie!"[36]

In the early 2010s, Glover hoped that the epic would still be made. In 2013, he spoke about the project in the present tense. However, by 2015, it became clear that he was no longer working on the project. He told interviewer Ariston Anderson: "The film that we always missed is a movie on the Haitian revolution and Toussaint Louverture." Some sources have claimed that Glover's effort to get funding from controversial Venezuelan leader Hugo Chávez—who offered $18 million, an insufficient sum for an epic—harmed him further with Hollywood funders.[37]

The Martinican director Euzhan Palcy has also stalled in her effort to make a Revolution epic. Palcy was the first woman of African descent to direct a Hollywood film (1989's *A Dry White Season*) and the first Black director to win a French César Award, for her masterful 1984 *Sugar Cane Alley*, about the persistence of racial inequality in Martinique decades after abolition. She initially partnered with Glover on Toussaint, but they had a falling out. As she explained in 2015 to interviewer Martine Jean:

> I've had that project for more than 20 years. It was very difficult to get people to finance it. . . . Danny Glover and I had the same project. In fact, we were partners. Things didn't work out well between us . . . so he went his way and I went my way. I never gave up on it because I truly believe Toussaint Louverture is a very important character in world history. People . . . have to know about that man.

Asked if she was working with Haitian collaborators, Palcy responded: "Of course. . . . You cannot make a movie about Toussaint and do it from America. That's stupid. . . . You need to do the right thing." Though she insisted in 2015 that she was still working on this film, she had said the same thing in 1999–2001; the project remains unfinished.[38]

Another filmmaker who initially sought to collaborate with Glover on a Haitian Revolution film was French-Mauritanian director Med Hondo, who had made the remarkable 1979 film *West Indies* (mentioned in the introduction). In the early 1990s, Tambay Obenson has reported, Hondo showed

Glover a script he had written about Toussaint Louverture, hoping that Glover might star. But Hondo later claimed that Glover had stolen the script, using it as the basis for his *Toussaint* project. Hondo's own efforts to make a Toussaint film never bore fruit.[39]

Still another project that was announced with fanfare in 2013—but has not been completed—is the Nigerian director Jeta Amata's epic on Toussaint, produced with a white Hollywood screenwriter named Kyra Pahlen. Amata told NPR's Michel Martin that Toussaint's story is one that "the world has to know." Hinting at the funding problems that had plagued other such films, Amata commented, "It's a big endeavor, but big endeavors have never scared Nigerians." Pahlen stated that the film's budget would be $17–18 million—a small amount for an epic, but a sum that would have made it the grandest Haitian Revolution film ever. Pahlen's and Amata's project was endorsed by Haitian president Michel Martelly. Amata promised that the picture would be filmed in Haiti, with a Haitian crew, and that profits would help restore Haitian historic sites. Though 2013 reports stated that the film was being shot and would be released the next year, in 2014 Amata spoke of the movie in the future tense, as something "still in development." The IMDb page for the film in 2019 showed it as "in development," without any confirmed cast; the IMDb Pro page for the film indicated only that Wyclef was rumored to be playing the revolutionary Boukman.[40]

• • •

This chapter has shown the repeated failure of funders to greenlight epics on the Haitian Revolution. In the twenty-first century, Hollywood films have begun featuring more serious plotlines about racism and the history of slavery. However, the Revolution (with its violence by enslaved people against racist white colonists, and its lack of a white savior) has seemed too radioactive a topic for white funders. *Lydia Bailey* had centered on the Haitian Revolution for practical reasons, not by design. In contrast, cinema legends seeking funding for Revolution epics have failed. Given the popularity of history films more generally, this omission is serious; the Revolution remains unthinkable to white non-Haitians when it is not shown on screen.

Topics related to racism have long been fodder, though, for cathartic humor by African Americans; this topic is no different. In practical terms, it is easier to joke about *not* being able to make a film on Haiti's revolution, than to actually make such a film. We turn in the next chapter to a film highlighting this very issue, Chris Rock's *Top Five*.

5

BLACK LIVES MATTERED IN THE HAITIAN REVOLUTION

Hollywood and Slavery in Chris Rock's *Top Five*

If you look at my comedy, it was always serious.
—Chris Rock as André Allen, *Top Five*

Filmmakers hoping to make Haitian Revolution epics have encountered numerous obstacles. These have included ignorance about the subject among non-Haitians, as well as white funders' unwillingness to make dramas about slave revolt, especially without friendly white characters. Where chapter 4 treated real projects that were thwarted by such reluctance, this chapter revisits the subject as turned into parody, in Chris Rock's 2014 film *Top Five*.[1] In this comedy, Rock highlighted the difficulty of making a Haitian Revolution film in Hollywood, as he chronicled the failure of a fictional epic on the event.

At first glance, *Top Five* might not seem to be about the Revolution at all. The film's trailer does not mention the topic; it positions the film as a comedy filled with profanity, alcohol, and romance. *Top Five* centers on André Allen, a Black comedian and movie star. The trailer shows André hanging out with friends played by Tracy Morgan and Leslie Jones, getting marriage advice from Whoopi Goldberg (playing herself), and partying in clubs. The film has several story lines unrelated to the Revolution. It unfolds on a single day in Manhattan, as Allen promotes his latest film, does an extended interview with a *New York Times* reporter, and prepares for his wedding to a reality TV star. *Top Five* also features plenty of physical comedy, built around André's most famous movie character, Hammy the Bear. One of *Top Five*'s main themes is that André wants to do serious work, but audiences only want to see him as Hammy, the machine gun–firing bear-cop whose films have raked in $600 million worldwide (figure 5.1). Leading film critics noticed that *Top Five* was deeper than the typical Hollywood comedy; they pointed to issues Rock raises, such as the difficulties of celebrity, the beauty of hip-hop, and the challenges of sobriety.[2]

Yet while *Top Five* treats all of these issues, an overlooked theme concerns history and memory and the extent to which Black lives matter in white views of history. The film that André promotes in *Top Five*, *Uprize!*, is a Haitian Revolution epic. Paralleling Rock's own work on *Top Five*, *Uprize!* is André Allen's labor of love. André wrote *Uprize!* and stars in it as Boukman, the self-educated slave who played a key role in launching the Revolution. Unfortunately, *Uprize!* turns out to be as much of a flop as the Nat Turner film *The Birth of a Nation* would be in real life two years later, something Rock commented on in a November 2016 tweet. Fleeing *Uprize!* as they later would *The Birth of a Nation*, audiences showed a preference for comedy over a serious drama about slave revolt (figure 5.2).[3]

This chapter focuses on Rock's aims in making a film with a fictional Haitian Revolution movie at its center. I show how he used the Revolution as a signifier of white disinterest in the history of slavery, as well as of hostility to serious films on Black History more generally. To decode his meaning, I read *Top Five* against other statements on history and race by Rock, from his stand-up to his Twitter feed.[4]

Why did Rock make a film about slavery and memory that focuses on the Haitian Revolution, rather than on US history? Certainly, Rock has shown an interest in Haiti over many years.[5] He visited the country in the early 2000s and is an admirer of Haitian director Raoul Peck. Moreover, in 2003, in his film *Head of State*, Rock's character responds to a nationalist politician whose slogan is "God bless America, and no place else!" with the question, "How about 'God bless Haiti' or 'God bless Africa'?"[6]

However, Rock himself is less interested in Haiti's history for its own sake than are Haitians themselves; the Revolution serves other purposes for him. In addition to how it signals white ignorance about Black History generally, Rock is acutely aware of the Revolution's particularity. He knows that it involved a real-life uprising by enslaved Africans, which not only abolished slavery but also led to national independence. He also knows that the Revolution's story line does not fit the cinematic tradition of slaves suffering patiently while singing spirituals (a pet peeve of one character in *Top Five*) or Blaxploitation fantasies of slave revolt as in *Django Unchained*. For him, the Revolution forces consideration not only of whites' lack of knowledge of

Figure 5.1. Screenshot of Hammy the Bear posters. *Top Five*. © IAC Films/Paramount, 2014.

the history of slavery, but also their discomfort with violence by Blacks, even when the latter were enslaved people yearning for freedom.

One reason Rock's aims are not completely transparent in the film is that it falls into the trickster tradition of African humor in the Americas. Rock cracks jokes that seem to be about himself, while actually shining a brutal spotlight on white *mentalités*. He follows a long tradition, dating from slavery, in which jokes are told in a "doubled" way. That is, jokes express resistance, while protecting the teller from harm by making him seem to be the butt of the joke. As Glenda Carpio has commented, "Until well into the twentieth century, [African American humor] had to be cloaked in secrecy lest it be read as transgressive and punished by violence. Hence the popular slave aphorism 'Got one mind for white folk to see / 'Nother for what I know is me.'" As an example, Carpio cites a classic joke in which an enslaved person is caught eating one of his master's pigs. The slave admits his guilt, saying "Yes, suh, Master, you got less pig now but you sho' got more n***." Carpio explains the joke's doubled nature: whites overhearing the joke would think it was about a shifty, thieving slave, thus "catering to whites' belief in the inferiority of blacks." But Blacks would read a different meaning in the joke; for them, the enslaved person's response "effectively burlesques 'the entire notion

Figure 5.2. Chris Rock tweet comparing the box office struggles of *The Birth of a Nation* (2016) and *Uprize!* (*Top Five*'s film within a film). Screenshot.

of ownership in human beings,' as the slave carries the master's objectification of his body to its outmost absurdity."[7]

Top Five draws heavily on this tradition of doubled or double-voiced humor, which is linked to the larger African American tradition of signifyin(g).[8] Rock skewers white memory on the Revolution and on slavery in general, while seeming to be self-effacing. He has frequently used double-voiced humor with regard to topics of race and injustice in other venues. Indeed, underneath his coarser punchlines when he hosted the 2016 Oscars (where he came on stage to Public Enemy's "Fight the Power") were biting denunciations of Hollywood racism. Rock is painfully conscious of how difficult it is for African Americans to tell their own stories in Hollywood, and of how distorted whites' views of African American realities can be. He has specifically chastised Hollywood treatments of slavery, a topic previously mined in comedy by the legendary "Black Acting School" scene in Robert Townsend's film *Hollywood Shuffle*.[9]

In *Top Five*, Rock continues this double-voiced commentary. Instead of actually making a film about the Haitian Revolution, he goes meta. By making a film *about* making a film about the Haitian Revolution—and predicting that the latter would bomb spectacularly—Rock appeared to be mocking himself, a safe topic for white audiences. His real target, however, is those whites who are unaware of—and unwilling to learn about—the history of slavery and of why the Haitian Revolution has world historical significance. *Top Five* thus functions as commentary on the failure of filmmakers like Glover to get funding for Haitian Revolution movies. Amid its nudity and broad comedy are subversive lines about the Revolution and about whites' views of Black History more generally.

The following scene offers a prime example of Rock's trickster humor. André speaks on the phone with his agent Charles, played by Kevin Hart. On its first day in theaters, *Uprize!* does not seem to be attracting many ticket buyers.

> CHARLES: Now, when you told me you wanted to do that movie about the Haitian Revolution, André, what did I say to you?
> ANDRÉ: You said it wasn't a good idea, OK?
> CHARLES: No, no, no, no, no, you're wrong, André, that's not what I said. I said: "N***, is you crazy?!" (7:38)

Here, Charles appears to suggest that André is crazy for even thinking of making a film on the Haitian Revolution.

Under the surface, the line's humor is doubled. It is intended to be read by whites as an innocuous joke, a self-effacement in which Rock invites others to mock his ridiculous idea. But the line offers a different meaning to Blacks or others with a greater awareness of Black History. For them, the reason Charles calls André a crazy n*** is because he knows that whites will not be willing to see a film on the Revolution. The line can also be read in light of two other uses of the phrase. One is Malcolm X's comment in his address to Mississippi youth: "You get freedom by letting your enemy know that you'll do anything to get your freedom; then you'll get it. . . . When you get that kind of attitude, they'll label you as a 'crazy Negro,' or they'll call you a 'crazy n***'—they don't say Negro. . . . But when you stay radical long enough, and get enough people to be like you, you'll get your freedom."[10] The line also evokes the title of an album made by one of Rock's comedy idols, Richard Pryor's 1974 *That N***'s Crazy*.[11] André thus fits into a long line of "crazy n***s," as he highlights the amnesia of most whites about the realities of slavery.[12]

While Rock has not commented explicitly about this joke, he has suggested that he learned to double his humor by necessity. Rock has explained that, when he started out as a comic in the 1980s, there were no spaces where African Americans could only entertain other African Americans. There were no Black comedy clubs, no *Def Comedy Jam* or UPN, and two Black comedians were not even allowed on the same lineup. Noting that "you had to figure out how to make other people laugh beside black people," Rock commented that "we had to swing two bats." Working on *Saturday Night Live* (1990–93) likely also helped Rock perfect this doubling. The show's producer, Lorne Michaels, long had a reputation for tokenism in hiring Black comedians and for not affording them the same creative freedom as others. On *SNL*, Rock often deployed doubled humor, especially in his Nat X sketches.[13]

Alongside the doubled parts of the script, other parts of *Top Five* speak more overtly to the gap between the Revolution's importance and whites' knowledge of it. As he promotes *Uprize!*, André tries to educate interviewers about the Revolution's significance. He explains that he made *Uprize!* so that people will know about the Revolution, "the greatest slave rebellion of all time" (42:51). André adds that he researched the film's central character, the revolutionary Boukman, and long wanted to make a film about him (43:10). André is eager to share this history, which he learned, he emphasizes, outside of school.

Rock is careful in *Top Five* not to criticize every white person. The character in *Top Five* most eager to see *Uprize!* is in fact a white man familiar with Haitian history. The *Times* reporter's boyfriend, a DJ named Brad, tells André: "I cannot wait to see the movie. I'm so glad someone is finally telling Boukman's story. . . . I mean, no one talks about the maroon slaves!" (53:10).

It is possible that Rock is mocking Brad as a cultural appropriator; Brad, who turns out to be secretly gay, is someone who not only dates a Black woman but makes his living spinning Black music. However, Rock has made it a point in other contexts to exempt individual whites from the generic ones he skewers. In his 1999 HBO special *Bigger and Blacker*, Rock told his audience, "Racism everywhere. Who's the maddest people? White people. Not y'all, y'all all right. You paid money to see me; we cool."[14] Rock has also called out African Americans when he thinks they are more interested in entertainment than in history. When André sees a long line on *Uprize!*'s opening day, he is disappointed to discover that they are not at the theater to learn about Haiti but to see a fictional Tyler Perry movie called *Boo! A Madea Halloween*.[15]

Despite acknowledging individual exceptions, however, Rock stresses that whites have been indifferent or hostile to learning about the history of people of African descent. The whites who interview Rock share neither his enthusiasm for Boukman nor for the Revolution. For one thing, they don't even know what a slave rebellion means (André patiently explains: "It's when slaves . . . rebel" [42:46]). More importantly, to them, the Haitian Revolution is a story about one thing and one thing only: Blacks killing whites. In their view, it is inconceivable that whites will want to see it.

One key scene involves André's visit to the radio hosts Opie and Anthony at Sirius XM, where he excitedly describes *Uprize!* Anthony responds skeptically, "What do you have to say to the white audience here that is insulted, disgusted, by your movie, watching 50,000 of their people being killed?" (32:43). Rock gives André a powerful—and undoubled—retort. André tells Anthony: "George [W.] Bush kills a lot of brown people! Nobody had a problem with that (32:50). . . . He *really* killed 'em! I fake kill white people and it's a problem?!" Here, Rock is complaining that when US forces kill civilians of color in war zones such as Iraq, little indignation follows. And yet when enslaved people killed those who tortured them because it was the only way to become free, their agency is considered beyond the pale. Rock draws attention to the hypocrisy of whites who are horrified by the deaths of other whites, but oblivious to the suffering of people of color.[16] Rock has Anthony respond, "There's outrage!" But before white audiences can absorb Rock's critique enough to be angered, the editing cuts away to another interview. None of the reviews of *Top Five* that I have found have remarked on this exchange. Rock drops this bomb into *Top Five*, but in trickster style, he allows Anthony to condemn his comments—and then moves away at lightning speed before it can explode.

Most reviews of *Top Five* by professional film critics, as I have noted, left the Haitian Revolution component of the film unexamined. When they mentioned *Uprize!* in passing, they seemed never to have heard of the Haitian Revolution; just like the whites in the film, they said it concerned "a slave revolt" or "rebellion" that happened in Haiti.[17] Whereas professional critics did not notice what Rock was doing historiographically, perceptive Twitter users did. They highlighted the subtle way that Rock was educating viewers about Haiti and Black History while ostensibly inviting them to mock himself. One wrote, "Shoutout to @chrisrock for slipping in details about the Haitian Revolution into the plot of the movie Top Five." Another wrote that Rock was: "Lettin' 'em know about the Haitian Revolution, and they won't even know they received it. Go see Top Five." Still another wrote, "In Top Five, Chris Rock jokes about making a film about the Haitian Revolution, knowing full well that wouldn't be accepted in Hollywood."[18] These tweets confirm that Rock's doubled humor read differently to different audiences.

If Rock's thinking on history and memory was often only signified in *Top Five*, he was more explicit in interviews on the film. He bluntly conceded that studios were not initially interested in a movie that had the Revolution even as a secondary theme: "No, no studio would do a movie with a subplot about a Haitian revolution. Are you kidding me?"[19] Rock made *Top Five* outside the studio system, beginning with his own seed money; the producers he recruited included Jay-Z and Kanye West. Only after Rock completed the film and screened it at the Toronto International Film Festival did Paramount buy *Top Five* and fund its distribution.

Rock also emphasized in interviews that Black freedom—and white fear of it—is a central element of the film. He stressed this especially when speaking about the place of rap in *Top Five*. The film's title refers to hip-hop: throughout the movie, André asks others to name their top five rappers of all time. Rock told an Australian interviewer about this element of the film: "Rap, for the most part, is made by free people. Free black people. That's what scares people so much about it. That's what pisses people off so much about it, it's like, 'Oh my God, it's fucking black freedom. Turn it down.'"[20] Rock's implication, I would suggest, is that if Black freedom is threatening in music, then Black agency in revolution is far scarier.

Rock's comments on rap illuminate yet another layer of the film: whites expect André to keep playing Hammy the Bear, so they can laugh. They want a modern-day Sambo, rather than meaningful Black self-expression.[21] André's desire to make a serious movie about Black revolutionaries does not interest them; therefore, it cannot be successful. Andre's experiences seem to parallel Rock's own. Rock's highest-grossing role has been as Marty the Zebra in the *Madagascar* films, each of which grossed approximately $200 million.

In contrast, Rock's documentary *Good Hair* (which analyzed the desire of African American women, including one of his daughters, to use weaves and dangerous straightening chemicals to conform to white beauty standards) grossed approximately $4 million, while *Top Five* itself earned $25 million.[22] Like André, Rock earns more as a cartoonish animal character than when making serious films about Black History and culture.

Finally, Rock's interviews gave more detail on his views about how films on slavery tend to minimize its horrors. In *New York* magazine, Frank Rich asked Rock about recent films on racism and slavery, from *The Butler* to *12 Years a Slave*. Rock commented that they might help some white Americans be more enlightened about historical realities. However, he stated: "Of the ones you just mentioned, the only one I really liked is *12 Years a Slave*, because it just didn't feel the need to make people feel comfortable." Rock insisted that whites needed to "own" what happened during slavery.[23]

Several film critics assumed that Rock was merely poking fun of the idea of a Haitian Revolution film in *Top Five*. For instance, Stephen Whitty described André Allen as a character whose interest in the Revolution resulted from a "desperate bid for seriousness," something he thought Rock was mocking.[24] Certainly, *Uprize!* is a bad parody of what a Haitian Revolution film would look like. Its poster shows André as Boukman, brandishing a machete with a goofy expression; the one clip we see involves slaves yelling repeatedly, "Kill the white man!" (*Top Five* 1:09:24). Nevertheless, Rock made clear in interviews that *Top Five*'s Haitian theme is not a joke signaling André's pathetic attempt at gravitas.

Indeed, Rock has indicated that he would love to do a real film on slave revolt, but has been thwarted because of Hollywood realities. Rock told the *Los Angeles Times* of "his dream of making a biopic about the slave-rebellion leader Nat Turner, though he acknowledged that one may be a hard sell. 'If somebody lets me make it, I'll make it,' he said, 'but that ain't happening.'" In a radio interview, Rock underlined the differences between Hollywood fantasies of an enslaved insurgent like Django and what a real revolutionary like Turner was like: "Nat Turner could read! . . . Nat Turner spoke different languages. . . . Django was nothing compared to Nat Turner." In 2016, after Nate Parker released his Nat Turner biopic, *The Birth of a Nation*, Rock lamented that it only proved *Top Five*'s point. Like *Top Five*, that film turned out to be a flop at the box office; the same year, Tyler Perry had released a real film called *Boo! A Madea Halloween* (in homage to the fake version in *Top Five*). The real *Boo!* drew audiences away from *The Birth of a Nation* much like its fictional counterpart had done to *Uprize!*[25]

Alongside his interviews, Rock's stand-up shows his interest in race and slavery. His routines can be raw, and he has faced criticism for his "regressive" treatment of gender issues.[26] Nevertheless, some critics who call attention to his stereotyping on gender have acclaimed his observations on race.[27] Indeed, he has been widely acclaimed by fellow comedians—as well as African American intellectuals—for the intelligence in his comedy, even as he embeds political jokes in lewd ones. According to comedian Katt Williams, Rock "brought intelligence back to stand-up comedy. He would talk about intellectual things and yet he was funny and would talk about n***a shit at the same time." For Robert Townsend, "Chris is a jedi master. He elevates the game." The social impact of Rock's comedy also earned him praise from Congressman Elijah Cummings, who stated, "Chris Rock has said things that I use in speeches. There's so much truth in what he says." When Kara Hunt, a specialist in African American comedy, interviewed Rock in 2014, she emphasized his associations with the intellectuals Nelson George and Cornel West.[28]

That Rock meant to speak on historiographical and political themes in *Top Five* can also be seen in his comedy oeuvre. While a young performer on *Saturday Night Live*, Rock inserted counter-narratives on history into his sketches, for instance questioning Columbus's reputation and blasting US treatment of Native Americans.[29] He deepened such critiques in his stand-up, most notably in his 1996 HBO special, *Bring the Pain*, and his 1997 book, *Rock This!* Sandwiching his comments between coarse jokes on prison sex and on infidelity, Rock called attention to the gap between Black History and white memory:

> I once took a black history class. I figured since I'm black I already knew everything. I figured I'd pass just by showing up.
>
> Failed it. Isn't that sad, a black man failing black history? But I didn't know anything about Africa.
>
> When you go to white schools you learn about Europe up the ass, but you don't learn that much about Africa. The only thing I know about Africa is that it's far, far away. A 35-hour flight. Imagine the boat ride. The boat ride's so long there's still slaves on their way here.
>
> All I learned in school about being black was Martin Luther King. That's all they ever teach. Martin Luther King. He was the answer to everything.
>
> TEACHER: What's the capital of Zaire?
>
> ME: Martin Luther King.
>
> TEACHER: Tell us the name of the woman who would not give up her seat on the bus.

ME: Oh, that's hard. Are ya sure it was a woman? Okay. I got it. Martin*a* Luther King.[30]

This routine operates similarly to *Top Five*. At first glance, Rock appears to be mocking himself. He failed the Black History class; he doesn't know any historical figures other than Martin Luther King, not even Rosa Parks. But embedded in this mockery is a harsh criticism of American education ("white schools"). Rock notes that schools teach a great deal about Europe, but nothing about Black History except for Martin Luther King. He also sneaks in a signifying reference to the Atlantic slave trade.[31] Clearly, Rock's discussion of the Haitian Revolution in *Top Five* is not random. As Rock sought to educate himself about Black History, he learned about Haiti's revolution but recognized that white schools (at least when he was a child) never taught it. Martin Luther King was the only subject of Black History that seemed nonthreatening to whites, since his movement was based on nonviolence. Haitian revolutionaries, in contrast, epitomized white fears about Blacks and were never discussed.

Another early bit by Rock highlighted the gap between white and Black memories of slavery, with regard to reparations. On a 2000 episode of *The Chris Rock Show*, Rock interviewed African Americans and whites in New York City about whether Blacks were owed compensation for slavery. He highlighted Blacks remembering that they were never given the "40 acres and a mule" promised them as compensation for slavery, versus whites insisting that they bore no responsibility for this history.[32]

Rock's stand-up has echoed still other themes in *Top Five*, for instance concerning white fears of Black men and boys. In *Rock This!* he suggested that whites fear Blacks gathering, no matter who they are: "White people don't know how to tell the difference between one black man and another. . . . They see two black men together and it's a crowd. A dangerous mob. To white people, even Ed Bradley and Bryant Gumbel hanging out, waiting to cross the street together, is potentially scary." Rock indicated here that, since the era of slavery, African American men (even genteel newscasters) are seen as threatening. Rock has also made jokes about how he himself has been perceived. Another classic bit in *Rock This!* was the following:

Sometimes I hate life because I was born a suspect. All black men are born suspects.

When I came out of my mother, right away, if anything happened within a three-block radius, I was a suspect. . . .

> If you're born a suspect, everybody's scared of you. . . . If I look up into the windows of the apartments I pass by I can see old ladies on the phone. They've already called 9-1 . . . and are just waiting for me to do something wrong.

Rock's comments here were not hypothetical; in 2015 on Twitter, Rock began chronicling each time he was stopped by police while driving.[33]

Around the same time as *Top Five* was made, Rock's Twitter feed amplified his concerns about how little African American lives are valued by many whites. *Top Five* was filmed at the same time as the rise of the Black Lives Matter movement, and Rock frequently tweeted in solidarity with it. In November 2014, after a grand jury declined to charge the officer who killed Michael Brown, Rock tweeted a quote from W. E. B. Du Bois: "A system cannot fail those it was never meant to protect." On December 2014, as *Top Five* began to screen, Rock tweeted about the NYPD's refusal to press charges against the officer who killed Eric Garner: "This one was on film." In June 2015, Rock juxtaposed photos of police treatment of Garner (who was killed while under arrest for selling contraband cigarettes) and Dylann Roof (who was arrested peacefully after murdering nine people at a church): "This is how you arrest a white man who shot 9 people, and this is how you arrest a black man for selling cigarettes." Following the killing of Sandra Bland in police custody in July 2015, Rock tweeted: "If I were to die in police custody, know this. . . . I did not commit suicide." In August 2016, he decried the fatal shooting of Korryn Gaines by tweeting, "WTF. It's gotta stop." And two years before *Top Five* was made, in the midst of the uproar over Trayvon Martin's death, Rock harkened back to slavery with a provocative tweet: "Happy white peoples independence day the slaves weren't free but I'm sure they enjoyed fireworks."[34]

Top Five was thus clearly a historiographical intervention, even if framed profanely and satirically. Building on comments he had made elsewhere, Rock underscored the difficulty of making serious films in Hollywood about Black History. He highlighted how Black lives are discounted not only in the present but also in the past; for whites like *Top Five*'s radio hosts, white lives matter more than Black ones, even when the former brutalized the latter. If other revolutions are seen as attractive topics for Hollywood, Rock made clear that Haiti's is not. Ever the trickster, Rock thus served as a pop-culture analog to the anthropologist Michel-Rolph Trouillot. Using the Revolution to signify white fears of Black freedom, Rock pushed audiences to confront why there has not yet been a successful Haitian Revolution film—one that values enslaved Black lives as much as those of their white enslavers.

6

REMEMBERING HAITI'S REVOLUTION IN FRANCE AND NORTH AMERICA

Documentaries, Dramatic Shorts, and Animation

As we have seen, there have been more unmade feature films on the Haitian Revolution than completed ones. The reluctance to fund and support such a film, whether encountered by real filmmakers or by *Top Five*'s fictional André Allen, has kept the topic largely off screen. In the absence of epics, directors have completed other kinds of films on the Revolution. I focus in this chapter on these projects: documentaries, dramatic shorts, and animated shorts. These films reach more limited audiences than historical feature films. However, they remain important to study for what they reveal about memories of slavery and the Haitian Revolution in France and North America. Most of them were made entirely by French and American filmmakers. However, some involved collaboration with Haitian scholars and artists, which makes them a valuable complement to the Haitian films discussed in part II.

While independent filmmakers everywhere struggle to raise money, I want to emphasize that those in France and the US can draw upon many more funding sources than their Haitian counterparts, even without major studio support. To make documentaries and shorts, which are far less expensive than features, French and North American filmmakers have procured funds from public television stations, universities, government agencies, crowdfunding, or their families and friends. These institutions have far greater resources than comparable ones in Haiti, a result of the wealth differentials bequeathed by slavery and colonialism. Thus, even today, filmmakers from these countries have greater power to tell Haiti's history on screen than do Haitians themselves.

Teaching French Audiences about Haiti in Documentary Film

Despite the general amnesia about Haiti's revolution in France, French directors have made a few full-length documentaries on the subject. These include one made for the French Revolution's Bicentennial in 1989, a second after the bicentennial of Toussaint Louverture's death in 2003, and two more in the wake of increased interest in French slavery in the late 2010s.[1] These documentaries have been aided by the greater government support that French filmmakers enjoy compared to both their Haitian and US counterparts. As I noted in chapter 1, the French have had difficulty grappling with their history of slavery in Saint-Domingue without whitewashing it. These films have sought to rectify French ignorance about Haiti and to make its history known to more French people, but still reflect the "limits" of French memory.

In December 1989, French television aired a program called *Toussaint Louverture* by filmmaker Claude Moreau. Sponsors included the Committee for the Bicentennial of the Revolution; several French ministries, including Culture and Foreign Affairs; the City of Lille; the Region Nord-Pas-de-Calais; the Conseil Général du Nord; the telecommunications company Alcatel; and two television stations. The film grew out of a multimedia production mounted in May in Dakar, Senegal, and in June in Lille.[2]

Moreau's film was significant in reclaiming Toussaint and the Haitian Revolution well before others in France began to pay attention to these subjects.[3] Aside from the sponsorship of Moreau's film, the official Bicentennial commemorations largely ignored slavery and the French Revolution's impact in the colonies; Caribbean scholars, along with sympathetic metropolitan colleagues like Marcel Dorigny and Yves Benot, were left to invoke these topics on their own.[4] Toussaint was relatively unknown in France at this time, and the 2001 Taubira Law (which recognized slavery as a crime against humanity and mandated that schools teach about it) did not yet exist. While most invocations of Toussaint and slavery during the Bicentennial came from grassroots groups,[5] the film was part of an official event, the Third Summit of Francophone Countries in Dakar. At this summit, organized by France and attended by President François Mitterrand, France asserted its continued leadership of Francophone countries. Moreau's "Toussaint Louverture" spectacle was a summit highlight, attended by more than forty heads of state. A two-hour extravaganza costing seven million francs (then equivalent to about $1.1 million), it combined filmed segments (made with actors and projected onto giant screens) and live performances from the National Ballet of Senegal, the Haitian singer Toto Bissainthe, a Senegalese choir, and others. These included

Camerounian actor Gérard Essomba playing Toussaint, and a multiracial cast. The television version blended the advance-filmed and live components.[6]

Given the film's funding sources, it is not surprising that it glorified France, even while raising the then-taboo subject of French slaveholding. Moreau highlighted Toussaint's story, but in a manner conforming to official French narratives about the French Revolution's liberating role worldwide. The film suggested that the Revolution had freed enslaved people not from "French" subjection per se, but from that of the Bourbon monarchy, who were then replaced by freedom-loving republicans. The white abolitionist priest and revolutionary abbé Henri Grégoire loomed large in this narrative. Though he had been denounced for his abolitionism during his lifetime, this approach made Grégoire seem typical of French ideals.[7]

White heroes like Grégoire figured prominently in this production, even as the writers (Pierre Sauvageot and Jean-Louis Sagot-Duvauroux) also included proslavery whites. In addition to Grégoire, the film's "good" whites included Robespierre, Mirabeau, and General Laveaux. Grégoire blasts white colonists who refuse to treat people of color equally, and declares that slaves wish only to "wear the *cocarde* and the *tricouleur*" (emblems indicating support for the French Revolution). Enslaved women wail while Vincent Ogé is prepared for execution; metropolitan revolutionaries try to save him, while colonists tell them to stop meddling. Toussaint emerges to speak for the "silent" slaves; he fights for French values against those who deny them: "I have taken up arms for the freedom of my color, which only France has proclaimed and which no one has the right to rescind."[8]

Moreau's work thus was avant-garde in 1989 in invoking Haiti. But it also fit into what Nicola Frith and Kate Hodgson have called "the instrumentalization of memories of slavery by state discourses" in France. As Christine Chivallon has remarked, French republican commemorations of slavery often make "the slave past visible only so that its glorious defeat [by French abolitionism] can be all the more celebrated"; Crystal Fleming has added that the state's deploying "color-blind ideology" during such commemorations has served to "grossly minimize France's history of racism" and to bolster narratives of white superiority.[9] Indeed, the production does not seem to have had any Haitian input aside from the casting of Bissainthe (who had also appeared in Hondo's *West Indies*). Moreover, except for Essomba as Toussaint, performers of color often danced and sang while words and arguments were left to white actors. A review of the performance in *Le monde*'s Bicentennial coverage noted that "the most beautiful scene in this vein is when a 'Messenger' makes people aware of the passage of the abolition decree [in Paris in 1794]. . . .

His announcement is constantly interrupted by the *han-han* of the crowd." This suggested that the French had gifted liberation to passive and grateful Haitians, rather than that Haitians had won it themselves, fighting *against* the French (with the latter acknowledging this fact only retroactively).[10]

Fifteen years later, a pair of French filmmakers, Laurent Lutaud and Georges Nivoix, returned to what remained an essentially unknown subject. Their 2004 film, *Toussaint Louverture: Haïti et la France*, was funded by agencies in the same region as Fort de Joux, the prison where Toussaint died, as well as some national agencies. The film aired numerous times on French television. It also had an English-language version, *Toussaint Louverture, Haiti, Destiny of a Nation*, created for France 3 Méditerranée.[11] The film improved on Moreau's film by acknowledging Haitian agency and colonial brutality, but still illustrated gaps in French memory about colonial Saint-Domingue.

Toussaint Louverture: Haïti et la France focused not just on Toussaint but on the general relationship between the Haitian and French Revolutions. The film's impetus was a 2003 ceremony held at Fort de Joux by the Haitian commission in honor of the bicentennial of Toussaint's death, in conjunction with local French officials. This ceremony prompted Lutaud, a French citizen, to wonder who Toussaint was. He states in a voiceover, "His name sounded vaguely familiar to me, but I didn't know anything about this former black slave who became general of the French army in Saint-Domingue" (1:22). Lutaud asserted that, while officials had come from Haiti, Africa, and the French Antilles for the ceremony, "in France, no one cares in the least; apart from a few scholars, no one knows Toussaint Louverture" (1:49).

Even two years after the Taubira Law's enactment, the fact that Saint-Domingue had been part of France was still not widely known. As noted in chapter 1, French president Jacques Chirac had shockingly claimed in 2000 that Haiti had never been a French colony. *Toussaint Louverture: Haïti et la France* thus represented Lutaud's journey to learn not just about Toussaint, but also about France's history in Haiti. Lutaud directed the film and cowrote its script with Nivoix, a filmmaker working for the Academy of Besançon's pedagogical division. Together, they aimed to educate French students and the public about this history.

Toussaint Louverture: Haïti et la France includes interviews with Haitian, French Antillean, and metropolitan intellectuals. The Haitians interviewed include historians Sabine Manigat and Pierre Buteau; architect Gérard Fombrun; curator Michel-Philippe Lerebours of the Musée d'art haïtien; painter Donald Obin; literary giant Frankétienne; and Kendy Vérilus, a young filmmaker discussed in chapter 8. In addition to these and other Haitians, Lutaud interviewed three French citizens who were central to efforts to revive the memory of slavery at the turn of the twenty-first century: Christiane Taubira, the author of the Taubira Law as a National Assembly deputy from Guyane (and later France's justice minister); legendary Martinican poet and statesman Aimé Césaire; and French historian Marcel Dorigny.

Lutaud's and Nivoix's film is earnest in many respects. Lutaud travels from France to Haiti to Martinique, visiting multiple *lieux de mémoire*. After filming the prison cell where Toussaint took his final breaths, Lutaud goes to Haiti to find out about the general's life. He visits the Bréda Plantation, where Toussaint was enslaved; he finds a modern monument to Toussaint but no colonial-era buildings. He journeys to central Haiti, where Gérard Fombrun has restored a plantation house and created a museum (Musée Ogier-Fombrun) commemorating the lives of enslaved people. He also visits the Galerie Nader in Port-au-Prince to see artistic representations of Toussaint Louverture. And he goes to the Bois Caïman and to Vertières, where independence was won.[12]

The film's interviewees discuss issues ranging from the suffering of enslaved people to the inconsistences of French universalism—topics not always acknowledged in French public discussions of slavery. Manigat calls colonial Saint-Domingue "a factory that consumed *les nègres* at a frightful pace" (12:44). Buteau tells horrifying stories about enslavers' cruelty. Dorigny notes that, despite the French Revolution's liberating rhetoric, the deputies "were in no hurry" to abolish slavery (24:23); they did so only after the insurrection pushed them to "reconsider their vision of human rights" (24:42). Eric Caberia, from the Comité Devoir de Mémoire in Martinique, explains that "Toussaint was a great man, and Napoleon an ethical dwarf" (32:01). Taubira, Dorigny, and others blast the indemnity agreement, indicating how Haitians suffered for generations for the sin of liberating themselves.

Despite including this crucial information, the film's perspective remains startlingly naive in other respects. It is shocking when Lutaud says in voiceover, while Fombrun is explaining some basic facts about slavery (not the most horrifying ones), that "I thought I knew all there is to know about slavery. I'd seen [D. W.] Griffith's films. I'd seen *Gone with the Wind* and Spielberg's *The Color Purple*. But no—in real life, slavery must have been very different from the master and servant relation I knew from the movies" (11:25). One can scarcely imagine a Haitian (let alone US) filmmaker declaring that Griffith's ferociously racist *The Birth of a Nation* had provided her knowledge about slavery. Later, the director seems most concerned with whether Toussaint remained faithful to France, and to what extent French ideals guided him.

Like Moreau's *Toussaint Louverture*, Lutaud's and Nivoix's film thus performed a service in helping some French audiences learn about Haiti. However, it still portrayed the Haitian Revolution as a product of the French, and measured it by its fidelity to French values. Rather than acknowledging Haitians' struggle against French racism, the filmmakers celebrated Haiti as a "child of the French Revolution" whose people remained devoted to French ideals but whom the *patrie* had abandoned (52:12).

As the Taubira Law has increased interest in the history of slavery in France, other French documentaries have offered more sophisticated perspectives on Saint-Domingue and the Haitian Revolution. These include Dominique Maestrati's 2016 *Bonaparte, côté noir* (Bonaparte, the Dark Side), whose funding sources included French television and the Corsican regional government. *Bonaparte, côté noir* examines Napoleon's reimposition of slavery and its impact throughout the French Antilles, with help from talking-head historians such as Dorigny, Bernard Gainot, and Frédéric Regent. The film also includes actors playing Napoleon, Toussaint Louverture, and the abbé Grégoire. The latter (played by Jean-Michel Ropers) gives several antiracist orations, while Toussaint (Martinican actor Christian Julien) is shown giving his "tree of liberty" speech while in prison (38:38). Notably for a French film highlighting an abolitionist like Grégoire, the narrator concedes that Haiti's eventual freedom came "not from the Enlightenment, or abolitionist laws, but from [former] slaves themselves" (43:21). And both Dorigny and Ropers-as-Grégoire mention France's inhumane use of slave-chasing dogs (47:52).[13]

Another recent documentary also refers to the Revolution while highlighting the flaws in official French commemorations of slavery. Filmed in Nantes and Bordeaux, 2019's *L'impasse Toussaint-Louverture* asks why state commemorations have focused on white French abolitionists like Victor Schœlcher, while marginalizing Toussaint and other Caribbean figures who battled for freedom against France. The film offers an excellent analysis of gaps in French memory of slavery, with the help of citizen-activists such as Octave Cestor and Karfa Diallo, who have pushed for more multifaceted commemorations of this history.[14]

Remembering Haitian Revolutionaries in US Documentaries

Despite fewer government subsidies for film, US documentarians can seek support from public television agencies and foundations. In the late 2000s Noland Walker and Margaret Koval made a television documentary on the Haitian

Revolution. Their cowritten *Égalité for All: Toussaint Louverture and the Haitian Revolution* benefited from funding from the Independent Television Service (ITVS) of the Corporation for Public Broadcasting, Oregon Public Broadcasting, and the National Black Programming Consortium. Walker, the director, had previously worked on the PBS series *Africans in America*; Koval, the executive producer, had previously made documentaries on the Roman Empire and World War I. *Égalité for All* aired nationally on PBS in 2009.[15]

Égalité for All offers an accessible sixty-minute introduction to Saint-Domingue and the Revolution. The filmmakers partnered with historian Laurent Dubois; his 2004 history of the Revolution, *Avengers of the New World*, is described as the film's "companion book" (though, as I will note, the filmmakers departed in some ways from Dubois's own historiographical perspective).[16] In addition, Walker and Koval recruited a high-profile narrator, the acclaimed Haitian American author Edwidge Danticat. Interspersed with her voiceovers, which are frequently paired with ominous-sounding music, *Égalité for All* includes interviews with scholars and artists. These include English-speaking Haitian intellectuals (poet Jean-Claude Martineau, sociologist Jean Casimir, and painter Edouard Duval-Carrié) as well as US-based writers (Dubois, the novelist Madison Smartt Bell, and the Haitian-descended scholars Chantalle Verna and Colin Dayan).

Though the dramatizations and costumes in *Égalité for All* are more elaborate than in many other documentaries on the Revolution, Walker has stated that budgetary constraints still limited his choices. He seems to have had funding for shooting exterior scenes in Paris, but insisted that filming in Haiti would have been too expensive. He instead shot the scenes about Haiti in the Dominican Republic. The film does not appear to have included any Haitian crew members, though the directors cast some Haitian-descended actors in the dramatizations.[17]

As its title suggests, *Égalité for All* portrays the Haitian Revolution as an outgrowth—and fulfillment—of French revolutionary ideals. It begins with the Revolution in Paris before shifting to Haiti. In this way, it resembles French documentaries and feature films on the Haitian Revolution more than the Haitian films I treat in chapters 7 and 8. The narration portrays French ideas of inequality as prompting Haiti's revolution ("what was a dangerous idea in France [equality] was even more dangerous in its slaveholding colonies off the Coast of Florida" [5:13]). It also suggests that enslaved people learned about ideas of liberty from their enslavers, even if the latter had not intended this (6:08). The film focuses on the Revolution's "great men," without much focus on its grassroots soldiers or on women revolutionaries.

The film also shares with other non-Haitian films an emphasis on the violence of the Haitian Revolution, even while Martineau, Dubois, and others point out that the colonists had themselves been brutal. *Égalité for All* includes numerous dramatizations of revolutionary battles, blood, and fire. The opening scene features Bell describing the Revolution as "a wholesale massacre on a really, really enormous scale. It was big, big, major payback time" (2:44). The filmmakers show actors playing slaves attacking white colonists sleeping in bed. They also recreate the Bois Caïman ceremony, complete with its infamous pig slaughter.

Égalité for All takes pains not to heroicize Toussaint; it praises his leadership while emphasizing his flaws. This strategy reflects recent scholarship on Toussaint, including works published by Dubois and Bell before the film. But it results in a more negative portrayal of Toussaint than in other non-Haitian films on the Revolution—with the exception of *1804*, discussed below. The film's opening credits scroll across water that Toussaint has made bloody by striking someone with his sword (3:11). Dubois and others explain that Toussaint initially would have been willing to settle for freedom for the Revolution's leaders only, while the rest of the colony's population remained enslaved with moderate reforms; however, once the colony's whites rejected compromise, Toussaint became more radical. The script has Danticat state that Toussaint had a "profound attachment to democratic ideals," but that "there was another side to Toussaint too" (40:04). Bell notes that Toussaint abhorred violence and sought diplomacy before resorting to it, but that "if that didn't work he would kill you" (26:57). He adds that "anybody who looked like they threatened Toussaint either ended up dead or deported" (40:11). The film also explores the controversy over Toussaint's efforts to force former slaves to return to plantation work after abolition, to raise funds for national defense. This highlighting of Toussaint's complexity has led some viewers to appraise him negatively. One IMDb.com reviewer remarked without any irony that "Louverture was NOT exactly the black George Washington, but was deeply flawed—and set the stage for centuries of misrule in this island nation. See the show and you'll know what I mean." The film's emphasis on Louverture's "other side," as this quote indicates, made some viewers see him as more flawed than a Southern slaveowner.[18]

Though some of *Égalité for All*'s narrative strategies paralleled other non-Haitian films on the Revolution, others departed from them. Unlike Niang's *Toussaint Louverture* miniseries, *Égalité for All* did not flinch from acknowledging slavery's brutality. Casimir notes that enslaved peoples were "expected to live like [animals]" (1:37). Martineau details how sugarcane could cut into and burn enslaved people's skin, leaving spaces in which biting ants could crawl (7:41). Dubois describes tortures used by enslavers, like rubbing hot pepper into wounds (9:30). Verna explains that, even when revolutionaries set fires, it was not wanton destruction but a specific targeting of the "mechanisms of [sugar] production" (2:30). Those interviewed stress the difficult circumstances in which Toussaint found himself, and his being a master of leadership and organization. And Bell defends Dessalines against charges that he was genocidal; he notes that Dessalines did not seek to kill all whites during the War of Independence, but only French ones who sought to reenslave Haitians (50:22). The film closes with stirring proclamations from Dubois and Martineau about the long-term importance of the Haitian Revolution for humanity, but also a scroll indicating that "a long line of authoritarian rulers [in Haiti] trampled rights and worsened race and class divides," causing "violence, poverty and environmental degradation" (53:46).

Overall, *Égalité for All* offers Anglophone viewers a helpful overview of the Revolution, and it is more sophisticated than Moreau's film or that of Lutaud and Nivoix. Nevertheless, it suggested that Haitians rebelled after borrowing French ideals, and it emphasized the revolutionaries' violence. This emphasis departed from Dubois's own scholarship, which has cautioned others not to overemphasize or decontextualize such violence.[19]

African American filmmaker Tariq Nasheed's film *1804: The Hidden History of Haiti* differs in a number of ways from *Égalité for All*, stemming in part from its funding source. So that he did not need to make his narrative palatable to the mostly white funders at institutions like the Corporation for Public Broadcasting, Nasheed crowdfunded among Black audiences. Nasheed had gained followers from dating manuals like *The Art of Mackin'*, as well as his series *Hidden Colors*, which chronicled "the real and untold history of people of color around the world." Directing his efforts at his fans as well as others interested in Haiti, Nasheed raised $261,945 on Indiegogo and successfully released *1804* in 2017 as a 110-minute documentary.[20]

In some respects, Nasheed's film parallels other documentaries on the Revolution, including those by Haitians that I discuss in part II. The film starts with the Tainos, continues through the horrors of slavery, and discusses the Revolution's major figures, before turning to Haiti's postrevolutionary fate. Like other documentaries, *1804* combines interviews with talking heads, short dramatizations with actors, engravings from the eighteenth century, and some animation. The film emphasizes the resistance of enslaved peoples before 1789, celebrates the revolutionaries, discusses how the Revolution has been forgotten outside Haiti, and introduces the Revolution's impact on enslaved peoples worldwide. It also challenges Western stereotypes about Vodou, while highlighting its role in resistance.

In other ways, the film differs markedly from other documentaries and dramas on the Revolution. Since Nasheed and his target audience were African Americans, he had little need to make white audiences feel comfortable. Nasheed does not disdain the violence of the revolutionaries but celebrates it. Many of the film's reenactments show Black actors playing enslaved peoples gleefully attacking white actors playing colonists, with a variety of weapons. Some of these scenes look like they could have been lifted from André Allen's *Uprize!*, if only it had been a real film. In addition, when Toussaint is introduced, his name is spelled out with swords as letters, in a title card with video game–style animation (37:33). Nasheed's approach seems designed to fulfill the kinds of anticolonial revenge fantasies that some gamers of color have sought in slave revolt video games (see chapter 9).

As part of cheering on the revolutionaries' violence, *1804* has a section on "Fighting styles used by the Haitians" (52:07), something that might appeal to African Americans who love martial arts films and want to know how enslaved peoples defeated Napoleon's army. Interviewees describe enslaved people's prior experiences in African wars, their "guerilla warfare" tactics, and their "mastery of the terrain" (53:39). They also invoke women's contributions to revolutionary battles. African American educator Kaba Kamene says that the "sisters . . . created the environment for the men to do what needed to be done" (53:44). Bayyinah Bello, a Haitian professor discussed in chapter 7, and Ezili Danto (who is identified as a "Haitian historian/lawyer" but is not an academic) are more specific about women fighters in the Revolution. They emphasize the fierceness of Sanité Bélair and of the Dahomeyan woman (Tante Toya) who raised Dessalines, rather than depicting women as auxiliary helpers.

Though Bello and Danto are Haitian, the film's talking heads are mostly African Americans, which gives *1804* a different perspective than other films discussed so far. Given the film's emphasis, it is not surprising that Nasheed bypasses the white scholars of the Revolution who appear in other documentaries. But, more unusually, instead of Haitian American experts in Haitian Studies such as Patrick Bellegarde-Smith, Gina Ulysse, or Chantalle Verna, or leading scholars in Haiti, the film features Afrocentric US professors like Leonard Jeffries who do not specialize in Haiti. The film's only Haitian talking head besides Bello or Danto is the musician Wyclef Jean. Though *1804*'s African American interviewees retell Haiti's history as best as they understand it, a reviewer at the *Haitian History Blog* lamented that this "odd assortment of African American Afrocentric academics and speakers, including Nasheed himself," did not add "much of substance or interest beyond a summary of the Revolution." The reviewer stated further that, "the appearance of so few Haitian intellectuals, historians, and scholars weaken[s]" the film.[21]

The director's serving as his own talking head provides some of the film's most problematic interpretations. *1804*'s strengths come from Nasheed's ability to translate the Haitian Revolution into accessible terms; he and interviewees such as the British rapper Akala compellingly explain why Haitian history—though it might seem remote to young African Americans—relates to their lives. But Nasheed's effort to connect eighteenth-century events to contemporary crises in the Black community—for instance the presence of "collaborators" willing to sell out their community for "trinkets"—sometimes leads him to surprising assertions. After denouncing "house Negroes" who did not care about other enslaved peoples, Nasheed suggests that Toussaint wanted so badly to be "accepted as French" (42:56) that he fell for Napoleon's flattery and stumbled into being captured. Rather than a master of strategy who triangulated foreign powers—and sacrificed himself so the fight for freedom could continue—Nasheed's Toussaint was a dupe who did not want to displease the French. *1804* does not mention Toussaint's switch to the Spanish before his carefully negotiated return to the French—nor his continuing efforts to defy Napoleon and other French leaders, particularly by writing a constitution in 1801. For Nasheed, Dessalines was a savvy hero, but Toussaint was not: "Now, Dessalines would not fall for [Napoleon's] trick" (43:36). Nasheed also contrasts Toussaint's efforts to make "deals" with Europeans to Dessalines. He states that Dessalines alone understood that "you cannot make deals with terrorists . . . and white supremacy is the ultimate form of terrorism" (55:29).[22]

Another striking part of the film is Nasheed's use of blanket generalizations about "mulattoes," a word whose negative connotations he ignores.[23] He declares that "the only thing that's worse than a white supremacist [his term in the film for colonists] is a wannabe white supremacist. . . . They'll sabotage anything for a fantasy [of something they can't be]. And that's what [mulattoes] did after the Haitian Revolution" (1:19:01). Nasheed also suggests that people of mixed race had been whites' allies until late in the Revolution (when General Rochambeau arrived from France). This statement ignores the diverse views of mixed-race people and the different factions in which they fought. The *Haitian History Blog* has pointed to other "uproariously outrageous" or dubious assertions in the film, such as the idea that "August 'electrifies' our melanin so that August is a propitious time of the year for revolutionary action among Black people," as well as Danto's reference to Africans living on Hispaniola before Columbus.[24]

Ultimately, the film offers a clear introduction to the Revolution, even if parts are problematic. In addition to Bello's important analysis of Haitian history, Gerald Horne offers nuance to complicate Nasheed's own comments. So does Wyclef, whose knowledge of Haitian history is deeper than most of the film's other interviewees (see for instance his comments on Toussaint and Dessalines, 46:19, 1:09:40). Perhaps the film's most important line is when Akala challenges those who dismiss the Haitian revolutionaries as brutal. "How," he asks incredulously, "are you going to get free of slavery without brutality?" (1:23:02). Akala also contrasts the labeling of Haitian revolutionaries as violent with other revolutionaries who are celebrated: "The French Revolution was incredibly brutal, yet it's treated with respect in historiography, as producing ideas that were influential for humanity. The Chinese Revolution, the Russian Revolution: similar, all treated with respect. The Haitian Revolution, until very recently . . . , has been treated like some, you know, n***s in the Caribbean rebelling, when actually it is arguably the greatest challenge to the dominant global order in the last two hundred years" (1:43:16).

Commemorating Toussaint in Cheaper Formats: Dramatic and Documentary Shorts

In addition to directors who have made feature-length documentaries on the Revolution, others have made dramatic shorts, or shorts mixing talking heads and reenactment. One such dramatic short is Derick Alexander's twenty-four-minute *The Last Days of Toussaint L'Ouverture*, made with a budget of approximately $7,500. Alexander is an African American actor who has had small parts on television series such as *ER* and *Parenthood*. This film, his directorial debut, premiered in Anaheim, California, in 2009; it is not clear whether it screened again publicly. The action unfolds entirely in the Fort de Joux prison. Given the film's budget, it was filmed not on location but on a California soundstage.[25]

Compared to Nasheed and Walker, Alexander venerates Toussaint more unreservedly. The action centers on Toussaint and his loyal servant Mars Plaisir. Alexander did include a white hero, perhaps in hopes of attracting funds to turn the short into a feature. He has written that "*The Last Days of Toussaint L'Ouverture* is the only film of its kind about Haiti's first Black leader, who was kidnapped and then killed by Napoleon. Our film chronicles the last desperate days of a proud Haitian man who refused to back down to the most powerful leader in the world at that time in history." While highlighting

Toussaint's bravery, Alexander explained that he crafted the story from a white perspective, that of Napoleonic General Cafarelli: "How director Derick Alexander brings a fresh perspective to this historic Haitian, American and European story is that the film is written from the eyes of General Cafarelli, who was sent by Napoleon to make a deal with Toussaint from inside the former general's cold and moldy cell located in France's ominous Jura Mountains." The *Last Days of Toussaint L'Ouverture* casts a Nigerian model, Joseph Ademola Adeyemo—considerably younger than Toussaint was in the 1800s—in the lead role. Adeyemo's Toussaint argues with Cafarelli, who seems chiefly interested in recovering treasure that Louverture is said to have buried.[26]

Another short celebrating Toussaint was produced by the Museum of the African Diaspora (MoAD) in San Francisco. *Toussaint: The Heartbeat of Freedom* (2005) runs fifteen minutes. Its director, Douglas McHenry, is a noted African American filmmaker who has worked on films like *New Jack City*. *Toussaint: The Heartbeat of Freedom* screened onsite at MoAD for several years after the museum opened; it aimed to introduce "older children" to this central episode in African diaspora history. The museum also posted the film on Vimeo.[27] Because of McHenry's connections and MoAD's unique mission, he was able to gather a more prominent cast than Alexander. Danny Glover, who has strong connections to San Francisco as a native of the city, served as narrator.

Toussaint: The Heartbeat of Freedom blends talking-head and reenactment segments. It opens with a rap song and a mural about Toussaint by an artist named Menaz. It includes interviews with Cornel West and Wyclef, as well as dramatized scenes featuring Bay Area native Glenn Plummer as Toussaint Louverture, suffering in his prison cell. Against a backdrop of images from Jacob Lawrence as well as Haitian artists like Edouard Duval-Carrié and Ulrick Jean-Pierre, Glover recounts Toussaint's story, appraising him more positively than in *1804*. West links Toussaint to the struggles of African Americans today, calling him "the first modern man in the Western hemisphere" (2:46) and "a precursor of what we're dealing with right now" (0:17).

Because *Toussaint: The Heartbeat of Freedom* has not been released theatrically or shown at festivals, it has received little attention; unlike Alexander's film, it is not included in the Internet Movie Database. The film was, however, mentioned in initial press coverage of the museum. When Edward Rothstein of the *New York Times* reviewed MoAD's opening, he found the short to be one of the museum's less compelling offerings: "A stylized short film about Toussaint L'Ouverture, made by Doug McHenry, filters out so much detail and eccentricity that this complex 18th-century leader of Haiti's slave revolution becomes a cartoon martyr packaged for contemporary tastes." The *Mercury News*, in contrast, found the film to be one of MoAD's "hidden gems." When a Duke University student argued in 2014 on a course blog that the film oversimplified the Revolution by focusing only on Toussaint and overlooking other revolutionaries, McHenry found her page and called the criticism unfair. He had not aimed to give a definitive history of the Revolution in fifteen minutes, he said, but to offer an "imaginary narrative of what Toussaint may have been thinking during his last moments."[28]

Animating the Haitian Revolution in North America, from the 1970s to the #BLM Era

While the dramatic shorts we have considered so far were made in the twenty-first century, the first—and most ambitious—short on the Revolution dates from 1978. *Black Dawn*, an eighteen-minute animated feature by Robin Lloyd and Doreen Kraft (white filmmakers and peace activists from the US) aimed to teach young people about the Revolution. Unlike Alexander's and McHenry's shorts, made with US-based casts and crews, Lloyd and Kraft produced much of their film in Haiti, working with Haitians. Their film was singled out by Arnold Antonin (the pioneering Haitian director discussed in chapter 7) as a rare example of serious foreign collaboration with Haitians; it reflects Haitian perspectives more than most other non-Haitian films on the Revolution.[29]

Lloyd and Kraft made the film as a labor of love, on a "shoestring" budget. They began with a small grant from the Vermont Council of the Arts, which enabled them to travel to Haiti to collaborate with Haitian artists. Because the film was animated, they did not need cameras or a crew; they simply bought paper and paint. At first, they did not even have money for an animation stand; after returning to Vermont, they lucked into a secondhand one from some Massachusetts animators who no longer needed it.[30]

What made *Black Dawn* exceptional among US films on the Revolution was Lloyd's and Kraft's eagerness to learn from Haitians. Lloyd and Kraft had spent time in Haiti before deciding to make *Black Dawn*, and had developed a fascination with Vodou. Having met *vodouisants* and acquired an admiration for the religion, Lloyd and Kraft did not intend to portray Vodou as bizarre. Lloyd notes that two young US white women eager to make a respectful film about Haitian culture, featuring Haitian perspectives, was a novelty. Lloyd's fluent French also helped. She and Kraft made their way into the most rarefied intellectual circles in Port-au-Prince. They spent time with the poet

René Depestre, the pioneering journalist and filmmaker Jean Dominique, and Frankétienne, now considered to be Haiti's greatest living writer. Another key connection was Francine Murat, director of the Haitian Centre d'Art. In the "Interview with the Directors" special feature on *Black Dawn*'s DVD, Kraft explained that Haitians like Dominique and Murat were "so excited that two American film artists were interested in really understanding what the role of Vodou was in the Revolution and were so respectful of their culture. . . . They really . . . put a lot of investment in this film."[31]

Lloyd and Kraft developed *Black Dawn* in collaboration with their Haitian friends. Lloyd recalls that, in discussing what kind of Vodou-related film to make, Haitians kept returning to the Revolution. Ultimately, Lloyd and Kraft directed the film and oversaw its animation and production, but they entrusted the rest of the project—from scriptwriting to art and music—to Haitians. For the script, Lloyd and Kraft recruited an all-star team: Dominique, who later became the subject of Jonathan Demme's documentary *The Agronomist*; Frankétienne; and Franck Fouché, a Haitian playwright living in Montreal.[32] Their Haitian friends also connected Lloyd and Kraft with the Haitian musicians (some living abroad) who created the soundtrack. Among these artists was a young Michel-Rolph Trouillot, singing with his group Tanbou Libète before beginning his graduate work in anthropology.[33]

For the film's animation, Lloyd and Kraft commissioned work from some of Haiti's most prominent painters. These included Philomé Obin, Rigaud Benoit, Salnave Philippe-Auguste, André Pierre, and Célestin Faustin. To make their paintings come alive, Lloyd and Kraft used cutout animation, which involved adding movable cutouts to paintings—for instance to show a character walking. The filmmakers also experimented with other types of animation. To show Boukman and others being possessed by the *lwa* in the film's Bois Caïman scene, Lloyd and Kraft filmed Faustin dancing, projected his performance onto a screen, and hand-drew each frame to turn it into cel animation. After the artists finished their paintings, Lloyd and Kraft returned to Vermont to complete the film. Faustin and another artist, Dieujuste Cadet, returned with them and helped Lloyd, Kraft, and friends finish the film's animation and editing.[34]

Black Dawn was designed to be accessible to Haitian as well as foreign audiences, a delicate task under the Duvalier dictatorship. The script by Dominique, Frankétienne, and the others was recorded with four different language tracks: English, Spanish, French, and Kreyòl. To give the film a familiar feel for Haitian audiences, *Black Dawn* took on the structure of a Kreyòl folktale; classic Haitian characters named Bouki and Ti Malice recount the story of the

Revolution. Lloyd and Kraft had to be careful in how they showed Bouki and Ti Malice recalling this history. Dominique told them that if they included the original blue and red flag of 1804, he could not participate. Duvalier had changed Haiti's flag to black and red, and the original flag was considered treasonous. Not wanting to endanger their Haitian colleagues, Lloyd and Kraft labored to create an ambiguous bluish-black for the flag. When the dictatorship ended and they released the film on DVD, they recolored the cel blue.[35]

Black Dawn begins with a "Once upon a time" opening, introducing Bouki, Ti Malice, and their island. The viewer learns that they are peasants who need to bring mangoes to market in Port-au-Prince, but they have an uncooperative donkey. The men rest under a palm tree and realize that it is Independence Day. Ti Malice tells Bouki the "story of the beginning" of their country. Rather than start with French colonization or 1791, Ti Malice's story extends back to Haitians' ancestors in Africa. Ti Malice tells Bouki that their ancestors lived peacefully in a "rich and beautiful" land, until a man from another tribe "who was working for the white people who wanted to enslave the blacks" (4:00) began kidnapping people.

Given recent live-action depictions of the Middle Passage, it may seem strange to see this journey—and plantation slavery—animated. *Black Dawn* uses cutout animation for the Middle Passage scene, eschewing the explicit violence of films like *Amistad* or *Middle Passage*. Instead, *Black Dawn* tries to communicate the horrors of the journey by showing a woman below deck, sitting amid others with bound feet, sobbing as a mournful song plays (5:04). Once the Africans arrive in Haiti and are forced to labor on plantations, *Black Dawn* shows them being whipped (6:37); through cutout animation, the effect is much less harsh than in films like *Roots* (1977 and 2016) and Nate Parker's *The Birth of a Nation* (2016), where lashings leave a trail of blood. Before dismissing these comparatively gentle visuals, it is important to keep a few things in mind. First, the film was intended for even young audiences to learn about the Revolution. Second, it was Haitian artists who designed these images of the Middle Passage and slavery (in the case of the former, Jacques-Richard Chery, a protégé of Philomé Obin).[36] Third, the film's accompanying narration—penned by Haitian literary giants—eloquently conveys the injustice of slavery.

Black Dawn's adoption of Haitian perspectives on the Revolution extends to its discussion of the event's origins. In contrast to the films discussed in chapter 1 or the documentary *Égalité for All*, France's revolution is not highlighted; the Haitian Revolution is explained by slaves' miserable condition as well as by the way Vodou helped them organize. Though the cutout animation only hints at colonial brutality, the narration powerfully condemns the slave system: "It was as if the soil in which the sugar cane grew was fed by the blood of the slaves" (6:45). The film is also unusual in acclaiming Dessalines alongside Toussaint—something common in Haiti but not abroad. Among non-Haitians, Dessalines is often portrayed as much more savage than Toussaint;[37] *Black Dawn* extols both men. The film describes Toussaint as "a great man" who was "strengthened by his people's courage" and who came "out of the flames" to lead Haitians to independence (13:12). Dessalines is shown as the "hero" who fulfilled Toussaint's prediction that the tree of liberty would continue to grow in Haiti even after his death.

Black Dawn also offers Haitian perspectives on Vodou. During the Middle Passage scenes, the narrator (in English and Kreyòl, Haitian actor Ali Maurice André) explains, "our people called out to their gods to help, but this was a time when even the gods were powerless" (4:15). The film also shows the *lwa* Erzulie Freda looking angelic as she sings a song of sorrow during the Middle Passage (5:22). Catholicism, in contrast, is portrayed as nefarious; once the Africans land in Haiti, viewers are told that they were forcibly converted and "forbidden to practice" their own religion (5:50).

Lloyd, Kraft, and their Haitian partners also portrayed the Bois Caïman ceremony more respectfully than in films such as Niang's. Ti Malice tells Bouki that "one night a very special Vodou ceremony was held deep in the forest to invite the gods to come and help the people gather their strength to fight the white colonists" (9:30). The scene shows men and women engaged in spiritual dancing but not the violent debauchery that permeates most foreign depictions of the ceremony. Viewers are told that Erzulie possessed a woman at the ceremony, but not in a way that sounds sinister; as we hear her sing to beautiful guitar music, we learn that she "gave the woman the wisdom and strength to fight" (10:27).[38]

Ultimately, if the film's animation depicted violence less explicitly than in non-animated films, this is precisely what enabled *Black Dawn* to exist. Lloyd has explained that one reason she and Kraft could successfully complete their project in the 1970s was because it was not live-action and did not literally reenact the violence against white enslavers that has scared off film funders. Reflecting on failed Haitian Revolution projects before and after *Black Dawn*, Lloyd has mused that "it's easier [to make a film on the Revolution] when it's animated"; otherwise, the funders see the film as one "about a lot of black people killing white people, and that gets awkward when you're trying to raise money."[39]

More than forty years after *Black Dawn*, an animated short on the Revolution was made in 2017 by Black Lives Matter Toronto's Freedom School program, this time only for North American consumption. The Freedom School's website notes that this three-week program, for children from age four to ten, is "designed to teach children [in the Greater Toronto Area] about Black Canadian and diasporic history, to engage children in political resistance to anti-Black racism and state violence through a trans-feminist lens, and to offer children an entry point into the #BlackLivesMatter movement." As part of these goals, the school commissioned a six-minute English-language animated short called *Aiyiti* (2017). This digital short introduces the Haitian Revolution in the context of pan-African struggles for liberation. *Aiyiti* was written by Leroi Newbold, a teacher at the Africentric Alternative School, with art direction and animation by Amber Williams-King, an Antiguan artist based in Canada.[40]

Aiyiti celebrates the Revolution's contemporary relevance, in an age-appropriate manner. Unlike *Black Dawn*, *Aiyiti* does not seem to have been made with Haitian partners. Because its funders came from the Black Lives Matter movement, they seem not to have shared other funders' worries regarding Black violence. Still, unlike *1804*, the film does not include explicit scenes of violence. Because of its intended audience, it chooses happier images like Toussaint reading a proclamation, or abstract ones like enslaved peoples with fists and swords raised in the air—but without being used against cartoon colonists.

Though *Aiyiti* has some factual inaccuracies, its narrative offers children a useful introduction to slavery in Haiti, as well as the resistance of African peoples. *Aiyiti* begins with the Tainos. It explains how they "took care of the land" (0:16) and "built beautiful houses shaded with palm leaves" (0:23) until a "ship reached Aiyiti that would change the land forever" (0:32). The film notes that Columbus and other "Spanish white people did not share [the Tainos'] generous spirit" (0:45) and enslaved them. *Aiyiti* then introduces the arrival of the French. Though the French became rich from gold, the film asserts, they were not rich enough "for their liking," so they began "steal[ing] Yoruban people and other Africans" (1:27) to work on sugar and coffee plantations.

Aiyiti describes white colonists' violent treatment of enslaved peoples, and the fact that "often they were not allowed to go to school" (2:44), before turning to their different forms of resistance.[41] Lest children think of enslaved people only as victims, the film notes that they "were powerful!" (2:55) and that they "fought back against their master, all the time, every day, in big and small ways, trying to get free" (3:17). The film covers the rise of Boukman; it presents the Bois Caïman ceremony as a model for grassroots organizing. *Aiyiti* mentions that, even when Boukman died, others "kept the fight for freedom going" (4:11), most notably Toussaint. *Aiyiti* mentions the abolition of slavery in 1794 and Napoleon's subsequent efforts to reimpose slavery in the colony.

The film explains that independence was eventually won, though strangely it does not mention Dessalines.[42] Perhaps the filmmakers did not realize his importance, or they read older sources that made him sound murderous and chose to highlight Toussaint instead. The film ends cheerfully, with a declaration, over the Fugees' "Ready or Not," that the Haitian Revolution "changed the entire world, because enslaved people from all around the world were watching and they too wanted freedom" (5:40).

The films chronicled in this chapter offer diverse approaches to the story of the Haitian Revolution. Though they have generally been seen by smaller audiences than feature films, they have made the Revolution's story accessible to viewers who might otherwise know nothing about it. Their directors have used a variety of funding strategies, whether crowdfunding, making their narratives innocuous enough for public television, or self-financing (which is easier for shorts than feature-length films). They have also taken different approaches to the Revolution's violence, depending on their audiences. As Robin Lloyd noted, her film's being animated seemed less threatening to white funders than if she had included live-action reenactments of anticolonial violence. These films show a willingness among filmmakers in former slaveholding countries to remember the struggles of Haitian revolutionaries, even if their depictions of slavery and the Revolution are sometimes imperfect.

The films I have discussed thus far in this book are not the only ones on the Revolution; though they are generally lesser known, films relating to the Revolution have also been made by Haitians. Such films do not reflect foreign efforts to learn about the Revolution, but Haitians' own analyses of the Revolution and its legacy. We turn to these films—made by Haiti's leading directors as well as diaspora Haitians and emerging filmmakers—in part II.

Part II

HAITIAN CINEMATIC PERSPECTIVES

7

FROM THE DUVALIER YEARS THROUGH THE 2004 BICENTENNIAL

Haitian Reflections on the Revolution's Legacy

Part II (chapters 7 and 8) explores films about the Revolution by Haitians. Though they are less well known than the films discussed in part I, they offer some of the best cinematic depictions of the Revolution. It is thus crucial to examine these overlooked films alongside those by foreigners. Where foreigners tend to read Haiti's revolution symbolically, as a story of slave revolt in a far-off land, the Revolution is more personal for Haitians. Haitian artists do not just read about the Revolution in books; they live its legacy each day.

This chapter and the next explore an array of Haitian perspectives on the Revolution. The directors treated range from Haiti's most eminent (Arnold Antonin and Raoul Peck) to emerging filmmakers working on shoestring budgets. In this chapter, I chronicle the circumstances that have prevented the production of more Haitian films. I then turn to films by Haitians (made alone or in collaboration with foreign filmmakers) that assess the Revolution's legacy. Many of the films I discuss in this chapter have been made by Haitians living outside the country, using non-Haitian funding. In chapter 8, I examine efforts by a younger generation of Haitian directors—working in Haiti itself—to make films on the Revolution in a more difficult environment. That chapter also examines unmade Haitian films on the Revolution.

The History of Haitian Cinema: An Overview

Why have Haitians not made more films on the Revolution? Haiti's cinematic tradition has been far more limited than that of Brazil and Cuba, let alone

France. A comprehensive history of Haitian cinema has not yet been written, in part because Film Studies has had little standing in Haitian universities.[1] However, I offer here an initial overview of this history, pieced together from articles by Antonin and others interested in Haitian cinema.

As Michaëlle Lafontant-Médard has noted, film technology was introduced in Haiti soon after its invention; a representative of the French Lumière Brothers company hosted Haiti's first screening in 1899. However, the Haitian film industry was subsequently hampered both by economic factors and political repression (external and internal). As cinema flourished in Hollywood and elsewhere during the interwar years, Haiti was occupied by the United States (1915–34). The US government was more concerned with turning Haitians into consumers of US products (including movies) than in helping them tell their own stories.[2] After the occupation ended, US agencies continued to encourage the sale of US-made films in Haiti, as in other parts of the world.[3]

Beginning in the late 1950s, brutal censorship by the Duvaliers further thwarted the development of a Haitian film industry. This repression existed first under François Duvalier ("Papa Doc"), who ruled from 1957 until his death in 1971, and then under his son, Jean-Claude Duvalier ("Baby Doc"), who ruled from 1971 until a popular uprising toppled him in 1986. The law of April 28, 1969, passed under Papa Doc's rule, threatened the death penalty (not to mention confiscation of property) to anyone guilty of spreading "Communist" ideas in print or other media. The law also prescribed the death penalty to any librarian or theater owner who provided a forum for such works. As Arnold Antonin commented in 1981, "The rigorous application of this law explains quite clearly why, nearly a century after the discoveries of the Lumière brothers, there is still no real national cinema in Haiti." According to Antonin, only three films were made by Haitians during the twenty-nine years that Duvaliers reigned (though others were made abroad by émigrés like Antonin and Peck).[4]

After Baby Doc's fall in 1986, Haitian filmmakers technically gained artistic freedom. No longer did they need to worry about being sentenced to death for perceived Communist ideas in their scripts. Still, violence by surviving *Tontons Macoutes* (Duvalierist death squads) meant that this freedom was more theoretical than real. Based on their opposition to Duvalier, Arnold Antonin and Jean Dominique were reportedly included on a 1988 hit list. Dominique (the crusading journalist who had cowritten *Black Dawn*, the 1978 animated short about the Revolution) was brutally assassinated on air in 2000, after criticizing the injustices of Aristide's regime as he had those of the Duvaliers.[5]

Other factors also prevented the creation of a national cinema after 1986. The cost of film remained prohibitive for most Haitians; the lack of venues and distribution channels also impeded production. As Antonin explained, most Haitians did not own a television, let alone have access to cinemas; radio was the king of media. In early 2008, Antonin noted that there was no formal filmmaking instruction in the country. Moreover, Antonin lamented, "audio-visual creativity does not enjoy the same reputation as the plastic arts," let alone literature. Even television owners, Antonin reported, could not see quality programs on Haitian history. He reported that Haitian television did not pay filmmakers to show their work (as on PBS or the BBC) but expected payment for timeslots. In Antonin's words, Haitian television was not a venue for preserving historical memory, but "a medium that up until now, just like the state, seems to be more concerned with organizing the erasure of memory."[6]

In the 2000s, new developments heralded change. In Jacmel, Haiti's southern tourism and cultural center, a film festival opened in 2004 (though it ceased operating after 2007). Cheaper digital technologies made purchasing acetate unnecessary; however, as Hancy Pierre has noted, the use of digital filmmaking technologies still disadvantages a country like Haiti, where they are unavailable to most citizens. In late 2008, US documentarian David Belle and other US-based funders and Haitian artists founded a cinema school in Jacmel, the Ciné Institute. This institute aimed to train a new generation of Haitians to make films as cheaply as possible, using local resources. Christening itself "Jollywood," the community around the institute sent graduates to Cannes and other festivals and created a hub for creativity.[7]

Nevertheless, challenges persist, especially funding. Though some cultural institutions aid would-be Haitian filmmakers (such as FOKAL in Port-au-Prince, the NGO founded by former Haitian prime minister Michèle Pierre-Louis with support from George Soros's Open Society Institute),[8] Haitian filmmakers cannot look to their government for the subsidies that have aided their French or Cuban counterparts. Given pressing social needs in Haiti—which have intensified since the catastrophic 2010 earthquake—film funding has not been a national priority. Compounding the lack of subsidies, Haitian filmmakers typically lack access to the corporate capital that funds films elsewhere.

Contemporary filmmakers in Haiti face other obstacles. Meredith Robinson has pointed to the problem of reliable electricity. Since the earthquake, the problems of funding and venues have worsened considerably. In 2008, the country had several cinemas. But the historic Paramount and Rex theaters in Port-au-Prince were leveled by the earthquake, and other cinemas have since closed. As Pierre has noted, closings have been accelerated by the growing use of home video and video games; wealthier Haitians who could afford cinema tickets no longer wish to brave traffic when they can consume media at home. Screenings are often held instead in informal spaces, which range (as Doris Posch has noted) from "renovated dance halls and clubs" to "pop-up screenings organized via grassroots networks." However, as Hancy Pierre argues, such efforts have contributed further to forcing cinemas to close.[9] As of fall 2018, there seemed to be only a handful of formal cinemas in the country: Versailles Ciné in Cap Haïtien, Colombes Ciné in Saint-Marc, Rev Cinéma in Pétionville, and Ciné Triomphe in Port-au-Prince. Yet these theaters were not open consistently. Indeed, after opening with great fanfare in 2015, Ciné Triomphe closed multiple times and remained open mainly for special events.[10] Even the Ciné Institute, faced with a lack of funding in the post-earthquake era, has had difficulty maintaining its services. As of 2019, it had temporarily stopped its signature two-year program offering free instruction to promising filmmakers, though it was continuing fee-based short-term programs in subjects like editing and screenwriting.[11]

Consequently, even though Haitian scholars can publish written analyses of the Revolution to complement or challenge those by foreigners, it is much more difficult for them to offer their views of the Revolution in film.[12] Some of the most important films about Haitian history have been made by Haitians working abroad such as Antonin or Peck. Both men tend to focus their work on contemporary themes; however, their films often refer to the Revolution's legacy. Just as Haitian scholars who study the Revolution are often less concerned with its origins than with its aftermath, Haitian films touching upon the Revolution more commonly examine its legacy than the colonialism that preceded it or its day-to-day development. Still, when Haitian filmmakers consider the Revolution's origins, they are more likely to invoke the brutal conditions of slavery from which enslaved people yearned to be free, than to stress the French Revolution's ideals of liberty.

The Revolution as Inspiration during the Duvalier Years

Antonin's documentary *Ayiti, men chimen libète/Haïti, le chemin de la liberté* (Haiti: The Way to Freedom) was one of the earliest full-length films by a Haitian. This 1974 film, chronicling the Haitian people's long struggle for liberty, was produced while the director was in exile from the dictatorship. Since Antonin is one of Haiti's most celebrated directors, the film has had multiple editions (VHS and later DVD) and been shown at international film festivals. Encouraging his countrymen to rise against their dictator, Antonin reminded them of Haitians' revolutionary past. Even under threat of torture, the film's narrator noted, "the masses of slaves, who never ceased to rebel, realized that the dances of Vodou . . . could not help them to obtain freedom, and they started to organize and to arm themselves" (11:17). In contrast to films such as *Burn!*, Antonin depicted Haitians as the sole authors of their revolution; no European was needed to spark the Revolution or ensure its success. In addition, unlike *Black Dawn*, which stressed Vodou's role in the Revolution, Antonin's leftist politics led him to emphasize human agency over prayers to the *lwa*. Still, despite celebrating the revolutionaries' feats, Antonin had no qualms about highlighting tensions among them. In his view, Haitian history was an ongoing struggle between descendants of the formerly enslaved, fighting for self-determination, and descendants of freedmen who had seized power only for themselves.[13]

Another 1974 documentary, the short *Simparele (If I Don't Cry Out)*, similarly discussed the Revolution while urging Haitians to drive Baby Doc from power. A Haitian-Cuban collaboration, the film was directed by Humberto Solás in partnership with the eminent Haitian performer Martha Jean-Claude. Solás would later make a more problematic film mentioning the Revolution, the 1992 miniseries *El siglo de las luces* (discussed in chapter 2). But in this thirty-one-minute short, the Cuban director featured Haitian artists' interpretations of their country's history.

Simparele is not well known abroad; it has no DVD edition, and WorldCat lists only one library in the world with a VHS copy.[14] However, the film offers a rare cinematic glimpse into how leftist Haitians viewed the revolutionary past and how they connected it to life under the Duvaliers. The film featured a troupe of Haitian singers and dancers living in exile in Cuba, led by Martha Jean-Claude. Jean-Claude, who rose to fame during Haiti's Golden Age of Tourism, had gone into exile even before François Duvalier's rise, for speaking out against the Magloire government's exploitation of the poor.[15] From Cuba, she continued to promote Haitian culture and to speak about conditions in her homeland. *Simparele*, made under the aegis of official Cuban institutions such as El instituto Cubano de arte e industria cinematográficos, gave Jean-Claude and her troupe a platform from which to chronicle Haitian history.

Simparele begins with Jean-Claude singing mournfully in Kreyòl about the Haitian people's enduring struggles. "If I do not cry out," she laments, "it will drown me." She then explains in French (which is subtitled in Spanish) that "singing is the refuge of the Haitian people." Jean-Claude declares that Haitians have sung their joys and pains for centuries, but that Haiti has an even greater source of richness than its music: "its history." She tells her Spanish-speaking audience that "the Haitian Revolution was the torch of liberty [that sparked] the Latin American Revolutions." She describes "heroes such as Toussaint, Dessalines, Pétion, and Christophe . . . who roused the people and led the mass of suffering slaves to break the chains of colonial humiliation" (6:45).

One scene artistically reenacts the Revolution, beginning with the Bois Caïman ceremony. A man representing Boukman sounds a conch shell. He declares in Kreyòl, "Vengeance! The time has come! . . . There has been a revolution in France. . . . And yet there is more and more oppression in the colony." The man details how enslavers speak of liberty but punish slaves savagely; they "bury men up to their necks" and "cover them with syrup to be eaten by ants" (7:17). "Who wants to continue bearing the abuses of these accursed people?" he cries. The crowd yells back, "No one!" (7:31). A woman voices the suffering of those ripped from their homes in Africa. "I left my daughters in Dahomey," she wails. "They do not know where I am!" (7:39). Next, several men and women declare their desire to strike back against their oppressors. One man screams, "I'll kill ten Frenchmen and then I'll rise up in the jungle like a maroon!" (7:49). Another cries, "I'll rise up like Makandal!" (7:52). The Boukman stand-in says, "At my signal, you'll all go to the plain near the Cap. We'll burn and massacre without pity as they have done to us. Remember that if you do not kill them, they will kill us!" (8:05).

While illustrating the revolutionaries' plan to kill their enslavers, *Simparele*'s Bois Caïman ceremony is far less exoticizing than most foreign depictions of the ceremony. As in the *Toussaint Louverture* miniseries, *Simparele*'s Bois Caïman participants dance, and they carry a pig whose blood they will drink. However, their dancing—indicating their desire for freedom from the atrocities outlined before dancing began—is more joyous and less sinister than in most other representations of the ceremony.

Like *Black Dawn*, *Simparele* recognized the role of Vodou in the Revolution. However, typifying the socialism of the film's Haitian Cubans (and paralleling Antonin's *Ayiti, men chimen libète*), it also reflected a suspicion of religion and an emphasis on human agency. The film's narration describes Toussaint, Boukman, and Christophe as working in conjunction with the *lwa* Ogun, Erzuli, Legba, and Baron LaCroix. However, after deploying classic imagery of these Vodou spirits guiding the Revolution, Jean-Claude depicts the Revolution's heroes as proto-Communists who knew how to channel popular religiosity while not believing in it themselves: "Toussaint knew that the gods do not exist, Pétion knew that men invented all of that to ease their misery. . . . Boukman, you turned the gods into soldiers! Makandal, you are Ogun; because Ogun was a man and not a god, he was the representative of the just, or in other words: Ogun means Freedom!" (10:30). Without treating Vodou as savage, this film suggested that humans drove the Revolution; religion was a man-made creation, pressed into service in the fight.

After depicting the Revolution, *Simparele* turns to its legacy. Jean-Claude surveys Haitian history after independence (including the US occupation) and declares that the Duvaliers have perverted the country's heritage. "Duvalier!" she cries, speaking to Baby Doc as much as to his father. "You have turned what had been a source of light [Vodou] into an opiate." She continues, "Duvalier, . . . Lucifer is you!" (15:32). Jean-Claude speaks of efforts by Charlemagne Péralte and others to carry on the legacy of Dessalines, Pétion, Christophe, and Toussaint against those who have betrayed it; she differs from others who have seen the Revolution as sparking division between the heirs of Pétion and of Dessalines. She denounces Haitian leaders (of any skin shade) who have mistreated ordinary Haitians and sold the country to foreign business interests. Urging Haitians to rise against Duvalier, she says, "Toussaint is not dead. . . . Charlemagne is not dead. . . . In each Haitian, there remains a little of him" (28:55).

Since both *Ayiti, men chimen libète* and *Simparele* were made from the safety of exile, Antonin and Jean-Claude could identify discrepancies between Duvalierist Haiti and the Revolution's promises. For those still in Haiti, speaking out was more difficult. As Antonin noted, only a handful of films were made in the country during the Duvalier years; references to political topics, such as the revolutionary heritage, were virtually nonexistent.[16]

One Haitian film of this era did refer obliquely to continuing injustices: Rassoul Labuchin's *Anita, fille d'Haïti*. This film was made during a transitional moment in 1980. When filming began in January, the death penalty was still in force for filmmakers seen as hostile to the government. By its September release, however, pressure against Baby Doc had resulted in the end of formal censorship.[17]

In many respects, *Anita* focused on social rather than political problems. It highlighted the abuse of poor children in Haiti, who are sent to live with better-off families in hopes that they will be well fed and sent to school, but who often end up in servitude. The film follows the relationship between Choupette, a beloved child who wears ribbons in her hair and attends school, and Anita, the peasant girl whom Choupette's mother has taken in. Anita wears rags and is beaten if she rests from her labors for even a moment; she is not sent to school with Choupette. Labuchin dedicated the film to "the children of Haiti and the world" (45:26). *Anita* was made with financial assistance from a Dutch NGO focused on children's well-being, as part of the International Year of the Children in 1979.[18]

Though the film focused on children, it engaged in political commentary on the Revolution's legacy, through the use of symbols. Michaëlle Lafontant-Médard, *Anita*'s coproducer, has explained that the use of masks in certain scenes, representing different countries, indicated the illusory nature of Haitian "independence," given that foreign interests still owned many of the country's resources. The film was set in Miragoâne, where US interests controlled the mines where the film's workers toiled. Lafontant-Médard explains that Labuchin sought to comment on "the exploitation of the working class" by "foreign lords and local Caesars."[19]

Another symbol in the film—so quick that one might blink and miss it—spoke more explicitly to the failures of Haitian independence. Some of *Anita*'s characters are poor laborers who spend their days drenched in sweat. One shot shows the license plate of the wheelbarrow they push: "1804" (43:48). This highly charged image suggested that the inequalities of the colonial period persisted; Haitian masses toiled while foreigners profited. The plate also highlighted how the promises of independence were not fulfilled by Haitian leaders. Lafontant-Médard has commented on the "evocative number" chosen:

> 1804! A date we trumpet around proudly. . . . 1804! The right to live free under the sun! And here the symbolism of the scene of the wheelbarrow carriers emerges admirably: should not the independence for which our ancestors fought so hard entitle us today to rule and determine the destiny of this land where we live? . . . These wheelbarrow carriers . . . are there to remind us that we are far from the dream of equality and fraternity that our flag symbolizes. What have we done since 1804? . . . . Our ancestors gave us 1804, what will we leave in legacy for our own descendants?[20]

An expert on Haitian cinema as well as *Anita*'s coproducer, Lafontant-Médard has stated that this scene resonated particularly with Haitian audiences. Because *Anita* was released after the censorship law was withdrawn, the film could be shown in theaters (which then still existed); however, they pulled it after two weeks in favor of less controversial fare. In addition to screening the film abroad at festivals, Labuchin, Lafontant-Médard, and their colleagues used informal circuits for domestic screenings, showing *Anita* to small gatherings of peasants. Lafontant-Médard reports that these workers found the wheelbarrow image to be especially meaningful: "They said: 'We are those people dragging their wheelbarrows bearing the plate No. 1804! We, the exploited modern slaves who carry the burden of society on our weak shoulders.'" Lafontant-Médard argued that the film opened up discussions of inequality since many of the peasants "confessed to us [after the screenings] that they had no idea that their children were subjected to such cruel treatment by people in the city."[21]

Unfortunately, even Labuchin's hesitant criticism earned him the enmity of the regime. He was arrested and imprisoned in 1981–82, and freed only because of intervention by French President François Mitterrand. Labuchin then left for exile in France, returning after the fall of the Duvaliers in 1986.[22]

1804/2004: Exploring the Revolution through the Bicentennial's Turmoil

Decades after *Ayiti, men chimen libète*, *Simparele*, and *Anita* had invoked the Revolution while commenting on Duvalierist Haiti, a new crop of films discussed the Revolution's legacy while exposing the conflicts of the 2004 Bicentennial. These films, made by Haitians or in partnership with them, include Antonin's *GNB kont Attila*, Peck's *Moloch Tropical*, and others.

Antonin was one of the first to focus his lens on the battles raging during the Bicentennial. With funding from FOKAL and his own film foundation (the Centre Pétion Bolivar, founded in 1986), Antonin made a 2004 documentary called *GNB kont Attila/GNB contre Attila, ou une autre Haïti est possible* (GNB v. Attila, or Another Haiti is Possible).[23] This film renewed his earlier discussion of the Revolution's legacy and of despotic tendencies by Haitian leaders.

Where *Ayiti, men chimen libète* had looked at the Duvaliers as thwarting revolutionary ideals, *GNB v. Attila* focused on Aristide. Though he had been bitterly anti-Duvalier, Antonin had become disillusioned with Aristide's rule. *GNB v. Attila* provides documentary footage of the anti-Aristide student protests of 2003–4. The Attila of the title referred pejoratively to President Aristide; GNB was an abbreviation of the Kreyòl expression *grenn nan bouda*. That term (which can be translated literally as "balls up the ass") was a slogan of the protesters from the Université d'État d'Haïti. The movement that came to be called GNB declared that, even against police shooting to kill, students would go "balls out" in the streets to seek a more just Haiti.[24] Antonin explained that he made the film to honor the courage of murdered protesters, who fought for justice "knowing that the official history would never remember them" (1:45).

Before chronicling these protests, *GNB v. Attila* turns to the Revolution. Antonin explains, "Two hundred years ago, Haiti became the first independent country in Latin America when an army of former slaves imported from Africa defeated Napoleon's colonial army in a series of extraordinary epic battles." He continues, "However, during the past two hundred years, most

Haitian leaders remained essentially preoccupied by personal gain and sterile power struggles" (0:09). In this view, the Revolution was cause for celebration, but the leaders who took power afterward betrayed the hopes of its martyrs.

GNB v. Attila placed Aristide squarely in this tradition of postrevolutionary Haitian leaders. Antonin argued that Aristide's election had elated his supporters, but that the president had ultimately "given in to his deeper tyrannical tendencies." Abandoning his commitment to the poor, he had made himself "one of the wealthiest men in Haiti" (0:39). Antonin described the GNB movement as "three years of struggle on the part of the Haitian people for emancipation from this last oppressor" (1:01).[25] Antonin showed the young men and women of GNB massing in the streets, cheered on by Boukman Eksperyans, the Haitian supergroup named for the revolutionary hero.

In Antonin's view, if anyone embodied the revolutionary spirit, it was not Aristide but the students. Filming them against the backdrop of a statue of King Henri Christophe on his horse, Antonin depicted these young people as incarnating an alternate tradition of the Revolution, grassroots activism. Antonin contrasted their democratic spirit with official declarations about the Bicentennial. While Aristide stared down on high from billboards proclaiming that the Haitian government was the source of Black freedom worldwide, GNB students marched beneath, seeking to win freedom from his repression. In juxtaposing these images, Antonin highlighted the difference between official commemorations of the Revolution and the battles that the Haitian people themselves still waged.

Like Antonin, Raoul Peck used the occasion of the Bicentennial to consider the Revolution's legacy; his 2009 drama *Moloch Tropical* offers another glimpse into how contemporary Haitians understand the Revolution. Peck is Haiti's most famous director internationally; he has produced films in and out of Haiti. His first shorts were made in Germany in the early 1980s, and his first-full length film, *Haitian Corner*, in Brooklyn in 1988. Peck's masterworks include *Sometimes in April*, made for HBO in 2005 about the Rwandan genocide; the documentary *Fatal Assistance*, about the international community's failures after the 2010 earthquake; and *I Am Not Your Negro*, his 2017 Oscar-nominated documentary about James Baldwin.[26] Peck's films tend to focus on recent history. Still, when he treats the recent past, the Revolution's legacy bubbles near the surface.

As president of the French film school La Fémis, Peck has been the only Haitian director with regular access to multinational film capital. Peck made *Moloch Tropical* with funding from his production company, Velvet Film, and from the French Centre national du cinéma et de l'image animée (CNC), a part of the French Ministry of Culture.[27] He based *Moloch Tropical* on his own experiences close to power, as Haiti's culture minister (1996–97); *Moloch Tropical* has often been seen as a merciless parody of Aristide. More generally, it lacerates what Robert Fatton has called the *authoritarian habitus* in Haitian history, by which even well-meaning leaders end up becoming tyrants.[28] Peck cowrote *Moloch Tropical*'s script with Haitian playwright Jean-René Lemoine.

Moloch Tropical is set on the eve of the Bicentennial. The film's fictional dictator Jean-de-Dieu Théogène lounges in silk pajamas in his palace, isolated from his people, and behaves lecherously toward his female staff. Théogène learns what happens outside his palace only by watching television. And even as he organizes a gala celebration of the Bicentennial, he is torturing his fiercest critic (formerly a close friend) in his basement (played, interestingly, by Jimmy Jean-Louis, a few years before he became Toussaint in Niang's miniseries). In short, Théogène invokes democracy while living a monarch's lifestyle and trashing democratic institutions.

In *Moloch Tropical*, Peck shows how invoking 1804 and colonialism can be a cover for Haitian leaders diverting attention from their failings. Théogène's critics challenge his claim to be the heir to the Revolution. They say that "President Théogène is no credit to our heritage" (6:29), and ask, "Is this what we fought for?" (6:40). But even as television news showcases the suffering of Haitians, Théogène exploits the Revolution to repress protestors. He cynically invokes Toussaint Louverture to portray them as betraying the general. In a televised address from his palace (figure 7.1), Théogène declares,

> Sisters and brothers, we celebrate today the anniversary of our beautiful country's independence, and the memory of its Black hero, Toussaint Louverture. . . . After two hundred years of political violence . . . only one road can lead us to a true . . . deliverance: the road of peace. . . . We must be unified even in our guts [*entrailles*], united with the police to control insecurity and free the country. (15:50)

Théogène also blasts Haiti's former colonizer, in hopes of distracting Haitians from his own failures: "After independence, France condemned us to pay 150 million gold francs to compensate the colonists whom we had chased from our island. France must pay restitution to us for this money" (17:17). During another address from the palace, Théogène declares, "Colonization is like terrorism, like barbarity." He says that Haitians should have been free after 1804, but that foreigners conspired to keep it poor (1:26:29).

For Peck and Lemoine, Haitian leaders have too often used anticolonial bluster and invocations of the Revolution to mask repressive policies. The

Figure 7.1. Jean-de-Dieu Théogane (fictional Haitian president in *Moloch Tropical*, © Velvet Film, 2009) draping himself in revolutionary symbols during the Bicentennial. Presskit.

director shows Théogène as profane and incompetent, someone who hurls anti-gay slurs at his staff and insists that there can be no true "popular uprisings" against him since "the people" voted for him (19:39). "Since when do the people know what they want?" he huffs (20:07). Théogène cannot understand that the poor could be unhappy with his rule, blaming protests on "the petite bourgeoisie," "mulattoes," and academics (20:31).

Rather than criticizing only Haitian leaders, Peck also mocked what he saw as African Americans' simplistic views of Haiti. The film includes an African American actor/director, John Baker, who is collaborating with Théogène on a Revolution-themed film (modeled perhaps after Danny Glover, who was seeking to make his Toussaint film in this era and was famously close to Aristide). Dressed up as Toussaint, Baker overacts badly and shows a naive view of contemporary Haiti. Baker's Black costar speaks condescendingly of Haitians on the phone—right in front of them. Peck suggests here that African Americans may celebrate the Revolution more than other foreigners, but they misunderstand Haitian realities.

Peck, like Antonin, ultimately suggests that Haitian leaders have sought to enrich themselves since 1804, while destroying their country. He shows Jean-de-Dieu harming the average Haitians who had placed their faith in him, suggesting that this tradition has endured since the Revolution. Théogène's elderly mother stands in for the Haitian people when she tells her son: "You're cruel. My heart is breaking. . . . How can you be like this? Where does all this cursed madness come from? Two hundred years of it! I'm tired, I'm worn out!" (1:40:56). The film closes with Théogène and his family heading to a forced exile, from the comfort of an imported SUV. Peck juxtaposes their exit with that of a palace servant whose happiness Théogène has destroyed. She dreamed of escaping the country with her boyfriend, but Théogène's henchmen killed him after he sought to shield her from Théogène's lechery (1:32:02). While Théogène and his family ride off in the SUV, the young woman must leave on foot, carrying her belongings away for what will not be a comfortable life abroad but a return to poverty.[29]

Another Bicentennial-themed drama that considers the Revolution's legacy is *Port-au-Prince, Dimanche 4 janvier* (2015).[30] While the film's director is not Haitian, it was adapted from Haitian writer Lyonel Trouillot's novel *Bicentenaire*. Director François Marthouret filmed in Haiti and Guadeloupe, with assistance from Trouillot.[31] An established French filmmaker, Marthouret was able to draw on multiple funding sources.[32] Though *Le Monde* called the film a faithful adaptation of the novel, I would argue that Marthouret's film offers a less sophisticated take on Haitian politics than Trouillot's original. Still, *Port-au-Prince, Dimanche 4 janvier* reflects Haitian perspectives on the Revolution more than the films discussed in part I, both because of its source material and its heavy collaboration with Haitians.[33] The film examines the conflict between two young brothers, one supporting Aristide and the other opposed to him.

Like *Moloch Tropical*, *Port-au-Prince, Dimanche 4 janvier* links the Revolution's legacy to the twenty-first century. The film begins by introducing Haiti's history to foreign audiences and explaining the context of 2004: "Haiti, a former French colony, is celebrating the Bicentennial of its independence" (0:45). The narrator explains that Napoleon's attempt to reimpose slavery in 1802 prompted Haitians to battle France and later declare independence.

After this introduction, the film focuses on battles in 2003–4 over the question of who were the true heirs of the Revolution's spirit. Where Aristide portrayed himself as its natural inheritor, the film (like the novel upon which it was based) suggested that the students better reflected revolutionary values. *Port-au-Prince, Dimanche 4 janvier* is even more sharply anti-Aristide than *Moloch Tropical* (which set its sights on both Aristide and the Duvaliers). The film does not portray any supporters of Aristide positively; it shows only the young male *chimères* (members of pro-Aristide paramilitary groups) paid to beat up his opponents. Similarly, in portraying the president's detractors, the film focuses on the university students who formed the grassroots, democratic portion of the opposition rather than the wealthy elites and military leaders who sought to resuscitate Duvalierism. The film's selectivity extends also to the clips shown from Aristide's speeches. Rather than showing him champion the people eloquently, but then not fulfill his promises (as in Peck's film), *Port-au-Prince, Dimanche 4 janvier* shows Aristide only as power-hungry (yelling, for instance, "I am the one in charge of the state!"). Against this nefarious leader, the students serve as the film's heroes.[34]

The two brothers at the film's center come from modest circumstances in rural Haiti; their mother has sent them to Port-au-Prince for a chance at a better life. Lucien, the anti-Aristide brother, studies law and philosophy. In the tin shack he shares with his brother Joe Joe, Lucien's most treasured possessions are his textbooks. Joe Joe, in contrast, is a *chimère* who earns a living beating up people like his brother. He scoffs at Lucien's books, declaring that his gun "is my diploma" (3:55).[35]

The film shows Aristide supporters repeatedly justifying his rule by referring to the Revolution. At police headquarters, a high-ranking official prepares his men for suppressing the protests by invoking 1804. "Today," he tells them, "we are celebrating the 200th anniversary of our republic, which put an end to slavery. . . . We set an example for the entire world, and we need to show that we are still a country on the forefront of progress" (36:18). He says that we must stop "those who want to sabotage our celebration, these *petits privilégiés* who live off of Daddy's money" (36:58).

Against these official declarations, the film depicts Lucien and his friends as the real heirs of the Revolution's spirit. At a student party in Port-au-Prince that resembles its counterparts in Europe, students drink, dance, and discuss politics. A French journalist at the party interviews Lucien; he tells her that the country needs to "drive out the dictator" (27:51). When she asks him to respond to Aristide's charge that opponents of his political party (Lavalas) are bourgeois liars, he responds, "My parents don't even know how to read!" Lucien says that they are called "bourgeois" only because they refuse to let Aristide manipulate them (28:06).

Against Aristide's populist claims, *Port-au-Prince, Dimanche 4 janvier* seeks to show a malevolent reality. A higher-ranking *chimère*, irritated by Joe Joe's cockiness, rapes him. Aristide is shown giving his famous "Père Lebrun" speech, urging supporters to give his opponents what they "deserve."[36] The police, after having been exhorted to defend democracy and the heritage of 1804, use their machine guns to massacre peaceful protestors. On behalf of his employers, Joe Joe himself assassinates Lucien, fulfilling the words of a student banner shown earlier: "Lavalas: Betrayer of hopes" (44:45). For Marthouret as for Lyonel Trouillot, these hopes were not only those of the people who voted for Aristide and then felt deceived, but also those of the Revolution itself.

Charles Najman explored similar territory to Antonin and Marthouret in his 2004 documentary *Haïti, la fin des chimères?*[37] Like Solás, Najman had made an earlier dramatic film touching upon the Revolution (*Royal Bonbon*, discussed in chapter 1), which exemplified the idea of the Revolution as unthinkable to many foreigners. However, also like Solás, Najman collaborated with Haitians to make a separate documentary that better reflected Haitian perspectives. Rather than illustrate foreign ideas about figures such as Christophe, Najman's *Haiti: la fin des chimères?* showcased diverse Haitian viewpoints on the Revolution and its legacy. Najman was able to use French film subsidies to make a film paralleling *Moloch Tropical*, *GNB v. Attila*, and *Port-au-Prince, Dimanche 4 janvier*, while offering a wider array of views, including those of Aristide's supporters.[38]

Haiti: la fin des chimères? begins on January 1, 2004, with Aristide's invocations of the history of slavery and the Revolution. In his speech that day, the two hundredth anniversary of Dessalines's Declaration of Independence, Aristide tells a massive crowd about the horrors of the slave trade. He describes how "three hundred years ago, fifteen million Africans were trapped inside cargo holds, and transported across the Atlantic Ocean like cattle" (0:47). The president argues that "genocidal trade" was a more appropriate name than "slave trade" (0:52). He then shifts to a more hopeful note, telling his followers to "remember that here . . . here! . . . in 1804, from the darkness of this history emerged the dawn of liberty" (1:26).

Subsequent parts of *Haïti: la fin des chimères?* present the views of Aristide and his supporters on the meaning of 1804. The film highlights the president's declaration that France must pay reparations to compensate Haiti for the 1825 indemnity. Leslie Voltaire, Aristide's minister of education, states that Haiti was the only country that, after winning independence, "had to pay other countries to be accepted in the community of nations" (17:17). Paul Raymond, identified as "Head of the Chimères," declares that instead of encouraging Aristide's opponents, France "should return the $21,685,135,571.48 that she stole in 1825 with a knife to our throats" (19:05). Aristide supporters also discuss other aspects of the revolutionary heritage. Leslie Voltaire explains that Haitian independence was not only a strike against slavery but also against Europeans' genocide of the Tainos (7:48). He argues that the Revolution is part of the world's universal heritage: "It was in Haiti that [the category] of 'man' was created, because, before that, 'man' was white" (8:00).

Against the views of Aristide's supporters, Najman intersperses those of their opponents. Where Aristide claimed in his January 1, 2004, speech that Haitians were united (2:50), Najman highlights the student protests of that month. Using footage similar to Antonin's, he shows how peaceful demonstrators were massacred. In contrast to Aristide's insistence on national unity, they had cried, "Too much blood has been shed! Aristide must go!" (*Trop de sang a coulé! Aristide doit s'en aller*!) (3:20).

Haiti: la fin des chimères? also includes prominent Haitian intellectuals discussing why they refused to participate in official celebrations. Laënnec Hurbon tells Najman that "the political parties [other than Lavalas] agree on one point: that it is not possible to celebrate the Bicentennial together with Aristide. Why is that? Because the Bicentennial is about the ideals of equality and liberty that founded the Haitian Republic, whereas we are now in a situation where basic liberties are systematically denied" (4:38). The novelist Gary Victor also insists that the hopes of the revolutionary masses have not been achieved. Paralleling the arguments of Michel-Rolph Trouillot's *Haiti: State Against Nation*,[39] Victor argues that 1804 was not a victory for enslaved people, but "for a class of owners, the freed slaves allied to the generals who had been officers in the French army. The majority of Black slaves ended up in the same situation if not worse" (12:21). In fact, Victor argued, "all of Haitian history has been a quest for freedom by the Black masses, after finally realizing they had been robbed of power, of their country, and of their state." Victor also attacks Aristide's campaign for reparations. While agreeing that France owes Haiti a great debt, Victor states that the notion of France sending $21 billion to Haiti in 2004 would be ridiculous. The only ones who would benefit would be corrupt officials; any such recompense "would only be effective once we have good government" (20:04).

Some former Aristide officials voice similar sentiments. Gérard Pierre-Charles, a prominent Haitian Communist and former aide to Aristide who had lived in exile under the Duvalier regime, remarks that most Haitians realized that the Bicentennial was being celebrated "against a backdrop of great imposture" and did not want to attend ceremonies presided over by Aristide. However, he states that the juxtaposition of 1804 and 2004 is a "powerful stimulant to the people's fight for change," giving them a renewed will to fight for freedom (4:53). Another former official, Evans Lescouflair, who had survived an assassination attempt two weeks earlier after daring to disagree with Aristide, asks, "Can we celebrate freedom from slavery when we have no freedom of speech?" (5:10).

Like Najman, the US filmmaker Robin Lloyd showcased diverse Haitian voices reflecting on the Revolution during the Bicentennial. As she prepared a

DVD edition of *Black Dawn* in 2003 to replace the original VHS, she traveled to Haiti to record extras. A featurette called "Haitian Voices on Slavery and Revolution" includes interviews with Haitian artists, scholars, and schoolchildren. Djaloki Dessables, identified as a "researcher in native/African spirituality," argues in Kreyòl that little has changed since 1804, since "we are still in slavery" (0:35). In his view, the masters have changed only somewhat; those prospering remain the descendants of enslavers, while those suffering are descendants of slaves. Another interviewee, Harry Nicolas, a *houngan* (Vodou priest), explains that whites have never forgiven Haitians for disrupting the plantation system (3:29). Since Haitians continue to suffer, he argues, they do not have the right to celebrate their independence (4:13). Gody Boursiquot, identified as an alternative educator, argues that, to honor Dessalines and Toussaint, it is not enough to place flowers on a statue.[40] Speaking in French (aiming presumably at educated urban Haitians), he insists that, to truly honor Dessalines, Haitians must go help peasants in the countryside (4:57). Lloyd also interviewed high school students in Cité Soleil, one of Port-au-Prince's poorest neighborhoods. A student named Bethany tells Lloyd that Haitians have been living in misery since 1804, and that their situation would be better if Dessalines had not been assassinated. Since his death, she states, Haitians "are mistreated and miserable" (1:56).

Lloyd also included a DVD extra called a "People's History of Haiti." It features an extended interview with Haitian scholar Bayyinah Bello (who was later featured in Nasheed's *1804* and Dudley Alexis's *Liberty in a Soup*). Bello's English-language overview of the Revolution differs sharply from most of the foreign films chronicled in part I. She offers a powerful rejoinder to the idea that resistance in Haiti began only after 1789:

> The Haitian Revolution did not begin in 1791. It began the day that the first white person went to Africa and began to kidnap people in Africa. They did not just sit down and let themselves be taken away; they fought. They fought all the way to the boat, they fought on the boat, they killed themselves throughout the trip . . . , or killed whoever was tying them up. So the fight began the day [of] the aggression, the kidnapping. (0:32)

Bello, who lived for many years in West Africa, links the Revolution to wider struggles by enslaved people. Making the Revolution into an iconic story, she argues, hid the fact that enslaved people elsewhere had similarly battled for their lives. She comments that Jamaicans and Cubans had fought even more than enslaved Haitians had; the only difference was that Haitians succeeded (0:52). Bello concludes that "the Haitian Revolution is just one tip of the revolution against slavery that went throughout the world" (1:30).

While emphasizing the prerevolutionary roots of resistance, Bello highlights women's leadership. She speaks not only of Boukman but also his mother in Jamaica, whom she calls "a great revolutionary woman" (1:54). As she would later do in Nasheed's film, Bello also invokes the woman who raised Dessalines. She explains that he was raised for his revolutionary future by a Dahomeyan military woman, Agbaraya (Adbaraya) Toya. This woman, nicknamed Tante Toya, "reminded him throughout his life that his destiny [was] to bring liberty to this land" (8:44). Bello adds that Toussaint had said that women composed one-third of the Revolution's soldiers.

Bello also speaks on the *Black Dawn* "People's History of Haiti" DVD extra about ongoing battles to realize the Revolution's ideals. She states that each revolutionary leader, from Boukman to Christophe, had continued the battle waged by his predecessors. Unlike Martha Jean-Claude and Arnold Antonin, Bello emphasizes the role of the Vodou *lwa* in the Revolution; she calls Toussaint a "pure living Legba" (10:07) and Dessalines an incarnation of Ogun (10:11). Also in contrast to Jean-Claude, Bello does not see Pétion as part of the revolutionary tradition. To her, he was not a revolutionary hero but a "confused person," eager for his white father to recognize him rather than proud of his Africanness. She argues that Pétion's "sickness of wanting to be white" (13:35) led him to consider paying France the absurd sum of "150 million gold francs for an independence that we earned" (13:54).

From New Jersey to Montreal: Diasporic Reflections on the Revolution

Like their counterparts in Haiti, diaspora Haitian artists often invoke the Revolution while speaking about contemporary issues. New Jersey–based musician Wyclef Jean is one such Haitian with a deep interest in his country's history. As we have seen, Wyclef served as a talking head in Nasheed's *1804* and MoAD's short *Toussaint: The Heartbeat of Freedom*; he also reportedly agreed to play Boukman in Amata's Toussaint film. While that project remains unmade, Wyclef has found ways to reference the Revolution in his music videos. His 2019 slavery-themed video "Baba" begins with him about to be lynched before he "free[s] myself like Nat Turner" and becomes a "General like Toussaint Louverture." In "Nou Pare" (2014), he declares, "I was born with the blood of a slave in my veins," warning, "Stay all up on me, see my army." Wyclef adds that social media negativity will not faze him, since it is nothing compared to what was done to Dessalines.[41] Régine Jean-Charles has pointed to Wyclef's recurring invocations of the revolutionary generals both as an expression of Haitian pride and a kind of "performed masculinity."[42]

In addition to such fleeting references, Haitians living in diaspora have made longer films related to the Revolution.[43] Miami-based director Dudley Alexis made a fascinating feature-length documentary (*Liberty in a Soup*) in 2017 about Haitian foodways and traditions stemming from the Revolution. Alexis, who has a background in television production, centered his documentary around soup joumou, a pumpkin soup eaten by Haitians on New Year's Day. To understand the soup's cultural meaning and historical origins, Alexis interviews prominent Haitian Americans and scholars in Florida, the writer Edwidge Danticat, Bayyinah Bello, and internationally known Haitian chefs. The film also shows Alexis traveling to Gonaïves, the birthplace of Haitian independence. He learns from Bello and others in Gonaïves that Dessalines's wife, Marie-Claire Heureuse, created a culinary tradition among the Haitian people on January 1, 1804. Masses had streamed into that city anticipating Dessalines's Declaration of Independence that day. Marie-Claire wanted them to enjoy a food that the French had forbidden them: soup, which the colonizers had deemed too civilized for slaves. Marie-Claire organized a mass distribution of this highly symbolic meal, thus launching the tradition of making soup joumou on New Year's Day and sharing it with loved ones and those in need. In addition to Marie-Claire, the director highlights other important women involved in the Haitian Revolution. Danticat talks about Sanité Bélair and other women warriors; she insists that the Revolution's history must not be told so that only men are remembered as soldiers, while women are depicted in domestic roles like preparing soup (25:37). In addition to these other components, *Liberty in a Soup* offers a chronological overview of the Revolution from 1791 to 1804.[44]

As a Haitian living in diaspora, Alexis relied more on Haitian and Haitian American authorities than did films such as Nasheed's *1804*. The film offers a nuanced examination of the Revolution, as well as one of the more creative approaches to the Revolution of any film. Without crowdfunding or government grants, Alexis and his father (Frédéric Chery, who has a doctorate in economics and appears in the film as a talking head) tapped their savings. Alexis did a lot of the production work himself and with aid from friends, because of their passion for Haitian culture. Since its release, *Liberty in a Soup* has been selected for festivals from Santa Barbara to Washington, DC, and had screenings from Manhattan to Miami; it remains available on Vimeo On Demand. The film gave Alexis great exposure despite being financially taxing; he hopes to be able to make more films on the Revolution and other aspects of Haitian history.[45]

Haitian Canadians have also made films that discuss the Revolution while exploring contemporary Haiti and their own ancestry. Joseph Hillel's *Ayiti Toma: In the Land of the Living* (2013) explores the beauty of Haitian culture and the problems of post-earthquake Haiti. It examines foreign exploitation of the country and how foreign efforts at reconstruction neglect Vodou and other aspects of Haitian culture. Hillel was born in Port-au-Prince, before his family moved to Quebec in the 1960s. Hillel has explained that the film reflects his search to understand his roots. His Catholic parents looked down on Vodou and wanted the family to assimilate, but his grandmother kept Haitian culture alive for him. Hillel was able to benefit from Canadian government subsidies in making his film, including from Quebec agencies, Telefilm Canada, and the National Film Board.[46]

Ayiti Toma mostly focuses on the present, mixing interviews with Laënnec Hurbon and other Haitians with those of North Americans described as experts on Haiti. These include scholars specializing in Haitian Studies (such as historian Laurent Dubois and anthropologist Timothy Schwartz) but also the actor Sean Penn. The film has a short section on colonial Saint-Domingue and the Revolution; it aims to trace the roots of the international community's exploitation of Haiti. In this section Hillel turns mostly to non-Haitians; he has Dubois, Schwartz, and especially anthropologist Ira Lowenthal (an American living in Haiti) explain the Revolution. Though Hillel is himself of Haitian origin, he follows the pattern Gina Ulysse has identified of non-Haitian media relying on white male scholars (in this case, plus Sean Penn) to explain Haiti. Hillel also differs from Haitians who have been more critical of Penn's purported expertise.[47]

Lowenthal, who has worked for NGOs like USAID, calls slavery "the most voracious eater of people and human beings that ever existed in the world" (1:05:23). Dubois explains the Bois Caïman ceremony as symbolizing the fusion of different African cultures into something new in the New World; he calls the beautiful culture created then "a gift that we receive from the revolutionary period" (1:09:53). The only Haitian voices in this section are an unidentified Kreyòl speaker (possibly a fisherman) who insists upon Vodou's centrality in the Bois Caïman ceremony and thus in Haitian history (1:08:31), and Camille Chalmers, an economist and activist. Chalmers describes the international community's punishing Haiti after the Revolution, and how debt service on the indemnity drained Haitian resources (1:13:25).

Where Hillel's film touches upon the Revolution only briefly, a deeper discussion of the Revolution's importance in the diaspora comes in the Canadian film *Haïti—La Route* (*Le Chemin Parcouru*) (Haiti—The Road We Have Traveled).[48] This 2016 film explores efforts to ensure that children born in Quebec of Haitian descent will know their ancestors' history. Though *Haïti—La Route* is a documentary short (33 min.), it has one of the most fascinating and original narratives of any Haitian Revolution film. It reveals Haitian views of the Revolution, and integrates the history of women in the Revolution, more than most other films. While *Haïti—La Route* is aimed primarily at Canadian youth, it offers a fascinating glimpse for adults into how the Revolution is memorialized by diasporic Haitians. The French Revolution barely figures here; the roots of the Revolution are attributed to the terrible conditions of slavery rather than ideas borrowed from foreigners. The film offers a fresh perspective on the Revolution, incorporating several topics missing from foreign documentaries.

Haïti—La Route introduces viewers to a summer camp at the Maison d'Haïti of Montreal (a Haitian community center) led by Ralph Maingrette, a Haitian-born conceptual artist.[49] The film was directed by Francine Saillant (a non-Haitian anthropologist at Université Laval), in collaboration with Maingrette and Frantz Voltaire. Voltaire, the virtual dean of Haitian intellectual life in Canada, has made several documentaries on Haitian history; he also runs the Montreal-based archive and publishing house CIDIHCA (Centre International de Documentation et d'Information Haïtienne, Caribéenne et Afro-canadienne).[50] Their film grew out of Saillant's ethnographic research on memory and slavery, first in Brazil and then in Montreal. Saillant's interests overlapped with those of Maingrette and Voltaire; as she sought to chronicle the children's reactions to what they were learning in the camp, she enlisted both men as codirectors.[51] *Haïti—La Route* was produced by CIDIHCA in partnership with York University's Harriet Tubman Institute, the Maison d'Haïti, and CELAT-Université Laval.[52]

The film seeks to preserve a record of what children were taught in Maingrette's camp, while adding material to help future generations of Haitian Quebecois learn the same history. The filmmakers wanted to chronicle the students' journey, but "insert it in a larger framework." Saillant and the others were committed to the film's "telling Haitian history [from the perspective] of members of the Haitian community."[53]

Haïti—La Route begins with street scenes in Port-au-Prince, followed by family photos of Haitians in Montreal. Marjorie Villefranche, director of Maison d'Haïti, explains how Haitian émigrés have enriched Montreal, forging a hybrid Afro-Quebecoise culture. Alix Jean, who directs the Maison's youth programs, speaks of the self-esteem one gains from knowing one's roots.

Maingrette adds that he had "noticed a lack of knowledge about the history of Haiti among young children born in Quebec of Haitian origin" (4:02) and that they "did not know what a slave was" (5:22). So in 2015, the Maison chose the theme "La route d'esclave" (The Slave Route) for its summer program, Kan Lakay. Maingrette called the 2015 program "Le chemin parcouru de 1492–1804" (The Road Traveled from 1492 to 1804).

Haïti—La Route chronicles the 2015 camp, while serving as an accessible stand-alone overview of Haitian history from the Tainos to the dawn of independence. Maingrette's original curriculum covered several themes:

1. Encounter—Christopher Columbus
2. Tainos
3. The Crossing (Ship)
4. In the Ship
5. Field Slaves
6. Treatment of Slaves
7. Bois Caïman Ceremony
8. Toussaint Louverture
9. Jean-Jacques Dessalines
10. Battle of Vertières
11. Catherine Flon—Haitian Flag[54]

Maingrette explains how he created sets and costumes reflecting this history and photographed the children. He then blanked out parts of these images using Photoshop, so the students could paint or draw on them. The students were then asked to present their pictures orally to become more connected to this history.

Beyond footage of Kan Lakay, *Haïti—La Route* integrates material created for the film by Dany Laferrière, the legendary Haitian novelist, and Rhodnie Désir, a Haitian Canadian dancer. The film streamlines Maingrette's curriculum into four parts, with Laferrière as narrator. Laferrière improvises from a script by Maingrette, describing this history in his own words.[55]

Part 1 of the film is called "The Tainos and the Collision of Two Worlds." Laferrière speaks engagingly about Haitian history, while the screen shows images from CIDIHCA archives (as well as paintings by artists such as Henri-Claude Obin, Edouard Duval-Carrié, and Ulrick Jean-Pierre). Laferrière describes the Tainos' culture and the arrival and greed of the Spanish, as well as the diseases and atrocities they inflicted on the Tainos. Part 1 also introduces us to Désir, who interprets each section of history through movement.

In part 2, "The Arrival of the Slaves and the Triangular Trade," Laferrière discusses the arrival of enslaved Africans on the island after the extermination of the Tainos, and the lucrative agricultural products that Europeans forced them to produce. Laferrière uses words—and Désir movements—to communicate the terrifying journey across the Atlantic.

Part 3, the film's longest, covers "Slaves' Lives and Revolts." Laferrière explains the colonists' cruelty toward enslaved people. He explains how traumatic it was to be ripped from one's home and forced into exhausting labor. Rather than shy away from history's harsh realities, Maingrette and his colleagues wanted young Haitian Canadians to grasp what slavery meant; they tasked Laferrière with explaining it in an age-appropriate but frank way. He explains that the slave system's punishments included rapes, whippings, and having limbs cut off. "This is a horrible history," he tells the children, "but . . . it is important to know" (14:16). After cutting from Laferrière to campers' explanations of slave life, *Haïti—La Route* returns to Laferrière; he explains that "these slaves were human beings, just like you and me" (14:41). He talks about their falling in love, having children, and creating daily lives "away from the eyes of the master" (14:46). At the same time, he notes that "it was unlivable," and that "something had to be changed completely" (15:12).

Like *Liberty in a Soup* and Bello's extra on the *Black Dawn* DVD, *Haïti—La Route* also integrates enslaved women into its narrative. As Maingrette has explained, "La Maison d'Haïti has a feminist mission [*vocation féministe*]," so it was only natural that his curriculum spoke of women's participation in the Revolution.[56] Laferrière tells the audience not only about Boukman—but also Cécile Fatiman (15:18). Together, he notes, they organized a ceremony at a plantation called Lenormand de Mezy, where slaves were given whispered invitations to the Bois Caïman ceremony.[57] Laferrière also discusses Catherine Flon, the seamstress who made Haiti's first flag. While Flon is a revolutionary icon for Haitians, akin to Betsy Ross, she is not mentioned in foreign films. *Haïti—La Route* shows numerous portraits of her by Haitian artists, and Désir offers a modern dance interpretation of Flon's sewing the flag.

While including revolutionaries less well known to foreigners, the film does not neglect Toussaint and Dessalines. Laferrière introduces Toussaint as having succeeded Boukman. He explains that Toussaint was a slave who was sickly but brave, and who learned to read and write and to be the best horseman in the colony. Toussaint "was an extraordinary leader; no one knew what he was thinking" (18:38), and the French were afraid of him. Laferrière describes Toussaint's deportation to France, and his declaration that the tree of liberty would survive in the colony since its roots were "deep and numerous."

Laferrière comments that "every young Haitian knows this sentence by heart" and that "it must remain in the heart of every young Haitian today" (20:23). He explains that Dessalines took up this challenge after Toussaint's death. He focused on attaining independence "so that this would be finished once and for all. There would never again be 'masters' on . . . this island" (21:54).

In part 4 ("A New Country"), *Haïti—La Route* turns to the struggle for independence. Here too, the narration notes that there were male and female warriors—all unified under Flon's flag. Laferrière talks about the Battle of Vertières and the courageous generals who defeated Rochambeau's armies. He lauds not only Dessalines, Pétion, and Christophe, but also Capois-la-mort (François Capois), a general often overlooked by foreigners. Laferrière extols Capois's courage in the face of cannon fire, calling him "the hero of heroes" (27:11). The film closes with Laferrière remarking that, "for the first time in human history, slaves became citizens by their own will" (28:54), and with a student extolling his ancestors' bravery.

A final short from the diaspora, connecting the earthquake in Haiti with colonial times, comes from New York City. *Ayiti: The Awakening* (2019) was made by a Haitian-born, Brooklyn-raised artist named Sage Love, who describes himself as a direct descendant of Dessalines. For his senior thesis at New York's School of Visual Arts, Sage Love sought to rediscover his roots; he reflects on the history of Haiti, from the 2010 earthquake back to colonial times. *Ayiti: The Awakening* blends first-person, arthouse, and talking-head documentary styles. It intersperses historical information with Haitian-contemporary-fusion dance segments, featuring dancer Lynette Elouise and striking animation from artist Josette Roberts. Like Joseph Hillel's *Ayiti Toma*, Sage Love's *Ayiti: The Awakening* emphasizes the long roots of foreign mistreatment of Haiti. Like *Liberty in a Soup* and *Haïti—La Route*, *Ayiti: The Awakening* also takes care to emphasize the role of women in the Revolution, such as Cécile Fatiman.[58]

As we have seen in this chapter, Haitian filmmakers (and foreigners with whom Haitians have collaborated) have made several films related to the Revolution. Even without funding for epics, they have referred to the event's legacy in documentaries and dramas. Their films differ in many ways from those discussed in part I. In general, Haitians emphasize Haitian agency in the Revolution—and struggles under French enslavement—to a greater extent than in foreign films. Haitian films also do not emphasize white heroes who were supposedly instrumental in the Revolution. In addition, rather than just invoking Toussaint, Dessalines, and Christophe, these films present a range of heroes, from Boukman to Pétion and from Fatiman to Flon, as well as the unnamed foot soldiers of the Revolution.

Nevertheless, while having some commonalities, Haitian films reveal a diversity of perspectives. One area of divergence relates to Vodou. Some Haitian films emphasize the role of the *lwa* in the Revolution's success, while filmmakers with a Marxist bent have deemphasized Vodou. Still, even the latter group of films treats Vodou more respectfully than foreign films; the Bois Caïman ceremony appears in them not as the bizarre spectacle of the *Toussaint Louverture* miniseries (or *AC Liberation*, discussed in chapter 9) but as a national milestone, the day Haitians gained the courage to launch their struggle.

Invocations of the Revolution by Haitians also differ depending on the era in which they were made. Speaking of the Revolution has served different purposes at different moments. Under the Duvaliers, exiled Haitians such as Arnold Antonin and Martha Jean-Claude invoked the Revolution's memory to encourage compatriots to rise against the regime. Films made in Haiti during this era, like *Anita*, were more subtle in referencing the Revolution's heritage. Under Aristide, filmmakers had more artistic freedom; they showed competing views of the Revolution's legacy, reflecting deep divides in Haitian society. Filmmakers such as Antonin and Peck portrayed Aristide as betraying revolutionary values while claiming to incarnate them.

Outside of Haiti, diaspora filmmakers have emphasized the Revolution's importance to their identities. Their perspectives also vary, reflecting the diaspora's own diversity. *Haïti—La Route* has perhaps the best and most detailed interpretation of the Revolution of any film. In contrast, *Ayiti Toma* shows the disconnection of some second-generation Haitians from their ancestral culture.

In presenting their visions of the Revolution, the filmmakers discussed in this chapter have been aided by sympathetic foreigners eager to bring Haitian perspectives to the screen, or by their own income earned abroad. Emerging filmmakers within Haiti have struggled far more to obtain funding; yet even without ready access to foreign capital, they have labored to make films on the Revolution. We turn next to their efforts, as well as to some unmade Haitian epics on the Revolution.

8

THE RISING GENERATION, TOUSSAINT LOUVERTURE, AND THE PROBLEM OF FUNDING

In the last chapter, we explored films by Haitians that comment on the Revolution, even while focusing on the present. This chapter centers on a new generation in Haiti who have made films on Toussaint Louverture and the Revolution itself. Though their works are less well known than Niang's *Toussaint Louverture* miniseries, this younger generation has been eager to honor Louverture and keep his memory alive. Indeed, even as Toussaint is unknown to many outside the country, within Haiti he is often eclipsed by Dessalines, who remained alive to declare independence.

Haitians who have made documentaries on Toussaint include Maksaens Denis, Kendy Vérilus, and Pierre Lucson Bellegarde. These filmmakers have been recognized by peers outside Haiti and have screened their films at international festivals that help compensate for the dearth of Haitian screening venues.[1] However, funding remains an enormous challenge. Young Haitian documentarians work with much smaller budgets than foreign counterparts or more established Haitian directors like Antonin and Peck. In contrast to the US-made documentaries discussed in chapter 6, these documentaries do not show elaborately costumed actors reenacting the Revolution. Moreover, some directors have settled for shorts while hoping to make feature-length films. Whatever format their works are in, I argue, it is essential to study them. Aside from *Haïti—La Route* and *Liberty in a Soup*, they are the only films by Haitians directly on the Revolution, and they have much to teach us about Haitian memory of this event.

In this chapter, I analyze these films by young Haitians, drawing on their content as well as on interviews I have conducted with their directors. I note that, like the films discussed in chapter 7, the young generation's films do not dwell on France's revolution as causing Haiti's; they focus on the longer roots of resistance in the colony. I also discuss other digital genres in which young Haitians have presented interpretations of colonial Saint-Domingue and the Revolution. Finally, I focus on thwarted Haitian feature films analogous to the non-Haitian projects discussed in chapter 4. I argue that one of them, by Raoul Peck, could have at last produced a high-quality epic on the Revolution. However, it was not completed in its hoped-for form.

The Rising Generation in the Early Twenty-First Century

The most well-known member of this young generation is Maksaens Denis (b. 1968), who has been called Haiti's "leading multimedia artist."[2] Denis's cutting-edge works range from documentaries and electronic installations to mixed-media sculpture; he was selected for Haiti's first exhibition at the Venice Biennale in 2011. Denis has worked in France and in Haiti. He began his career as a filmmaker with training obtained in Paris, at the École Supérieure de l'Audiovisuel (ESRA). After graduating in 1992, he worked for many years as a director and editor for French television stations. Denis also participated in the 1990s techno rave scene in Paris, where he developed and pioneered his audiovisual style. Since then, Denis has worked as an artist in residence in Mali, Congo, South Africa, Canada, and the United States. He has also made several short films. These include a documentary, *E pluribus unum* (2002), about the Haitian sculptors André Eugène and Jean Hérard Céleur, and his four-minute film *Marchons unis* (2017), a powerful experimental meditation contrasting the promises of Haitian independence ("L'union fait la force") with the chaotic realities of modern Haitian life.[3]

Denis's most important film on the Revolution is his documentary *L'arbre de la liberté* (The Tree of Liberty, 2004). Denis made it while living in France at the time of the bicentennial of Toussaint's death. He first considered producing a news segment about the discovery in France of a cane that had belonged to Toussaint. But, once he read books on Louverture, Denis decided that a full-length documentary was needed: "The more I 'attacked' history, the more conscious I was that I was explaining something that was poorly documented in both [contexts], Haitian and French."[4] Especially with the Taubira Law only a few years old, French awareness of Toussaint was minimal.

Denis aimed the film at French and Haitian audiences, and he made the film in French rather than Kreyòl. To tell this "common history," he remarked, "I needed the common language." Denis also wanted to bring the story to audiences in Martinique and Guadeloupe (who, he noted, "have given a very enthusiastic welcome to this film, because it chronicles history in a very different way than they learn in school"), as well as to Francophone Africans. Denis considered making a second version with Kreyòl narration, but even without it, the film was shown several times on Haitian television. Overall, Denis wanted to arrive at a nuanced view of history, which recognized that not all white colonists had opposed emancipation:

> For me, it was important to show . . . that one should not simplistically explain this history as a [battle] between whites and blacks. . . . There were colonists who were slaveholders and others who battled against slavery and for liberty. Just like today, there are inhumane people for whom their own interests are more important than a life.[5]

Compared to Denis's other films and installations, *L'arbre de la liberté* is a relatively conventional documentary, though admirers of his oeuvre will notice some characteristic touches. These include inventive montages and electronic mixed-media images of figures like Toussaint as backdrops for the interviewees. Denis filmed in France and Haiti, and his film combines narration, images, and interviews with scholars, artists, and statesmen. *L'arbre de la liberté* also features occasional scenes of an actor riding through the countryside on horseback as Toussaint, as well as Haitian children playing in the water. They represent the movement of peoples and the various foreign ships arriving in and leaving colonial Saint-Domingue.

Denis wanted the film's narrative to begin before the Revolution. In this decision, he was particularly influenced by Aimé Césaire, whose writings showed him that "one cannot explain the life of Toussaint without explaining the context of colonial life in Saint-Domingue." To provide this context, Denis interviewed French academics specializing in this period, including Jacques de Cauna, Jean-Louis Donnadieu, and Florence Gauthier. He credits Gauthier, the film's historical consultant, for helping shape his vision. Denis also learned a great deal from Christiane Taubira, who delivers some of the film's most powerful lines.[6]

Rather than only interviewing white French scholars, Denis also interviewed Haitian scholars who could place the colonial period into a larger context. Chief among them were Pierre Buteau, a historian and former education minister, and Odette Roy Fombrun, a revered educator whose textbooks are used widely in Haitian schools. Both are so iconic that they appear in all three Toussaint films discussed in this chapter. For Denis, Roy Fombrun was not only a national icon, but also his cousin; he remembered that, "since I was a child, she had often spoken to me of Haiti's 'Indians.'" Inspired by Roy Fombrun, Denis was determined to highlight the Native peoples of the island and their lives before Columbus. In contrast to non-Haitians who hold Columbus in great esteem, Denis wanted to acknowledge "this great genocide" around which there was still much silence. Denis also pressed into service Jacqueline Scott-Lemoine, a Haitian actress who had emigrated to Senegal; like Roy Fombrun, she was also his cousin.[7]

L'arbre de la liberté begins with Scott-Lemoine and Roy Fombrun discussing Native peoples' lives hunting, fishing, and farming in this "beautiful countryside, blessed by God" (0:42). Combining panoramic shots of the Haitian countryside with paintings and artifacts, the film notes their welcoming the Spaniards, who responded by enslaving them. Roy Fombrun notes that, long before the French formulated these ideals, the Native peoples of Hispaniola fought for "freedom" and "the rights of man" (7:43). After explaining how the Native peoples were exterminated by violence and disease, *L'arbre de la liberté* turns to the Triangular Trade. The film shows images of the fortress at Gorée and of slave ships, and describes the plantation system and its horrors. Taubira tells Denis that this was "the only economic system in the world that was founded on forced exile and legal murder" (21:45). Images of enslaved people being tortured appear on screen as she describes the punishments prescribed by the Code Noir (23:09).

L'arbre de la liberté then moves to the French Revolution and to arguments in the colony over the Declaration of the Rights of Man. Gauthier explains that, as conflicts between different factions of whites and *libres de couleur* continued in 1791, enslaved people understood that the conditions for a revolt were "extremely favorable, for the first time" (29:42). This perspective, it should be emphasized, differs sharply from the idea that they came up with the idea of rebelling only after learning about French ideals; it parallels Carolyn Fick's emphasis on the Revolution as a moment when enslaved people simply saw the greatest opportunity of success for an insurrection. After depicting Boukman, the Bois Caïman ceremony, and the outbreak of revolution on Haiti's Northern Plain, the film passes to Toussaint's rise. Buteau introduces the Haitian Revolution's other generals, and the film traces the stages of the abolition of slavery. *L'arbre de la liberté* also covers attempts by the British and Spanish to conquer the colony, the War of Independence against France, and the death of Toussaint. The film ends with independence and Toussaint's famous quote warning foreigners that "the tree of the liberty of blacks" would continue to grow after his death, because of its "deep and numerous roots."

Denis was able to complete a full-length documentary because of his reputation in the French television industry, and because he could benefit from some French film subsidies. Nevertheless, he still struggled to complete the film. Denis explained:

> I had a French producer who financed the first stages of production. . . . He gave the necessary amount so that we could get a subsidy from the CNC [Centre national de la cinématographie]. But this production company had some serious problems [and] filed for bankruptcy. . . . Eventually the producer disappeared, and I finished the film alone, with help from a few friends.

Denis also obtained some funding from FOKAL. When he shifted from France and Gorée to film part of *L'arbre de la liberté* in Haiti, FOKAL generously supported his work. Denis was then able to complete the film, and he screened it at festivals in France, Belgium, and Switzerland.[8]

While Denis was able to make a feature-length documentary on Toussaint, other young Haitians have struggled just to complete short films on the subject. At the same time as Denis planned his documentary, Haitian filmmaker Kendy Vérilus was making a twenty-minute short, *Toussaint Louverture, par devoir de mémoire* (Toussaint Louverture, A Duty to Remember 2003).[9] Like Denis, Vérilus works in multiple media, including painting, film, and photography. In addition to *Toussaint Louverture*, he has made several other documentaries that have been shown at festivals, such as the New York Film Festival and HCX Haiti Film Fest. These include the shorts *Haiti, Year Zero* (2013), about the 2010 earthquake; and another, *Une voix pour les sans voix* (A Voice for the Voiceless, 2017), about the plight of the mentally ill. Vérilus has also worked on the Massachusetts Institute of Technology's MIT-Haiti Initiative.[10]

Despite gaining recognition abroad, Vérilus notes that funding challenges endure. He told a Haitian reporter that he used his own savings to make *Haiti, Year Zero*, doing so as a "duty of memory" toward earthquake victims. Vérilus had similar problems making his Toussaint film. As he explained in 2017, "Right now, I have three documentary film projects [languishing] on the shelf, and two others in the process of being filmed. I have received not a single penny [from others] for finishing them. You can imagine how hard it was in 2003 to find financing. I had to cover the expenses myself."[11]

Vérilus made his film in French, which resulted from circumstance rather than design. He wanted the film to be shown to Haitian schoolchildren, so Kreyòl would have seemed a better choice. But Haitian interviewees opted to speak in French, so Vérilus also wrote the film's voiceovers in French, while still hoping to make later a second Kreyòl version. Unfortunately, he notes, "this was never done, due to a lack of funding."[12]

Vérilus aimed to make Toussaint better known at a time when his importance was neglected inside and outside of Haiti. Though a Haitian commission had been set up for the bicentennial of Toussaint's death, Vérilus felt that the government was not doing enough to honor this "precursor of the independence of Haiti." Vérilus wanted to emphasize Toussaint's primacy over figures like Dessalines, who are more commonly celebrated in Haiti. He also wanted to make sure that foreigners did not control Toussaint's image. While feeling strongly that "no one has a monopoly on Toussaint" and that foreign filmmakers have the right to make films on him, Vérilus noted that foreigners often depicted the general in racial caricatures: "I don't need to tell you that numerous engravings from that era by French artists depict a Toussaint Louverture whose facial features too closely resemble that of an ape." As the film's title indicates, Vérilus viewed the film as a historical duty, one that would "quite simply, pay homage" to Toussaint.[13]

Toussaint Louverture, par devoir de mémoire has a chronological structure, moving from the 1790s into the early 1800s. Talking heads such as Odette Roy Fombrun, Pierre Buteau, Georges Corvington, Jacques-Antoine Auguste, and Rony Durand (president of the Haitian commission for the bicentennial of Toussaint's death) appraise Toussaint's actions and legacy. The film also intersperses historic images of Toussaint with modern monuments like his statue on the Champ de Mars, dedicated in 1954 by President Magloire. Not surprisingly for a self-financed film, the production values are not as high as *L'arbre de la liberté*'s, something the director says he would change if he had more resources. In addition, where Denis had earned a degree in audiovisual production in France, Vérilus was more self-taught; he took a correspondence course in film from France, before later getting to take a directing course at the New York Film Academy.[14] Still, *Toussaint Louverture, par devoir de mémoire* has an earnest quality and clear structure, and it includes some details beyond those of *L'arbre de la liberté*.

As *Toussaint Louverture, par devoir de mémoire* begins, the narrator states that slavery was an assault on Haitians' human dignity. The film introduces the Revolution's heroes, singling out Dessalines, Christophe, Pétion, and Toussaint. It then offers an overview of Louverture's life, as the screen shows images from Jacob Lawrence's *The Life of Toussaint L'Ouverture* series as well as work by other artists. The film discusses how Toussaint learned to read, his becoming free, and his marrying Suzanne, before describing his switch to the Spanish army and his return to French forces. Roy Fombrun explains that, though Toussaint was free before the Revolution, he cast his lot with enslaved peoples rather than free people of color (3:24). Durand tells the filmmaker that Toussaint is the "only man in Haitian national history who can be spoken of as an equal to [other world revolutionaries], like George Washington, Saint-Just, and Vladimir [Lenin]" (4:53). As might be expected from someone employed at the Banque de la République d'Haïti, Vérilus also includes a topic absent from other documentaries we have examined: he interviews Guerdy Lissade, an expert in Haitian currency. Lissade explains Louverture's role in stabilizing currency values throughout Hispaniola when his armies ruled over Spanish Santo Domingo.

The film then turns to the early 1800s. It discusses the Leclerc expedition, Toussaint's imprisonment, and the return of his remains to Haiti in 1983. Jacques-Antoine Auguste discusses the phenomenon of France reclaiming Toussaint in the twenty-first century. He reminds his viewers that France betrayed Toussaint while he was alive, and he insists that Louverture must be seen "as a Haitian head of state, not a French general" (17:03). The narrator reads quotes by Toussaint about his wishes for the happiness of Saint-Domingue's inhabitants, while the camera pans over some of his possessions (such as weapons) that are still in Haiti, at MUPANAH (the Musée du Panthéon National Haïtien).

The film closes with laments about Toussaint's fading memory in Haiti. Vérilus interviews Michel-Philippe Lerebours, director of the Musée d'art haïtien. Lerebours complains that schoolchildren and others know Toussaint's name, but do not understand who he was, especially compared to Dessalines. Lerebours laments that some people "pass his statue on the Champ de Mars [in Port-au-Prince] and . . . don't even realize what they are looking at. . . . They regard it with indifference, as if it were the statue of a foreigner" (19:26). He concludes that "our [historical] memory is seriously in peril, and something must be done so that this memory survives." The film's last word goes to Durand, who was later a victim of the 2010 earthquake; he calls Toussaint not just a "planetary genius," but a "cosmic one" (20:03).

Even if it had not been Vérilus's intention, using French made it easier for foreigners to view the film. French documentarians Laurent Lutaud and Georges Nivoix saw Vérilus's film, then invited him to collaborate on their documentary on Toussaint (discussed in chapter 6). Vérilus's short did not screen as widely as Denis's *L'arbre de la liberté*, but it was shown at the Musée d'art haïtien, in private homes and gatherings, and in some schools. Vérilus notes that the film had a warm reception, especially because there were few comparable films. Since then, the film has been unavailable to the public.[15]

Pierre Lucson Bellegarde and the Jollywood Movement

More recently, another young filmmaker has turned to Toussaint Louverture. In 2016, Pierre Lucson Bellegarde released *Toussaint Louverture: Miroir d'une société* (Toussaint Louverture: Mirror of a Society), a twelve-minute documentary short. This first-person documentary was produced by a Haitian crew in Gonaïves, Léogâne, Ennery, Cap-Haïtien, Port-au-Prince, and Jacmel; it features Kreyòl narration with French subtitles.

Born in 1985 as Baby Doc's regime was ending, Bellegarde is part of the new generation of filmmakers based in Jacmel. The Jollywood movement (as I noted in chapter 7) grows out of Jacmel's Ciné Institute, where Bellegarde was one of the first graduates. As Doris Posch notes, the Ciné Institute curriculum has emphasized a "lowest-budget and fast-track production model." It created a "Manifes Jollywood" (Jollywood Manifesto), pressing filmmakers to "recognize and use the local resources around you . . . use only nearby locations . . . [and] use natural light. We do NOT rely on generators or electricity." The manifesto also proclaims: "We are rebranding Haiti and showing the world the richness of our country."[16]

Bellegarde's work fits well with these Jollywood ideals, though he has no objection to filming farther from Jacmel when he can get resources. He decided to make his films in Kreyòl because "the main audience that I am targeting is the Haitian public." He explains that "I want to educate, instruct, entertain, and raise awareness . . . among my compatriots through my films. Practicing the 'Seventh Art' [cinema] is my way of contributing also to the reconstruction of Haiti."[17]

Bellegarde has begun to achieve the international recognition that other young Haitian filmmakers dream of. Under Raoul Peck's sponsorship, he was one of two Haitians chosen to screen an early version of his first feature film, *Carmen*, at Cannes in 2013. In the section "La Fabrique des Cinémas du Monde," featuring new directors in world cinema, Bellegarde's script won the Prix Éclair. He has also been included in international workshops, and he was able to take a master class with Peck. Bellegarde's prominence among Ciné Institute graduates has made him one of Jollywood's greatest success stories.[18]

Despite this recognition, Bellegarde still finds raising funds to be extremely challenging. He noted that "funding is the major problem that all Haitian filmmakers face daily. There is no government or private fund [in Haiti] dedicated to supporting cinematic works. We have so many scripts which remain hidden away in drawers because of a lack of funding." After taking a documentary workshop at FOKAL with the Emmy-winning director Anne Aghion, Bellegarde wanted to turn his attentions toward Toussaint. He hoped to produce a full-length documentary called *Le vrai visage de Toussaint Louverture* (Toussaint Louverture's True Face). However, even with seed funding from FOKAL, he was unable to produce the film on the scale he envisioned, with footage from France, Haiti, the US, and Canada. Thanks to a small grant ($6,000) from Caribbean film-funding agency Sparring Partners, Bellegarde decided to release a short version of this project, filmed only in Haiti; this version became *Toussaint Louverture: Miroir d'une société*. The twelve-minute short screened in 2017 at the Vues d'Afrique Film Festival in Montreal, the HCX Haiti Film Fest in New York City, and festivals in France. Bellegarde also released it on YouTube.[19]

Toussaint Louverture: Miroir d'une société is a different kind of Toussaint short than the US-made ones discussed in chapter 6. Where those introduced Toussaint to foreigners unfamiliar with him, Bellegarde's film helps Haitian audiences break through the mythology about Toussaint. Bellegarde was particularly interested in a question that others might consider a minor detail but which he considered of "capital importance for me, for collective memory, and for our identity as a people": What did Toussaint really look like? Bellegarde recalled noticing as a youth that there were about a dozen images of Toussaint, each with different faces. "Knowing what Toussaint Louverture represents for humanity and for Blacks worldwide," Bellegarde wanted to understand "why there could not exist a single depiction of our national hero—who is also an international hero."[20]

Toussaint Louverture: Miroir d'une société presents Bellegarde's journey to better understand this father of Haiti. The film begins with shots of Haitian schoolchildren reading about Toussaint. In unison, they chant his iconic line that his capture by the French "only cut the trunk of the tree of liberty" in Haiti, and that it will surely regrow because its roots "are deep and numerous."

After Bellegarde explains the confusion about Toussaint's appearance, he interviews several Haitian scholars. These include Pierre Buteau, Odette Roy Fombrun, Gaetan Mentor (an author and collector), and Guerdy Lissade (the numismatist and collector interviewed by Vérilus). The choice of these interviewees parallels Denis's and Vérilus's films—but with a difference. Here, all four speak in Kreyòl; their comments are thus more accessible to Bellegarde's target audience. Buteau and Roy Fombrun discuss the different representations of Toussaint and offer their views on his appearance. Bellegarde visits a library, where he reads some facts about Toussaint's life. But he notes that he is "skeptical like Saint Thomas" (4:15) and does not blindly trust official textbooks. Bellegarde then does something possible only for a filmmaker shooting in Haiti: he drives to Toussaint's home in Ennery. If he cannot be sure what Toussaint looked like, he can at least see the physical environment in which the icon lived. He also visits the site where Toussaint was arrested in 1802 in Gonaïves. Here, he declares, "the *mama tambour* [the mother drum] was punctured, the tree of liberty was knocked down" (7:41).

After visiting these sites, Bellegarde turns to representations of Toussaint as a French general. Given the reclaiming of Toussaint in France, the director considers, as did Vérilus, how the man could be seen as a hero by both Haitians and their former colonizers. He refers to the 2009 inclusion of Toussaint in the Pantheon in Paris and the exhibit devoted to him at Fort de Joux. He films a 2015 ceremony where French president François Hollande paid homage to Toussaint, during a historic visit to Port-au-Prince (figure 8.1). Bellegarde notes that Haitians who see Toussaint depicted in a French uniform—and who learn that he ran a plantation after he obtained his own freedom—might wonder whether he was a French or a Haitian hero. Buteau notes that Toussaint alone, unlike Dessalines and others, is claimed by both countries. Odette Roy Fombrun explains that the French celebration of Toussaint began only recently. She declares passionately that, despite recent praise of Toussaint by Hollande and others, the French government mistreated the general during his lifetime (figure 8.2): "He should have had a trial! He never got a trial!" (9:32). *Toussaint Louverture: Miroir d'une société* ends with Odette Roy Fombrun's calling French efforts to honor Toussaint hypocritical; she declares him a "Haitian hero," not a French one (9:58). As Bellegarde has explained, this scene is not what he originally envisioned for the film's ending; the short is an intermediate step toward the longer documentary he wants to finish.[21]

According to Bellegarde, audiences in Haiti and abroad who have seen *Toussaint Louverture: Miroir d'une société* have praised it, both because of its production quality and its originality. However, many told Bellegarde that the thirteen-minute version was too short. With further assistance from FOKAL, Bellegarde shot additional footage on location in France and New York. This material includes interviews with Haitian artists living abroad, such as Edouard Duval-Carrié and Dominique Dennery, to understand how they choose to depict Toussaint. Bellegarde also benefited from Ciné Institute

Figure 8.1. French president François Hollande pays homage to Toussaint Louverture during a 2015 visit to Port-au-Prince. *Toussaint Louverture: Miroir d'une société*. © Pierre Lucson Bellegarde, 2016. Screenshot.

colleagues donating their time. As of 2019, despite having finished shooting his full-length documentary, he lacked funds for postproduction and editing.[22]

Bellegarde adds that, though funding for Haitian cinema has always been a challenge, the post-earthquake years have been particularly difficult. He notes, "There are no longer theaters to show our films, which we labored to complete in lamentable conditions." Bellegarde remains optimistic that the situation can change, and that Haitians will be able to produce more works about their country's history. He is working on a "cooperative cinema project to try to produce high-quality films on a small budget," whereby filmmakers would aid others reciprocally. "With this project," he explains, "we expect to create a film industry in Haiti, which can boost the country's economy." He adds that young filmmakers "do not want to leave Haiti," because "we can change certain things in the country with our art." But he laments that challenges remain, given that government cultural subsidies go only to Carnival and Rara music festivals.[23]

Noir et Blanc: Animating Colonial History on YouTube

In addition to these documentaries, young Haitians have used other forms of digital media to reclaim the history of colonial Saint-Domingue and the

Figure 8.2. Odette Roy Fombrun describes the hypocrisy behind the recent French reclaiming of Toussaint Louverture. *Toussaint Louverture: Miroir d'une société.* © Pierre Lucson Bellegarde, 2016. Screenshot.

Revolution from foreigners. Making films remains prohibitively expensive for many Haitians, even when using digital instead of analog technologies. Young artists have thus found alternate ways to tell stories about the end of slavery,[24] and to turn them into short films. In 2014, graphic artist Kendy Joseph, working for the Haitian studio Chevelin Illustration, produced a powerful series of illustrations about life under French colonialism. These images, a fusion of historical commentary and sexually explicit art, were called *Noir et Blanc* (Black and white) and later published in the magazine *Haiti Open*.[25] A fan of *Noir et Blanc*, probably a Haitian American, turned the illustrations into a short film on YouTube, with a North American R&B soundtrack matched to its story line. Joseph later posted his own version using "Ken Burns effect" animatics such as close-ups and panning, paired with a Kreyòl-language soundtrack.[26] These videos do not focus on Toussaint but on average Haitians experiencing colonialism. They reflect the way young Haitians have worked creatively to make films about the Revolution, in the absence of funding for epics.

Noir et Blanc focuses on an enslaved couple on a sugar plantation. The images are not accompanied by text, so Haitian audiences of all education levels can understand them. The woman is a house slave, and the man a field hand. Despite slavery's humiliations, they try to carve out space, far from their enslavers, for human behaviors like making each other laugh and having sex. Their hopes of being together are threatened after a drunken overseer tries to rape the woman, and the man rises to protect her. While beating the overseer may seem honorable, the woman is angry with her love, because she knows he will be punished for not swallowing his pride and abiding the rape. In the next frame, a colonist prepares a noose to hang the man. She begs the overseer for mercy, ready to submit to his disgusting urges on condition that he release her beloved. We next see the satisfied overseer pulling up his pants, while the man has been saved—though his back is now riddled with scars from the colonist's whip. The couple embraces while the overseer leers.

The couple's respite from being made sexual prey is short lived. While walking near the fields, the woman's mistress is attacked by an ox. The man, carrying a load of firewood nearby, rushes to attend to her wounds. Seeing how handsome he is, the mistress (in her nightgown) later makes the woman take her to his quarters. She flirts with him, then presses her body against him, while the woman is forced to sit nearby in silence (in the fan version, the scene is accompanied by Glenn Lewis's song "It's Not Fair," as the lyrics say, "I was true to you. . . . You betrayed the trust I had in you"). We then learn that the woman has become pregnant, and she is devastated by the man's having seemed to enjoy her mistress's overtures. His choice had a fortunate consequence for him, though; by giving into the mistress's desires, he seems to have won his freedom. The mistress is shown with a notary certifying a document; we then see the man leave the plantation with a sack of belongings—and a piece of paper, presumably a manumission. The woman, left behind, watches from the cane fields.

Lest we think that the man has abandoned the woman and others still enslaved, the next scene shows him communing off the plantation with an elder; they seem to be planning something. In the next scene, we see that the Revolution has broken out. The man returns to the plantation, torch in hand, to help launch the struggle. Meanwhile, the woman and her mistress flee, unsure what is happening. An armed insurgent appears and aims a pistol at the women; unfortunately, his bullet hits the enslaved woman rather than her mistress. The man arrives just in time to attack the shooter, and he holds his beloved while a healer attends to her wounds. In the final frame, it seems that the woman has survived. She and her lover are now free, in revolutionary Haiti, where he wears a military uniform and they are with their children. The Revolution has given them the right to be together as a family.

The fan-made version of *Noir et Blanc* focuses on the emotional content of Joseph's illustrations, with a soundtrack by R&B singers Tank, Glenn Lewis, and Whitney Houston. However, the film version made by Joseph and his colleagues at Chevelin Illustration uses different music, stressing *Noir et Blanc*'s political and historical content. Rather than North American love songs, Joseph accompanies the illustrations with Haitian singer John Steve Brunache's song "Linyon." "Linyon" emphasizes how Haitian families were torn apart by enslavement. The singer laments that "it has been a long time since they separated us, since we had to leave Africa, when the colonists bound us like animals." Brunache notes that colonists had tried to make Haitians "believe that we are worthless." He sings of those who still try to "separate" and "divide us"; he urges Haitians to find unity through love and to seek justice and respect for human rights. This message parallels that of the Bicentennial films, which traced the roots of contemporary inequalities in Haiti to the colonial and revolutionary era.

From Roger Gaillard to Raoul Peck: Unmade Toussaint Epics

So far I have focused on documentaries and shorts by Haitian filmmakers about Toussaint. I do not want to suggest, however, that Haitians have never tried to make an epic centered on Toussaint or the Revolution. According to Lafontant-Médard, a Toussaint epic was first discussed in Haiti in the early 1970s. The French actor Jacques Charrier visited in 1971 and explored the possibility of making a film there. Lafontant-Médard reports that Roger Gaillard (longtime president of the Université d'État d'Haïti as well as of the Société Haïtienne d'Histoire et de Géographie) and other Haitians encouraged Charrier to make a biopic of Toussaint. However, she reports, "after learning more about his life, Charrier said: 'Only a Haitian should make a movie about Toussaint. An outsider will not be able to understand, feel or do justice to such a man.'" Without understanding how Duvalierist censorship complicated the production of films, Charrier continued, "Why can't Haitians themselves produce movies about their country? . . . Only a Haitian can speak with genuine love of his country."[27]

The noted Haitian director Elsie Haas also tried and failed to make a slave revolt epic with parallels to the Haitian Revolution. As she recalled:

> I wrote a superb fictional scenario about the story of Boni, the maroons . . . of Surinam. It was a true epic, [depicting] their struggles for freedom in the eighteenth century. They fought against not only an expeditionary regiment sent from Holland to suppress their rebellion, but also to establish a civilization in the middle of the forest. It is a little known but passionate story; but of course I could not find a producer.[28]

In the early twenty-first century, as European interest in the history of slavery increased, Haitians tried again to make an epic on Toussaint. While this detail seems to have gone unnoticed by others who have discussed the 2012 French *Toussaint Louverture* miniseries, Niang was not originally named as its director; early reports indicated that Peck had been tapped for this project. In 2009, a French film site announced that "Raoul Peck is in the middle of writing Toussaint's story in collaboration with Jean-René Lemoine [his cowriter on *Moloch Tropical*], for a 2x90 [two parts of ninety minutes] film destined for France 2. Title of the miniseries: *Toussaint Louverture*." A Haitian website offered further information on this miniseries, listing the same producers later credited for Niang's film.[29]

There has been no public explanation of why Peck ceased work on this project and Niang helmed it instead. A source close to the production reported to me that Peck was indeed the initial director of the miniseries, but was removed after his and Lemoine's script seemed to portray the French slave system too harshly and he refused to change it. Even without confirmation of this report, the film's producers have publicly acknowledged that the script took many years to perfect and underwent many revisions; they wanted to make a film that was both "educational and *populaire*," meaning one that could appeal broadly to French television audiences.[30]

An early copy of Peck's unfilmed script—which he reportedly developed in consultation with some of Haiti's most distinguished historians—offers a fascinating glimpse into what his version of the film would have looked like.[31] This film could have become the kind of high-quality epic that has not yet been made, surpassing all previous dramas on the subject. The script fit the third wave Trouillot dreamed of in "Unthinkable History"; it offered Haitian perspectives on this history while also reflecting the best foreign scholarship.[32] And, in accordance with Robert Rosenstone's ideals for history films, the script was lively and compelling. It brought history alive without becoming a hodgepodge of facts with an overstuffed cast of characters.

Some lines from this unfilmed screenplay remained verbatim in Niang's miniseries; others explaining the evils of slavery and the duplicity of French whites were eliminated. This earlier version, I would argue, offered a more complex view of the Revolution than any other feature, reflecting the best recent historiography by both Haitian and foreign scholars. Where Niang professed disinterest in accuracy, Peck's script seemed to reflect scholarly input. It hewed as closely as possible to the historical record, given that films inevitably depend, as Rosenstone explained, on compression of facts to fit movie length.[33] The script outlined useful text scrolls, as well as voiceovers that would help viewers understand the Revolution's context. Peck's script did not feature the white heroes who would appear in Niang's miniseries.[34]

Overall, Peck's and Lemoine's original script avoided the trope of banalization as well as that of making enslaved people into mimics: it did not suggest that Haitians copied French ideals, but it also did not make African cultural practices seem frightening. The script's revolutionaries were neither African buffoons nor naive figures whose ideas of freedom were imported from France. For instance, Vodou was acknowledged as a central part of slave *mentalités*, without caricature, as when one woman assures Toussaint that "Legba will protect you." In another instance, paralleling John Thornton's work, slaves' African heritages were introduced as helping to organize the revolt, as when Ibo characters pledge to coordinate with others of their heritage.[35]

Their screenplay also portrayed the horrors of slavery plainly. Rather than presenting slaves as happy until French books taught them to feel otherwise, this version presented slavery as self-evidently wrong. Like the other Haitian-made films, it rooted the Revolution in the awful conditions of slavery rather than imported ideals. While one cannot know exactly what a filmed version of this script would have looked like, the script hints at images that were absent from the televised miniseries. For instance, episode 2 begins with Toussaint in the Fort de Joux prison, weak and fragile—but bearing on his chest the words branded on him with a red-hot iron, "Bayon de Libertat" (the Bréda plantation manager). Such a palpable reminder of slavery's brutality did not appear in Niang's version.

Peck's and Lemoine's script thus grounded the motivations of the Revolution's leaders in their experiences while enslaved. Notably, it did so without oversanitizing them, something Trouillot said Haitian scholars sometimes tend to do.[36] The draft's treatment of Biassou and Dessalines, for example, was markedly different than in Niang's miniseries. As in the latter work, the revolutionary Biassou appears in the early script as bloodthirsty and flawed. However, in Peck's and Lemoine's version, the audience could see why Biassou would want revenge against whites. In their script, we see a group of elderly slaves being "terrorized"; Biassou notes that his mother is among them. This treatment of the harshness of slavery differed sharply from the Niang version's *Gone with the Wind*–style nostalgia for plantation life. Where Peck's Biassou described this trauma as the cause of his retributive violence ("The whites massacred my family. And so I will massacre whites."), this explanation did not appear in Niang's miniseries. The Dessalines of Peck's and Lemoine's script was also more nuanced than Niang's Dessalines—or *Lydia Bailey*'s Dessalines-as-Mirabeau. Rather than a villain embodying Black racism against whites, Peck's and Lemoine's Dessalines spotlighted French whites as racists. Where Niang's miniseries tried to paint most French colonists as antiracist, Peck's and Lemoine's Dessalines commented sarcastically, "I will trust the French when they give their daughters in marriage to black men."

Peck's and Lemoine's screenplay similarly led audiences to empathize with Toussaint, without oversimplifying him. Their script made clear that Louverture had run his own plantation and employed slaves after obtaining his own freedom, so as not to romanticize him as having categorically opposed slavery. And it outlined the sensitive debates among the Revolution's leaders about whether they were fighting only for their own freedom, or for that of all enslaved people. One scene shows Toussaint, Dessalines, and others arguing about whether slavery should be abolished—or the condition of slaves simply ameliorated.

The script also offered a nuanced depiction of Toussaint by referencing debates among newly freed slaves about Toussaint's labor policies. Toussaint explains that he wants "to show all of Europe that slavery is not necessary to a plantation economy. . . . We can restart the production of sugar and of coffee." But the script revealed the human costs of forced labor schemes. One scene in episode 1 has Dessalines, then one of Toussaint's chief aides, instructing an overseer to make sure anyone who tries to avoid working on plantations will be "denounced to the gendarmerie," and that children must begin plantation work at age ten. In episode 2, we see a plantation manager beating unhappy former slaves; they explain that freedom has evaporated in Toussaint's plantation system.

Suzanne Louverture, too, received a more compelling treatment from Peck and Lemoine. Their Suzanne offered a more realistic look at Haitian women's ideas about the Revolution than in Niang's miniseries. In the Haitian script, Suzanne approves of her husband's efforts to liberate Saint-Domingue's slaves. She represents the many women involved in the Haitian struggle for independence, a fact underscored in scholarship as well as in films such as *Haïti—La Route*, *Liberty in a Soup*, and Bello's extra on the *Black Dawn* DVD.[37] In Niang's version, in contrast, Suzanne criticizes Toussaint for what she considers a needless war against the peaceful French. Several lines that I highlighted in chapter 1 (for instance, Suzanne urging Toussaint to "stop meddling in whites' affairs" and crying, "You have a wife and kids and land! Are you even thinking of us?") did not appear in Peck's and Lemoine's script.

In addition, the script by Peck and his collaborators emphasized Haitians as authors of their own liberation. The French revolutionary emissary Sonthonax appears not as Haitians' liberator but as a hothead who wants to guillotine all whites and people of mixed race. When Sonthonax declares in this script that he has come to "return dignity to this people," Toussaint retorts, "They recaptured their dignity before you even arrived!" This script made clear that enslaved people in Saint-Domingue had not waited to be liberated by French universal ideals, since the revolutionaries had resisted applying these ideals to them from 1789 to 1793.

Peck's and Lemoine's screenplay pointed to the limits of French universalism in still other ways. It presented key revolutionaries, like Vincent Ogé, who were absent from the final miniseries. Only a few pages into the script, Ogé appears at the Club Massiac in Paris (a political club dominated by white colonists) and calls attention to the hypocrisies buried beneath the universalism of the Declaration of the Rights of Man. Facing jeers from slaveowners, he declares that, despite French proclamations about "all men" being free and equal, wealthy *gens de couleur* are still treated differently than whites. Such language disappeared from Niang's version.

The Haitian script also better reflected eighteenth-century racist discourse by colonists about people of color. In this older version of *Toussaint Louverture*, colonists call slaves "monkeys" and make jokes about how *les nègres* would do anything for *tafia* (cheap rum). Slaveowners also state that they would use violence against any attempt by enslaved people to seek change. As one colonist says to another, "Good men do not speak with their domestics. They kick them in the ass!" In Niang's version, pervasive racism disappeared; isolated comments by racist whites are dismissed by the film's good whites. The differences between this early version and the televised miniseries seem to reflect what we have noted in previous chapters about gaps in French memory of slavery. The televised version highlighted French abolitionists, while consigning to oblivion Haitians who challenged French hypocrisy.

• • •

We have seen in part II a range of depictions of the Revolution by Haitian artists. They have varied in their approach to revolutionaries like Toussaint and Dessalines. What they share, especially compared to most non-Haitian films, is an emphasis on the horrors of colonial slavery and the agency of Haitians. Despite their quality, these films have had greater difficulty reaching audiences than those by their foreign counterparts.

We have also seen that the lack of a Haitian epic on the Revolution is not because Haitians have not tried to make one, nor because they lack cinematic talent. Peck's and Lemoine's unfilmed script could have been the best Haitian Revolution film yet made. It had a powerful and sophisticated narrative, one that could have translated into a drama as high-quality as Peck's other historical films. These writers managed to squeeze an accurate overview of the Revolution—and plenty of drama and snappy dialogue—into a 180-minute timeframe. Their script reflected recent historiographical perspectives, while avoiding narrative problems plaguing other Revolution-themed films. It showed the revolutionaries neither as overly Europeanized and dependent on French ideals of liberty, nor as exoticized Africans whose culture was barbaric.

The fact that this script was left unmade further highlights the problem of getting funding for Haitian Revolution films. Even a giant of world cinema like Peck, who can generally fund films that fit his vision, seems to have had his project disrupted when he would not change the Revolution's story line to satisfy funders.[38] His experience seems to reinforce Chris Rock's pessimism about the possibility of making films on the Revolution and on slave revolt, from the perspective of enslaved people.

Remarkably, however, there are other funding sources ready to tell cinematic stories about slave revolt in Saint-Domingue and elsewhere, stories centering on the perspectives of enslaved people rather than their enslavers. We turn in this book's final section (part III) to this surprising source of depictions: video games.

Part III

VIDEO GAMES ON SLAVERY AND THE HAITIAN REVOLUTION

9

NORTH AMERICAN AND EUROPEAN GAMES

From MECC's *Freedom!* to *Assassin's Creed: Freedom Cry*

Thus far, I have discussed the lack of a high-quality epic film on the Revolution, despite some compelling films in other formats. Part III moves from the world of cinema to that of video games. This section analyzes several games dealing with slave resistance in Saint-Domingue and the French Caribbean. Because historians have not yet analyzed games on Atlantic slavery in general, I begin by discussing several such games, to contextualize those related to Saint-Domingue.[1] Chapter 9 discusses games made by North Americans and Europeans, while chapter 10 turns to games by developers from the Caribbean.

Though the games I analyze are not of equal quality, I argue that two of them, the well-known *Assassin's Creed: Freedom Cry* (Ubisoft, 2013, discussed in this chapter) and the long-forgotten *Freedom: Rebels in the Darkness* (Coktel, 1988, discussed in chapter 10), make the Haitian Revolution more thinkable than nearly all non-Haitian films. Ubisoft and Coktel did not share film funders' reluctance about depicting slave revolt—and doing so from the perspective of the enslaved. Indeed, as Marc Bernardin of the *Hollywood Reporter* wrote of *Assassin's Creed: Freedom Cry*, "The game was, literally, kill whitey. And it was a game produced by a billion-dollar, international outfit." Bernardin—a journalist, comic book writer, and TV scriptwriter who is of Haitian and Trinidadian descent—marveled at how different Ubisoft was from the Hollywood studios he normally interacted with: "Can you imagine thinking that you can make money and be 'woke' at the same time?"[2]

Assassin's Creed: Freedom Cry was made by Canadian developers, collaborating with Quebec-based scholars of Haiti and people of Haitian descent, while *Freedom: Rebels in the Darkness* was made by French Caribbean developers. Both games seek to honor the memory of slavery and to help players understand Saint-Domingue's brutal plantation system. Reaction to them has been markedly different than for other slavery-related video games. Notwithstanding some reservations about *Freedom Cry*, both have been received enthusiastically by gamers, including Haitians and others of African descent.

In examining games on Saint-Domingue and comparing them to others on Atlantic slavery, I ask: Do they allow people to understand the Revolution better than films by non-Haitians? Do they lead players to empathize with enslaved peoples and freed slaves more than with slaveowners, and do they show them as the architects of their own resistance? Do they contextualize the revolutionaries' retributive violence by recognizing the brutality that preceded it—or do they portray Haitian revolutionaries as savage and bloodthirsty?

Video games might seem an unlikely place to find high-quality representations of slave revolt and of the Haitian Revolution. For one thing, the notion of a "game" related to slavery can seem utterly distasteful, especially to non-gamers. Discussing one game on slavery, *Playing History 2—Slave Trade*, a commenter remarked that the developers seemed to be "still making money off black chattel slavery . . . in 2015!" Another wrote of the same game, "Countless lives lost to the Middle Passage, lost to the bottom of the sea . . . , and the makers of this thing wanted to gamify the experience?"[3]

Another reason why one might not expect a game to have historiographical value is that historians have traditionally disdained video games. Certainly, as Joshua Holdenried and Nicholas Trépanier have acknowledged, recounting history in a game format has inherent limits:

> The centrality of gameplay (games . . . *must* be fun if they are to find any success) can lead game designers to overlook or even contradict the consensus conclusions of historians. . . . Furthermore game designers often integrate, willingly or not, myths and inaccuracies into products that are sold as "historically accurate."[4]

Historians rightly fear that gamifications of slavery will trivialize the past.

However, as Game Studies has become a cutting-edge field, an increasingly sophisticated literature on historical games has developed. This work has shown that historical games can have pedagogical value, both for showing lived experience (if they are well made) and for helping students think about the construction of historical narratives (even if they are awful). This literature has also noted that, by simulating the past and giving players agency within limits, games can help students escape teleology. They can help students understand cause and effect, contingency, and counterfactuals.[5] Holdenried and Trépanier argue further that we must recognize that written texts have their own limits; they flatten the *experience* of history and make it hard to imagine concretely. A well-constructed game, they argue, can mimic lived experience "more accurately than almost any scholarly monograph or article." Michael Hattem, an early Americanist, explained that he was not a game aficionado until discovering *Assassin's Creed III*, which centers on the American Revolution. He found that

> the gaming experience of walking around Boston . . . [was] both personally thrilling and historically enlightening. The cities were designed from historical maps. . . . But it's not just the layouts that are accurate. Walking down the streets of Boston in 1754, one witnesses robberies . . . , random dogs and pigs wandering the streets, small groups of children in ripped clothing and no shoes harassing passers-by, and groups of British soldiers marching through the streets.

Hattem concluded, "It really brings to life the . . . Wild-West nature of colonial urban life."[6]

Historians engaged in Game Studies have also maintained that scholars need to be realists. We live in an age, as Trépanier has noted, when students "come to college interested in history precisely because they've played historically themed video games." It is also true that K-12 curricula increasingly feature software gamifications, which turn subjects like multiplication into games with animation and rewards. Moreover, younger generations increasingly learn history through bestselling games such as *Sid Meier's Civilization* and the *Assassin's Creed* franchise, just as older generations acquired their knowledge of history through films and even Disneyland. As Sarah Zaidan noted in the *Journal of Popular Culture*, "Although [video games] have often been derided as time-wasters that atrophy social skills or promote violent mentalities," scholars need to realize that "video games are presently the number one most-used form of entertainment worldwide." High-profile games can have budgets that eclipse their cinematic counterparts; one 2014 game, *Destiny*, had a budget of nearly half a billion dollars. As Robert Whitaker argued in the American Historical Association's magazine, *Perspectives*, in 2016, "Video games will prove to be one of the most popular mediums of the 21st century. . . . It is well past time for historians to actively engage with that medium and its audience."[7]

Certainly, one might argue that video games' promise to help players "experience" the past—particularly on a subject like slavery—is inherently doomed. A game may purport to immerse players in the past, but they will never know what it was actually like to be there. No matter how "accurate" a game attempts to be, players will never experience the brutality of the slave system.

On the other hand, the problem of false verisimilitude applies not only to games, but also to films and even primary sources. Elie Wiesel famously lambasted Holocaust films in 1989 for pretending that they could show viewers what happened during the Shoah: "Auschwitz is . . . a universe outside the universe, a creation that exists parallel to creation." He blasted the attempt to depict it in film:

> Why this determination to show "everything'" in pictures? . . . How can one "stage" a convoy of uprooted deportees . . . , or the liquidation of thousands and thousands of men, women and children? How can one "produce" the machine-gunned, the gassed, the mutilated corpses, when the viewer knows that they are all actors, and that after the filming they will return to the hotel for a well-deserved bath and a meal?

Wiesel argued that direct contact with survivors was the best way to learn about the Holocaust.[8] Later in his life, however, Wiesel expressed concern that even survivors' own words could not fully convey the horrors of the Holocaust: "No one has ever really translated the experience of the Holocaust—it's impossible, there are no words."[9]

While recognizing that video games can never recreate the past, and that—like films and texts about atrocities—they can only allude to them in a mediated form, I would argue that historians must acknowledge games on slavery and on the Revolution, to evaluate them for the public. Such analyses should parallel the approach Rosenstone advocated for cinema; historians should assess video games not simply for whether they adhere strictly to facts, but also for how well they make historical processes vivid, helping players understand them better than if they did not play.[10]

Why did games on slavery emerge? Traditionally, historical video games—like other game genres—have privileged white male experiences. Dom Ford has described a 4X genre (eXplore, eXpand, eXploit, eXterminate), in which "imperialist narrative[s]" are "coded into" game mechanics. Similarly, Rebecca Mir and Trevor Owens have pointed to the way that the bestselling game *Sid Meier's Colonization* glorifies conquest and colonialism."[11]

In this context, gamers of color have often felt unrepresented in the games they play. Orpheus Hanley, a Black game designer, told the *New York Times*, "In the 80s and 90s you never saw black characters. If there were any black ones, they would get beat up." Anna Everett, a leading scholar of gender and race in new media and a gamer herself, noted that "I am acutely aware that my mature, black, and female body is marked and thus marginalized in the gaming industry's multibillion dollar marketplace."[12]

In recent years, game studios have added more diverse characters to satisfy nonwhite gamers' hunger to feel represented. While there is a risk of what Adam Clayton Powell III has called "high-tech blackface," sociologists like Elijah Anderson have suggested that adding characters of color can be positive, if done well. Despite backlash from the white male gamers who propelled #Gamergate, games now offer more diverse protagonists. There have also been efforts to create "videogames of the oppressed," to quote Gonzalo Frasca, which could be "tools for education and sociopolitical awareness." As Kishonna Gray and David Leonard have written, games can challenge racist ideologies and be "teachers of alternative narratives and histories."[13]

As designers have created games from nondominant perspectives, some have concerned slavery. The topic is challenging to treat in a game, and many games on the subject have provoked criticism. Before turning to video games dealing with slavery and slave revolt in Saint-Domingue, I want to consider others that treat African slavery in the Americas, whether marketed for educational or leisure use.

Should Slavery Be Gamified? Slavery and Slave Resistance in Educational Software

Most efforts to make video games on slavery have proven bitterly disappointing. In 1992, an organization called MECC (the Minnesota Educational Computing Corporation) released a "history-based simulation" for the Apple II called *Freedom!* The game sought to teach fifth- to ninth-grade students about slavery by assigning them the role of an enslaved person escaping along the Underground Railroad. An introductory screen explained, "When one of your grandfathers was young, he was kidnapped and brought to America. Your other grandfather was a free black man who was forced into slavery after he was accused of breaking a law (which he had not done)."[14]

Freedom! seems to have been designed to show children that escaping from slavery was nearly impossible. The manual cautioned, "As you travel, you must be very careful. Patrollers (figure 9.1) are all over. . . . Often, they would rather see you dead than let you successfully escape." The game's outcomes included being told, "You have been recaptured, whipped and returned to your master. The master decides you cannot be trusted and decides to sell you to another man in the deep south. It is extremely difficult to escape from slavery that far south."[15]

Though MECC's *Freedom!* seems to have been well intentioned, its design was ill conceived. The game aimed to help students understand how enslaved people's forced illiteracy limited their chances for emancipation: How could an enslaved person gain freedom if she could not read signs or documents? But the developers' decision to use dialect to illustrate a lack of education was not received by students in the way they had imagined. Elders said things like, "I sees a runnin' look in yo' eyes, chile"—and the player had to respond in kind, choosing from options such as "Do yuh have anythin' that'd help me?" Black students whose schools used *Freedom!* found that their classmates mocked them and asked why they did not talk that way; they did not seem to gain any appreciation of slavery's horrors from the game. As the *New York Times* reported, "The software company pulled [*Freedom!*] off the market in 1993 and said it had instructed school districts to destroy any copies they had."[16]

In 2013, a Danish maker of educational software, Serious Games, released an even more troubling game, *Playing History 2—Slave Trade*. As the company describes it, "The Playing History game series revolves around experiencing engaging and personal stories set in exhilarating points in world history." The company encourages teachers to adopt its games to make history more engaging than in traditional curricula: "Why play Playing History? . . . To take part in history, within in a living breathing world." Serious Games promised that students would "travel back to the 18th century and experience the horrors of the transatlantic slave trade."[17]

As critics pointed out almost immediately, *Slave Trade* offered a callous approach to its subject. One section, derisively nicknamed "Slave Tetris," drew particular infamy. The player (an enslaved boy assigned to help his owner, an English ship's captain) is charged with squeezing as many African captives as he can onto a slave ship embarking on the Middle Passage. The graphics, widely panned as outrageous, involved dropping cube-shaped slaves into moving slots on the ship. In August 2015, a backlash erupted over this part of the game, with critics calling it "dehumanising" and "sick." As media reported on the controversy, Serious Games CEO Simon Egenfeldt-Nielsen (himself a former Game Studies professor) defended the game. He insisted, "It has to be

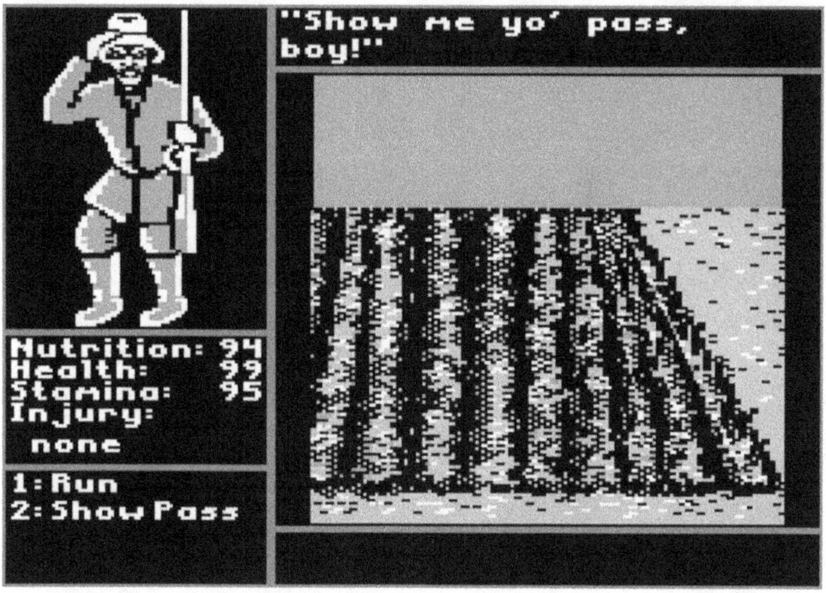

Figure 9.1. Patrollers in *Freedom!* © MECC, 1992. Screenshot, MobyGames.

like this to show what was done to load slave ships," and that "the reactions people have to this game [are] something they will never forget." But as criticism raged, Serious Games pulled that task from *Slave Trade*, while keeping the rest of the game available for purchase.[18]

Even without "Slave Tetris," the game's other components hardly educated students about the brutality of the trade. The game's trailer invites students to "join Tim and his sister on an adventure like no other. . . . Experience the time of the slave trade." The marketing materials declare, "Playing History 2: Slave Trade is a casual point 'n click adventure . . . [which] approach[es] an important topic in [an] engaging, fun and humoristic way." While a game might strive for many things when trying to help students "experience" the slave trade, fun and humoristic are not among them. The game's cartoonish graphics, whimsical music, and images of what it called "bizarre" African chiefs fulfilled the worst fears of game critics.[19]

Dexter Thomas, an African American *Los Angeles Times* reporter and doctoral candidate in East Asian studies, decided to play *Slave Trade* to investigate if removing "Slave Tetris" could solve the game's problems. He found that it remained appalling:

> In the game, you play as a young slave boy named Tim. . . . Along the way, you discover that your sister is being sold as well. Instead of taking the guns and

> rebelling or freeing her immediately, you stuff her into a slave ship and sail her across the Atlantic.
>
> Yes—you, a black slave, pilot the slave ship. Twice. To "win" this section, you are literally tasked with being a good slave driver. . . . If you try to go back to Africa, you fail. If you don't sail your boat fast enough, you fail. . . . "Winning" here means getting all of the slaves (including yourself) to America.

Thomas continued, "The most disturbing thing is that this is one of the most engaging and 'fun' parts of the game." He added that, "in a game that claims to portray horrors of the transatlantic slave trade, the slave owners in 'Slave Trade' are pretty nice. If you complete a simple task for even the meanest white person, they are kinder to you. In fact, some of the rudest characters in the game are not white slavers but black slave characters, who sometimes refer to white characters as 'white devils.'"[20]

Slave Trade does not depict slave revolt at all, since players "win" by being obedient slave children. As Dexter Thomas indicated, overall the game cleanses slavery of its horrors. It explains that when Tim's master goes to Africa to get more slaves, "Tim tags along on the journey," as if enslaved peoples had any control over their destinations. Moreover, the Africans whom Tim meets seem as bad as the "mean" whites. One exchange includes Tim meeting an African chief while trying to help his master buy more slaves. The chief (evidently hoping that one day he will time travel and be cast in the TV program *The A-Team*), declares, "I pity the fool who messes with Chief Janto." To which Tim can only answer, "Good to know, bye." Even when Tim's owner uses racist language, it fits the game's "humoristic" tone; he calls Tim "you lazy little son of a jungle-jingle."[21]

Slave Trade thus whitewashed slavery even more than the Toussaint miniseries discussed in chapter 1. If MECC's *Freedom!* and Serious Games' *Slave Trade* were the best that game designers could muster to show the "horrors of the transatlantic slave trade," then critics of games were absolutely right.

Mission US 2: Flight to Freedom, created by New York PBS station WNET in 2012 with funding from the National Endowment for the Humanities, was a more serious interactive fiction. This freeware text-based exploration game, part of the Mission US series of interactive history games, was created by historians at the CUNY Graduate Center's American Social History Project/Center for Media & Learning (ASHP). That center collaborated with several eminent historians of slavery, including Ira Berlin, Nikki Taylor, and Christopher Moore.[22] The developers explained that *Flight to Freedom* "immerses users in historical and contemporary problems in ways that encourage perspective-taking, discussion, and weighing of multiple kinds of evidence." They stated that the game was "informed by the latest scholarship," as well as classic works by John Hope Franklin and others. As of 2015, *Flight to Freedom* had close to one million users.[23] The game, I would argue, was flawed in several respects, but still represented an improvement over MECC's *Freedom!* and *Slave Trade*.

Covering 1848 to 1850, *Flight to Freedom* introduced players to a fourteen-year-old enslaved girl in Kentucky named Lucy (figure 9.2). In a prologue that is one of the game's weakest sections, Lucy explains the difficulty of her workday on the plantation. She has to wake up early and then "collect the eggs, do the wash, fetch water, feed the hogs, scrub the pots, and even more than that." Unfortunately, the developers made her life as an enslaved person sound no worse than that of children on farms. Regarding the overseer, Lucy complains simply that he "works us hard." The prologue did introduce a few other hardships that farm children do not have. Lucy only occasionally gets "a road pass so I can go visit my papa," who lives on a different plantation. If the game were to end after the prologue, it would be nearly as bad as *Slave Trade*. In that section of the game, no real horrors are shown; slavery seems like "hard work" with a boss who looks severe and says that he prefers "quiet Negroes."[24]

Flight to Freedom improves somewhat in part 1, "Behind the Big House." Though there is still no real trauma, this section introduces at least some of the horrors of the slave system. Brutality is not visible in this game aimed at middle schoolers, but we hear about whippings secondhand. Lucy's mother asks her to get comfrey root to heal a friend, Henry, whose back is scarred. Henry declares, "I'm tired of being treated worse than they treat mules. We work, work, work and get nothing but whippings." Players also learn something of the arbitrariness of slave life. Children playing as Lucy discover quickly that, even if they obey the overseer, they will still be blamed for sabotage done by others. When Lucy is threatened with being sold south to a cotton plantation, she makes the difficult decision to leave her family to try to reach freedom in Ohio.

Once Lucy leaves the plantation in part 2 ("Runaway!"), the game's activities and dialogue become more compelling. Escaping alone through the forest is frightening, and Lucy has to make difficult decisions as she encounters whites: Pretend she is supposed to be there, or run? Players find that, mirroring reality, there is no logic to the consequences of Lucy's choices. The game design seems to randomize results; running sometimes yields the best outcomes, but other times results are better when Lucy pretends to be on an errand for her master, since her running raises suspicions. To reach Ohio successfully, players likely need to restart the chapter several times and try alternate choices—an option that the real Lucy did not have.

When Lucy finally reaches Ohio in part 3, "Free and Not Free," she meets several new characters—some real and some fictional composites. The first person she meets is the kindly white Reverend John Rankin, a real historical figure who worked on the Underground Railroad. Rankin introduces her to a fictional free Black couple, Abigail and Morgan Wright, who then pretend that Lucy is their niece. Lucy also befriends John Parker, a real African American, in addition to a kindly white composite, an abolitionist educator named Millie Hatcher. The game also introduces a white villain, a slave catcher named T. C. Bercham. Bercham has the power to return Lucy to her plantation if he finds out who she really is. The game also includes future president Benjamin Harrison, at that time an Ohio congressman. In part 4, "Gathering Forces," *Flight to Freedom* shows Harrison opposing the extension of slavery to additional states, but also believing that whites and Blacks cannot live together and that freed Blacks must go back to Africa.

As Lucy seeks freedom in Ohio, and tries to free her mother and brother, the game highlights the capricious injustices that even free Blacks faced. Though her friend Morgan Wright is free, the Fugitive Slave Law's passage emboldens slave catchers to fabricate evidence. Consequently, in part 5, "New Times, New Troubles," Morgan is kidnapped and sold into slavery. Lucy herself is eventually captured, though the game offers alternate endings for her. If Millie purchases her at auction, she can have a peaceful, free life, even if she never again sees her mother. Or she can resist being sold, flee, and work on the Underground Railroad. Or she can be sold south and die without ever knowing freedom again.

Though professional historians largely ignored *Flight to Freedom*, many education and game reviewers appraised it positively. Common Sense Media called it a "powerful" simulation. Common Sense reviewer Christy Matte cautioned that "kids might find the experience to be emotionally intense; families are torn apart, people are treated poorly, and characters are unfairly imprisoned." While *Flight to Freedom* does not confront children with slavery's harshest realities, Matte argued that

> because no simulation can or should adequately convey the full depth of slavery or the escape to freedom, this shouldn't serve as a stand-alone experience. . . . When it's paired with a strong curriculum unit—or discussions and research as a family—*Flight to Freedom* has the ability to humanize the people of the time and can serve as a springboard for further learning.

Kirk Hamilton of gaming site *Kotaku* said that the game surprised him; it helped him, a white male, place himself in the shoes of an enslaved girl in a way he had not imagined: "The game's presentational simplicity forced me to use my imagination, and I imagined very scary things. This was real, I kept reminding myself, people lived this, they lived under these laws and with this kind of fear."[25]

However, *Flight to Freedom* also was condemned by those who believe that slavery should never be gamified, or that it was a poor gamification. Rafranz Davis, a Black educational technology expert, noted that the game "features everything the 'edtech' buzzword community loves . . . role playing, badges, student choice and reevaluation of failure." But Davis maintained that this type of activity was completely inappropriate for the subject of slavery. Others argued that *Flight to Freedom* was egregious in removing the "torture, rape and murder" at slavery's core. Furthermore, as reporter Joseph Williams explained, critics felt that, "by avoiding the perspective of Lucy's master . . . the game doesn't compel students to consider how or why whites perpetuated the oppression."[26] After a few school districts removed the game following complaints from parents, Nikki Taylor (the scholar who had consulted on the game) said she understood their objections. She told *Current* in 2017 that "*Flight to Freedom* was done in a different period and may no longer be appropriate." She also asked whether animation had been the best choice, as opposed to "real images of slavery."[27]

The game's producers at WNET Education insisted that such critiques were unfair. *Flight to Freedom*, they said, could not be expected to teach students everything about slavery: "Although geared to children, the mission tells some ugly truths about slavery. . . . The mission also aims to humanize enslaved people and present them with dignity, courage, fear, and real human emotions like love and hate."[28] Sandra Sheppard of WNET told *Current* that educational studies had shown that "playing the game helped students understand how slavery worked 'and the ways that enslaved and free people struggled against it.'" She added that, in the climate of the late 2010s, "there is an urgent need to facilitate more dialogue . . . about our painful history of race and slavery in America," and that animation was a valuable tool for engaging young people.[29]

Still, even if *Flight to Freedom* improved on MECC's *Freedom!* and *Slave Trade*, especially in its later sections, the teacher's guides accompanying it had major flaws. Some of this material reduced the study of slavery to trite "lessons." In one recommended pre-game activity, teachers were told, "A core element of 'Flight to Freedom' is the notion of 'cause and effect' in history." While cause and effect are important concepts for historical thinking, the guide's examples were banal. For instance, "CAUSE: You didn't check the weather before you left for school/EFFECT: Your clothes are soaked because you were caught in a sudden rainstorm. . . . CAUSE: You got a job after school/EFFECT: You were able to save enough money to buy an iPad." Other parts of the lesson plan questioned the unique evils of slavery; one troubling prompt asked students whether slavery was necessarily worse than indentured servitude. Another part of the curriculum told students that the Civil War happened because the North and South had different views of states' rights and slaves were "caught in the middle."[30]

It is important to note that, while MECC's *Freedom!*, *Slave Trade*, and *Flight to Freedom* all discussed slavery and even slave resistance, they did not tackle armed slave revolt. Nat Turner's, Denmark Vesey's, and other slave revolts in the United States have not been the subjects of any game, let alone one marketed for educational use.[31] Whether because schools avoid the subject of violence in general—or because enslaved revolutionaries are not extolled in curricula in the way that white revolutionaries like George Washington are—educational software on slavery has steered clear of slave revolt.[32]

The Haitian Revolution in Commercial Games: *Age of Empires III: The WarChiefs*, *Assassin's Creed III: Liberation*, and *Assassin's Creed: Freedom Cry*

Whereas educational games avoid slave revolt, a few commercial games have treated this subject. Some even involve slave resistance in Saint-Domingue. These games have emerged from major franchises created by the wealthiest game studios. Unlike a film on the Haitian Revolution, which would be released outside of a blockbuster franchise like *Star Wars* or *Marvel Cinematic Universe* and would need to build its own audience, these games have appeared within already successful franchises. Incorporating these titles into series whose players have demonstrated an interest in early modern world history and prefer violent games, game producers have found slave revolt a less worrisome topic than their counterparts in film or educational software.

One might expect that these games would be just as appalling as MECC's *Freedom!* and *Slave Trade*. Indeed, not all invocations of the Revolution have had laudable results. The strategy game *Age of Empires III* (2005), which has sold a few million copies, alluded to the Revolution problematically. *Age of Empires* is a major franchise created by Ensemble Studios, then part of Microsoft. The game's *WarChiefs* expansion pack, released in 2006, included a Toussaint Louverture character, as part of what Forsdick has called the twenty-first-century iconization of Toussaint.[33] The addition of a Toussaint character did not change the colonialist structure of *Age of Empires*; players colonize territory and build an army to defend their empires from Natives or rival empires who might attack. The game's Toussaint has no dialogue or personalized features, other than brown skin and a distinctive uniform. He is simply one interchangeable "revolutionary politician" available to help the player's army, if the player advances far enough to "earn" him. More importantly, the character does not control himself; whether gamers play as the French or British Empire, Toussaint simply follows their orders in fighting their enemies.

Other attempts to gamify the Revolution have also proven troubling. The magazine *Wargames Illustrated* suggested a way to play the Revolution as a tabletop game; its approach was based on colonialist paradigms. This game asked players to choose between being a French officer trying to "snuff out the rebellion" or being one of the hordes of African warriors who "charg[ed] forward in a wild rush." This perspective hardly humanized enslaved people. Another video game that alluded to Haiti stereotypically was *80 Days*, *Time* magazine's 2014 Game of the Year.[34]

However, the 2013 video game *Assassin's Creed: Freedom Cry* is far superior to other attempts to gamify slavery and the Revolution. While the game takes creative liberties with facts, I argue that it offers a better representation of Haitian slave resistance than most other depictions by foreigners. Without sanitizing slavery or creating white heroes, it plunges players into plantation society and tasks them with helping enslaved people escape their oppressors.

Freedom Cry comes from a hugely successful franchise, Ubisoft's *Assassin's Creed* series (henceforth *AC*). *AC* releases are so-called AAA games, akin to blockbuster films in two ways. First, AAA games can have development budgets in the hundreds of millions of dollars. Second, they offer a more cinematic aesthetic than lower-tech games. *AC* games have been a spectacular success, with more than 93 million copies sold by 2015. They also regularly win awards such as Xbox or GameSpot Game of the Year. In 2016, Fox released a movie version of the series (*Assassin's Creed*), set during the Spanish Inquisition; it grossed approximately $240 million. *AC* games focus on the battles between two fictional orders, the Assassins and the Templars, while incorporating real historical events from the Renaissance to the French Revolution. Where filmmakers such as Niang have flouted historians' suggestions, Ubisoft seeks help from professional historians, such as Jean-Clément Martin, former chair of the History of the French Revolution at the Sorbonne.[35]

The quality of *AC Freedom Cry* is especially remarkable, given that an earlier *AC* game invoking Saint-Dominguan slave resistance, *AC Liberation* (2012), was less compelling historiographically. An adjunct to the main *AC III* game, *AC Liberation* was set in New Orleans, but featured characters who had migrated from Saint-Domingue. Set between 1765 and 1777, *Liberation* centered on Aveline, a biracial female Assassin and daughter of an enslaved woman from Saint-Domingue. Aveline moves through New Orleans and its surroundings, clandestinely killing Templars and freeing slaves while helping her white father with his business. *Liberation* also had a subplot involving the famous Haitian rebel François Makandal.

Liberation garnered much acclaim after its release, both for treating slavery in a new way and for having an intelligent Black woman as protagonist. As Anna Everett has noted, the game was a landmark in the industry. Everett called Aveline a "kickass black heroine," noting that "now, males of all racial and ethnic groups confess online to enjoying gameplay as a powerful black female MPC [must-play character]." In 2013, *Liberation* received a Writers Guild of America award—alongside the film *Argo* and the television show *Breaking Bad*—for Outstanding Achievement in Videogame Writing.[36] In retrospect, the game's choice of protagonist looks even more radical, given the struggles that women developers have reported facing in the game industry, including in creating female avatars.[37]

Still, despite the game's breaking ground with regard to gender, its treatments of slavery and of Saint-Domingue were problematic. In the game, Aveline lives in privilege in her white father's mansion; his slaveowning is presented as incidental. The information provided explains that Aveline's mother, Jeanne, was scared of Makandal, who had been her mentor in planning slave revolt in Saint-Domingue; she was thrilled to be bought by a new enslaver, Philippe de Grandpré, who whisked her away from Makandal and took her "to safety" in New Orleans. Subsequent sexual encounters between de Grandpré and his slave Jeanne are presented as consensual; de Grandpré is depicted as a good white for having manumitted Jeanne and their baby Aveline. In portraying de Grandpré as Aveline's doting "Papa," the game evades his continuing to own others; it shows neither his running his plantation, nor the overseers who discipline in his stead. Aveline makes some casual antislavery pronouncements. However, we do not see her begin this campaign at home by urging her father to manumit their slaves.[38]

Another weakness of *Liberation* was its refraining from confronting the slave system's racist underpinnings. The game's depiction of slavery paralleled what Chivallon has observed about French memorials on slavery, which act "'as if' this suffering [of slavery] were acknowledged, without that acknowledgement genuinely taking place."[39] While ostensibly opposing slavery, the game avoided blaming whites for the institution. Instead, *Liberation* included many nice whites who help Aveline, including her father's assistant Gérard, a spunky smuggler named Elise, and Aveline's kindly slaveowning father.

Several of *Liberation*'s villains were not in fact whites but enslaved Blacks. The game introduces players to a "false Mackandal" in Louisiana named Baptiste. It explains in a cutscene that Baptiste, a former student of the real Makandal, now lives outside New Orleans, pretending to be his former mentor. (Of course, the real Makandal was burned at the stake in Cap Haïtien in 1758 after being captured by slaveowners.) In this guise of "François Mackandal," Baptiste aims to convince enslaved Louisianans to poison their masters and revolt; however, unbeknownst to them, he plans to lead them not to freedom but into the hands of different enslavers, for his own profit. As Aveline hunts for this false Makandal, she finds him at a "voodoo ceremony," which resembles the Bois Caïman ceremony in Niang's miniseries. Instead of spiritual communion with the Vodou *lwa*, this ceremony offers drinking, dancing, creepy makeup, and the throwing of poison darts.[40] One might explain away the game's treatment of "Makandal," since Baptiste is an impostor. However, the real Makandal is not described as "the false Makandal's" opposite, but as a bloodthirsty person from whom Aveline's mother yearned to flee. In addition, Sarah Lauro has pointed to the troubling connotations of *Liberation*'s referring to Baptiste's men as "thugs."[41] Ultimately, despite its larger significance in the history of gaming, *Liberation* distorted the history of slave revolt in Saint-Domingue. It suggested that nice slaveowners were needed to rescue enslaved people from evil rebels like Makandal.

Given *Liberation*'s flaws, Ubisoft's decision to make a game set entirely in Saint-Domingue might not have seemed cause for celebration. However, *Freedom Cry*—which, as a game for the main PlayStation console, had a fuller development budget and more extensive historical input—presented a wholly different view of the background to the Haitian Revolution than did *AC Liberation*. *Freedom Cry* is an offshoot of *AC IV Black Flag*.[42] That game, focused on eighteenth-century Caribbean piracy, had a few passing mentions of slavery. *Freedom Cry* follows a fan-favorite character from *Black Flag* (Adéwalé, a freed Trinidadian slave turned pirate turned Assassin) as he travels to Saint-Domingue. Because *AC* games focus on violence, and Adéwalé was already well liked from previous *AC* games, Ubisoft did not share film funders' worries about white audiences' reactions to a Black man killing white enslavers.

Haitian gamers and others welcomed the game, indicating that Ubisoft was filling a void in the market. Evan Narcisse, a Haitian American journalist (and grandson of Haitian dance pioneer André Narcisse), had famously lamented the lack of compelling Black protagonists in games. In a 2012 essay called "Come On, Video Games, Let's See Some Black People I'm Not Embarrassed by," Narcisse stated, "I've never played as a black video game character who's made me feel like he was cool. . . . Video games just don't get black people." When *Freedom Cry* was issued, however, Narcisse (who has since become an important comic book and game writer) found it a revelation:

> I'm a Haitian-American child of immigrants and, personally, Freedom Cry felt like a deeply resonant fictionalization of the history my ancestors came from. Hearing passers-by discuss the sub-humanity of the slaves doing backbreaking labor and giving chase to the slave catchers pursuing runaways trying to escape to freedom gave me motivations I never had before in playing video games.

Narcisse noted that hearing characters talk in Kreyòl was especially unexpected. The game's language and feel, he remarked,

> reminds me of going to church with my mother. It makes me happy and sad at the same time. Whether it was a first communion, wedding or funeral, someone nestled in the crowd . . . would start singing the Haitian national anthem. For no reason other than a deep longing for the home they'd left behind. *Freedom Cry* calls up the same combination of mournfulness and pride that I'd hear in those moments of song.

Similarly, Marc Bernardin, the Haitian American journalist and writer who had been amazed at the existence of *Freedom Cry*, called the game "the first time I'd ever felt seen in a medium I loved."[43] Non-gamers might be surprised to hear such emotional reactions from players. But *Freedom Cry* is designed to elicit intense reactions, from Haitians and non-Haitians alike.

Certainly from a historiographical standpoint, *Freedom Cry* is imperfect. First, it fictionalized the Revolution by rooting it in something entirely fantastical, the Templar-Assassin war that lies at the core of the *AC* series. In addition, the game makes specific errors, such as in its timing. *Freedom Cry* claims to be set at a moment when "the French are in panic," because slaves and maroons are conspiring to kill whites. But this panic happened not in the 1730s but the 1750s, at the height of Makandal's conspiracy.[44] There are other glaring inauthenticities, such as an actor referring to the *lwa* (Vodou spirits) and pronouncing it "I-wa" instead of like the French word *loi*. The game also includes counterfactual fantasies, like maroons capturing slave ships; in reality, maroons stayed in mountains far from the coast, to avoid capture. In addition, *Freedom Cry* can be accused of commodifying Black bodies and exploiting slavery for commercial purposes.[45] Finally, in contrast to other games that have treated slavery, the game is a third-person shooter or stabber game, which is anachronistic when representing a time when enslaved people's recourse to overt violence was rare.

However, *Freedom Cry* has many startlingly good aspects; its representations of the slave system in Saint-Domingue are better than in most non-Haitian films—and certainly than in *Age of Empires III* or *AC Liberation*. While it involves invented characters and situations, I would argue that it has a firm historical grounding. Compared to most non-Haitian films, *Freedom Cry* offers a much more humanizing view of Saint-Domingue's enslaved people and their ability to organize resistance themselves. The game's white colonists are neither brilliant puppet masters (à la *Burn!*) or kindly mentors dispensing needed advice (as in the *Toussaint* miniseries).

Unlike Niang's film, the game does not hide slavery's brutality. As soon as Adéwalé falls overboard and washes up on Saint-Domingue, he witnesses a slave auction (figure 9.3). Players are immediately led to empathize with caged human beings whom they will try to liberate.[46] Next, players observe an overseer pursuing an enslaved woman, presumably in order to rape her. When she fights back, the overseer yells, "This will cost you an ear!" and chases her (mission 2, "A Common Enemy").[47] Where the producers whom Danny Glover met could only imagine a film on Haitian slave revolt if it had a white hero, *Freedom Cry* places players in the role of a subaltern.[48] No matter their own gender or skin shade, players become Adéwalé, tracking down the overseer and avenging his treatment of the woman.[49] As Adéwalé engages in retributive violence, liberating enslaved people and meeting maroon leaders, players become invested in their success.[50]

Second, the game highlights women of color as having intelligence and agency, while acknowledging that they operated within limits. The game's female protagonist is Bastienne Josèphe, the madam of a Port-au-Prince brothel serving high-ranking French officials. The depiction of Saint-Domingue's women of color as prostitutes or madams would normally be a red flag to a Haitian historian. Recent scholarship has labored against the image of women of color on the island, popularized by Moreau de Saint-Méry, as prostitutes who lived for the love of white men. Combating such stereotypes, Dominique Rogers and Stewart King have offered a fuller picture of Saint-Domingue's free

Figure 9.3. Witnessing a slave auction as *Assassin's Creed: Freedom Cry* begins. © Ubisoft, 2013. Screenshot, PS4 version, 2014.

women of color, highlighting the range of professions in which they worked, from midwives to merchants.[51] Bastienne also might not seem unusual on the surface since she falls into a long tradition of buxom women in video games.[52]

And yet Bastienne Josèphe is no ordinary prostitute (figure 9.4). Clever and strategic, Bastienne uses her position to ply information from clients such as the island's Governor de Fayet and feed it to the maroons. In real life, as I have noted in previous chapters, many Haitian women were involved in resistance against the French; in most films, we see only men.[53] *Freedom Cry* is thus truer to the historical record than these films, in including a woman of color resisting the slave system. In highlighting women's agency in history, Bastienne subverts expectations of video game sex workers. She is also a useful analyst of the complexities of resistance. When Adéwalé impetuously wants to keep killing enslavers to liberate the enslaved, she cautions him about the collective punishment meted out to those left behind: "You help the ones you freed, but at what cost to the ones you can't?" (mission 8, "Down with the Ship").

Like Raoul Peck's unfilmed miniseries script (discussed in the last chapter), *Freedom Cry* also makes vivid colonists' worldviews, in ways that mirror real eighteenth-century discourse. When Bastienne tells de Fayet that enslaved people are rebelling because they are unhappy with their treatment, he responds that such treatment is necessary: "It is their animal nature. Violence is the only currency that motivates them" (mission 2, "A Common Enemy"). The game also

Figure 9.4. Adéwalé and Bastienne discuss strategy. *Assassin's Creed: Freedom Cry*. © Ubisoft, 2013. Screenshot, Windows version, MobyGames.

highlights slaveowners' greed. Speaking with maroon leader Augustin Dieufort, Adéwalé expresses his frustration at not being able to convince whites to stop the trade: "I once hoped men of education could be made to see the cost. But profit makes them ignorant" (mission 4, "A Ship of His Own").

In addition, *Freedom Cry* shows the human cost of these enslavers' views, while leading the player to identify with those challenging them. The game's cutscenes include powerful cinematic images of enslaved people dying in the hold of a ship as Adéwalé and Augustin cannot rescue them in time. Adéwalé, Augustin, and Bastienne argue passionately about the wisdom of seeking to avenge the deaths of these kidnapped Africans:

> AUGUSTIN: Revenge is cold comfort. Once de Fayet is gone, another tyrant will take his place.
> ADÉWALÉ: His death must give this generation of warriors hope. They must not abandon the goal of independence.
> BASTIENNE: And the death of these souls? Some barely knew life.
> AUGUSTIN: We will always mourn them. (mission 8, "Down with the Ship")

Adéwalé fulfills gamers' fantasies by obtaining the vengeance that enslaved people in the 1730s could not. He tracks down de Fayet and overhears the governor pressing an enslaved person to tell him about resistance. As we hear heart-piercing wails from others being tortured, Adéwalé decides to kill de Fayet—but not without letting him suffer first (figure 9.5):

DE FAYET: Help!

ADÉWALÉ: Who will come to your rescue? Your slaves? The overseers who follow your orders? Pathetic. What kind of man does not fight for himself? . . .

ADÉWALÉ: (stabbing de Fayet) I have killed many men on principle, but never have I wanted one to suffer as much as you—to understand what it is to gasp and beg for your life, like the innocents you drowned!

DE FAYET: (before dying) You mean those slaves? That ship? But they are not even human! (mission 9, "De Fayet's Last Stand")

Another admirable aspect of *Freedom Cry* is that players are not simply assigned shooting missions, but encouraged to learn more history. While playing *AC* games, players can choose between only doing required missions and charging through a game, or taking time to do optional missions. They earn information as they complete tasks, which unlocks entries in the game's Animus Database, an in-game wiki. As game-site moderator and *AC* fan Olivia Salazar explains, while some players prefer to reach a game's end quickly, many others enjoy collecting the Animus material. When they are rewarded with this information, they are more motivated to read it and to learn about Haitian history than if they were tasked with reading a history textbook, or given a torrent of unearned text from the beginning.[54] Players are thus more likely to want to read Animus sections such as "Code Noir" and "Maroons" (figure 9.6).

The Animus entries offer much useful background. "Plantation Life" tells players that "slaves collapsed from exhaustion regularly and sometimes got into horrible accidents with . . . primitive machinery." The entry also explains enslaved people's tenacity in creating spaces of their own, away from their oppressors: "Friends and family units were created in the barracks, and children were reared and taught the dangers and risks of the harsh life they were being brought into. These barracks were the focal point for developing slave communities." The "Plantation Life" entry also describes religion's role on the plantation: "Faith offered the slaves a form of escapism from their harsh lives and masters," but scripture could also be used as a "code" among slaves, sometimes "sparking . . . rebellion." Certainly, Animus entries have occasional mistakes, and some information could be nuanced. The material in "Plantation Life" on family and religion, for instance, needs to be complemented by more negative information. For example, even if enslaved peoples built families,

Figure 9.5. Adéwalé avenges murdered enslaved people by killing Saint-Domingue's governor. *Assassin's Creed: Freedom Cry*. © Ubisoft, 2013. Screenshot, Windows version, MobyGames.

slaveowners could break them up on a whim. In addition, faith was used to scare slaves into submission. The entry on "Maroons" also includes some debatable assertions.[55] Still, the Animus offers players high-quality information on Saint-Domingue society, in a way that non-gamers would not expect.

Players were so enthusiastic about the Animus information that Ubisoft added further information on the Revolution in *AC Initiates*, a section of Ubisoft's website with bonus content. This content fictionalized portions of the Haitian Revolution, appropriating it into the *Freedom Cry* story line. While the forum is defunct, fan pages reproducing this material indicate that it identified Toussaint himself as a member of the Brotherhood of Assassins. The developers thus explicitly tied the actions of Adéwalé, Bastienne, and Augustin to the struggles of the 1790s. *Initiates* also claimed other revolutionaries, including Boukman and Biassou, as Assassins. Adéwalé's and Bastienne's contribution to the Revolution's origins were depicted as not only theoretical; *Initiates* told fans that the two conceived a child together during Adéwalé's stay on the island, and that their grandson became one of the Revolution's leaders. According to this bit of historical invention, their grandson Eseosa, son of their love child Babatunde, was an Assassin; he was the person who bought Toussaint's freedom from Bayon de Libertat. Eseosa is further identified as having succeeded

Figure 9.6. Information on Maroons from *Assassin's Creed: Freedom Cry*'s Animus Database. © Ubisoft, 2013. Screenshot, PS4 version (2014).

Makandal as leader of Saint-Domingue's Brotherhood of Assassins chapter, and having worked with Boukman to organize the Bois Caïman ceremony.[56]

While this information is fictional, it did introduce more Haitian Revolution content to *AC* players. It also created the possibility that players might seek to learn about these real figures from more reliable sources. Because of gamers' enthusiasm for *Freedom Cry*'s Haitian story line, Ubisoft later added Haitian Revolution elements to other parts of the *AC* franchise. The 2014 game *Assassin's Creed: Rogue* included brief references to Makandal and to slave resistance in colonial Saint-Domingue.[57]

Freedom Cry tries to offer Haitian studies immersion in still other ways. The developers sought to include authentic Haitian culture in the game—not only through using Kreyòl, but also by including eighteenth-century Vodou songs. Though they were not initially told what project they were working on, singers associated with the famous Afro-Haitian ensemble La Troupe Makandal were hired to record songs for the soundtrack, which were then mixed with a European orchestral score. The singers included prominent Haitian artist Monvelyno Alexis, who is deeply interested in the colonial history of Saint-Domingue. Lois Wilcken, La Troupe Makandal's executive director and an expert in Haitian ethnomusicology, has explained that the group was very deliberate in choosing what to include. They opted for Rada songs, one of the main types of Vodou music, from the Guinea Gulf region (Wilcken notes that Rada songs "have a lot of *fongbe* words in them, and we know that the Fon [an important West African ethnic group] and related people were coming in large numbers in the mid-eighteenth century"), as well as another type of eighteenth-century Vodou resistance music, a Congo song.[58] Using real Haitian music was in contrast to films such as *Lydia Bailey*, which invented songs that were supposed to sound Haitian. The effect impressed listeners emotionally. One reviewer called *Freedom Cry*'s soundtrack "one of the strongest video game scores I've ever heard."[59]

Freedom Cry's deep engagement with Haitian culture and history might at first seem puzzling: How could a game offer a more complex view of the Revolution than so many films and texts? Given that the game was made by Anglophones in Montreal,[60] one might guess that the developers had been students of Carolyn Fick, the eminent historian of Haiti who teaches at Montreal's Concordia University. However, Jill Murray, the game's lead scriptwriter, offered a different answer. She explained that Ubisoft (which works with professional historians on each *AC* title) had hired not Fick, but another Quebec expert on the Revolution, Jean-Pierre Le Glaunec of the University of Sherbrooke.[61] Author of an important book on the Haitian army's victory against

Napoleon, Le Glaunec was initially skeptical about a game based on the Revolution. His main objective in consulting was to help Ubisoft "avoid caricaturing" slaves. He wanted also to ensure that the game did not depict them as debased persons (*êtres abattus*), without dignity. However, he was impressed by the game's structure as well as by the input that Ubisoft allowed him to have: "Their research has been exemplary. I am not saying that just for PR's sake! . . . They permit themselves certain liberties [with facts, but] as much as possible, they want the game to be historically accurate. And it is not easy to represent those who resisted slavery." For Le Glaunec, *Freedom Cry*'s beauty lies in the fact that players act not only to liberate enslaved people, but also to help "plant the seeds for the Haitian Revolution."[62]

Murray also did a great deal of research on her own to write *Freedom Cry*. Interestingly, she had also cowritten *AC Liberation*. However, she was not present at that game's inception; Aveline was conceived at Ubisoft Sofia before Murray joined the project. As she "had to get up to speed very quickly," her research for *Liberation* was limited. For *Freedom Cry*, in contrast, Murray had more time to develop a complex and respectful story line about slave resistance in Haiti. In addition to working with Le Glaunec, Murray "read about Haitian revolutionaries, their descendants across the diaspora. . . . I've read slave narratives. I've read the Code Noir." In addition, her team drew upon the marronage database that Le Glaunec had codeveloped. Interestingly, Murray based Bastienne Josèphe on a real person she discovered in her research. Murray explained, "I actually set out to avoid writing any more prostitutes into *Assassin's Creed*." But when her team researched scientist Louis Godin's expedition to measure the world's circumference, which is integrated into the game, Murray found mention of a wealthy brothel owner named Bastienne Josèphe. Murray was fascinated by a story about a scientist on Godin's expedition who fell so deeply in love with one of Bastienne's prostitutes that he stole funds to buy her a gigantic diamond. Murray decided to include Bastienne to illustrate the way that power could be exercised in unexpected ways.[63]

Being based in Montreal, a center of the Haitian diaspora, Murray had more insight into Haitian culture than the Sofia-based developers who conceived *AC Liberation*. She was thus eager to fulfill Haitian expectations for such a game. Murray has young relatives of Haitian descent and wanted "to be an ally" in "build[ing] a world" without racism.

> We can't go back in time, but we can talk to Haitian Canadians and Haitian Americans today. . . . They tell us things like they don't ever expect to see themselves as the protagonist of a videogame, . . . that they certainly never in

> a million years expect to see Creole coming back at them out of an Assassin's Creed game. It's heartbreaking to hear that. . . . [We] set out to . . . make a game that would make people feel seen. . . . We're really going to focus on . . . what would [people] like us to communicate of their . . . community, of their history.

Murray added that *Freedom Cry* was developed because, when Adéwalé was a supporting character in *AC IV Black Flag*, "many fans wonder[ed] what Adewale . . . would do when confronted with slavery if he was the captain of his own ship." She explained that *Freedom Cry* sends Adéwalé to confront slave society years after winning his own freedom, in the hopes that players will grapple with the ethical questions he faces.[64]

AC Freedom Cry received enthusiastic reviews from critics, gamers, and students using it in the classroom. As lead scriptwriter, Murray and her team earned a repeat nomination in 2014 for the Writers Guild of America Outstanding Achievement in Videogame Writing Award. Gamers also reported finding the game rewarding. Reviewer Mike Williams wrote of how much he learned while playing: "Freedom Cry breathes in the reality of its setting: the enslaved people in Saint Domingue outnumbered their masters and other freed people of color ten to one." He felt that the game also confronted some important moral debates surrounding slave resistance: "While Adewale calls for direct action and the immediate strengthening of the Maroon rebellion, Bastienne advocates for a slower path without [upending] the current status quo. . . . Both characters are proven right and wrong, because there is no easy answer." An early assessment of the game's impact in the classroom has been offered by social studies education scholar Lisa Gilbert. In her fieldwork, she found that *AC* games created historical empathy. She quoted one student who described "in vivid detail" how Adéwalé had made him understand "how serious" slavery was for the first time, even though he had learned about it previously in school.[65]

On Twitter, those who represent themselves as subscribers of color expressed their amazement about playing the game—or just learning about its existence. One exclaimed, "My dream came true. In the new AC 4 DLC [downloadable content], you get to play [as] Adewale liberating slaves in Haiti. F–ing awesome." Another wrote that he was dying to play *Freedom Cry* after realizing that "you free slaves in Haiti for 10 hours."[66] Haitians in particular discussed their excitement about the game.[67]

Players self-identifying as white also expressed enthusiasm for *Freedom Cry*'s concept. IT developer and game aficionado Scott Murray reported being astonished by being placed in Adéwalé's shoes: "Fiiiinally playing

#assassinscreed freedom cry. Holy crap. Holy. Crap. You play a former slave freeing slaves in 18th cent. Haiti." Another Twitter user noted that the game combated colonial revisionism: "Assassin's Creed IV: Black Flag: Video Game depicting Haiti's fight for freedom from France. Things . . . some of my French relatives are in denial about. Over 11 million copies sold so far."[68]

Though these gamers and bloggers were enthusiastic about *Freedom Cry*, some still had reservations about it. Narcisse expressed some qualms after considering how "the game's mechanics essentially has the player treating freed slaves like a resource to purchase stuff. That mechanic is uncomfortably close to the way that slaves were used in the bondage that players are supposed to be freeing them from." So did Scott Murray, the gamer who had initially been so enthusiastic about playing, tweeting, "This is a lot to process. The gameplay rewards you for freeing slaves. It's like I love the idea but it makes me queasy?" Game Studies scholar Souvik Mukherjee has made similar claims; he notes that in *Freedom Cry*, as in another Ubisoft game set in central Africa, "the ostensible act of liberation from the bondage imposed by the elite actually becomes a mechanism of generating in-game capital."[69]

Writers have pointed to other shortcomings. Game critic Amanda Kerri argued that *Freedom Cry* "glosses over some of the worst aspects of [slave] ownership," including "the separation and destruction of families." Chris Franklin, who runs a gaming-related YouTube channel, expressed similar reservations. For Game Studies scholar Emil Hammar, the game's avoiding racist language was problematic; it sanitized slavery. Kishonna Gray worried that, even as "black gamers in particular may laud Adéwalé," he might simply "[replicate] the dominant visual paradigm," of Black men as violent killers.[70]

The Haitians who performed on *Freedom Cry*'s soundtrack also expressed some ambivalence. Once the game was released, Monvelyno Alexis was disappointed by its fictionalized treatment of Haitian history; he wished it had featured real heroes like Boukman instead of imaginary ones. Lamenting the game's violence, Alexis added that if the developers really wanted to show battles between Haitians and colonists, they should have set their game during the Revolution, focusing on the Battle of Vertières (the 1803 turning point where Haitians defeated the French). Furthermore, Alexis lamented, though the creators included authentic Haitian music in the soundtrack, they had submerged it in European orchestrations. To him, the result sounded "corny."[71]

Nevertheless, Alexis was grateful for the game's introducing Haitian culture to foreign audiences. He notes that his main reason for participating was to give greater exposure to Haitian Vodou music: "Every nation has its own culture; I would like the Haitian culture to be [better] known." Alexis was particularly eager to ensure that the soundtrack included "Ogou O," a song for the *lwa* most associated with war; he felt that a game about Haitian rebels could not be made without reference to Ogou (also spelled Ogun). He reports that *Freedom Cry* has been successful in making Vodou music better known; in recent travels to Europe, he met fans who knew his work from the game. Alexis was also gratified to learn that, after playing *Freedom Cry*, one of his Swedish fans had bought a history of the Revolution.[72]

Bloggers and scholars have also agreed that the game deserves respect, notwithstanding its flaws. For Amanda Kerri, *Freedom Cry* is "not a perfect game, but it goes places where others would not, and for that it does deserve recognition." Despite his apprehensions about its mechanics, Chris Franklin still felt that *Freedom Cry* was "fairly nuanced and fleshed out"; he particularly liked the debates between Adéwalé, Augustin, and Bastienne about how to challenge slavery. For Narcisse, both *Freedom Cry* and *Liberation* deserve credit "for talking about historical practices of white hegemony"; he called the *AC* franchise "singular" in daring to approach these issues. Hammar noted that, even if *Freedom Cry* could have included more information on Haitian history, it still allowed players to engage in "counter-hegemonic commemoration" of slavery.[73]

Ultimately, despite misdating the height of French "panic" over slave resistance by two decades, *Freedom Cry*, I would argue, powerfully represents ongoing resistance in Haiti. By being set in the 1730s and not the 1780s, the game is able to divorce the French Revolution from the Haitian Revolution, thus avoiding the notion that enslaved people were simply copying French ideals. *Freedom Cry* shows the brutality of slavery and the fact that resistance existed long before 1789. It also shows women's agency in resisting this system. In my view, where *Freedom Cry* is most inaccurate is not in its misdating, but in making violent slave resistance appear more feasible than it was. But this is perhaps part of the game's appeal, that players (particularly of African descent) can do things in *Freedom Cry* that their ancestors could not. Indeed, as Game Studies scholar Kevin Schut has noted, one of the most popular aspects of historical games is that they are counterfactual and allow players to imagine that they could have changed history.[74]

Ubisoft's *Freedom Cry* thus embraces the challenge of portraying slave revolt positively, something other games have avoided. It makes the Haitian Revolution far more thinkable than most films by non-Haitians. Unlike in *Burn!*, the African-descended men and women in this story are thinking agents of change planning their own resistance, not tools of Europeans. Furthermore, the game had no need for a white hero; players were made to identify with Saint-Domingue's people of color, not its colonists. Given the millions who have played it, *AC Freedom Cry* has introduced the Revolution to a far greater audience than any film.

However, even though it is better than other games discussed in this chapter, *Freedom Cry* is still the creation of developers of European descent—notwithstanding the input from Haitian Canadians and a soundtrack including Haitian musicians. In our final chapter, we turn toward a different set of games, created by descendants of enslaved people from the French Caribbean, to explore how and why they put slave revolt into a video game format.

10

FRENCH CARIBBEAN GAMES

Honoring Rebel Ancestors in *Mẽwilo* and *Freedom: Rebels in the Darkness*

This chapter turns from video games produced by North American and European developers to those authored by Caribbean writers. Since Haitians have not yet designed video games about the Revolution, these games help us see how other French Caribbean artists have created digital treatments of slave resistance in Haiti and beyond.

I highlight here two largely forgotten slavery-related games from the 1980s: *Méwilo* (1987) and *Freedom: Rebels in the Darkness* (1988; not to be confused with MECC's 1992 *Freedom!*). These games, created by a pair of important Martinican intellectuals, lack the flaws of *AC Freedom Cry* and *Liberation*. Like *AC Freedom Cry*, *Freedom: Rebels in the Darkness* involves killing white colonists to gain freedom, and it offers subaltern perspectives on slave revolt. Yet where *Freedom Cry* made assassinating overseers relatively easy for an experienced gamer, *Freedom: Rebels in the Darkness* made slave resistance less likely to be successful, no matter a player's skill level. The game celebrated the courageous resistance of enslaved peoples while highlighting the real obstacles blocking their success.

To create *Freedom*, Muriel Tramis, a trailblazing figure in game design, collaborated with the great Caribbean writer Patrick Chamoiseau. Tramis was one of the first women—not to mention one of the first Black women—to find success in that field. Long before the 2001 Taubira Law, Tramis and Chamoiseau utilized this new media form to preserve the memory of slavery; they sought to educate metropolitan French citizens and others about Caribbean history. Tramis and Chamoiseau made *Méwilo* and *Freedom* together (along with illustrator Philippe Truca); Tramis later created a third slavery-related game without Chamoiseau, the groundbreaking *Lost in Time* (1993). Each of these games included Makandal as a character, whether as an avatar choice (*Freedom*) or in cameo roles (*Méwilo* and *Lost in Time*).

Tramis's and Chamoiseau's pioneering video games are crucial to examine—not only because they may be the earliest games ever made on Atlantic slavery, predating those in chapter 9, but also because their authors are descendants of enslaved people. A trailblazing French game company, Coktel Vision, recognized Tramis's talent and creativity and gave her the freedom to make any kind of game she wanted. Martinican and Guadeloupean people's identities are not identical to those of Haitians; they diverged in many ways after 1804, as Haiti became independent while those islands remained part of France, with slavery still in force. Even after abolition in 1848, Parisian authorities controlled education in the Antilles; Haiti was made a bogeyman, a place where dangerous Blacks had murdered whites and suffered the consequences of poverty. Nevertheless, these games by Tramis and Chamoiseau highlight enduring counter-images of Haiti among Antillean peoples. They showed that memories of Haitian revolutionaries—not just Toussaint and Dessalines but also Makandal—were kept alive underground, as symbols of freedom.[1]

In addition to their key place in the history of video games and of Antillean ideas about Haiti, *Freedom: Rebels in the Darkness* and *Méwilo* represent overlooked portions of Chamoiseau's oeuvre. Chamoiseau's novels, including 1988's *Solibo Magnifique* and his 1992 Prix-Goncourt-winning opus *Texaco*, have been translated into multiple languages. *Texaco* spans two centuries as it alternates between the story of an improvised neighborhood sprouting near a Texaco refinery in Martinique, and the lives of residents' enslaved ancestors. A linguistic virtuoso and trickster, Chamoiseau has called himself a mere "word scratcher" (*marqueur des paroles*) as he transcribes oral traditions shared with him by older Martinicans, both in *Texaco* and in his book *Creole Folktales*. With Jean Bernabé and Raphaël Confiant, Chamoiseau is also a founder of the Créolité movement. The trio's famous *Éloge de la Créolité* (1989) argued for a middle ground between those who embrace Martinique's French heritage and those who argue for reclaiming African culture (*négritude*). The *Éloge* noted that the Caribbean has been subject to fusion and *métissage* (mixing) for centuries, and that instead of having to choose between monolithic options, Caribbean peoples should embrace their *créolité* (mixedness).[2]

Alongside his novels and other works, Chamoiseau has embraced popular culture and audiovisual media. His contributions vary from comic books written pseudonymously in the 1980s with Tony Delsham (a noted Martinican writer as well as Tramis's cousin) to screenplays. Chamoiseau's most famous film collaboration, *Passage du milieu* (*Middle Passage*, 1999, dir. Guy Deslauriers), aired on HBO in 2002.[3] As Christopher Miller has written, *Middle Passage* was a highly unusual representation of slavery on screen; in contrast to films such as *Amistad*, *Middle Passage* had an "unrelenting, punishing tone" in which "no white heroes intervene on behalf of the slaves as a sop to the viewer's conscience."[4] Despite scholars' attention to other popular media through which Chamoiseau has explored the history of slavery, this part of his oeuvre has escaped notice outside the gaming world.[5]

Beyond expanding our understanding of Chamoiseau's work, these games help us discover a Caribbean intellectual who has explored slavery's legacy digitally since the 1980s: Tramis herself. Tramis has had a distinguished career bringing French Caribbean culture to the public. However, because she has used computer code rather than words, she has been less well known outside gaming circles than other Martinican intellectuals of her generation. In 2018, she received overdue national recognition when she was named a Chevalier of the French Legion of Honor, one of the first game designers ever honored.[6]

Tramis studied electrical engineering and computer science in France at a time when few women entered those fields. Early in her career, she worked for the French military, designing weapons systems. After five years, she sought to do something more "peaceful" with her engineering skills; amid the PC revolution, she changed careers to game design. Tramis did not want to make generic games in the mold of *Donkey Kong* or *Pong*; she sought to make creative and educational adventure games that could teach a larger public about the Creole culture she held dear.[7]

Working for Coktel, Tramis made several groundbreaking games about slavery. As she later reflected, "We were all aware at [Coktel] that we were in an era of innovation and that we were going to create something totally new in edutainment." While film studios were avoiding explosive topics such as slave revolt, Tramis found herself in a world where fresh ideas were welcomed. A French citizen with a strong Antillean identity, Tramis aimed to integrate into games the history of her enslaved ancestors, which was discussed privately but not taught in schools. Indeed, Tramis notes that even in the twenty-first century, when US "universities are willingly studying slavery or African culture, in France, this does not happen." Tramis explained that "it is for this reason that the work of black French intellectuals [has been] important," in filling silences.[8]

Rather than seeing games as illegitimate media in which to explore these histories, Tramis determined that "books, film, and video games [were all appropriate] media in which to explain and keep the memory" of slavery.

Where other Caribbean intellectuals used traditional prose to explore this heritage, Tramis "chose interactive writing instead of novels because I wanted to express myself with the [technological] tools on which I had been trained." Her work shared much in common with peers who used print forms. Like Chamoiseau, Évelyne Trouillot, and other acclaimed Caribbean novelists, Tramis sought to overcome archival silences; she wanted to bring enslaved people to life by drawing from community memory rather than documents left by colonists. In addition, Tramis felt that Caribbean peoples must narrate stories about slavery themselves, to avoid the exploitation of this history by white artists such as Tarantino in 2012's *Django Unchained*.[9]

Before examining these games, we should recognize that it is no small achievement that, more than twenty-five years before the release of *AC Freedom Cry*, Tramis persuaded a French company to release a game that tasked players with kidnapping or slaying French colonists on the way to freedom. Tramis has credited Coktel founder Roland Oskian, a French citizen of Armenian descent, for giving her the freedom to tell stories about slavery—and those who resisted it—that she felt "deep in my guts." Oskian hired developers of every skin shade for Coktel. Tramis likened the creative latitude she found there to that which Woody Allen had for his films.[10] And because her games were cutting-edge narratively and visually, they were received positively by the company and by gamers.

For her first game, the interactive fiction/adventure *Méwilo*, Tramis tapped her old friend Chamoiseau as a collaborator.[11] At this time, Chamoiseau had written graphic novels and plays, and published his novel *Chroniques des sept misères* (1986). But he had not attained the renown he has today. Tramis was a fan of her friend's "metaphorical literary style" and felt that he was the right person to collaborate with. She notes that, "after some discussion," she and Chamoiseau settled on the topic of slavery for their creation: "[The game] should be about slavery because slavery had built us."[12]

Tramis's and Chamoiseau's choice was shaped by their identities as Antillean citizens of France. Where some young Caribbean professionals might have felt that they needed to choose integrationist topics while building a career with a metropolitan company, Tramis explains, "we were not ashamed [to choose slavery as the theme] because we had already settled the issue of our Creole identity." She adds that, while there was an abundant mythological literature on Greek, Roman, Arab, and Chinese heroes, she and Chamoiseau felt that there was a "great emptiness" (*vide*) with regard to that of French Caribbean peoples. The two were eager to reclaim the Creole heroes whose memory had been suppressed by colonialism, and to restore the humanity of Caribbean peoples for those unaware of this history. Tramis created and programmed *Méwilo*, something that was both challenging and liberating in an era with no precedent for such a game: "With just my computer science training, I worked only with intuition, because this game designer job did not exist yet. There was no guide, no recipe, no training. Everything had to be invented."[13]

Méwilo takes place in 1902 rather than the eighteenth century; unlike their later game, *Freedom*, which treats slave resistance in Saint-Domingue and other islands, *Méwilo* concerns only Martinique.[14] However, *Méwilo* still centers on slave revolt, exploring several themes that would recur in Chamoiseau's and Tramis's later works. Tramis tapped her friend Philippe Truca to collaborate on the illustrations. Chamoiseau wrote *Méwilo*'s dialogue in addition to a short story included in the game's manual.[15] Fans of Chamoiseau may spot him in the game; Truca drew the bespectacled writer as character Papa Echevin. Truca used his own likeness for Michel Hubert-Destouches, one of the game's *béké* protagonists (descendants of white colonists), though he himself was from metropolitan France. And Truca turned Tramis into Pélagie St-Just, the beautiful proprietor of a bird store (figure 10.1).[16]

Méwilo was a groundbreaking game not only in treating slavery, but also in being multimedia and multisensory. The game immersed players in Creole culture, requiring them to become familiar with Martinican history and culture to advance and win.[17] In addition to the game disk, *Méwilo*'s packaging included a cassette soundtrack by Martinican band Malavoi, to create an immersive Antillean experience; unlike for *AC Freedom Cry*, Malavoi's music was not mixed with a European score. *Méwilo*'s manual also contained multiple components. One was Chamoiseau's story, "Les derniers jours d'un mulâtresse" (The Final Days of a Mulatto Woman"), which offered more information about turn-of-the-century Martinique. Tramis wrote the other parts of the manual. These included a glossary of Creole expressions, a recipe for calalou (which was missing an ingredient that players needed to identify during the game), and the game's address on Minitel (an antecedent of the internet used widely in France of the 1980s).[18]

Méwilo also forced players to learn about other aspects of Antillean culture. To advance, players needed to answer several randomly generated questions. These ranged from identifying flora and fauna of the Antilles to knowing the date of France's abolition of slavery.[19] As game bloggers Oli and Ilmari Jauhiainen have commented, this feature may seem simplistic from a twenty-first-century vantage point, given the efficiency of search engines; however, in an era before Google, answering such questions was decidedly more challenging.[20] By

Figure 10.1. Muriel Tramis as Pélagie St-Just. *Méwilo.* © Coktel Vision, 1987. Screenshot, Atari ST version, courtesy of Ilmari Jauhiainen.

forcing players to leave the console and go to a well-stocked library—or *Méwilo*'s Minitel site—*Méwilo* was doing something pathbreaking.[21]

In setting the game in 1902, more than fifty years after abolition, Tramis and Chamoiseau made a different choice than would the creators of the games discussed in chapter 9. Though *Méwilo*'s gameplay does not unfold within the era of slavery, the duo emphasized the ever-present legacy of slavery in the Caribbean. *Méwilo* is set in northern Martinique, near Saint-Pierre, the site of a famous 1831 slave revolt.[22] Homeowners Geneviève and Michel Hubert-Destouches move into a plantation home inherited from their slaveowning ancestors, and discover a ghost in one bedroom and a *zombi* haunting the grounds. The gamer plays as a paranormal psychologist hired by Geneviève and Michel to investigate why the house is haunted and to end these disturbances. To solve the mystery and free the ghostly souls from torment, players must travel through northern Martinique, interacting with different residents.

Several components of *Méwilo* stressed the enduring weight of slavery on the lives of those in the post-emancipation Caribbean. For one thing, the haunting turns out to have resulted from a crime committed by one of Geneviève's ancestors. During the 1831 revolt, the game's story goes, French colonist Arnaud de Ronan tasked an enslaved person named Méwilo with hiding his riches to keep them away from rebels. However, consumed with fear after discovering slaves' rebellious spirit, Arnaud worried that Méwilo would reveal the treasure's location. As soon as Méwilo finished burying it, therefore, Arnaud murdered him. Players need to solve this mystery, and to realize that Méwilo is the *zombi* haunting the grounds, while Arnaud is the ghost wracked with guilt.[23]

Not only is the Hubert-Destouches home literally haunted by slavery's horrors, but the game's characters reference this past continually. An elderly Martinican named Alcipe Condette (descended from the leader of the 1831 revolt, who is suggestively named Makandal) tells the player that little has changed since 1848. Referring to the fact that descendants of enslaved people often found themselves working on the same plantations as their ancestors, for less than subsistence wages, Condette cries, "People say, 'Abolition, Abolition!' What has changed? I am still the Béké's *nègre*" (figure 10.2). In contrast, plantation owner Laurent de Banville, a descendant of the de Ronans, laments that free blacks no longer want to cut cane: "Blacks (*nègres*) do not want to work the land anymore! Luckily, we can get contracts with *coolies*" (a derogatory name for laborers imported from India after 1848).[24]

Another way Chamoiseau and Tramis highlighted slavery's harmful legacy was through rum. A character named Clarisse instructs the player to obtain key information from a seer named Papa Echevin, the character with Chamoiseau's likeness. But Clarisse adds that Echevin "will not move his tongue" unless the player brings rum to quench his thirst. This might seem a playful joke by Chamoiseau about his love for Martinique's most famous beverage. Commenting on this line of dialogue, the blogger Ilmari asked, "What is it with French games encouraging abuse of alcohol?"[25] However, Tramis has explained that Echevin's request for rum was neither a joke nor a sign of Gallic love for alcohol. Rather, the developers inserted rum into *Méwilo* to symbolize the injustices left by the slave trade: "The agricultural rum . . . for which the French Antilles are famed comes from the sugar cultivation which has produced misery for black people. It was in order to grow sugar that Africans were deported to the Caribbean. And it is this same rum which then permits blacks to drown their sorrows."[26]

Though *Méwilo* did not obtain the multimillion-dollar sales figures of an *Age of Empires* or *Assassin's Creed* title (games were less embedded in popular culture in the 1980s than in the 2000s, and fewer people owned consoles), the game was a success for its time. As one Parisian gaming magazine declared, "Sweeping aside . . . enduring clichés about the Antilles ([for instance, that its residents are] naive, dancing creatures), *Méwilo* represents a true immersion into the Antillean soul. . . . The complex social hierarchy and power relations between different elements of the population are skillfully revealed." The gaming magazine *Génération4* called *Méwilo* "original and educational."

Figure 10.2. Alcipe Condette talks about continuing injustices after emancipation. *Méwilo.* © Coktel Vision, 1987. Screenshot, Atari ST version, courtesy of Ilmari Jauhiainen.

Though *Génération4*'s reviewers found the game better suited for beginners than advanced gamers, they called it a "success" for introducing the culture of a "sadly unknown" part of France and for taking gamers beyond the usual adventure-game terrain of "castles and ships." *Méwilo*, *Génération4* explained, carries players "into a troubling [world of] mystery where the abuses of slavery, abolished only recently . . . are still very present in the memory of those who suffered from them."[27]

The first video game by French Caribbean developers, *Méwilo* elevated Tramis's reputation. It won a Médaille d'argent from the City of Paris, an award bestowed for remarkable acts or services. The game also attracted positive attention in Germany, where Tramis appeared on television. *Méwilo* received a further publicity boost when the Conseil Général de la Martinique (the equivalent of an US state legislature) sponsored a gaming contest for it, the "Prix de la Liberté." As part of Antillean commemorations of the French Revolution's Bicentennial, the contest aimed to build excitement about computing in the Antilles. Tramis later reflected that the contest was "a sign that [the release of] *Méwilo* was perceived as a major event," marking a "local girl bringing home honors for Martinique." A similar competition was held for the game in Paris.[28]

Fresh from this success, Tramis, Chamoiseau, and Truca collaborated in 1988 on a second slavery-related game for Coktel, *Freedom: Rebels in the Darkness* (called *Freedom: Les Guerriers de l'ombre* in French). In contrast to *Méwilo*, which took place wholly in twentieth-century Martinique, *Freedom* was broader in its geographic scope and more daring in its setting. Where *Méwilo* dealt with slavery's legacy from the vantage point of the twentieth century, *Freedom* was set at the height of the plantation era. It tasked players with organizing a slave revolt and possibly killing colonists, rather than simply learning about a slave revolt from a seventy-year distance. Where *Méwilo* looked at slavery's painful legacy, *Freedom: Rebels* asked players to act out enslaved people's "desire to escape from a cruel and unbearable situation."[29]

Tramis designed *Freedom: Rebels in the Darkness* as a "war game" to honor her ancestors. She told journalist Tristan Donovan, "Fugitive slaves, my ancestors, were true warriors that I had to pay tribute to." Pointing to the disparity between commemorations of slavery today in France and the silence that reigned in the 1980s, she commented that *Freedom* was a means for her to "speak" on the subject: "At the time I made the game, these stories were not known because they were hidden. Today, the official recognition of slavery as a crime against humanity [in the Taubira Law] has changed the world, people are aware now. . . . At a time when the subject was still painful [it] was my duty to remember."[30]

Where *Méwilo* had been released only in French and German, Coktel funded *Freedom*'s release in these languages as well as English and Spanish. Tramis conceived the game, led the design team, and wrote the manual. Graphics were done by Truca, Yannick Chosse, and Kaki Chapouillié, and programming by Roland Lacoste. Just as for *Méwilo*, Tramis tapped Chamoiseau to write the game's dialogue and text boxes (figure 10.3). The game was released in several now-obsolete formats: Commodore Amiga, Atari ST, Amstrad CPC, and DOS.[31]

Once these consoles became obsolete and Windows supplanted DOS, *Freedom* fell out of usage. However, gamers began to rediscover it in the twenty-first century. As early as 2007, gamers began uploading screenshots of *Freedom* to sites like MobyGames. In 2014, a Greek YouTuber uploaded two walk-throughs, played on different systems.[32] *Freedom: Rebels in the Darkness* was further rescued from oblivion in 2015 when Phil Salvador, a game enthusiast and librarian, blogged about its Amiga version. The following year, game aficionado Anatoly Shashkin recovered a DOS version and posted it to the Internet Archive.[33]

Consequently, even though playing *Freedom* on its original platforms is impossible for most people, the playing experience can be approximated in other ways. It can be emulated on PCs using the files Shashkin posted at the Internet Archive, and the game's code can be downloaded there.[34] French and UK versions of the manual remain accessible, either digitized on gaming sites

Figure 10.3. Title screen with credits. *Freedom: Rebels in the Darkness*. © Coktel Vision, 1988. Screenshot, French version, Amstrad CPC, MobyGames.

or from collectors.[35] My analysis draws upon all of these sources, as well as information provided by Tramis.

To twenty-first-century eyes, *Freedom*'s graphics may appear old-fashioned, especially compared to the state-of-the-art animation and epic-cinema style of *AC Freedom Cry*. However, it is important to recall that technology was far less advanced in the 1980s. Tramis notes that Truca's pixel art "was remarkable [at the time] because there were so many constraints imposed by the computers of that era." In addition, where Ubisoft spends $10–100 million or more developing *Assassin's Creed* titles, Coktel had much smaller budgets. *Freedom* also did not make as much of a splash as *Méwilo*; a year after *Méwilo*'s innovations, reviews for *Freedom* were more mixed. *Amiga Computing*'s reviewer found *Freedom* "engrossing," while the reviewer for *Computer + Video Games* found its design "somewhat lacking." As technology changed in the early 1990s, *Freedom* stopped being issued for new systems; Tramis left pixel art behind and turned to newer forms of animation for *Lost in Time*.[36] In retrospect, however, the game's concept appears more radical.

Unlike *Méwilo*, *Freedom: Rebels in the Darkness* does not specify on which French Caribbean isle it takes place; it announces simply that it is set on a plantation in the eighteenth-century Antilles. Still, the game has a clear link to Saint-Domingue: one of the four playable character choices (two women and two men) is Makandal, the most iconic symbol of slave resistance in

Saint-Domingue before Boukman. Offering a different view of him than in *AC Liberation*, Tramis and Chamoiseau resuscitate Makandal so that he can again fight the slaveowners of Saint-Domingue—and of the entire French Caribbean.

Tramis included female avatars—the Guadeloupian rebel Solitude and a maroon named Délia—because she wanted players to appreciate the fighting spirit of enslaved women as well as men.[37] "I did not want people to think," she notes, "that the fight for freedom was only the concern of men." The decision was reinforced by Tramis's temperament as a "feminist militant," forged from needing to prove herself in the male-dominated worlds of engineering and computer science. In addition, Tramis felt it was essential to include Haitian rebels alongside those from the other French Antilles: "The heroes of Martinique, Haiti, or any colonized island of the Caribbean have a common destiny: they all fought for their freedom. It is not useful to make distinctions." With Makandal, Solitude, Sechou, or Délia as avatars, a player can choose which island to play from—or rise in pan-Antillean solidarity for all enslaved peoples.[38]

Freedom's manual and opening scenes offer more information on the game's setting. The manual explains that the game takes place on an extremely profitable plantation, Grand Parnasse. Despite its ostensible flourishing, "sometimes violent nocturnal outbreaks arise . . . the slaves revolt." The player is told, "You are the leader of the rebellion and, at the head of your group, you are trying to make a heroic escape towards Freedom" (emphasis in original).[39] The game then begins with the sound of drums and an opening frame designed to look like a parchment document, which explains the game's setting:

> Night is falling over the prosperous Grand Parnasse plantation. The slaves, under their supervisor's thumb, have left the carts of cane and gone back to their huts. Meanwhile, the owner sips his rum on the veranda and the director rubs his hands [with glee]; the plantation makes a considerable profit. The accountant finishes his records; there are 200 casks of sugar piled up in the buildings. [But] the supervisor is worried. The lashes of his whip are no longer enough to keep the rhythm in the fields. The wind of rebellion is blowing over [Black Shack Alley]! But who would dare become the leader of a rebellion?[40]

Freedom asks players to choose a skill level: How rebellious do they wish to be (Rebellious, Defiant, or Fanatical)? Next, players choose an avatar and receive an overview of the plantation hierarchy.

With this background, players receive a map and begin to explore Grand Parnasse. In a superficial sense, movement around the map resembles that

Figure 10.4. Setting fire to a hut. *Freedom: Rebels in the Darkness.* © Coktel Vision, 1988. Screenshot, English version, Amiga, MobyGames.

in *Pac-Man*—but without whimsical music or dots to consume. Instead, the drums alternate with the sound of menacing dogs barking, as the player searches for others willing to join a revolution. The overseers use dogs to control slaves; they are players' main obstacle in trying to spark a revolution.

In making dogs a mortal danger, something absent from *AC Freedom Cry*, Chamoiseau and Tramis were referencing the use of dogs as ferocious slave hunters throughout the Americas. Enslaved people's fear of these creatures would later become a key theme of Chamoiseau's novel *L'esclave vieil homme et le molosse* (The Old Slave Man and the Mastiff). That work's antagonist was a mastiff described as a "monster"; its "terrifying tracking" skills and thirst for blood foiled the plans of would-be maroons. The novel described the plantation's other dogs as "barbarous" creatures who "amused themselves by chomping on one of the house slaves. . . . The slaves hated these dogs in a way that can no longer be imagined."[41] The inclusion of these beasts made the game much more historically realistic than *AC Freedom Cry*.

As players move around the plantation, hoping to be noticed by neither mastiffs nor colonists, they must develop a strategy: they may look for other enslaved people to join with them, or begin sabotage activities alone. These can include setting the plantation afire (figure 10.4) or picking locks and breaking into buildings. If players stumble upon a colonist, a duel ensues. If they defeat him, they have a choice of holding him hostage or executing him;

they also get his weapon and live to continue the rebellion. However, if they lose, the dogs are unleashed and the game ends. Players can also confront the plantation owner directly at the big house. As the code and screenshots suggest, it is likely that players will lose if they seek to confront their enslaver; they will be told, "You have grown too weak and the master is invincible. You are quickly captured, whipped and condemned to have your bones broken by a hammer, without having [last] Rites."[42]

If players encounter others before being discovered by dogs or colonists, they can invite them to join the Revolution. Some of Grand Parnasse's enslaved people are overjoyed to learn of a possible uprising. One field hand declares, "Yes, we're ready to die for our freedom. We'll go with you." Similarly, a craftsman says, "Yes! You need our strength to win your freedom. Take us with you!"[43] But most others, terrorized by the plantation's brutality, are more apprehensive. A different field hand says, "Oh no! Just what kind of trouble are you trying to get us into? Aren't our lives miserable enough?"[44] A house slave named Timolet—who, like Echevin in *Méwilo*, is Chamoiseau's spitting image—exclaims, "Oh no! I can't betray the master who is so good to me" (figure 10.5).[45] When playing as Solitude or Délia, players encounter another enslaved person, Aimable, who responds, "Oh no! Freedom holds nothing tender for us. Running is dangerous, sister!"[46]

Freedom: Rebels in the Darkness also offered a glimpse into colonists' mentalities by including racist dialogue from plantation whites. The game contained two priests, Père Labat (a real cleric who helped spur the Martinican sugar industry and also spent time in Saint-Domingue) and the abbé de l'Etang. Unlike the kindly priest in the *Toussaint Louverture* miniseries—or the Presbyterian minister who is the only cleric in *Mission US: Flight to Freedom*—these Catholics illustrated the Church's backing of slavery. When the abbé de l'Etang discovers a player planning revolt, he rails at them, "Oh sweet Jesus! God is looking at you and judging you at this moment, my negroes!" Père Labat has even less regard for enslaved people's humanity; against the kind of Christian universalism espoused by the French abolitionist priest abbé Grégoire, Labat cries, "Dear n***s, the Holy Spirit has told me about this crazy undertaking of yours."[47]

Freedom included fewer textual elements than *Méwilo*, and its manual was more straightforward, with no short story, recipes, or Minitel site. However, pan-Antillean Creole culture was integrated into the game in a few ways. The rebel plays under time pressure; the Revolution has to succeed under cover of darkness, before the break of dawn. If players are doing well, they can get some assistance. Manman-Dlo, a water spirit called Mamiwata in parts of

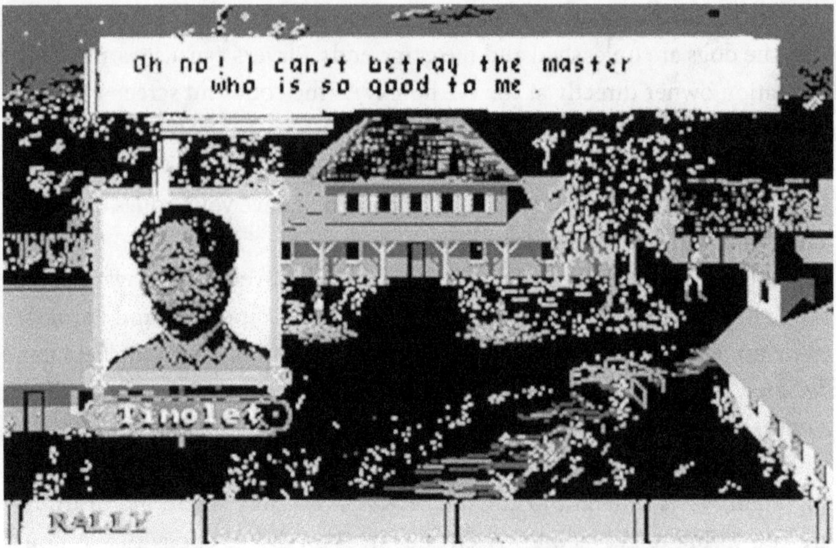

Figure 10.5. Patrick Chamoiseau as a field hand reluctant to join the revolt. *Freedom: Rebels in the Darkness*. © Coktel Vision, 1988. Screenshot, English version, DOS, MobyGames.

Africa, and La Sirène or La Baleine in Haitian Vodou, will turn back the clock to give players more time.[48]

Although many gamers report having had only losing outcomes, with game-over messages pervading uploaded screenshots, walk-through videos, and blog comments,[49] *Freedom*'s code does allow for the possibility of winning. If players defeat the plantation owner in a duel, they can be told: "VICTORY! You fought heroically and have beaten the owner. The dogs are going mad and the troops are getting nowhere. You can walk down the road to Freedom without turning back!" Alternately, if they burn down the plantation without alerting the dogs, a message would read "VICTORY! You've reached the road to Freedom! The owner is crying over his devastated plantation. Never again will you know slavery. You're free!"[50] The game's manual outlined specific conditions by which the game can be won. Either the plantation owner must be killed, or players must kill all dogs and then either destroy a certain percentage of the cane fields and buildings or persuade at least 75 percent of the plantation's enslaved people to join the Revolution.[51]

It seems more likely, however, that players will lose. In contrast to Ubisoft's designers, Tramis and Chamoiseau emphasized the very real obstacles their ancestors had to overcome as they dreamed of freedom. Convincing enslaved people to risk torture and join the Revolution, not being discovered by ferocious dogs, and winning every fight against colonists who are better fed and not exhausted from work proves daunting.[52]

If the dogs are unleashed on players, the game's most likely outcome, they learn their gruesome fate. Echoing the horrifying punishments offered by French slave codes, one message explains, "It's an unfair fight. You don't have the same weapon as your adversary. You are immediately captured, whipped and condemned to have your feet and legs burned and to be buried alive." Another announces, "The pipiri bird is singing. It's dawn! The plantation wakes up and the troops come running. You are quickly captured, imprisoned, whipped and condemned to have your ears cut off and a lys flower tattooed on your shoulder."[53] While these are horrific outcomes, they mirror what happened to rebellious slaves much more than in *AC Freedom Cry*, where Adéwalé simply is told "Game Over" and permitted to restart a game chapter if he fails to kill enough overseers.

Twenty-first-century gamers who have discovered *Freedom* have been extremely enthusiastic. Phil Salvador declared in 2016, after the DOS version was located, that "this is an enormously historically significant game with major implications for the discussion of race and intersectionality in gaming history." Salvador explained why he found this 1988 game amazing:

> The world continues to grapple with the aftermath of the Western slave trade. As the recent challenges to removing the Confederate Flag from public spaces demonstrate, we still often don't know how to discuss or even acknowledge Western civilization's deep history of racial division. . . . The gaming world's well-publicized dismissiveness towards diversity concerns makes it generally inhospitable to socially charged, historically conscious work.
>
> In these circumstances, the existence of *Freedom: Rebels in the Darkness* . . . is a miracle.

The blogger Ilmari noted that historical games usually forced him to "take the unjust side," which made him feel uneasy. *Freedom: Rebels* was different: "Just let me play a rebel who will throw away her chains, cut the throat of her oppressors and lead her enslaved people to freedom and I am hooked." In addition to these enthusiasts, Tramis is frequently contacted by gamers, from Europe to Japan, who express their love for the game. In the wake of slavery being more discussed in France, Tramis noted, many players seem eager to "incarnate a slave who is fighting for his freedom." Tramis's body of work has also been rediscovered by French Game Studies scholars Sebastian Genvo and Alexis Blanchet.[54]

Tramis also has been acclaimed for her third slavery-related game, the science fiction puzzler *Lost in Time*. That game was innovative in 1993 in blending live action and animation, and for integrating film clips into gameplay to create the interactive multimedia experience that twenty-first-century players take for granted. *Lost in Time*'s plot paralleled Ellen Holly's never-made Christophe film and *Sankofa*—not to mention the French comedy *Case départ*[55]—in depicting slavery through a time-travel device. *Lost in Time* concerned a mixed-race French woman named Doralice, sucked back from 1992 to the era of slavery to meet her ancestors.[56] Here also, Makandal and Délia made cameos, as enslaved healers on the game's fictional island of St. Cristobald who help Doralice mix potions.

Despite vintage game aficionados' admiration, the number of gamers who have access to these games today is small. Given the enthusiasm of those who have rediscovered *Freedom* and *Méwilo*, Tramis has indicated that she would be eager to remake them if she had funding. She has specific plans for improving both. With today's technology, she would "reinforce the strategic and tactical aspects that are somewhat limited in that version" [of *Freedom*]. She would also offer "a greater choice of characters with varied talents" as well as different "means of attack and defenses." In addition, she would add cinematic cutscenes, like those she introduced in *Lost in Time* and that have since become standard, to "pace the progression and [give] more interactivity in the encounters between characters." Tramis also would work with historians and ethno-sociologists to add more authenticity to both games, building on her collaborations with archaeologists on 3D projects.[57]

Tramis laments, however, that she does not have the resources that Ubisoft does. "With the state of computer graphics today," she muses, "one could do wonders with animation and special effects." Tramis wishes that she could hire Kendy Joseph, the Haitian graphic artist who created *Noir et Blanc* (chapter 8), to create a new look for *Freedom*. She also dreams of being able to redevelop the game along the model of *World of Warcraft*, a multiplayer online role-playing game (MMORPG). She imagines that players could "play on a larger scale," planning uprisings "not just [on] one plantation but several. At the beginning, one would be alone and the aim would be to trigger insurrections throughout the country until the enemy surrenders. Wouldn't it be nice to have the cooperation of players from around the world, all united to free a country from colonial domination?" Tramis is also considering a new slavery-related game to replace *Méwilo* and *Freedom*.[58]

♦ ♦ ♦

In the last two chapters, we have examined several interactive games depicting slavery or slave revolt in Haiti and elsewhere. In chapter 9, I argued that *AC Freedom Cry* surpassed other games by North American and European developers in leading players to empathize with Saint-Dominguans who challenged the slave system. In this chapter, I have argued that Tramis's and Chamoiseau's games were even better than *Freedom Cry*. For Tramis and Chamoiseau, the Antilles were not an abstract site, read about in history books, where a foreign company could set an edgy game featuring a nonwhite protagonist. The history in their games was personal. At a time when official narratives silenced the history of slavery, the pair spoke, through code and text, of the traumas and humanity of enslaved peoples. These games popularized Tramis's and Chamoiseau's ideas for players who would never read their analog writings.

Like *AC Freedom Cry*, Tramis's and Chamoiseau's *Freedom* also showed that it is possible to depict eighteenth-century slave revolt in the French Caribbean respectfully, and in more historically complex ways than in most foreign films discussed in this book. Both games honored Antillean women who challenged slavery alongside men. Both highlighted slave resistance throughout the eighteenth century, without suggesting that enslaved people began resisting only after contact with French ideals of freedom. In the Tramis/Chamoiseau games as well as in *Assassin's Creed*, freedom is a natural longing, common to all humans, not a buzzword circulated by the French Revolution; this is perhaps why the game's French title used the English word *Freedom*, rather than the French *liberté* (*Freedom: Les guerriers de l'ombre*). Most importantly, *AC Freedom Cry* and the ahead-of-their-time Tramis/Chamoiseau games made clear that it is possible to create depictions of the Haitian Revolution and of slave revolt that do not feature white heroes—and for audiences of all colors not to fear them, but to purchase them.

CONCLUSION

In 1952, 20th Century Fox (under Darryl Zanuck) released *Lydia Bailey*, a film that explored issues of race through the prism of Haiti's revolution. In 1968, 20th Century Fox (under Darryl's son Richard) would release *Planet of the Apes*, a film that explored issues of race through the prism of interspecies conflict. Unlike the quickly forgotten *Lydia*, that film would enter the Hollywood pantheon, with numerous sequels and remakes. In sixteen years, Fox had moved from justifying Black violence against white oppression to evoking Black Power as a terrifying specter, via science fiction. As Eric Greene has noted, *Planet of the Apes* (which drew on historically racist tropes linking Blacks and primates) was released just as "the racial power dynamics of the United States were under sustained, often furious, attack." From 1952 to 1968, African American challenges to white supremacy—whether peaceful à la Martin Luther King Jr. or "by any means necessary" like Malcolm X—had frightened many US whites. The contrast between the dystopian view of Black Power in *Planet of the Apes* and the dearth of epics on the Haitian Revolution did not escape the attention of Chris Rock's André Allen in *Top Five*.[1]

Anxieties about race made *Lydia Bailey* Hollywood's last film about Toussaint and the Revolution. Since then, as we have seen, Revolution-related films have been made outside Hollywood, with relatively small budgets. Most Revolution-related feature films (especially in the US and Europe) have downplayed the revolutionaries' agency and humanity. Though some better films exist from the Caribbean, they have treated the Revolution only indirectly. I have also identified films by Haitians that treat the revolutionaries more thoroughly and sympathetically, even while noting the internecine conflicts among them. Haitian films on the Revolution, however, have found far smaller audiences than *Burn!*, the *Toussaint Louverture* miniseries, or even *Égalité for All*. Many who would be interested in these films are not aware that they exist.

In considering the relative invisibility of the Haitian Revolution on the big screen, I have explored structural issues. These include *mentalités* that have rendered the Haitian Revolution frightening to many, though not all, whites, as well as funding systems. As Joe Feagin has noted, "The corporations that now control Hollywood's moviemaking and the other US mass media are increasingly in charge of global education. Something like half of Europe's entertainment programs . . . are based on US sources. . . . Growing billions of the world's peoples now get their entertainment from US movies, television programs and videos."[2] Despite their far-reaching influence on global popular culture and understandings of history, these corporations have not viewed the Revolution as an appealing subject. The Revolution's story, of enslaved Africans liberating themselves through violent struggle, does not fit the suffering-slaves-waiting-for-a-white-hero genre prevalent in Hollywood. I have argued that the unwillingness to fund films on the Revolution exemplifies a more general fear of greenlighting scripts about slave revolt (and Black History in general) that lack a white savior.

While I was working on this book, two films seemed poised to break these patterns. The first was Nate Parker's independently financed but studio-distributed 2016 film *The Birth of a Nation*. *Birth*, a stunning epic about the Nat Turner insurrection, received rave reviews and a rare standing ovation at the Sundance Film Festival. The film's reception suggested that white film insiders, sensitive to #OscarsSoWhite complaints and prepared by *12 Years a Slave*, could be willing to view a serious picture on slave revolt. It also indicated that, with evidence of audience interest and a compelling film, producers could fund it. *Vox* noted that "*The Birth of a Nation* is brutal and unflinching in its depiction of how slaves were treated. . . . Inside the theater [at Sundance], the response . . . was so ecstatic that a follow-up standing ovation began the minute the credits started to roll." *Variety* declared that "the response . . . was seismic and the Oscar buzz erupted as soon as the lights went up." *Birth* subsequently received a $17.5 million distribution deal from Fox Searchlight, the biggest in Sundance history.[3]

From *Lydia Bailey* . . . to *Planet of the Apes* to . . . the Nat Turner revolt? *Birth* showed the evolution of a studio like Fox, with a film that neither Zanuck (father or son) would have made. *Birth* featured enslaved protagonists, presenting their struggles sympathetically. It neither hid the brutality of slavery nor featured a white hero. Even the film's seemingly "kind" slaveowner proved violent and willing to subject his slaves to rape.[4]

Beyond Sundance, however, the film found far less success. *Birth* was ultimately deemed a flop, earning back less than its production and distribution costs. It ostensibly failed because Parker himself had been accused of rape in real life, something publicized ahead of the film's release; *Birth* faced separate criticism for its lack of strict fidelity to the details of Nat Turner's story. Of course, the white actor Casey Affleck was not punished by audiences that year despite similar allegations, and even received an Oscar. *New York Times* film critic A. O. Scott, who called *The Birth of a Nation* a "powerful" glimpse into the "everyday wickedness of 19th-century slavery," correctly predicted that the film would be the "must-see and won't-see" film of the year. White audiences seemed to take the controversy over Parker as license not to see a film that threatened to be disturbing.[5]

A second film that suggested a possible smashing of Hollywood patterns was Ryan Coogler's 2018 *Black Panther*. The film, starring the magisterial Chadwick Boseman, was heralded (as *Lydia Bailey* had been in 1952) as a milestone in Hollywood treatments of African Americans. In contrast to *Birth*, *Black Panther* was 2018's top-grossing film and one of the most successful of all time; it earned more than a billion dollars worldwide.[6]

The film represented progress in myriad ways and was embraced by audiences of color as well as whites. Boseman's title character (Black Panther/T'Challa) was a smart, kind, and fierce head of state who commands an impressive African army. Boseman gave Black audiences their first true superhero, shattering Hollywood formulas that have made violent Black men into nefarious bogeymen.

Nevertheless, despite the film's importance in so many ways, it retained a number of tropes we have discussed. Indeed, the film had built-in plot points that preempted white fears about such a protagonist. First, in contrast to the lack of white heroes in *Birth*, white audiences could feel comfortable in *Black Panther* since they knew that T'Challa had many white pals. Indeed, the Black Panther character was not new to action film and comic book fans, but a familiar friend to Marvel's white superheroes. Black Panther, who had appeared in other Marvel comic books and films as a supporting character, was in fact one of the last members of the Marvel Cinematic Universe to receive his own film.[7]

Second, the film featured Black Panther battling with the help of a friendly white CIA agent. Such a character would be preposterous in a Haitian context, given the CIA's record of supporting antidemocratic death squads there.[8] More generally, as the scholar Robyn C. Spencer has noted, making the CIA agent appear as a benign friend eager to help Africans conceals the organization's "well documented role in political repression, surveillance and disruption of foreign governments and murder of leaders" in Africa and elsewhere.[9]

Third, T'Challa does not fight against whites but other Blacks. Rather than seeking justice for African-descended peoples, he faces off against—and ultimately kills—a Black anti-hero (Killmonger) trying to do just that. Killmonger sees himself as avenging centuries of oppression against Blacks, against a less political T'Challa who wants peace with whites. As C. C. Saunders has noted, the battle between these two men "makes the film accessible to whites—as depicted in the dissonant phrase 'black on black crime.'" As historian Russell Rickford has pointed out, Killmonger "is depicted as deranged and his plot to arm those Frantz Fanon called 'the wretched of the earth' is cast as a bitter crusade for vengeance rather than as a rational response to the horrors of white supremacy and imperialism." While it is true that many African Americans (including Boseman) had a counter-reading of the film, in which Killmonger is more sympathetic than T'Challa because of his pursuit of social justice, such a reading did not predominate among white audiences or critics. As Grégory Pierrot has summed up Killmonger's place in the film: "Killmonger [who was trained by the CIA] wants to turn the master's tools against the master's house. . . . [He] cannot be allowed to be too sympathetic: he can ask the right questions but cannot possibly provide the right answers." The film, in Pierrot's view, necessitates Killmonger's death, since it would be too disturbing to the "international racial order" were viewers expected to cheer his victory over the more conciliatory T'Challa.[10]

In addition to the thundering acclaim for Boseman, the film's brilliant and fearless Black female characters drew further praise. The film reminded producers of the purchasing power of Black moviegoers and suggested that non-Black audiences worldwide would see at least some films with Black protagonists. Unfortunately, however, *Black Panther* did not reveal a complete upending of the patterns that I have discussed.

If Hollywood still has difficulty handling story lines like the Haitian Revolution's, what about other film hubs? Given the 2001 Taubira Law in France recognizing slavery as a crime against humanity, one might expect film funders there to be more willing to greenlight such a project. The existence of the *Toussaint Louverture* miniseries certainly indicated the stirrings of change, a desire to better acknowledge the history of French slavery. As I discussed in chapter 1, however, that film was deeply problematic in denying the brutality and racism of the slave system. Though better films on the Haitian Revolution (primarily television documentaries) have been made in France, many still exalt white abolitionists and liberating French ideals, rather than the agency of Africans. In the Netherlands, 2013's *Tula: The Revolt* (the Curaçao-made film produced with some Dutch crew and financing) showed at least some interest in funding an epic about the Haitian Revolution's Caribbean effects. The film was compelling in many ways, as one of the only feature films about slave revolt, and one that led audiences to root for enslaved people seeking freedom. However, Dutch audiences largely avoided the film, and the producers—after garnering acclaim at several international festivals—were unable to show it widely. While European countries have done much in the last decade to acknowledge their histories as slaveholding countries, plots highlighting the agency of enslaved people, rather than the kindness of abolitionists, still seem too radical to many funders and audiences.

As I have noted, creative young Haitians are more than willing to fill the gap left by the US and European film industries. However, Haitian filmmakers (particularly those working inside the country rather than the diaspora) have difficulty funding their works. Internal and external forces—from the legacy of French colonialism to the US occupation, the rise of the Duvaliers, and the 2010 earthquake—have combined to impoverish Haiti.[11] The NGO system, created ostensibly to help Haiti, has further damaged the country. As Claire Payton has shown, this system, created in Haiti by US diplomat Melville Osborne in 1965, "produced a 'parallel state'" that weakens Haitian institutions. As Raoul Peck, Mark Schuller, Jonathan Katz, and others have illustrated, government by a "republic of NGOs" proved particularly deadly after the 2010 earthquake.[12]

While the NGO system has had less deadly effects in cinema than in earthquake reconstruction, it still disrupts Haitians' ability to represent themselves to others. Without state cinema institutions, artists in Haiti are dependent on the same patchwork of foreign NGOs. And, as Doris Posch has indicated, NGOs prefer to fund PR films highlighting their benevolence, rather than support Haitians' perspectives on the past and present.[13] Haitians working inside the country thus suffer a kind of cinematic neocolonialism. They can resign themselves to letting wealthy foreigners define their history on screen, or they can try to make films representing Haiti to the world—but only if foreign NGOs or other funders find the content appealing.[14]

While this problem is particularly severe in Haiti, Haitians are not the only formerly colonized people with limited film capital. As Olivier Barlet has argued, funding inequities also shape African cinema; the French agencies that offer grants to African filmmakers have enormous power over which stories reach the screen. Ella Shohat and Robert Stam point out that "Western festivals, critics and funding agencies remain the gate-keepers and literally the 'judges' of world cinema. . . . The cultural centers of the 'Global North' hold the key that opens the door to artists from the 'Global South.'" A few countries like India or Nigeria, with more robust economies and much larger domestic viewing populations, have been able to create film industries rivaling those of

Hollywood or Paris. But they remain exceptions compared to other formerly colonized countries.[15]

The Haitian case thus reminds us of a more general truth: Long after political decolonization, former colonizing nations have greater ability to recount the history of slavery and colonialism on screen than most formerly colonized peoples. Indeed, optimism in Media Studies scholarship about digital technologies' ability to disrupt the power of conglomerates[16] applies more to countries where home computer systems and reliable electricity are widespread than to countries like Haiti where they are not. This postcolonial imbalance is especially problematic given that, as Vera and Gordon have noted, "much of what we know about people we consider to be 'others' we learn through the movies."[17]

Though I have focused on difficulties raising funds for films on the Revolution, we have also seen alternative representations on screen, from an industry in which funding is less of a problem. Video game companies, beginning with Coktel in the 1980s and extending recently to Ubisoft and others, have gone where film studios fear to tread, depicting Haitians and others of African descent rising up against oppressive white enslavers. In part III, I described some horrendous games on the topic of slavery. But I also presented more compelling games, such as those by the Martinican intellectuals Muriel Tramis and Patrick Chamoiseau. Tramis's and Chamoiseau's games anticipated the drive to tell diverse stories in video games by decades, and dispensed with white heroes; they focused on enslaved people's resistance as well as on constraints thwarting their yearnings for freedom. Their games were forgotten, even though *Assassin's Creed: Freedom Cry* later made headlines for treating slave revolt.

In the wake of *Freedom Cry*'s success, game companies seem to have embraced a new archetype, the Haitian revolutionary. Since *Freedom Cry*'s 2013 release, several new games have featured brave and likeable Haitian characters fighting for justice. Rockstar Games' *Red Dead Redemption* 2, released in late 2018, broke game industry records, earning $725 million in sales in its opening weekend alone.[18] Though the game takes place in the 1890s and 1900s, it had several Revolution-inspired components. *Red Dead Redemption* 2's protagonists, a gang of American outlaws on the run, sail to the Caribbean and wash up on an "old sugar plantation island . . . east of Cuba." Though the fictional island is called Guarma, and its evil rulers are Spanish, its terrain resembles Haiti's. Soon after arriving, the outlaws are captured by Guarma's dictator, Antonio Fussar—until a Haitian named Hercule Fontaine rescues them. Hercule, embodying the tradition of Haitian revolutionary heroes rising against slavery, has begun an "insurrection." He and his comrades seek to free other Haitians who have been trafficked to this island and are enduring terrible conditions on sugar plantations. Voiced by Haitian actor Guyviaud Joseph, Hercule is a kind of "Black hero" rescuing the gang—who then repay the favor, killing Fussar's henchmen to free other Haitian rebels. During the gang's tensest moments in Guarma, they hole up at a fortress resembling the Citadelle;[19] the outlaws are trying to reach a boat that will take them from Guarma, while Hercule is trying to help the unfortunate plantation laborers return to Haiti. Facing off against a larger and stronger army, Hercule and the outlaws kill Fussar, then part as friends.[20]

In addition, Blizzard Entertainment's blockbuster game *Overwatch* (which, as *Variety* notes, "topped 40 million players and . . . raked in more than a billion dollars in revenue" in 2018) added a Haitian character in 2019. *Overwatch* is more superficial than *Freedom Cry* or *Red Dead Redemption 2*, with less narrative content, but it features a Haitian character, Jean-Baptiste Augustin (Baptiste for short), a medic and ex-mercenary. Blizzard explains that "Baptiste now uses his skills to help those whose lives have been impacted by war."[21] Another recent game, 2019's *Anno 1800*, developed by Blue Byte and distributed by Ubisoft, includes a former slave colony named "High Mountain" (a translation of the Arawak/Taino word *Ayiti*). The game features an African-descended nonplayable character from High Mountain named Jean La Fortune. La Fortune's in-game bio tells players that he "escaped a life of slavery to become the leader of a fledgling nation on the isle his people call High Mountain. But his people cannot hope to grow while the Empire refuses to recognise their independence. With few allies in society, it seems Jean has little choice left but to fight."[22] These games mark a new direction for depictions of Haiti, in which Haitians are celebrated as brave warriors rather than marked as criminals or savages. This new image is particularly remarkable considering that Haitian appearances in games were typified previously by Rockstar's *Grand Theft Auto Vice City* (2002). That game featured Haitians as gang members stealing cars, as rival Cuban gangs exhorted the player to "KILL THE HAITIANS!"[23]

The success of these new games illustrates, like *Black Panther*, that there is a far greater market for content featuring Black heroes than studios had thought. Indeed, the reception of *Freedom Cry* illustrates that, for young audiences at least, Haitian characters engaged in retributive justice against oppressive whites are not problematic, as long as audiences understand the injustices they are fighting against. A generation raised on *Freedom Cry*'s Adéwalé and *Red Dead Redemption 2*'s Hercule may not share their elders' discomfort with slave revolt stories in film, nor expect white heroes in plotlines.

Game studios are thus likely to continue making games in which the humanity of Haitians and of enslaved people is acknowledged. And popular demand may push film studios in directions they have avoided. Indeed, even as they have criticized the white-savior genre, Vera and Gordon argue that "Hollywood racial representations may change in the future as the result of demographic and market pressures." They note that, because audience tastes are shaped by what the industry releases, those who want Hollywood to move beyond harmful tropes must engage in advocacy and commit to "educat[ing] ourselves and our children to view media critically."[24] Indeed, funders willing to move away from old tropes—as Fox Searchlight tried with *Birth*—will need audiences ready to see challenging films.

If producers prove willing to fund a new feature film on the Haitian Revolution, what should it look like? Ideally, there should be not one such new film on the Revolution, but dozens. The case of Holocaust cinema makes clear that one film alone will never capture the full scope of traumatic events like slavery, nor the courageous efforts of African-descended people to challenge it. Only a body of dramas, totaling more than one two-hour story, can help audiences understand the many dimensions of an upheaval like the Revolution and how it affected individuals differently.[25] New films can complement older ones like 1976's *The Last Supper* or 2013's *Tula*, in showing the Revolution's myriad effects around the Atlantic.

In the short term, the most promising movie would be the unfilmed *Toussaint Louverture* script by Raoul Peck and Jean-René Lemoine. Written by Haiti's most prominent director with a celebrated Haitian playwright, and reportedly in collaboration with leading Haitian historians, the script (which has the benefit of already existing) offered a lively and sophisticated account of the Revolution, condensed into a planned three-hour frame. It is not clear, however, if Peck is free to use this script, given that portions of its dialogue made their way into Niang's miniseries.

Even if Peck can make this film, other films should complement it. Multiple biopics could be made on different leaders of the Revolution, from Toussaint to Dessalines and Christophe, as well as Boukman, Cécile Fatiman, and Catherine Flon (some of which would require extra invention given gaps in the historical record). There could also be compelling films and games about fictional men and women of the Revolution, as there have been on other historical events, especially if these works are made with the input of historical consultants. For their part, historians will need to recognize that films and games require some compression, in which historical characters and events are collapsed together to streamline narratives. As Rosenstone has argued,

"Without the enormous amount of invention, condensation, and compression undertaken by even the most 'accurate' attempt at film, the historical would not be dramatic, but a loose, sprawling form far less able to make the past interesting, comprehensible and meaningful." For creative works to conform to standard lengths and reach audiences, some details inevitably need to be changed or glossed over.[26]

Other screenplays could be made from some of the hundreds of Revolution novels. I would argue that one of the best choices for cinematic treatment would be Évelyne Trouillot's *The Infamous Rosalie* (*Rosalie l'infâme*). While not epic in scope, this powerful and poignant novel depicts the experiences and inner life of Lisette, an enslaved woman in Saint-Domingue who dares dream of freedom. Trouillot's novel captures both the joys and traumas of an enslaved person's daily life; it is grounded in deep historical research but uses community memory to fill silences in the archival record. Another obvious choice would be Madison Smartt Bell's National Book Award–nominated *All Souls' Rising* trilogy, which would lend itself well to an epic. Though one of its main characters is a fictional benevolent white named Dr. Hébert, the trilogy also has a compelling depiction of Toussaint, around whom a film version could be centered. Another possibility would be Isabel Allende's novel *Island Beneath the Sea*, also set during the Revolution.[27]

Producers also could look further back to works from the 1930s or 1940s that supported decolonization and predated the fears of the 1960s and 1970s. One possibility would be *Babouk*, Guy Endore's 1934 novel about a fictional Haitian maroon, half modeled on Boukman and half invented. Endore himself was a leftist Ashkenazi Jew from New York rather than a Haitian. However, Michel-Rolph Trouillot, so often critical of foreigners' depictions of the Revolution, praised *Babouk* enthusiastically in 1991, because of its author's deep research, and because Endore had exposed the archival and historiographical silences about the Revolution that Trouillot would later highlight in *Silencing the Past* (1995). *Babouk* was ahead of its time in mocking then-conventional archetypes (like a "mammy song" thrown in to "show the sorrows of the Negro"), while highlighting Europeans' savagery. The novel also highlighted enslaved men like its protagonist, whose tears were "lost forever" and never recorded, while racist accounts left by Moreau de Saint-Méry and other colonists endure in the archives. CBS in fact made *Babouk* into a short radio drama in 1937, indicating that the story was not then seen as unpalatable for white audiences.[28] Indeed, ten years later, while *Lydia Bailey* was being developed, CBS made another compelling radio play sympathetic to the Revolution. *You Are There*'s episode "The Betrayal of Toussaint Louverture" featured news-report style accounts of Leclerc's meetings with Toussaint Louverture, before the French double-crossed and captured him.[29]

Despite the long history of the tropes I have described, there are signs that the future is arriving, and that film companies are catching up to game studios in understanding the hunger for media on this event. In fall 2018, Kwame Kwei-Armah, artistic director of London's Young Vic theater, announced that he was making a ten-part television series based on C. L. R. James's *Black Jacobins*, with funding from British production company Bryncoed. Bryncoed producer Foz Allen, who is white, declared that

> C. L. R. James' unflinching analysis of the Haitian Revolution captures what, in those days, must have been unthinkable—the liberation of the largest slave colony in the Americas and its transformation into a new nation. When I set up Bryncoed, my vision was to produce drama that reminds us of our humanity and shows us that there is more that unites than divides us. *The Black Jacobins* is exactly that drama.

Whether this production will be completed, or join the list of unfinished projects chronicled in chapter 4, remains to be seen; if it does reach the screen, it will mark an important step in cinematic depictions of the Revolution.[30]

In the US, while there have not been any television dramas on the Revolution, serious programs about slave resistance have begun to appear on television. These have included the CBC/BET miniseries *Book of Negroes* (2015), the WGN America drama *Underground* (2016–17), and the 2016 remake of the groundbreaking 1977 miniseries *Roots*.[31] Such programs may help shift *mentalités* further, making white audiences and producers more interested in films on the Revolution.

Adding their voices to those of Chris Rock and Danny Glover, social media users—many of whom are unaware that any films on the Revolution exist—have increasingly pushed for such films. The fervent desire to see the Revolution projected onto the big screen is exemplified in tweets such as "WHY LE FUQ HAVEN'T 1,000,000 FILMS/TV SERIES BEEN MADE ABOUT THE HAITIAN REVOLUTION" and "If I was a filmmaker with a budget, I would absolutely make a film on the Haitian revolution. [It's] amazing how there hasn't been a film on such a monumental historical event."[32]

Whether Hollywood studios heed such requests and break away from tired tropes remains to be seen. Hollywood's track record gives some cause for pessimism. The Public Archive may have been right in 2012 in predicting that "unless it can be cast as an inter-racial buddy film with a white lead a film about the Haitian Revolution will never be made in the US." Similarly, Greg Carr of Howard University made an excellent April Fools' joke in 2015 when he tweeted: "Danny Glover signs deal with Brad Pitt's 'Plan B Productions' to make Haitian Revolution Film. Pitt promises not to interfere. #AprilFools." Nevertheless, these very expressions of frustration—coupled with the incipient changes I have chronicled and the sudden explosion of white solidarity with the Black Lives Matter movement in spring 2020—may lead producers to fill this gap. In addition, as Brenda Stevenson has predicted, the momentum from recent new works on slavery and the growing clout in Hollywood of Black filmmakers may make it "difficult to turn back."[33] Still, those who care about history on screen must not only look to Hollywood, Paris, or Montreal; they must seek out the work of Haitians as well. Though we cannot instantly erase the resource inequities that confront Haitian artists, audiences can work to decolonize our viewing choices. Popular culture will be impoverished if films and games about slavery and slave revolt come only from Hollywood and not from Haitians.

ACKNOWLEDGMENTS

My father, Dr. Jerry Sepinwall, developed medications at Hoffman-LaRoche. As a scientist at a multinational company, Dad used computers long before the PC revolution of the 1980s. To access his data, he occasionally brought home a screenless terminal that printed out information like a typewriter. Sometimes he would give it to my brother Alan and me, to do something highly unusual at the time: play a game using the computer. Our choices were limited (*Pong* and possibly *Hangman*), and so were the terminal's black-ink-on-paper graphics. But, in playing over a dial-up modem in the late 1970s, Alan and I were among the world's first online gamers.[1] As the PC revolution arrived, Dad brought home newer machines for us and our sister Stacy: a VIC-20, then a ColecoVision. Movies were another Sepinwall family passion; lively discussions among us after a film (or TV program) helped launch Alan into a career as one of the country's most acclaimed television critics.

For many years, cinema was not part of my scholarly work—and video games were lost to me. I thank those who prompted me to revisit these childhood loves, in ways that connected so powerfully with my interests in Haitian and French history, slavery, and memory. These include my former student Nicklaus Boyens (who first informed me of the release of a game about eighteenth-century Saint-Domingue), as well as scholars who encouraged my work in Film and History (especially Lawrence Baron, Robert Rosenstone, and Liana Vardi).

It takes a village to write a book like this, unearthing and analyzing neglected titles. I benefited from suggestions and advice from Nadève Ménard, Philip Kaisary, Paul Clammer, Patrick Bellegarde-Smith, Stewart King, Sue Peabody, Charles Forsdick, Carolyn Fick, Grégory Pierrot, Jon Cowans, Marlene Daut, Nina Gelbart, Toni Pressley-Sanon, Millery Polyné, Évelyne Trouillot, Judith E. Smith, Matthew Smith, Duchess Harris, Pierre Serna, Mariana Past, Hadassah Saint-Hubert, David Geggus, Jean-Pierre Le Glaunec, Chris Kempshall, Marcel Dorigny, Manuel Covo, Nadège Clitandre,

Claudine Michel, Michael Vann, Rob Taber, Régine Jean-Charles, Nathan Dize, John Garrigus, Jeremy Popkin, Matthew Wysocki, Bernard Gainot, Tony Michels, Yun Kyoung Kwon, Kate Ramsey, Claire Payton, John Walsh, Jason Herbeck, Tony Acevedo, Brent Ashby, Nadège Volcy White, Annette Joseph-Gabriel, Oscar Moralde, Eric Jennings, Nancy Fitch, Douglas Daniels, Clément Thibaud, Paul Cheney, Charlene Regester, Michele Kipnis, Peter Lev, Alan Wald, Celucien Joseph, Andrew Daily, Jeffrey Rosenberg, Marilyn and Harvey Goldstein, and many others. In addition to those who commented on excerpts, a dream team of colleagues, Alex Dupuy, Claudy Delné, Dominique Rogers, Harriet Lipman Sepinwall, and Jennifer Heuer, read the entire manuscript and offered priceless suggestions.

I am deeply grateful to the filmmakers, game designers, and other participants in film and game projects who shared their works or answered questions: Muriel Tramis, Pierre Lucson Bellegarde, Maksaens Denis, Kendy Vérilus, Jill Murray, Robin Lloyd, Frantz Voltaire, Ralph Maingrette, Francine Saillant, Jean-Pierre Le Glaunec, Kendy Joseph, Lois Wilcken, Dudley Alexis, and Monvelyno Alexis. I am also grateful to Tariq Marshall, Cecilia Peck, Carey Peck, Susie Blankfort Camiel, Ellie Blankfort, Joyce Camiel, Dan Camiel, and Naftali Camiel for information and reminiscences about their fathers or grandfathers. My work on games could not have proceeded without Phil Salvador, Evan Narcisse, Ilmari Jauhiainen, and others who have contributed to game blogs and fan sites. This book greatly benefited from feedback by audiences at the Haitian Studies Association, Society for French Historical Studies, Popular Culture Association's Game Studies Section, French Colonial Historical Society, *Film & History* Conference, University of Central Lancashire, Seoul National University, Stanford University, University of California–Santa Barbara, and University of Wisconsin–Milwaukee.

I must also thank my California State University–San Marcos colleagues who read drafts or gave precious counsel (Jeff Charles, Katherine Hijar, Carmen Nava, Jill Watts, Kimber Quinney, David Avalos, Sharon Elise, Rebecca Lush, Suzanna Krivulskaya, Olga Gonzalez-Silen, and Anne Lombard), as well as several cohorts of students who explored this material with me (especially Oscar Canedo, Stephanie Williams, Alex Towey, Melissa Haire, Silvia Ramirez, John Ess, and Brent Ashby). Olivia Salazar, gamer-nanny extraordinaire, gave me invaluable time to write and shared her expertise during the early stages of this project.

In addition, I extend my deepest thanks to the librarians and archivists who made this work possible. These include the staffs of the Academy of Motion Picture Arts and Sciences' Margaret Herrick Library, Howard Gotlieb

Archival Research Center at Boston University, University of Iowa's Special Collections, Bibliothèque nationale de France, and New York Public Library (both the Schomburg Center's and main branch's Manuscript Divisions), and the University of Southern California's Cinematic Arts Library (especially the indefatigable Ned Comstock). I am also grateful to Tom Kennedy of 20th Century Fox for allowing me to consult *Lydia Bailey*'s final script. The CSUSM Library and Academic Computing teams remain my personal rock stars, especially Debbie Blair and Natalya Serge (interlibrary loan), and Damon Adamo and Charles Allen (academic technology). This project was also assisted by research and travel grants at CSUSM from the Office of the Provost; Office of Graduate Studies and Research; College of Humanities, Arts, Behavioral and Social Sciences; History Department; and Faculty Center.

At the University Press of Mississippi, Katie Keene willed this book into being with her enthusiasm. She and Lisa McMurtray helped shepherd it from embryonic form to a monograph covering several dozen films and games. I am so grateful to them, to book designer Jennifer Mixon, to copyeditor Nicholas Bergin, and to their colleagues, for supporting a topic that might have seemed esoteric and for understanding its larger twenty-first-century resonances.

During my research for this book, my family was a font of strength, even as my sister's battle against cancer consumed much of our energies. Stacy has been a model of courage and loving-kindness. Alan inspires me with his gorgeous writing style and devotion to family. My mother Harriet remains a great source of love and encouragement. My sweet husband Steve listened to me talk about films he had not seen, helped me think through several key arguments, and offered excellent suggestions on the penultimate draft. Not least of all, he was an ideal partner in parenting who helped me find time to write. My son Jacob grew while I was writing from a child coveting my Adéwalé action figure to a young man passionate about video games and history—and keenly attuned to silences (or questionable narratives) about slavery and Columbus in his textbooks. I could not have completed this book without them.

NOTES

Introduction

1. "Chris Rock's Opening Oscar Monologue: A Transcript," *New York Times*, Feb. 28, 2016, https://www.nytimes.com/2016/02/29/movies/chris-rock-monologue.html. The hashtag was created by activist and writer April Reign in 2015 but used more widely after 2016.

2. Though Haiti was known as Saint-Domingue while under French rule, I often use *Haitians* and *Haiti* to designate the country and its inhabitants even before independence. This convention is not only for ease of use, but also to echo contemporary Haitian scholars who use *Haiti* to describe the country's entire history, reflecting the island's precolonial name *Ayiti* and rejecting French renaming of the country.

3. For novels written just from 1787 to 1899, see Marlene Daut, "Fictions of the Haitian Revolution," https://www.haitianrevolutionaryfictions.com/, accessed Mar. 13, 2019.

4. VèVè Clark counts sixty-three plays on the Revolution performed around the world from 1796 to 1975. See "Haiti's Tragic Overture: (Mis)Representations of the Haitian Revolution in World Drama (1796–1975)," in *Representing the French Revolution: Literature, Historiography, and Art*, ed. James A. W. Heffernan (Hanover, NH: Univ. Press of New England, 1992), 240. On early twentieth-century plays related to Haiti, see also Maurice Jackson, "'No Man Could Hinder Him': Remembering Toussaint Louverture and the Haitian Revolution in the History and Culture of the African American People," in *African Americans and the Haitian Revolution: Selected Essays and Historical Documents*, ed. Jackson and Jacqueline Bacon (New York: Routledge, 2010), 141–64; Lindsay J. Twa, *Visualizing Haiti in U.S. Culture, 1910–1950* (Burlington, VT: Ashgate, 2014), ch. 5; and C. L. R. James, *Toussaint Louverture: The Story of the Only Successful Slave Revolt in History: A Play in Three Acts*, ed. Christian Høgsbjerg (Durham, NC: Duke Univ. Press, 2013).

5. See Robert Toplin, "In Defense of the Filmmakers," in *Lights, Camera, History: Portraying the Past in Film*, ed. Richard V. Francaviglia and Jerome L. Rodnitzky (College Station: Texas A&M Univ. Press, 2007), 125.

6. Charles Forsdick and Christian Høgsbjerg, "Sergei Eisenstein and the Haitian Revolution: 'The Confrontation between Black and White Explodes into Red,'" *History Workshop Journal* 78, no. 1 (2014): 178; see also Gina A. Ulysse, *Why Haiti Needs New Narratives: A Post-Quake Chronicle* (Middletown, CT: Wesleyan Univ. Press, 2015), 4.

7. While I have sought to be comprehensive, future scholars may uncover titles I overlooked. In addition, while I obtained some out-of-print films held in only one or two libraries, I was unable to view the following: Theodor Grädler's 1968 *Die Verlobung in San Domingo*, a

televised version of a 1960 German opera (based on an 1811 novel) set amid the Revolution; Jean Rouch's *Liberté, egalité, fraternité . . . et puis après* (1990), discussed in Charles Forsdick, "The Panthéon's Empty Plinth: Commemorating Slavery in Contemporary France," *Atlantic Studies* 9, no. 3 (2012): 285, and Jamie Berthe, "Disruptive Forms: The Cinema of Jean Rouch," *Studies in French Cinema* 18, no. 3 (2018): 248–51; Gian Godoy's *Three Dumas* (2007) and the Colonial Williamsburg Foundation's video *Flames of Freedom* (2001), both of which include Toussaint characters; and Charles Najman's thirty-three-minute documentary *Le serment du Bois Caïman* (1992). David Geggus gives a brief overview of the latter, noting that it includes "local people talking about the Bois Caïman ceremony," in *Haitian Revolutionary Studies* (Bloomington: Indiana Univ. Press, 2002), 85. Najman also discusses this film in his *Haïti, Dieu seul me voit* (Paris: Balland, 1995), 164–90.

8. See most recently Philip Kaisary, *The Haitian Revolution in the Literary Imagination: Radical Horizons, Conservative Constraints* (Charlottesville: Univ. of Virginia Press, 2014); Marlene Daut, *Tropics of Haiti: Race and the Literary History of the Haitian Revolution in the Atlantic World, 1789–1865* (Liverpool: Liverpool Univ. Press, 2015); Claudy Delné, *La Révolution haïtienne dans l'imaginaire occidental: Occultation, banalisation, trivialisation* (Port-au-Prince: Éditions de l'Université d'État d'Haïti, 2017); Víctor Figueroa, *Prophetic Visions of the Past: Pan-Caribbean Representations of the Haitian Revolution* (Columbus: Ohio State Univ. Press, 2015); Nadève Ménard, *Écrits d'Haïti: Perspectives sur la littérature haïtienne contemporaine (1986–2006)* (Paris: Karthala, 2012); and Mariana Past, "Reclaiming the Haitian Revolution: Race, Politics and History in Twentieth Century Caribbean Literature" (PhD diss., Duke Univ., 2006).

9. The only existing studies of cinema on the Haitian Revolution are Sepinwall, "Happy as a Slave: The Haitian Revolution, French Style," *Fiction and Film for French Historians: A Cultural Bulletin* 4, no. 1 (2013): https://h-france.net/fffh/maybe-missed/happy-as-a-slave-the-toussaint-louverture-miniseries/; Forsdick and Høgsbjerg, "Sergei Eisenstein"; Jude Ulysse, "'I Wait for Me': Visualizing the Absence of the Haitian Revolution in Cinematic Text" (PhD diss., Social Justice Education, Univ. of Toronto, 2017); and Kaisary, "The Haitian Revolution and Tomás Gutiérrez Alea's *La última cena*" in *Racialized Visions: Haiti and the Hispanic Caribbean*, ed. Vanessa K. Valdés (Albany: SUNY Press, 2020), 113–33. See also Sepinwall, "*Burn!*" in *Encyclopedia of Slave Resistance and Rebellions*, ed. Junius P. Rodriguez (Westport, CT: Greenwood, 2006), 1: 86–88. Forsdick's and Høgsbjerg's article chronicles one failed effort to make a film on the Revolution, while also discussing a few other failed projects. Ulysse's dissertation, though it focuses on a limited set of films, is a useful reflection on the absence of more films and what this gap means for Haitian identity. As a nonhistorian, Ulysse also specifies that he does not seek "to determine the historical (in)accuracies of the films" (160).

10. To my knowledge, the only monograph by a historian examining games on a particular topic is Chris Kempshall, *The First World War in Computer Games* (Basingstoke, UK: Palgrave Macmillan, 2015). For theoretical works on historical video games, see Matthew Kapell and Andrew B. R. Elliott, eds., *Playing with the Past: Digital Games and the Simulation of History* (New York: Bloomsbury, 2013); Tobias Winnerling and Florian Kerschbaumer, eds., *Early Modernity and Video Games* (Cambridge: Cambridge Scholars, 2014); Kevin Kee, ed., *Pastplay: Teaching and Learning History with Technology* (Ann Arbor: Univ. of Michigan Press, 2014); Adam Chapman, *Digital Games as History: How Video Games Represent the Past and Offer Access to Historical Practice* (New York: Routledge, 2016); A. Martin Wainwright, *Virtual History: How Videogames Portray the Past* (New York: Routledge, 2019); and Alexander von Lünen,

Katherine J. Lewis, Benjamin Litherland, and Pat Cullum, eds., *Historia Ludens: The Playing Historian* (New York: Routledge, 2019). A few of these authors are historians, but others earned their doctorates in other fields. As I note in chapter 9, scholars in other fields (Emil Hammar, Sarah Juliet Lauro, Kishonna Gray, and Souvik Mukherjee) have begun to publish on particular games on slavery and video games, but historians have not examined these games, nor have any scholars looked at the entire corpus that I identify here.

11. Natalie Zemon Davis, *Slaves on Screen: Film and Historical Vision* (Cambridge, MA: Harvard Univ. Press, 2000), 17. While Davis's work was groundbreaking in appraising slavery and film (and my title nods to her work), I have been less influenced by her mode of appraising historical films than that of Robert Rosenstone. For Rosenstone's respectful dissent from some of Davis's approaches, see his *History on Film/Film on History*, 3rd ed. (New York: Routledge, 2017), 22–27.

12. Brenda E. Stevenson, "Filming Black Voices and Stories: Slavery on America's Screens," *Journal of the Civil War Era* 8, no. 3 (2018): 488–520, quote 493–94. On the legacy of Griffith's *The Birth of a Nation* more generally, see Michael T. Martin, *The Birth of a Nation: The Cinematic Past in the Present* (Bloomington: Indiana Univ. Press, 2019).

13. For more on *Amistad*'s insistence on "the fundamental goodness of white American civilization," see Hernan Vera and Andrew Gordon, *Screen Saviors: Hollywood Fictions of Whiteness* (Lanham, MD: Rowman & Littlefield, 2003), 52–64. For further analysis of *12 Years a Slave*, see Kaisary, "The Slave Narrative and Filmic Aesthetics: Steve McQueen, Solomon Northup, and Colonial Violence," *MELUS* 42, no. 2 (2017): 94–114; and Janell Hobson, "This Film Called My Back: Black Pain and Painful History in *12 Years a Slave*," in *Celluloid Chains: Slavery in the Americas through Film*, ed. Rudyard J. Alcocer, Kristen Block, and Dawn Duke (Knoxville: Univ. of Tennessee Press, 2018), 262–76. On other recent slavery-related films, see Steven W. Thomas, "Cinematic Slavery and the Importance of *Belle*," in *The Cinematic Eighteenth Century*, ed. Srividhya Swaminathan and Steven W. Thomas (New York: Routledge, 2018), 170–86.

14. Vera and Gordon, *Screen Saviors*, 34; and Matthew W. Hughey, *The White Savior Film: Content, Critics, and Consumption* (Philadelphia: Temple Univ. Press, 2014), 1, 15. See also Michael T. Martin and David C. Wall, "The Politics of Cine-Memory: Signifying Slavery in the Historical Film," in *A Companion to the Historical Film*, ed. Robert A. Rosenstone and Constantin Parvulescu (Malden, MA: Wiley-Blackwell, 2013), 443–67. On the larger discomfort of whites with such stories, see Grégory Pierrot, *The Black Avenger in Atlantic Culture* (Athens: Univ. of Georgia Press, 2019).

15. Joe R. Feagin, foreword to Vera and Gordon, *Screen Saviors*, viii–ix.

16. *Tamango*, dir. John Berry (1958), 100 min., Fandor (via Amazon Prime); Christopher L. Miller, *The French Atlantic Triangle: Literature and Culture of the Slave Trade* (Durham, NC: Duke Univ. Press, 2008), 222–41. Stevenson also identifies earlier films that showed unsuccessful attempts at slave rebellion, such as 1937's *Souls at Sea* (dir. Henry Hathaway), 1935's *So Red the Rose* (dir. King Vidor), and Stan Lathan's 1982 *A House Divided* ("Filming Black Voices," 494, 507). Sarah Juliet Lauro has argued that *Get Out* (2017, dir. Jordan Peele) is a kind of slave revolt film; see "Specters of Slave Revolt," in *Jordan Peele's* Get Out*: Political Horror*, ed. Dawn Keetley (Columbus: Ohio State Univ. Press, 2020), 147–59.

17. Robert Weems, *Desegregating the Dollar: African American Consumerism in the Twentieth Century* (New York: New York Univ. Press, 1998), 125; Clarence Munford, *Race and Reparations: A Black Perspective for the 21st Century* (Trenton, NJ: Africa World Press, 1996), 417; Françoise

Pfaff, "The Films of Med Hondo: An African Filmmaker in Paris," *Jump Cut*, no. 31 (1986), 44–46; Tambay Obenson, "Med Hondo, the Firebrand Pioneer of African Cinema, Dies," *IndieWire*, Mar. 3, 2019, https://www.indiewire.com/2019/03/med-hondo-dead-african-cinema-1202048352/; and *West Indies: Les nègres marrons de la liberté*, dir. Med Hondo (1979), 112 min., YouTube, posted by danette le cinephile, August 10, 2020, https://www.youtube.com/watch?v=uNvoYqHImow. Before this copy was posted, *West Indies* seems to have been available only at two libraries (Harvard University and Université Laval), a telling sign for an epic with a slave revolt theme.

18. Joseph Vogel, "The Confessions of Quentin Tarantino: Whitewashing Slave Rebellion in *Django Unchained*," *Journal of American Culture* 41, no. 1 (2018): esp. 25–27 (including quote from Gay). For further criticism of *Django*, see Sharon Willis, "Moving Pictures: Spectacles of Enslavement in American Cinema," in *The Cambridge Companion to Slavery in American Literature*, ed. Ezra Tawil (New York: Cambridge Univ. Press, 2016), 232.

19. The original tweet has disappeared but is discussed in articles such as Adelle Platon, "Spike Lee Slams *Django Unchained*: 'I'm Not Gonna See It,'" *Vibe*, Dec. 21, 2012, https://www.vibe.com/2012/12/spike-lee-slams-django-unchained-im-not-gonna-see-it/.

20. See Sepinwall, *The Abbé Grégoire and the French Revolution: The Making of Modern Universalism* (Berkeley: Univ. of California Press, 2005); Sepinwall, "Atlantic Amnesia: French Historians, the Haitian Revolution and the 2004–6 CAPES Exam," *Proceedings of the Western Society for French History* 34 (2006): 300–314; Yves Benot, *La révolution française et la fin des colonies* (Paris: La Découverte, 1987); Michel-Rolph Trouillot, *Silencing the Past: Power and the Production of History* (Boston: Beacon, 1995); C. Miller, *French Atlantic Triangle*; Nicola Frith and Kate Hodgson, eds., *At the Limits of Memory: Legacies of Slavery in the Francophone World* (Liverpool: Liverpool Univ. Press, 2015); and Crystal M. Fleming, *Resurrecting Slavery: Racial Legacies and White Supremacy in France* (Philadelphia: Temple Univ. Press, 2017). On gaps in the memory of slavery outside France, see esp. Ana Lucia Araujo, *Shadows of the Slave Past: Memory, Heritage, and Slavery* (New York: Routledge, 2014).

21. For more on the evolution of this field, see Sepinwall, *Haitian History: New Perspectives* (New York: Routledge, 2012). For exceptions, see the works highlighted in section 2 of that book, as well as Laurent Dubois, *Haiti: The Aftershocks of History* (New York: Metropolitan, 2012); and Julia Gaffield, *Haitian Connections in the Atlantic World: Recognition after Revolution* (Chapel Hill: Univ. of North Carolina Press, 2015).

22. See especially G. Ulysse, *Why Haiti*; Millery Polyné, *The Idea of Haiti: Rethinking Crisis and Development* (Minneapolis: Univ. of Minneapolis Press, 2013); Nadège Clitandre, "Haitian Exceptionalism in the Caribbean and the Project of Rebuilding Haiti," *Journal of Haitian Studies* 17, no. 2 (2011): 146–55; Daut, *Tropics of Haiti*; Alessandra Benedicty-Kokken, Kaiama L. Glover, Mark Schuller, and Jhon Picard Byron, eds., *The Haiti Exception: Anthropology and the Predicament of Narrative* (Liverpool: Liverpool Univ. Press, 2016); Kaisary, *The Haitian Revolution in the Literary Imagination*; and Delné, *La Révolution haïtienne*, 25.

23. See Robert Toplin, *History by Hollywood: Screening the American Past*, 2nd ed. (Urbana: Univ. of Illinois Press, 2009); and Rosenstone, *History on Film*, xi.

24. Rosenstone, *Revisioning History: Film and the Construction of a New Past* (Princeton, NJ: Princeton Univ. Press, 1994), 6–7; and Rosenstone, "The Historical Film as Real History," *Film-Historia* 5, no. 1 (1995): 5–23. For similar analyses, see Toplin, "In Defense of the Filmmakers," 124; and Marcia Landy, ed., *The Historical Film: History and Memory in Media* (New Brunswick, NJ: Rutgers Univ. Press, 2001), 12–13.

25. See Rosenstone, "History in Images/History in Words: Reflections on the Possibility of Really Putting History onto Film," *American Historical Review* 93, no. 5 (1988): 1179–80; Rosenstone, *History on Film*, 63–78; Toplin, *History by Hollywood*, 13–14; and Jonathan Kahana, *The Documentary Film Reader: History, Theory, Criticism* (New York: Oxford Univ. Press, 2016).

26. Francaviglia and Rodnitzky, *Lights, Camera, History*, viii. See also Alison Landsberg, *Prosthetic Memory: The Transformation of American Remembrance in the Age of Mass Culture* (New York: Columbia Univ. Press, 2004); Landsberg, "Politics and the Historical Film: *Hotel Rwanda* and the Form of Engagement," in Rosenstone and Parvulescu, *Companion to the Historical Film*, 11.

27. Rosenstone, *Visions of the Past: The Challenge of Film to Our Idea of History* (Cambridge, MA: Harvard Univ. Press, 1995), 7, 12, 31; and Lawrence Baron, *Projecting the Holocaust into the Present: The Changing Focus of Contemporary Holocaust Cinema* (Lanham, MD: Rowman & Littlefield, 2005), viii–ix. See also K. R. M. Short, *Feature Films as History* (New York: Routledge, 2014); Landy, *The Historical Film*; Marnie Hughes-Warrington, *History Goes to the Movies: Studying History on Film* (London: Routledge, 2007); Rosenstone and Parvulescu, *Companion to the Historical Film*; and Jennie M. Carlsten and Fearghal McGarry, eds., *Film, History and Memory* (New York: Palgrave Macmillan, 2015).

28. See Carolyn Fick, *The Making of Haiti: The Saint Domingue Revolution from Below* (Knoxville: Univ. of Tennessee Press, 1990); John K. Thornton, "'I Am the Subject of the King of Congo': African Political Ideology and the Haitian Revolution," *Journal of World History* 4, no. 2 (1993): 181–214; Thornton, "African Soldiers in the Haitian Revolution," *Journal of Caribbean History* 25, nos. 1 and 2 (1991): 59–80; Laurent Dubois, *Avengers of the New World: The Story of the Haitian Revolution* (Cambridge, MA: Belknap Press/Harvard Univ. Press, 2004); and Chris Davis, "Before They Were Haitians: Examining Evidence for Kongolese Influence on the Haitian Revolution," *Journal of Haitian Studies* 22, no. 2 (2016): 4–36. On creolized African culture and Vodou in the Revolution's roots, see also Patrick Bellegarde-Smith, *Haiti: The Breached Citadel*, rev. ed. (Toronto: Canadian Scholars' Press, 2004); and Kate Ramsey, *The Spirits and the Law: Vodou and Power in Haiti* (Chicago: Univ. of Chicago Press, 2011), ch. 1.

29. Delné, *La Révolution haïtienne*, 19; Pierre Nora, *Les lieux de mémoire*, 3 vols. (Paris: Gallimard, 1992).

30. Toplin, "Cinematic History: Where Do We Go from Here?" *The Public Historian* 25, no. 3 (2003): 86–88.

31. In contrast to the PCA and SCMS, the AHA does not have an official Game Studies grouping. Past AHA annual meetings have included only a handful of panels on Game Studies, such as one in 2015 on "Scholars as Game Designers" and another in 2016 on "Historia Ludens: Games and Play in the Practice of History."

32. Scholarship by historians on games has often been pedagogically focused. See Aaron Whelchel, "Using Civilization Simulation Video Games in the World History Classroom," *World History Connected* 4, no. 2 (2007), https://worldhistoryconnected.press.uillinois.edu/4.2/whelchel.html; Jeremiah B. McCall, *Gaming the Past: Using Video Games to Teach Secondary History* (New York: Routledge, 2011); Nicolas Trépanier, "The Assassin's Perspective: Teaching History with Video Games," *Perspectives on History* 52, no. 5 (2014), https://www.historians.org/publications-and-directories/perspectives-on-history/may-2014/the-assassins-perspective; A. Martin Wainwright, "Teaching Historical Theory through Video Games," *The History Teacher* 47, no. 4 (2014), 579–612; Robert Whitaker, "Backward Compatible: Gamers as a Public

History Audience," *Perspectives on History* 54, no. 1 (2016), https://www.historians.org/publications-and-directories/perspectives-on-history/january-2016/backward-compatible-gamers-as-a-public-history-audience; and Scott A. Metzger and Richard J. Paxton, "Gaming History: A Framework for What Video Games Teach about the Past," *Theory and Research in Social Education* 44, no. 4 (2016): 532–64. As a sign of change, while this book was in press, the *American Historical Review* was set to publish its first issue centered on Game Studies.

33. Chapman, *Digital Games*, 14; Soraya Murray, *On Video Games: The Visual Politics of Race, Gender and Space* (London: I.B. Tauris, 2018), 15.

34. Mark J. P. Wolf, ed., *The Medium of the Video Game* (Austin: Univ. of Texas Press, 2001), 2; Stephen Keane, *CineTech: Film, Convergence and New Media* (New York: Palgrave Macmillan, 2007), 14, 97, 207. On "games-in-light-of-cinema," see Geoff King and Tanya Krzywinska, eds., *Screenplay: Cinema/Videogames/Interfaces* (London: Wallflower, 2002); on films through the prism of games, see Jasmina Kallay, *Gaming Film: How Games Are Reshaping Contemporary Cinema* (Basingstoke, UK: Palgrave Macmillan, 2013). For analysis of cinema and games on the same era from a Media Studies standpoint, see Tanine Allison, *Destructive Sublime: World War II in American Film and Media* (New Brunswick, NJ: Rutgers Univ. Press, 2018).

35. Rosenstone, epilogue to *History on Film*, 152–53.

36. For an overview of these terms, see Keane, *CineTech*, 103. "Interactive fiction" often refers to text-based adventure games like those I discuss in chapter 10; Keane defines "interactive cinema" as combining gameplay and cutscenes (like the *Assassin's Creed* games analyzed in chapter 9). Both are analogous to novels and films in having preplanned narratives (as opposed to genres such as the sandbox game, in which players can do many things in the game environment without a set teleology). See also Nick Montfort, *Twisty Little Passages: An Approach to Interactive Fiction* (Cambridge, MA: MIT Press, 2003).

37. On classic Game Studies debates on whether to adopt narratological or ludological approaches, see for instance Henry Jenkins, "Game Design as Narrative Architecture," in *First Person: New Media as Story, Performance, and Game*, ed. Noah Wardrip-Fruin and Pat Harrigan (Cambridge, MA: MIT Press, 2004), 118–130; and Matthew Kapell, ed., *The Play versus Story Divide in Game Studies: Critical Essays* (Jefferson, NC: McFarland, 2016). While focusing on games' narrative components, I integrate some discussion of the interactive (ludic) playing experience.

38. See especially M.-R. Trouillot, *Silencing the Past*; Antoinette M. Burton, *Archive Stories: Facts, Fictions, and the Writing of History* (Durham, NC: Duke Univ. Press, 2005); and Ann Laura Stoler, *Along the Archival Grain: Epistemic Anxieties and Colonial Common Sense* (Princeton, NJ: Princeton Univ. Press, 2009). For an inventive use of archives to overcome silences and reconstruct the lives of subaltern peoples, see Sue Peabody, *Madeleine's Children: Family, Freedom, Secrets, and Lies in France's Indian Ocean Colonies* (New York: Oxford Univ. Press, 2017).

39. For an overview, see Nicholas Mirzoeff and Jack Halberstam, "Decolonize Media: Tactics, Manifestos, Histories," *Cinema Journal* 57, no. 4 (2018): 120–23 (and the rest of the "In Focus: Decolonizing Media Studies" section of this issue).

40. See for instance Chuck Tryon, *Reinventing Cinema: Movies in the Age of Media Convergence* (New Brunswick, NJ: Rutgers Univ. Press, 2009); and Keane, *CineTech*.

41. For readers desiring further background, see Fick, *Making of Haiti*; Dubois, *Avengers*; Jeremy D. Popkin, *A Concise History of the Haitian Revolution* (Malden, MA: Wiley-Blackwell,

2012); and Geggus, *The Haitian Revolution: A Documentary History* (Indianapolis: Hackett, 2014). On the end of the Revolution, see also Philippe R. Girard, *The Slaves Who Defeated Napoleon: Toussaint Louverture and the Haitian War of Independence, 1801–1804* (Tuscaloosa: Univ. of Alabama Press, 2011). On the Revolution's legacy from the nineteenth century to the present, see Sepinwall, *Haitian History*; and Dubois, *Haiti: The Aftershocks.*

42. On other Caribbean slave revolts that did not result in independent states, see Gad Heuman, "Slave Rebellions," in *The Routledge History of Slavery*, ed. Heuman and Trevor G. Burnard (London: Routledge, 2011), 220–33; and Vincent Brown, *Tacky's Revolt: The Story of an Atlantic Slave War* (Cambridge, MA: Belknap Press/Harvard Univ. Press, 2020). On the Revolution's contribution to modern democracy, see Nick Nesbitt, *Universal Emancipation: The Haitian Revolution and the Radical Enlightenment* (Charlottesville: Univ. of Virginia Press, 2008); and Susan Buck-Morss, *Hegel, Haiti and Universal History* (Pittsburgh: Univ. of Pittsburgh Press, 2009).

43. Saint-Domingue has often been called the world's leading producer of these commodities. However, the statistics used to make this claim do not include production in India and elsewhere. I am grateful to Rob Taber for this insight, drawn from his conversations with David Geggus.

44. Fick, *Making of Haiti*, 45–75.

45. For more on slaveowners' violence, see especially Malick W. Ghachem, *The Old Regime and the Haitian Revolution* (New York: Cambridge Univ. Press, 2012). John Garrigus is preparing work suggesting that Makandal may not have sought to poison anyone, though he notes that his findings would not affect the fact that Makandal was seen this way by others (emails to author, Apr. 5, 2012, and June 6, 2017). An early version of this research was published in Trevor G. Burnard and John D. Garrigus, *The Plantation Machine: Atlantic Capitalism in French Saint-Domingue and British Jamaica* (Philadelphia: Univ. of Pennsylvania Press, 2016), ch. 5.

46. Fick, *Making of Haiti*; Thornton, "African Soldiers"; Thornton, "'I Am the Subject.'"

47. Though whites often used this term, people of mixed race in eighteenth-century Saint-Domingue disliked it, since *mulattoes* literally meant "mule people." Recent scholarship generally uses instead *gens de couleur* or *libres de couleur*, or the English expressions *people of mixed race* or *free coloreds*. Even though many people of mixed race were enslaved, and the "free people of color" included free Blacks, scholarship sometimes uses the terms *free people of color* and *people of mixed race* interchangeably. For a critique of racialist labels, see Daut, *Tropics of Haiti*, 17–19.

48. Since the French scholar Léon-François Hoffmann stunned a gathering of Haitians by asserting that the Bois Caïman ceremony never happened, there has been a lively debate on this topic, as well as about the ceremony's location, date, and larger importance. See esp. Geggus, "The Bois Caïman Ceremony," in *Haitian Revolutionary Studies*, 81–92 (which defends the idea that the ceremony happened, while acknowledging what is unknown about it); the 2002 forum on the Corbett listserv (Daniel Simidor [André Elizée], Rachel Beauvoir-Dominique, and Bob Corbett, "The Bois Caiman Ceremony: Fact or Myth," Mar./Apr. 2002, http://faculty.webster.edu/corbetre/haiti/history/revolution/caiman.htm); and the recent overviews by Delné (*La Révolution haïtienne*, 287–301) and Ramsey (*Spirits and the Law*, 42–45). Without seeking to resolve this controversy here, I will note that I am convinced by Geggus's argument that the ceremony happened. In analyzing onscreen representations of it, I do not dissect whether they match colonists' descriptions in every detail, but examine them as *lieux de mémoire* where directors and developers projected their ideas about what Haitians launching a revolution looked like.

49. Stewart King, "Toussaint L'Ouverture before 1791: Free Planter and Slave-Holder," *Journal of Haitian Studies* 3/4 (1997–98): 66–71; Philippe R. Girard and Jean-Louis Donnadieu, "Toussaint before Louverture: New Archival Findings on the Early Life of Toussaint Louverture," *William and Mary Quarterly* 70, no. 1 (2013): 71.

50. On this debate, see Sepinwall, *Haitian History*, 20.

51. Christophe's fame in this era was sparked especially by the Marines discovering the Citadelle when they invaded Haiti after 1915. Several popular histories and novels on Christophe were published in the 1920s and 1930s, including John W. Vandercook's bestselling *Black Majesty: The Life of Christophe, King of Haiti* (New York: Literary Guild of America, 1928). When the *Los Angeles Times* reviewed C. L. R. James's *The Black Jacobins: Toussaint L'Ouverture and the San Domingo Revolution* in 1939, it noted that most American readers probably thought of Christophe as the Revolution's leading figure (W. N., "Black Majesty's War Has Pointers for Today," *Los Angeles Times*, Jan. 8, 1939, C6). Christophe's legendary status was bolstered by the Citadelle's becoming a must-visit site for tourists, whereas Toussaint had not left any particular building.

52. The light-skinned *anciens libres* heroes of the Revolution, Ogé and Pétion, were fixtures of nineteenth-century accounts of the Revolution but have dropped out of more recent fiction, as memory has focused on former slaves. See John D. Garrigus, "Vincent Ogé Jeune (1757–91): Social Class and Free Colored Mobilization on the Eve of the Haitian Revolution," *Americas* 68, no. 1 (2011): 35; Daut, *Tropics of Haiti*; and Chris Bongie, *Friends and Enemies: The Scribal Politics of Post/Colonial Literature* (Liverpool: Liverpool Univ. Press, 2008), 25.

53. I distinguish *Lydia Bailey* from *The Emperor Jones*, which had wholly fictional characters but was inspired by the story of Christophe. *Lydia Bailey* includes real characters such as Toussaint and Leclerc and is set during the Revolution.

54. More obscure whites who supported the Revolution include Jean-Baptiste Picquenard (discussed by Bongie, *Friends and Enemies*, ch. 2, and Delné, *La Révolution haïtienne*, ch. 4); and those discussed by Erica R. Johnson, *Philanthropy and Race in the Haitian Revolution* (n.p.: Palgrave Macmillan, 2018).

55. V. Brown, *Tacky's Revolt*, 245.

Chapter 1. An Unthinkable Plot?
The Haitian Revolution in US and European Feature Films

1. The epic film has been defined in various ways—to denote high-budget films or simply to refer to a grand historically themed tale. Many planned films on the Revolution (see chapter 4) had characteristics associated with epics; they involved a sweeping historical saga, with a heroic character, amid turbulent events. As Robert J. Burgoyne has noted, the epic is often associated with "the birth of a nation, the emergence of a people, the fulfillment of a heroic destiny"; see *The Epic Film in World Culture* (New York: Routledge, 2011), 2. Andrew B. R. Elliott also characterizes epics as "costly"; see *Return of the Epic Film: Genre, Aesthetics and History in the 21st Century* (Edinburgh: Edinburgh Univ. Press, 2014), 1. On different genres of historical films, see Burgoyne, *The Hollywood Historical Film* (Malden, MA: Blackwell, 2008), 2–8.

2. On "the neo-colonization of finance capital" in cinema, see Mirzoeff and Halberstam, "Decolonize Media," 121; Olivier Barlet, "The Ambivalence of French Funding," *Black Camera* 3, no. 2 (2012): 205–16; and Randall Halle, "Offering Tales They Want to Hear: Transnational

European Film Funding as Neo-Orientalism," in *Global Art Cinema: New Theories and Histories*, ed. Rosalind Galt and Karl Schoonover (New York: Oxford Univ. Press, 2010), 303–19.

3. M.-R. Trouillot, *Silencing the Past*, 70–107.

4. M.-R. Trouillot, *Silencing the Past*, 96, 103. See also Marcus Wood's critique of the idea of abolition as a gift from erstwhile slave states in *The Horrible Gift of Freedom: Atlantic Slavery and the Representation of Emancipation* (Athens: Univ. of Georgia Press, 2010), 16; and also Araujo, *Shadows of the Slave Past*.

5. M.-R. Trouillot, *Silencing the Past*, 73, 96, 105–6.

6. Geggus, "Saint-Domingue on the Eve of the Haitian Revolution," and Ada Ferrer, "Talk about Haiti: The Archive and the Atlantic's Haitian Revolution," both in Sepinwall, *Haitian History*; Sibylle Fischer, "Unthinkable History? The Haitian Revolution, Historiography, and Modernity on the Periphery," in *A Companion to African-American Studies*, ed. Lewis R. Gordon and Jane Anna Gordon (Oxford: Blackwell, 2006), 360–76; and Yun Kyoung Kwon, "Ending Slavery, Narrating Emancipation: Revolutionary Legacies in the French Antislavery Debate and 'Silencing the Haitian Revolution,' 1814–48" (PhD diss., Univ. of Chicago, 2012). For further analysis of the reception of Trouillot's work, see Sepinwall, "Still Unthinkable? The Haitian Revolution and the Reception of Michel-Rolph Trouillot's *Silencing the Past*," *Journal of Haitian Studies* 19, no. 2 (2013): 75–103. My references to the Revolution being unthinkable to "most" whites depart slightly from Trouillot. As an intellectual historian, I do not see all people at a given time as necessarily sharing a single ontology. Though I agree strongly with Trouillot that the Revolution was unthinkable to many whites, I use "many" or "most" (rather than "all") because some whites, such as Abraham Bishop in the US in the 1790s, have been able to see outside dominant frameworks of their time and could imagine enslaved Africans planning a revolution.

7. On pre-1789 resistance, see Fick, *Making of Haiti*; Jean Fouchard, *The Haitian Maroons: Liberty or Death* (New York: E.W. Blyden, 1981); and Crystal N. Eddins, "Runaways, Repertoires, and Repression: Marronnage and the Haitian Revolution, 1766–1791," *Journal of Haitian Studies* 25, no. 1 (2019): 4–38. See also Figueroa, *Prophetic Visions*: "the [Haitian] revolution itself has sometimes been reduced (even by admirers) to an appendix of the French Revolution, as if the slaves needed to hear about 'liberty, fraternity and equality' from their French masters before they could truly aspire to them" (13–14).

8. Delné, *La Révolution haïtienne*, 15.

9. On the unevenness of this isolation, see Gaffield, *Haitian Connections*. For debates on whether paying the indemnity was necessary, see Alex Dupuy, *Rethinking the Haitian Revolution: Slavery, Independence, and the Struggle for Recognition* (Lanham, MD: Rowman & Littlefield, 2019).

10. *New York Herald*, Apr. 14, 1850, cited in Rayford W. Logan, *The Diplomatic Relations of the United States with Haiti, 1778–1841* (Chapel Hill: Univ. of North Carolina Press, 1941), 255. For more on the fears that the Haitian Revolution sparked in the US, see Sepinwall, "The Specter of Saint-Domingue: American and French Reactions to the Haitian Revolution," in *The World of the Haitian Revolution*, ed. Norman Fiering and David Geggus (Bloomington: Indiana Univ. Press, 2009), 317–38; and Ashli White, *Encountering Revolution: Haiti and the Making of the Early Republic* (Baltimore: Johns Hopkins Univ. Press, 2010).

11. Brenda Plummer, *Haiti and the United States: The Psychological Moment* (Athens: Univ. of Georgia Press, 1992), 108ff. For more on the occupation and its causes, see Mary A. Renda, *Taking Haiti: Military Occupation and the Culture of U.S. Imperialism, 1915–1940* (Chapel Hill:

Univ. of North Carolina Press, 2001); Yveline Alexis, "Nationalism and the Politics of Historical Memory: Charlemagne Péralte's Rebellion against the U.S. Occupation of Haiti, 1915–1986" (PhD diss., Univ. of Massachusetts, 2011); *Journal of Haitian Studies* special issue on the occupation (21, no. 2 [2015]); Jeffrey W. Sommers, *Race, Reality, and Realpolitik: U.S.-Haiti Relations in the Lead Up to the 1915 Occupation* (Lanham, MD: Lexington, 2016); and other works cited in Sepinwall, *Haitian History* (section 3, 215–40).

12. Toni Pressley-Sanon, *Zombifying a Nation: Race, Gender and the Haitian Loas on Screen* (Jefferson, NC: McFarland, 2016), 16, 8–9, 18; J. Ulysse, "'I Wait For Me,'" esp. ch. 4.

13. Academic works included Mary Bosworth Treudley, *The United States and Santo Domingo, 1789–1866* (Worcester, MA: n.p., 1916); Charles Callan Tansill, *The United States and Santo Domingo, 1798–1873: A Chapter in Caribbean Diplomacy* (Baltimore: Johns Hopkins Univ. Press, 1938); Ludwell Lee Montague, *Haiti and the United States, 1714–1938* (Durham, NC: Duke Univ. Press, 1940); and Logan, *Diplomatic Relations*.

14. Jackson and Bacon, *African Americans and the Haitian Revolution*, 1; see also Polyné, *From Douglass to Duvalier: U.S. African Americans, Haiti, and Pan Americanism, 1870–1964* (Gainesville: Univ. Press of Florida, 2010); and Brandon Byrd, *The Black Republic: African Americans and the Fate of Haiti* (Philadelphia: Univ. of Pennsylvania Press), 2020.

15. *The Emperor Jones* (1933, dir. Dudley Murphy, United Artists), 73 min. The film is in the public domain and streams on multiple platforms (timestamps are from Amazon Prime).

16. Twa, *Visualizing Haiti*, 32, 40; Clark, "Haiti's Tragic Overture," 247–48.

17. Twa, *Visualizing Haiti*, 32; Thomas Cripps, *Slow Fade to Black: The Negro in American Film, 1900–1942* (New York: Oxford Univ. Press, 1977), 183; Renda, *Taking Haiti*, 198.

18. Paul Robeson Jr., *The Undiscovered Paul Robeson: An Artist's Journey, 1898–1939* (New York: Wiley, 2001), 207.

19. Roland L. Williams Jr., *Black Male Frames: African Americans in a Century of Hollywood Cinema* (Syracuse, NY: Syracuse Univ. Press, 2015), 60, 65; Gerald Horne, *Paul Robeson: The Artist as Revolutionary* (London: Pluto, 2016), 23; Robeson Jr., *Undiscovered Paul Robeson*, 210.

20. Jerry Philogene, "'Dead Citizen' and the Abject Nation: Social Death, Haiti, and the Strategic Power of the Image," *Journal of Haitian Studies* 21, no. 1 (2015): 100–126 (quotes from 105).

21. Past, "Reclaiming the Haitian Revolution," 112–14, 116. For alternate readings of Christophe, see also Marlene Daut, "The King of Haiti's Dream," *Aeon* (July 14, 2020), https://aeon.co/essays/the-king-of-haiti-and-the-dilemmas-of-freedom-in-a-colonised-world.

22. The film's opening sequence (0:00–1:25), which links African backwardness and African American religiosity, has drawn much condemnation. See for instance Williams, *Black Male Frames*, 78.

23. *Burn! (Queimada)*, dir. Gillo Pontecorvo (1969), DVD, 112 min. (Culver City, CA: MGM, 2005). Unlike the more obscure films discussed in this book, *Burn!* is well known to scholars. See my initial analysis in Sepinwall, "*Burn!*," and the more sympathetic readings in N. Davis, *Slaves on Screen*, 41–55; Forsdick and Høgsbjerg, "Sergei Eisenstein," 157–58; Wood, *Horrible Gift*, 30–32; and M. Martin and Wall, "The Politics of Cine-Memory," 445–67. Though Haiti is the most obvious inspiration for the story, N. Davis has noted that Pontecorvo also drew on uprisings in Brazil, Jamaica, and Cuba (*Slaves on Screen*, 44).

24. *The Battle of Algiers*, dir. Pontecorvo (1966), DVD, 125 min. (Irvington, NY: Criterion Collection, 2004); Neelam Srivastava, "Anti-Colonial Violence and the 'Dictatorship of Truth' in the Films of Gillo Pontecorvo/Interview with Pontecorvo," *Interventions: International Journal*

of *Postcolonial Studies* 7, no. 1 (2005): 97–117; Ethan Katz, "Multi-Directional History in The Battle of Algiers," *Fiction and Film for Scholars of France* 9, no. 3 (2019), https://h-france.net/fffh/reviews/multi-directional-history-in-the-battle-of-algiers/; and Sohail Daulatzai, "The Screen and the Streets," *Baltimore Sun*, Nov. 22, 2016, http://www.baltimoresun.com/citypaper/bcp-112316-screens-battle-of-algiers-20161122-story.html.

25. Srivastava, "Interview," 115; Danny Peary, "*Burn!*," *Criterion Collection*, Dec. 10, 1991, https://www.criterion.com/current/posts/947-burn; Gerald Peary, "Talking with Pontecorvo" (1991), http://www.geraldpeary.com/interviews/pqr/pontecorvo.html.

26. Stevenson, "Filming Black Voices," 506–7; Alan Stone, "Last Battle: Gillo Pontecorvo's *Burn!*," *Boston Review* 29, no. 2 (2004), http://bostonreview.net/archives/BR29.2/stone.html; J. Ulysse, "'I Wait for Me,'" 187; and Delné, *La Révolution haïtienne*, 16.

27. See for instance M. Martin, "Podium for the Truth? Reading Slavery and the Neocolonial Project in the Historical Film: *Queimada!* (*Burn!*) and *Sankofa* in Counterpoint," *Third Text* 23, no. 6 (2009): 718.

28. See Moreau de Saint-Méry, *A Civilization that Perished: The Last Years of White Colonial Rule in Haiti* [originally published 1797–98], trans. and ed. Ivor D. Spencer (Lanham, MD: Univ. Press of America, 1985), esp. 62, 83. For critiques of Moreau's view, see Doris L. Garraway, *The Libertine Colony: Creolization in the Early French Caribbean* (Durham, NC: Duke Univ. Press, 2005); and Daut, *Tropics of Haiti*, 198ff.

29. Adam Alcorn, "BURN!"—A Review," *History through Film; Slaves on Screen and Political Violence* blog, Feb. 17, 2013, https://blogs.lt.vt.edu/adamalcorn/2013/02/17/burn-a-review-by-adam-alcorn/; and Robert Stam and Louise Spence, "Colonialism, Racism and Representation," *Screen* 24, no. 2 (1983): 18.

30. Roger Ebert, "Pontecorvo: 'We Trust the Face of Brando,'" *New York Times*, Apr. 13, 1969, D11; Marlon Brando and Robert Lindsay, *Brando: Songs My Mother Taught Me* (New York: Random House, 1994), 320–30; Richard E. Rubinstein, "Sputtering Fires of Black Revolution: *BURN!*" in *Film in Society*, ed. Arthur A. Berger (New Brunswick, NJ: Transaction Books, 1980), 79–84; and Marilyn G. Miller, "Truths, Lies and Telling Silences in Gutiérrez Alea's *The Last Supper* and Pontecorvo's *Burn!*," *Studies in Spanish & Latin American Cinemas* 10, no. 1 (2013): 59–74.

31. *Royal Bonbon*, dir. Charles Najman (2002), DVD, 85 min. (Paris: Malavida Films, 2004). For alternate readings of this film, see Gilbert Doho, "Le Fou, le rebelle, l'enfant et la Révolution haïtienne," *Présence africaine* n.s., 169 (2004): 227–40; Mariana Past, "What's in a Name? Reading Transformative Farce in Césaire's *La tragédie du roi Christophe* and Najman's *Royal Bonbon*," in *Latin American Studies: Critiques of Cinema, Literatures, Politics and Revolution*, ed. David Gallagher (Bethesda, MD: Academica, 2012), 183–99; and Meredith N. Wright, "Fugitive Filmmaking: Third Cinema and the Caribbean," in *Rethinking Third Cinema: The Role of Anti-Colonial Media and Aesthetics in Postmodernity*, ed. Frieda Ekotto and Adeline Koh (Berlin: Lit, 2009), 190–92.

32. On Najman's fascination with Makandal and other Haitian icons, see Najman, *Haïti, Dieu seul*, esp. 123–29.

33. Najman, "Reportage sur le tournage" extra, *Royal Bonbon* DVD (5:32). Najman's *Haïti, Dieu seul* offers insightful reflections about how Haitian history has been distorted. However, his book is also replete with foreign clichés about Haiti as the "land of Vodou" and of mulatto women with "inviting physiques" (see for instance 9, 196). For an unpacking of ideas about

Haitian "singularity," see M.-R. Trouillot, "The Odd and the Ordinary: Haiti, the Caribbean and the World," *Cimarrón* 2, no. 3 (1990): 3–12; and Clitandre, "Haitian Exceptionalism."

34. "Haïti-France-Cinéma: 2.9 millions de téléspectateurs pour le téléfilm sur 'Toussaint Louverture,'" *Haiti Press Network*, Feb. 16, 2012, http://www.hpnhaiti.com/site/index.php/hait-diaspora-trait-dunion/paris/5491-haiti-france-cinema-29-millions-de-telespectateurs-pour-le-telefilm-sur-qtoussaint-louvertureq.

35. *Toussaint Louverture*, dir. Philippe Niang, DVD, 180 min. ([Paris]: France Télévision, 2012). An earlier version of this section appeared as Sepinwall, "Happy as a Slave."

36. See Benot, *La révolution française*, ch. 10 (and further references in Sepinwall, "Atlantic Amnesia"; and Sepinwall, "The Specter of Saint-Domingue," 324–25); Press Conference of Jacques Chirac and Percival Patterson, Guadeloupe, Mar. 10, 2000, http://www.jacqueschirac-asso.fr/archives-elysee.fr/elysee/elysee.fr/francais/interventions/conferences_et_points_de_presse/2000/mars/fi002681.html; and Fleming, *Resurrecting Slavery*.

37. Since *Tropiques Amers* (dir. Claude Barny, DVD [Paris]: France télévisions, 2007) focuses on Martinique, I do not offer a detailed account of its six episodes. Certainly the miniseries, which begins its story line in 1788, offers a more realistic glimpse into the violence of slavery than does *Toussaint Louverture* (see for instance ep. 1, 1:18, 16:26), but it also presents, problematically, a "romance" between a house slave and a colonist (for instance ep. 1, 4:20). While noting that *Tropiques Amers* mostly erases Haiti's revolution from its narrative, Delné has pointed to passing references to Haiti in the episodes, for instance when colonists fearfully mention the name of the island (*La Révolution haïtienne*, 17). In referencing the fear that the Revolution generated among whites, *Tropiques Amers* parallels the Caribbean films discussed in the next chapter.

38. Quoted in Stéphanie Guerrin, "Le révolté d'Haïti," *Le Parisien*, Feb. 14, 2012, LexisNexis.

39. Madison Smartt Bell, *Toussaint Louverture: A Biography* (New York: Pantheon Books, 2007), 292, 298; see also Forsdick, "Situating Haiti: On Some Early Nineteenth-Century Representations of Toussaint Louverture," *International Journal of Francophone Studies* 10, nos. 1–2 (2007): 17–34; and John P. Walsh, *Free and French in the Caribbean: Toussaint Louverture, Aimé Césaire, and Narratives of Loyal Opposition* (Bloomington: Indiana Univ. Press, 2013).

40. See essays in Frith and Hodgson, *At the Limits of Memory*. On the flaws of French films in depicting slavery, see also C. Miller, *French Atlantic Triangle*.

41. Muriel Frat, "*Toussaint Louverture* provoque une polémique," *Le Figaro*, Feb. 15, 2012, http://tvmag.lefigaro.fr/programme-tv/article/fiction/67823/toussaint-louverture-provoque-une-polemique.html; and Ianis Mischi, "Trop de liberté tue Louverture," *L'Est Républicain*, Feb. 18, 2012, Lexis-Nexis.

42. Bell, *Toussaint Louverture*, 93.

43. On the omission of slaveowners' violence in French slavery commemorations, see Christine Chivallon, "Representing the Slave Past: The Limits of Museographical and Patrimonial Discourses," in Frith and Hodgson, *At the Limits*, 36.

44. See Fick, *Making of Haiti*, 34–38; Ghachem, *Old Regime*; and Marcel Dorigny's remarks on Saint-Domingue compared to other colonies ("Partie 2 ♥ TOUSSAINT LOUVERTURE ~ UN COMBAT POUR LA LIBERTE ♥," YouTube, posted Feb. 22, 2012, http://www.youtube.com/watch?v=8sQWK4MUkYc).

45. Daut, *Tropics of Haiti*, esp. 50–54.

46. *Réimpression de l'ancien Moniteur* (Paris: H. Plon, 1853–63), vol. 29 (no. 110, issue of Jan. 9, 1799), 585bis; Daniel Desormeaux, "The First of the (Black) Memorialists," *Yale French*

Studies, no. 107 (2005): 131–45; and Deborah Jenson, *Beyond the Slave Narrative: Politics, Sex, and Manuscripts in the Haitian Revolution* (Liverpool: Liverpool Univ. Press, 2011), 48–49.

47. On foreign iconography of the Bois Caïman ceremony, see Elizabeth McAlister, "From Slave Revolt to a Blood Pact with Satan: The Evangelical Rewriting of Haitian History," in Polyné, *The Idea of Haiti*, 203–42; on stereotypes about Vodou more generally, see Ramsey, *Spirits and the Law*; and Bellegarde-Smith and Claudine Michel, eds., *Haitian Vodou: Spirit, Myth, and Reality* (Bloomington: Indiana Univ. Press, 2006). On foreigners' tendency to overemphasize the revolutionaries' violence while ignoring that of colonists, see Dubois, *Avengers*, 5ff. On the "mulatto/a vengeance" narrative, see Daut, *Tropics of Haiti.*

48. See Benot, *La démence coloniale sous Napoléon* (Paris: La Découverte, 1991); and Girard, *Slaves Who Defeated Napoleon*, 86ff.

49. On these atrocities, see Benot, *Le démence coloniale*; and Girard, *Slaves Who Defeated Napoleon.*

50. Quoted in Frat, "*Toussaint Louverture* provoque," and in "Toussaint Louverture, téléfilm attendu et contesté," *France-Antilles*, Feb. 14, 2012, https://www.guadeloupe.franceantilles.fr/loisirs/une-tv-mag/toussaint-louverture-telefilm-attendu-et-conteste-14-02-2012-158390.php.

51. "Partie 2 ♥ TOUSSAINT LOUVERTURE," (comments at 11:10 and 14:08); and "Partie 3 ♥ TOUSSAINT LOUVERTURE ~ UN COMBAT POUR LA LIBERTE ♥ ~FIN," YouTube, posted Feb. 22, 2012, http://www.youtube.com/watch?v=SfK1CUw8YQg (8:07).

Chapter 2. Invoking the Revolution in Caribbean Feature Films

1. The French and Spanish versions of the miniseries and the shorter cinematic cut are available in different VHS and DVD editions. My analysis is based on the full French-language version of the miniseries: *El siglo de las luces/Le siècle des lumières*, dir. Humberto Solás, VHS, 3 videocassettes ([New York?]: [Videoteca del Sur], 1992).

2. Alejo Carpentier, *Explosion in a Cathedral* [1962], trans. John Sturrock (Minneapolis: Univ. of Minnesota Press, 2001). For a critique of this novel, see Bongie, *Islands and Exiles: The Creole Identities of Post/Colonial Literature* (Stanford, CA: Stanford Univ. Press, 1998).

3. Michael Chanan, *Cuban Cinema* (Minneapolis: Univ. of Minnesota Press, 2003), esp. 461–63; and Santiago Juan-Navarro, "Internacionalismo y revolución: Las intervenciones del ICAIC en la historia de las independencias," in *1808–1810: Cine e Independencias*, ed. Jorge Nieto Ferrando (Madrid: Acción Cultural Española, 2012), 197–201.

4. Alejo Carpentier, "The Victor Hughes of History," in *Explosion in a Cathedral* (2001), 350–51. On the real Victor Hugues, see Dubois, "'The Price of Liberty': Victor Hugues and the Administration of Freedom in Guadeloupe, 1794–1798," *William and Mary Quarterly* 56, no. 2 (1999): 363–92.

5. It is almost certainly an invention that Vincent Ogé had a physician brother. Garrigus has noted that Vincent's two older brothers, Joseph and Jacques, managed the family's coffee plantation ("Vincent Ogé," 40). Garrigus explains that, after the Makandal Affair, officials would have been unlikely to allow persons of color to practice as doctors, fearing that they could use medicines to poison whites (email to author, June 2, 2017). On discrimination against people of color in Saint-Domingue, see Garrigus, *Before Haiti: Race and Citizenship in French Saint-Domingue* (New York: Palgrave Macmillan, 2006).

6. On Enlightenment philosophers' ambiguous thinking on racism and slavery, see Louis Sala-Molins, *Dark Side of the Light: Slavery and the French Enlightenment* (Minneapolis: Univ. of Minnesota Press, 2006); and Bernard Gainot, Marcel Dorigny, Jean Ehrard and A. G. Sepinwall, "Lumières et esclavage," *Annales historiques de la Révolution française*, no. 380 (2015): 149–69.

7. The film reflects what Daut has described as an older tradition interpreting the Revolution as a "'mulatto/a' revolution for vengeance" rather than a "'black' slave revolution" (*Tropics of Haiti*, 11).

8. Garrigus, *Before Haiti*, 40.

9. *The Last Supper* (*La Última Cena*), dir. Tomás Gutiérrez Alea (1976), YouTube, 110 min., posted by opensourceguinea.org, Jan. 26, 2015, https://www.youtube.com/watch?v=g_CPbHIgnF4 (timestamps refer to this version). While this book was in press, a Haitian director released a film tracing connections between Haiti and Cuba after the Revolution: *Kafe Negro*, dir. Mario Delatour (2020). On this film, see my thread https://twitter.com/DrSepinwall/status/1332439638682738689.

10. Jorge Camacho, "The Falsification of History in Gutiérrez Alea's and Moreno Fraginals' *La última cena*," *Islas* 7, no. 21 (2012): 58–67, http://www.angelfire.com/planet/islas/Islas21/English/58-67.pdf.

11. Ferrer, *Freedom's Mirror: Cuba and Haiti in the Age of Revolution* (New York: Cambridge Univ. Press, 2014); on the larger impact of the Haitian Revolution in Cuba, see also Fischer, *Modernity Disavowed: Haiti and the Cultures of Slavery in the Age of Revolution* (Durham, NC: Duke Univ. Press, 2004).

12. Kaisary, "Haitian Revolution and Tomás Gutiérrez Alea's *La última cena*," 8, 20; J. Ulysse, "'I Wait for Me,'" 172–73, 180, 181–82. For positive appraisals of *The Last Supper* that do not center on Haiti, see Dennis West, "Slavery and Cinema in Cuba: The Case of Gutiérrez Alea's *The Last Supper*," *Western Journal of Black Studies* 3, no. 2 (1979): 128–33; M. Miller, "Truths, Lies and Telling Silences"; and N. Davis, *Slaves on Screen*, 42, 55–68.

13. Jean Antoine-Dunne, "Sex, Spirit and the Artist in the Films of Felix De Rooy," *Caribbean Quarterly* 61, no. 2/3 (2015): 66.

14. *Almacita di Desolato*, dir. Felix De Rooy (1985), DVD, 112 min. (New York: ArtMattan Productions, [200-?]); Gilberto M. Blasini, "Caribbean Cinematic *Créolité*," *Black Camera* n.s., 1 (2009): 81; and Antoine-Dunne, "Sex, Spirit and the Artist," 67. On the Revolution's impact in the Caribbean, see Geggus, ed., *The Impact of the Haitian Revolution in the Atlantic World* (Columbia: Univ. of South Carolina Press, 2001); and Ferrer, *Freedom's Mirror*.

15. *Tula: The Revolt*, dir. Jeroen Leinders, DVD, 98 min. ([Amsterdam]: A-Film/Fisheye Feature Films, 2013). On the actual revolt, see Gert Oostindie, "Slave Resistance, Colour Lines, and the Impact of the French and Haitian Revolutions in Curaçao," in *Curaçao in the Age of Revolutions, 1795–1800*, ed. Wim Klooster and Gert Oostindie (Leiden: KITLV, 2011), 1–22; and Junius P. Rodriguez, "Tula (Rigaud) (d. 1795)," in *Encyclopedia of Slave Resistance and Rebellion* (Westport, CT: Greenwood, 2006), 2: 525–26.

16. Hendrik Henrichs, "Review Essay: A Children's Book and a Soap Opera as Public History? Two Dutch Films on Slavery, *Tula, the Revolt*, *The Price of Sugar* (*Hoe duur was de suiker*)," *The Public Historian* 36, no. 2 (2014): 117–21; Oostindie, "Slave Resistance," 1; and Jeroen Leinders, *Tula: The Revolt* [henceforth *Tula* (novel)], trans. Brian Doyle-Du Breuil (London: HopeRoad Publishing, 2012), 189–90; "Q&A with Jeroen Leinders the Director of Tula—The Revolt," *HopeRoad Publishing* blog, Sept. 2, 2013, https://hoperoadpublishing.wordpress.com/2013/09/01/qa-with-jeroen-leinders-the-director-of-tula-the-revolt/.

17. Tambay A. Obenson, "First Trailer for Epic Slave Uprising Actioner 'Tula, The Revolt,'" *IndieWire*, May 10, 2013, https://www.indiewire.com/2013/05/first-trailer-for-epic-slave-uprising-actioner-tula-the-revolt-135634/ (discontinued); and list of corporate sponsors, http://www.tulathemovie.com/partners/sponsors/ (discontinued; accessed Apr. 13, 2018).

18. "Q&A with Jeroen Leinders"; Oostindie, "Slave Resistance," 8.

19. The novel *Tula* and the film version that Leinders developed with screenwriter Curtis Holt Hawkins are not identical. For instance, the novel shows Tula learning about the Haitian Revolution via Black sailors bringing the news from Saint-Domingue (Leinders, *Tula* [novel], 41–42), rather than from Speranza's overhearing plantation whites. I focus here on the film version.

20. Interview with Danny Glover, *Tula* website, http://www.tulathemovie.com/press/video-audio/ (discontinued; accessed Apr. 13, 2018).

21. This detail departs both from the historical record and from Leinders's novel; the historical priest claimed that Tula used biblical language to argue for equality, since he said all men descended from Adam and Eve (Henrichs, "Review Essay," 119; Leinders, *Tula* [novel], 53, 122).

22. Oostindie, "Slave Resistance," 10.

23. Henrichs offers a more unreservedly positive assessment of *Tula*. He considers only critiques that say the film is like a "simple children's book." He also argues that *Tula*, along with the Dutch film *The Price of Sugar*, are "both interesting, serious, and sometimes touching ways of coming to terms with the painful and, in the Dutch public domain, relatively unknown parts of the past" ("Review Essay," 118). Though analyzing *The Price of Sugar* falls outside the scope of this study, I find it far more flawed than *Tula*, for instance in celebrating the "romance" between a nice enslaver and his slave. *The Price of Sugar* (*Hoe duur was de suiker*), dir. Jean van de Velde [2013], 120 min., viewed at San Diego Jewish Film Festival, 2016; also on DVD ([Hilversum, Netherlands]: Entertainment One, 2013).

24. On Mrs. Lesire as the film's white savior, see also Daniel Arbino, "Telling the Tula Slave Revolt: A Creolizing Revolt with Neo-Colonial Implications," in *Celluloid Chains*, ed. Alcocer, Block, and Duke, 242–59.

25. The film won the Grand Jury Prize at the 2014 London Film Awards. It also screened at festivals in Trinidad and Tobago, San Diego, Montreal, Tehran, and elsewhere; in theaters in Holland, Curaçao, and Aruba; and on one Dutch television channel (https://www.facebook.com/Tula.TheRevolt/). However, the reception was far from what the filmmakers hoped. See Facebook post quoting the scholar Zihni Özdil (June 16, 2016, https://www.facebook.com/Tula.TheRevolt/posts/1168670059862577:0), who blasted the film's limited impact as a sign of the failures of Dutch memory; and Anouska Folkers, "Tepid Reviews For 'Tula: The Revolt' in Dutch Media," *IndieWire*, July 15, 2013, https://www.indiewire.com/2013/07/tepid-reviews-for-tula-the-revolt-in-dutch-media-236040/ (discontinued).

26. Glover's DVD extra, as well as some deleted scenes, remain available on *Tula*'s Facebook page. The film has been absent from most discussions of slavery on film. Beyond Arbino's article (see note 24), it is referenced only by a few scholars of the Netherlands; see Henrichs, "Review Essay," and the passing reference in Aspha Bijnaar, Karin Lurvink, and Katharina J. Joosen, "Reframing Criminalised Resistance Strategies of Female Slaves in the Dutch Caribbean and Suriname during the Era of Colonialism," *Caribbean Crime and Criminal Justice: Impacts of Post-Colonialism and Gender*, ed. Joosen and Corin Bailey (London: Routledge, 2018), 10, which emphasizes the film's focus on a heroic male rebel rather than on women resisters.

Chapter 3. Handling Haiti in HUAC-Era Hollywood: 20th Century Fox's *Lydia Bailey*

1. "President Magloire's Address to Visiting Journalists Sunday Morning," *Haiti Sun*, May 11, 1952, 5.

2. For brief exceptions, see Donald Bogle, "*Lydia Bailey* [1952]," in *Blacks in American Films and Television: An Encyclopedia* (New York: Garland, 1988), 140–41; Thomas Cripps, *Making Movies Black: The Hollywood Message Movie from World War II to the Civil Rights Era* (New York: Oxford Univ. Press, 1993), 256, 259–60; Kaisary, *The Haitian Revolution in the Literary Imagination*, 7–8; and Alan Thomas Lipke, "The Strange Life and Stranger Afterlife of King Dick Including His Adventures in Haiti and Hollywood with Observations on the Construction of Race, Class, Nationality, Gender, Slang Etymology and Religion" (MA thesis, Univ. of South Florida, 2013). As I completed this book, I learned that Judith E. Smith had been working on *Lydia Bailey* coterminously with me. I am grateful to Prof. Smith for her generosity in contacting me and sharing her conference paper ("What Happened to *Lydia Bailey* [1952]: White Adventure, the Haitian Revolution, and the Hollywood Blacklist" [Stars and Screen Film and Media History Conference, Rowan University, Sept. 29, 2018]) and her manuscript "Hollywood Imagines Revolutionary Haiti: The Forgotten Film *Lydia Bailey*" (forthcoming in the *Historical Journal of Film, Radio, and Television*). Notwithstanding similarities in our analyses, we worked independently; however, I have added citations to details Smith presented that I did not know about before reading her work.

3. A DVD was released in 2010, but it was sold only in Spain (PAL, Region-2; includes original English with Spanish subtitles). All timestamps below come from this edition: *Revuelta en Haití* [*Lydia Bailey*], dir. Jean Negulesco (1952), DVD, 89 min. (Madrid: Impulso Records, licensed from 20th Century Fox, 2010). A second DVD version was released in 2018 in Italy (*La Rivolta di Haiti*, Golem Video), but it is unclear whether Fox authorized it, as Fox's copyright is not acknowledged as with the Spanish edition. The film is periodically posted on YouTube, then removed per Fox's request. UCLA's Film and Television Archive was the only US library with a print of the film until the Art Institute of Chicago acquired the Spanish DVD.

4. A. H. Weiler, "By Way of Report," *New York Times*, Sept. 29, 1946, sec. 2:3.

5. Aubrey Solomon, *Twentieth Century-Fox: A Corporate and Financial History* (Metuchen, NJ: Scarecrow Press, 1988), 67, 69; Drew Casper, *Postwar Hollywood, 1946–1962* (Malden, MA: Blackwell, 2007), 23–24, 43–44; Peter Lev, *Twentieth Century-Fox: The Zanuck-Skouras Years, 1935–1965* (Austin: Univ. of Texas Press, 2013), 104–5, 111.

6. Solomon, *Twentieth Century-Fox*, 66–68.

7. George F. Custen, *Twentieth Century's Fox: Darryl F. Zanuck and the Culture of Hollywood* (New York: Basic Books, 1997), 4.

8. Sol Siegel to Darryl Zanuck, April 9, 1947, University of Southern California, Cinematic Arts Library (henceforth "USC"), 20th Century Fox Collection, Lydia Bailey Files (henceforth "Fox-LB"), 2483.1.

9. Siegel to Zanuck, Apr. 9, 1947, USC, Fox-LB, 2483.1; Zanuck to Siegel, Apr. 14, 1947, USC, Fox-LB, 2483.1; "*LB* Conference with Mr. Zanuck on Treatment of 4/9/47 [with Zanuck, Siegel, and Krims, prepared by Molly Mandaville]," Apr. 17, 1947, USC, Fox-LB, 2483.2.

10. Jeff Smith, *Film Criticism, the Cold War, and the Blacklist: Reading the Hollywood Reds* (Berkeley: Univ. of California Press, 2014), 1. On action movies as desirable for overseas audiences, see Solomon, *Twentieth-Century Fox*, 74.

11. Bernard F. Dick, *The Screen Is Red: Hollywood, Communism, and the Cold War* (Jackson: Univ. Press of Mississippi, 2016), 231; Cripps, *Making Movies Black*, ix, 160. On the rise of the social problem film in the 1930s, see Peter Roffman and Jim Purdy, *The Hollywood Social Problem Film: Madness, Despair, and Politics from the Depression to the Fifties* (Bloomington: Indiana Univ. Press, 1981).

12. Cripps, *Making Movies Black*, 55, 152; Ellen C. Scott, *Cinema Civil Rights: Regulation, Repression, and Race in the Classical Hollywood Era* (New Brunswick, NJ: Rutgers Univ. Press, 2015), 108–9, 178; Jon Cowans, *Empire Films and the Crisis of Colonialism, 1946–1959* (Baltimore: Johns Hopkins Univ. Press, 2015), 298.

13. Mary L. Dudziak, *Cold War Civil Rights: Race and the Image of American Democracy* (Princeton, NJ: Princeton Univ. Press, 2000).

14. *Gentleman's Agreement*, dir. Elia Kazan (1947), DVD, 118 min. (Beverly Hills, CA: 20th Century Fox, [2002]). On the pressure Zanuck faced while making this film, see Judith E. Smith, *Visions of Belonging: Family Stories, Popular Culture, and Postwar Democracy, 1940–1960* (New York: Columbia Univ. Press, 2004), 161.

15. Philip Dunne, *Take Two: A Life in Movies and Politics* (New York: McGraw-Hill, 1980), 61. For critical analysis of *Pinky*'s production and reception, see Scott, *Cinema Civil Rights*, 119–45; and Cowans, *Empire Films*, 300–307.

16. Solomon, *Twentieth Century-Fox*, 68.

17. David Eldridge, *Hollywood's History Films* (New York: Palgrave Macmillan, 2006), 102–3; Short, *Feature Films*, 32; Judith Smith, *Visions of Belonging*, 255.

18. Leonard Dinnerstein, *Antisemitism in America* (New York: Oxford Univ. Press, 1994), 94–95; Jack Bales, *Kenneth Roberts* (New York: Twayne, 1993), 17, 19; Kenneth L. Roberts, *Lydia Bailey* (Garden City, NY: Doubleday, 1947), 197, 75, 97; White to Joseph Charles, Sept. 20, 1947, National Association for the Advancement of Colored People Records, Library of Congress, via Proquest History Vault (henceforth "NAACP-LC") (General Office File [1940–1955], Haiti General, 1943–1949). On the NAACP and Haiti, see Polyné, *From Douglass to Duvalier*.

19. See Bales, *Kenneth Roberts*, 82 and 84; and Stacy E. Holden, "The Cold War in Barbary: Re-Casting the Tripolitan War in Kenneth Roberts's *Lydia Bailey*" (lecture presented in Casablanca, 2016; copy provided by author).

20. Lipke, "Strange Life," 91n210.

21. Milton Krims to Richard Zanuck, June 14, 1967, Milton Krims Papers, Margaret Herrick Library, Academy of Motion Picture Arts and Sciences (henceforth "AMPAS"), 18.f-290; Krims, Undated Statement [objecting to the Guild's criticizing HUAC in 1947], Krims Papers, AMPAS, 19.f-301, 1; and biographical information in Krims Papers inventory.

22. Krims, "Lydia Bailey [henceforth *LB*] Treatment," Apr. 15, 1947, 1; Krims, "*LB* Treatment" (undated), 1, 19, both in USC, Fox-LB, 2483.1. On the film's displacement of racism onto the French, see also Bogle, "Lydia Bailey"; on the larger pattern in postwar films of "locating . . . the germ of racism in foreign soil," see Cripps, *Making Movies Black*, 200. Southern papers did not seem to be offended by the film's slave revolt theme; see for instance Edith Lindeman, "Haitian Fight for Freedom Is Fine Film," *Richmond Times-Dispatch*, June 27, 1952, 36; and Robert Leidenheimer, "Amusements," *New Orleans Times-Picayune*, June 16, 1952, 16.

23. Krims, "*LB* Treatment," Apr. 15, 1947, 1; Krims, "*LB* Treatment" (undated), 1, 13; both in USC, Fox-LB, 2483.1.

24. Krims to Siegel, Jan. 5, 1948, Krims Papers, AMPAS, 4.f-32.

25. Thomas F. Brady, "Virginia Mayo Gets Warner Film Lead," *New York Times*, Apr. 22, 1948, 34; Dunne Contract, Apr. 23, 1948, USC, Philip Dunne Papers (henceforth "USC-Dunne") box 7, folder 13; Dunne, *Take Two*, 10–11, 8; Custen, *Twentieth Century's Fox*, 300.

26. Reynold Humphries, *Hollywood's Blacklists: A Political and Cultural History* (Edinburgh: Edinburgh Univ. Press, 2008), 103n29, 111, 88; and Dunne, *Take Two*, 109–10, 130, 193. For a sample of Dunne's opposition to fascism and Communism before the war, see Dunne to American League for Peace and Democracy, Oct. 30, 1939, USC-Dunne, box 3, folder 5.

27. Dunne, "Approach to Racism," *New York Times*, May 1, 1949, sec. 2:5.

28. Dunne, "*LB* First Draft," May 18, 1948, 35–36, USC, Fox-LB, 2483.3. On Dunne's trying to persuade Zanuck to make an entire anti-HUAC message picture in 1949, see Custen, *Twentieth Century's Fox*, 314–15.

29. Dunne, "*LB* First Draft," May 18, 1948, 39, 40b, 60, USC, Fox-LB, 2483.3.

30. Dunne, "*LB* First Draft," May 18, 1948, 64, USC, Fox-LB, 2483.3. Dunne built here on Krims, who also evoked the 1930s and 1940s when discussing Napoleonic expansionism (Krims, "*LB* treatment," undated, USC, Fox-LB, 2483.1).

31. Krims, "*LB* Treatment," undated, 39, Fox-LB, 2483.1.

32. Dunne, "*LB* First Draft [revised]," Aug. 19, 1948, 107, 47, USC, Fox-LB, 2483.3a; Dunne to Peter [a friend in Asia], Mar. 1950, 1, USC-Dunne, box 4, folder 17; and Dunne, *Take Two*, 338. Dunne's views on colonialism seem to have evolved; he had expressed a more procolonial viewpoint in his movies *The Last of the Mohicans* (1936), *Suez* (1938), and *Stanley and Livingstone* (1939). I am grateful to Jon Cowans for this observation.

33. Cowans, *Empire Films*, 2, 21, 336, 343, 22, 11; and Larry Ceplair and Steven Englund, *The Inquisition in Hollywood: Politics in the Film Community, 1930–1960* (Berkeley: Univ. of California Press, 1983), 247–48.

34. "*LB*, Conference on First Draft Continuity of 10/14/48 [with Zanuck, Siegel, and Dunne, prepared by Mandaville]," 1, USC, Fox-LB, 2483.4. Zanuck was corresponding with White at this time; White expressed enthusiasm that the film would lack the novel's racism (White to Zanuck, June 17, 1949, NAACP-LC, [General Office File 1940–1955, Film—General, 1952]). On Zanuck's letters to White in this period, see Cowans, *Empire Films*, 297–98.

35. "*LB* Conference on First Draft Continuity of 10/14/48," 1–2, USC, Fox-LB, 2483.4; "*LB*, Conference on Revised First Draft Continuity of 11/4/48 [with Zanuck, Siegel, and Dunne, prepared by Mandaville]," Nov. 10, 1948, 10, USC, Fox-LB, 2483.6.

36. Dunne, "*LB* Final Script," Nov. 16, 1948, 128, USC, Fox-LB, 2483.7.

37. Dunne, "*LB* Final Script," Nov. 16, 1948, 100, 144, USC, Fox-LB, 2483.7. Dunne had an earlier version of the line about killing whites in "*LB* Revised First Draft Continuity," Nov. 4, 1948, 102, USC, Fox-LB, 2483.6.

38. Brady, "Miss Darnell Gets Lydia Bailey Lead," *New York Times*, June 7, 1948, 16. On the freezing of assets, see Rebecca Prime, *Hollywood Exiles in Europe: The Blacklist and Cold War Film Culture* (New Brunswick, NJ: Rutgers Univ. Press, 2014).

39. Joseph Breen to Colonel Jason Joy, Nov. 2, 1948, 1–3, Motion Picture Association of America–Production Code Administration [MPAA-PCA] Papers, *LB* file, AMPAS. The same year that *Lydia Bailey* appeared, Roberts published a translation of Moreau: *Moreau De St. Méry's American Journey, 1793–1798*, trans. and ed. Kenneth L. Roberts and Anna M. Roberts (Garden City, NY: Doubleday, 1947). On the MPAA's more general opposition to "miscegenation," see Scott, *Cinema Civil Rights*, ch. 1.

40. See "$119 Million for 65 Pix; High Priced Films Lined up for '49," *Variety*, Dec. 2, 1948, 1, 14; Reba and Bonnie Churchill, "Hollywood Diary," *San Diego Union*, Feb. 7, 1949, 5; Edwin Schallert, "Hollywood Still Dominates World Film Market, Zanuck Learns," *Los Angeles Times*, Oct. 9, 1949, D1; R. and B. Churchill, "Power Soon to Go to Bermuda, Haiti," *San Diego Union*, Feb. 6, 1950, 5.

41. Charles O'Neal, "*LB* Story Outline," June 24, 1950, 1–2, USC, Fox-LB, 2483.8; and O'Neal, "*LB* First Draft Revised Screenplay," July 6, 1950, 2, 4, USC, Fox-LB, 2483.8a.

42. Schallert, "Niven Will Twice Star Abroad; 'Lydia Bailey' Hypoed; Bob Alda Wanted," *Los Angeles Times*, Nov. 9, 1950, A12. It is unclear why they opted for California over England.

43. Harry Brown, "*LB* Writer's Working Script," Dec. 1, 1950, 10, 12, 54, 16, USC, Fox-LB, 2483.10.

44. In contrast to the modern director-as-auteur style of film, Negulesco joined long after the scriptwriters and producers had developed the project. At Fox, Zanuck was the "one boss [and] arbiter of all disputes," and the script was more important than the direction (Dunne, *Take Two*, 45–46, 54).

45. Ceplair, "Who Wrote What? A Tale of a Blacklisted Screenwriter and His Front," *Cinéaste* 18, no. 2 (1991): 18–21.

46. Blankfort, "Partial Introduction of Philip Dunne," undated [likely between 1973 and 1980], and Blankfort to Dunne, Oct 18, 1980, both from the Michael Blankfort Collection, Howard Gotlieb Archival Research Center at Boston University (henceforth, "Blankfort-BUHG"), box 77, folder 5; "Michael Blankfort, 74; Novelist, Screenwriter," *New York Times*, July 16, 1982, B4.

47. Blankfort, "*LB* Writer's Working Script," Jan. 12, 1951, 1–2, USC, Fox-LB, 2483.11.

48. Blankfort was a fascinating thinker and person who deserves his own biography; until one is written, I offer this brief survey of his life, built from his personal papers, his publications, and recollections of him by the Blankfort-Camiel family.

49. S. Michael Blankfort, "In Memoriam: Free Speech," *Junto Literary Quarterly* (May 1928): 2–4, Blankfort-BUHG, box 67, folder 11; Robert C. Cottrell, *Izzy: A Biography of I. F. Stone* (New Brunswick, NJ: Rutgers Univ. Press, 1992), 26–28; Blankfort, Composition Notebook, Trip to Russia (1929), Blankfort-BU, box 56, folder 3, inside cover ms. note and p. 8; Blankfort, Diary (1929) [loose pages], Blankfort-BU, box 56, folder 4, entry for Nov. (Princeton).

50. Blankfort's byline appeared often in 1933 in *Modern Monthly*. See for instance Blankfort, "The Literary Caravan," *Modern Monthly* 7, no. 1 (1933): 62. On his leaving, see Cottrell, *Izzy*, 43. D. D. Guttenplan suggests that Blankfort was not a CPUSA member but moving "ever closer to the party" when he left the magazine; see *American Radical: The Life and Times of I. F. Stone* (New York: Farrar, Straus and Giroux, 2009), 65. Blankfort nevertheless remained friendly with Calverton, later telling him that he was going to try "getting paid for my writings by selling my soul to the movies" (Blankfort to Calverton, undated [presumed from 1937], New York Public Library, Manuscripts and Archives Division, V. F. Calverton Papers, box 2 [accessed courtesy of Tal Nadan, NYPL]).

51. See Ilka Saal, *New Deal Theater: The Vernacular Tradition in American Political Theater* (New York: Palgrave Macmillan, 2007), 83; Anne Fletcher and Cheryl Black, "The Color of Revolution: Race Trumps Class in Theatre Union's *Stevedore*, 1934," *New England Theatre Journal* 22 (2011): 23–51; Blankfort, "Behind the Scenes of *Stevedore*, a Play for Negro Rights," *Daily Worker*, Apr. 27, 1934, 5; Blankfort, "Facing the New Audience: Sketches toward an Aesthetic for the Revolutionary Theatre [pt. 1]," *New Theatre* 1 (June 1934): 11–12, continued in *New Theatre*

1 (July/Aug. and Nov. 1934): 14–15 and 25–27; Blankfort, "Epilogue to Propaganda," *New York Times*, Jan. 26, 1936, sec. 9:3; and John Flanagan, "The Folk Hero in Modern American Drama," *Modern Drama* 6, no. 4 (1964): 412–13.

52. Jean Negulesco to Jules Schermer, Jan. 11, 1951; Zanuck to Schermer, Jan. 11, 1951; Schermer to Zanuck, Jan. 12, 1951; Negulesco to Blankfort, Jan. 18, 1951; and Schermer to Blankfort, Jan. 19, 1951; all in Blankfort-BUHG, box 88, folder 1; and Blankfort, "*LB* Revised Writer's Working Script," Jan. 22, 1951, USC, Fox-LB, 2483.13. On Negulesco's view of the film as not about antiracism or slavery, but Albion's saving Lydia *from* Vodou and the Haitian Revolution, see his handwritten summary: "Dale Robertson['s] virility" as a "handy with his dukes hero fight[ing] Voodooism, save[s] helpless Lydia[,] heroine handy with her eyelashes[,] from massacre [by] Blacks," in "Things I Did . . . and Things I Think I Did . . . [Lydia Bailey]," Negulesco Papers, AMPAS, 95.f-1563.

53. *Alert*, no. 154 (Jan. 4, 1951); Blankfort to Zanuck, Jan. 17, 1951, and Jan. 22, 1951; and Blankfort to William Laffin, Jan. 19, 1951; all in Blankfort Papers, AMPAS, 11.f-86. Material prepared for Blankfort's case indicates that Blankfort had been criticized by *Alert* and other magazines as early as 1949; however, a formal campaign against him seems to have begun only after Jan. 1951 (see A. B. Leckie to Clore Warne, Feb. 6, 1951, enclosure, Blankfort Papers, AMPAS, 11.f-86, 1–3).

54. Negulesco to Schermer, Feb. 8, 1951 (Blankfort's copy with his penciled marginalia), Blankfort-BUHG, box 88, folder 1; Warne, "Michael Blankfort Problem," Mar. 5, 1951 (and other documents related to his case), Blankfort Papers, AMPAS, 11.f-87.

55. "If I were a native today, whose liberty was threatened by Napoleon's bully boys, I'd kill any white I could get my hands on" ("*LB* Final Script," March 10, 1951, 83, USC, Fox-LB, 2483.13a).

56. William Marshall headed the list of casting ideas for King Dick on Mar. 16; within a week, he and Anne Francis were hired. On a Mar. 23 cast roster, Tyrone Power appeared as Albion, and he would have made more than Marshall; however, at a later date, his name was crossed out and replaced with Robertson's—who, like Francis, received only one-third of Marshall's salary. By June 7, Robertson was formally listed on the roster. Marshall's weekly salary was exceeded only by Luis van Rooten, who was cast only for one week rather than Marshall's six ("Lydia Bailey [casting information]," Mar. 16, 1951; and Lydia Bailey cast rosters, Mar. 23, 1951, and June 7, 1951, all in William "Billy" Gordon Papers, AMPAS, 4.f-179). Power quit either because he did not want to do another costume picture (the explanation in most newspapers), or because he was angry that his African American costar Marshall had a more substantial role than him. Though I have found no firm evidence for the latter, the USC script files do offer some support for the rumor (Ruby B. Goodwin, "Show Business," *California Eagle*, June 21, 1951, 6) that Power quit because the size of Marshall's role displeased him and script changes failed to placate him.

57. Blankfort, "*LB* Final Script," Mar. 10, 1951, 25 and 108, USC, Fox-LB, 2483.13a; and Breen to Joy, Mar. 20, 1951, MPAA-PCA Papers, *LB* file, AMPAS.

58. House Un-American Activities Committee, "Testimony of Michael Blankfort, Wed. Apr. 4, 1951, Los Angeles, Ca.," 6–9, 29, Blankfort Papers, AMPAS, 11.f-87; J. K. H., "One Strike, Backstage," *New York Times*, Mar. 2, 1936, 12; J. K. H., "The Brave and the Blind," *New York Times*, Mar. 22, 1937, 26; Blankfort, "The Education of a Jew," in *Mid-Century: An Anthology of Jewish Life and Culture in Our Times*, ed. Harold U. Ribalow (New York: Beechhurst, 1955), 48. See also Blankfort to George Bernard Shaw, Mar. 28, 1944, Blankfort-BUHG, box 82, folder 8.

59. For competing positions on this issue, see Daniel Aaron, *Writers on the Left: Episodes in American Literary Communism* (New York: Octagon, 1974), 311–12; Judy Kutulas, *The Long War: The Intellectual People's Front and Anti-Stalinism, 1930–1940* (Durham, NC: Duke Univ. Press, 1995), 35, 49, 91; Guttenplan, *American Radical*, 65, 66, 276; Victor S. Navasky, *Naming Names* (New York: Viking, 1980), 377–78; and Leonard Wilcox, *V. F. Calverton: Radical in the American Grain* (Philadelphia: Temple Univ. Press, 1992), 177, 240.

60. Blankfort, *The Juggler* (Boston: Little, Brown, 1952); Ribalow, "American Jewish Writers and Their Judaism," *Judaism* 3, no. 4 (1954): 418–26.

61. Blankfort to Zanuck, May 2, 1951, Blankfort Papers, AMPAS, 11.f-87.

62. Navasky, *Naming Names*; Blankfort letters to Dunne, esp. Mar. 27, 1980, Blankfort-BUHG, box 77, folder 5; documents on HUAC in Blankfort Papers, AMPAS, 10.f-77; and Blankfort's FBI file, Blankfort-BUHG, box 70, fols. 5 and 8.

63. Dunne to Zanuck, May 7, 1951, USC-Dunne, box 4, folder 3; Dunne and Blankfort, "*LB* Revised Shooting Final," May 12, 1951, USC, Fox-LB, 2483.14; F. D. Langton to Dunne, June 5, 1951, USC-Dunne, box 6, folder 4. The latter document, which indicated that Blankfort pressed for his name to go first despite earlier arrangements, is one of the few records Dunne kept on *Lydia Bailey*, as if to document that the names had been switched against the original plan.

64. Zanuck to W. D. Maxwell, July 9, 1952 (defending himself after being attacked in the *Chicago Tribune* as a leftist), reprinted in *Memo from Darryl F. Zanuck: The Golden Years at Twentieth Century-Fox*, ed. Rudy Behlmer (New York: Grove, 1993), 209–13.

65. Harry Levette, "Gossip of the Movie Lots," *Plaindealer* (Kansas City), June 1, 1951, 5; "William 'De Lawd' Marshall Big Hit in His First Movie," *New York Amsterdam News*, July 28, 1951, 25, 36.

66. Schallert, "She's Anne of the 1000 Misfortunes: Newcomer's Movie Debut Marked by Series of Accidents," *Los Angeles Times*, June 24, 1951, D1; "*LB* Confs. with Mr. Zanuck [to discuss new scenes and retakes], screenings of 9/7 and 9/11/51," USC, Fox-LB, 2483.15; and "*LB* Confs. with Mr. Zanuck . . . combined notes of screenings of 9/7, 9/11, and 9/20/51," USC, Fox-LB, 2483.16.

67. Judith Smith, "What Happened to *Lydia Bailey*?", 9.

68. 20th Century Fox, Exhibitor's Campaign Book, *Lydia Bailey*, author's personal collection, 1; "William Marshal[l] Signed By 20th Century-Fox on Seven-Year Contract," *Los Angeles Sentinel*, Aug. 23, 1951, A11; "Lydia Bailey: Negro History Glorified in Superb New Movie on Haiti during Days of Toussaint," and "Historical Movie on Haiti Employees Large Negro Cast," both in *Ebony* 7, no. 3 (Jan. 1952): 39, 44.

69. I described the premiere in greater detail in "Hollywood Goes to Haiti: The Port-au-Prince Premiere of *Lydia Bailey* (1952)" (presented at the Haitian Studies Association, New Orleans, Nov. 3, 2017); I hope to publish more of this material in the future.

70. White to Zanuck, June 17, 1949; "Haiti Fits Bill for 'Lydia Bailey' Premiere," *Jet*, June 19, 1952, 12.

71. "Press Representatives Attend Haiti Opening," *Box Office*, May 3, 1952, 40; "William Marshall, Other 'Lydia Bailey' Stars Frolic in Haiti," *Plaindealer*, June 13, 1952, 6; Constance Curtis, "Haiti! Contrasts! Must See Again," *New York Amsterdam News*, May 10, 1952, 1. For a sample of other reports on the premiere, see W. Z., "Movie Junket Back in Full Glory: Reporter Goes to Haiti for Lavish Premiere—and Returns Alive," *New York Herald Tribune*, May 11, 1952, sec. 4:3; "Haiti Rolls Out Welcome Mat for Lydia Bailey," and George S. Schuyler, "Views and Reviews: 'Bailey' Premiere Wonderful in Haiti, But, Ah! That Joseph and Innocence!" both in *Pittsburgh*

Courier, May 17, 1952, 9, 17; Louis Berg, "Palomino Blonde," *Los Angeles Times*, June 29, 1952, 116; Chester Friedman, "Showmandiser: Haiti Debut," *Box Office*, May 16, 1952, 43.

72. "World Premiere 'Lydia Bailey' Tonight," *Haiti Sun*, May 4, 1952, 1, 3; "President Magloire's Address to Visiting Journalists Sunday Morning"; and Izzy Rowe, "Izzy Rowe's Notebook: Haiti in a Hurry," *Pittsburgh Courier*, May 17, 2017, 17. The premiere—and Francis's falling from a horse at the Citadelle—were widely covered in Haitian papers; see for instance "Anne Francis fait une terrible chute sur la route de la Citadelle," *Le Matin*, May 6, 1952, 1.

73. See Solomon, *Twentieth Century-Fox*, 246, 224; "Top Grossers of 1952," *Variety*, Jan. 7, 1953, 66; and reports about initial ticket sales in Negulesco Papers, AMPAS, 8.f-6.

74. This may reflect the shift in US foreign policy during the film's development. The US had a more supportive attitude toward decolonization in the French empire in the late 1940s. However, after 1950, the Truman administration began sending hundreds of millions of dollars in military assistance to French forces in Vietnam.

75. The dance historian Debra Levine has stated that the film's white American choreographer, Jack Cole, went to Haiti to research this scene ("Jack Cole [1911–1974]," Dance Heritage Coalition, 2012, https://web.archive.org/web/20180219104325/http://www.danceheritage.org/treasures/cole_essay_levine.pdf; and cited in Alison Durkee, review of "'All that Jack (Cole)' Film Series," *Critical Dance*, Feb. 7, 2016, http://criticaldance.org/jack-cole-films-jack-cole/). However, practioners and scholars of Vodou to whom I have shown the scene attest that the songs are not authentic, but reflect commodified "voodoo" ceremonies staged for tourists in the 1940s. Patrick Bellegarde-Smith told me that the costuming and dances were "all wrong," the movements "anemic and not at all African," the drumming "pitiful," and the language a nonsensical imitation of Kreyòl (email to author, April 3, 2014).

76. On King Dick as a "Black Buck," see Bogle, "Lydia Bailey." I owe the insight about Lydia's changed behavior when blacked up to conversation with Douglas Daniels. On minstrelsy more generally, see Mel Watkins, *On the Real Side: A History of African American Comedy, from Slavery to Chris Rock* (Chicago: Lawrence Hill Books, 1999); and Eric Lott, *Love and Theft: Blackface Minstrelsy and the American Working Class* (New York: Oxford Univ. Press, 1993).

77. Krims, "*LB* Treatment," Apr. 15, 1947, 5, and Krims, "*LB* Treatment" (undated), 5, both in USC, Fox-LB, 2483.1; Dunne, "*LB* First Draft [revised]," Aug. 19, 1948, 61-A, USC, Fox-LB, 2483.3a; Blankfort, "*LB* Writer's Working Script," Jan. 12, 1951, 39, USC, Fox-LB, 2483.11. The final film has the dogs jump on Albion, then stop to sniff him, before moving away—prompting Lydia to exclaim, "You're a white man!" In Blankfort's Mar. 10, 1951, script (p. 31), Lydia had added, "You are quite fortunate being a white. Otherwise my dogs would have eaten their fill of you by now"; Breen insisted that Fox remove this inflammatory line (Breen to Joy, Mar. 20, 1951, MPAA-PCA Papers, AMPAS, 3). Dunne had had a version of this scene that did not involve the idea of different racial smells, but only that dogs had been specially trained by colonists to see skin color difference (Dunne, "*LB* Revised First Draft Continuity," Nov. 4, 1948, 36, USC, Fox-LB, 2483.5).

78. Blankfort, "*LB* Final Script," Mar. 10, 1951, revision from 3/12/51, 7, USC, Fox-LB, 2483.13a; 20th Century Fox, Exhibitor's Campaign Book, 11. For further critiques of the film's depiction of Haitians, see Judith Smith, "What Happened to *Lydia Bailey*?"

79. Bogle, *Bright Boulevards, Bold Dreams: The Story of Black Hollywood* (New York: One World, 2005), 294.

80. "The Film," and Edith Efron, "Letter to the Editor," both in *Haiti Sun*, May 11, 1952, 4, 15.

81. "Critique des Films: Lydia Bailey," *Le Nouvelliste*, May 5, 1952, 6.

82. [Goodwin], "Show Business." For a parallel critique of the film's focus on whites, see "This is Hollywood," *Chicago Defender*, June 30, 1951, 22. On this as a more general flaw of studio message films, see Chris Cagle, *Sociology on Film: Postwar Hollywood's Prestige Commodity* (New Brunswick, NJ: Rutgers Univ. Press, 2017), 5.

83. Walter White, "'Lydia Bailey' Hailed as Stirring Picturization of Negro on Film," *Chicago Defender*, June 21, 1952, 11; and Marion B. Campfield, "Mostly about Women," *Chicago Defender*, May 31, 1952, 6. See also White to Magloire, Feb. 18, 1952, NAACP-LC (General Office File 1940–1955, Paul Magloire 1950–55); and Plummer, *Haiti and the United States*, 142.

84. "Movie of the Week: Lydia Bailey," *Jet*, June 12, 1952, 66; Hazel Lamarre, "All the World's a Stage," *Los Angeles Sentinel*, July 3, 1952, B2; "People and Places," *California Eagle*, July 3, 1952, 10.

85. "Lydia Bailey," *Film Daily*, June 2, 1952, 6; Schallert, "'Lydia Bailey' Rare Tale of Adventure," *Los Angeles Times*, June 28, 1952, 9; Earle Walbridge, "Lydia Bailey," *Library Journal* 77 (June 15, 1952): 1071; "Movies: Lydia Bailey," *Newsweek*, June 9, 1952, 89–90.

86. John Robertson, "'Lydia Bailey' Given Over to Adventure," *Cedar Rapids Gazette*, July 12, 1952, 5; John Rosenfeld, "Screen in Review: Has Anyone Here Seen Lydia?" *Dallas Morning News*, Aug. 28, 1952, 12; Hollis Alpert, "*SR* Goes to the Movies," *Saturday Review*, June 21, 1952, 33–34; "'Lydia Bailey' Routine Technicolor Historical Drama," *Film Bulletin* (New York), June 16, 1952, 14; Jonathan Kilbourn, "Movie Reviews: Lydia Bailey," *Modern Screen*, Aug. 1952, 20–21.

87. Ben Levine, "A Film about the Haitian Revolution," *Daily Worker*, July 17, 1952, 7; and David Platt, "The 'Lydia Bailey' Film and the Haitian Revolution," *Daily Worker*, July 31, 1952, 7.

88. "On the Screen," *Globe and Mail*, July 3, 1952, 19; Derek Walker, "*Lydia Bailey* Misses the Bus," *Picturegoer*, July 19, 1952, 12–13; S. D., "Lydia Bailey est une demi-sœur de Scarlet O'Hara," *Libération*, Oct. 21, 1952; Louis Chauvet, "Les films nouveaux: 'Lydia Bailey,'" *Le figaro*, Oct. 17, 1952, 6; Paul Sengissen, "Lydia Bailey," *Radio cinéma télévision*, Oct. 26, 1952, 39; and Pierre Kast, "Un technicolor pascalien," *Cahiers du cinéma* 3, no. 19 (1953): 20–25.

89. Handwritten notes in Negulesco, "Things I Did," Negulesco Papers, AMPAS, 95.f-1563; "Philip Dunne, Interviewed by Thomas Stempel, Darryl F. Zanuck Project, 1970–1971 Research Associateship, AFI, Louis B. Mayer Foundation," USC-Dunne, box 22, folder 1. In another interview, Dunne complained that Zanuck's "nervous scissors" had cut some early scenes that made the rest of the picture not make sense ("An Oral History with Philip Dunne, Interviewed by Douglas Bell," Oral History Program, Margaret Herrick Library, 1991, in USC-Dunne, box 25, folder 64).

90. *The Golden Mistress*, dir. Joel Judge [Abner Biberman] (1954), 82 min., R.K. Productions (distributed by United Artists), streaming, Amazon Prime. I am grateful to Evan Narcisse for first telling me about this film. Like Blankfort, Biberman was a Penn graduate who had been active in 1930s leftist theater circles; he had once acted in a Blankfort-penned play for Theatre Union ("Sailors of Cattaro," *New York Times*, Dec. 11, 1934, 28).

91. Tom Weaver, "Rosemarie Bowe on *The Golden Mistress* (1954)," in *A Sci-Fi Swarm and Horror Horde: Interviews with 62 Filmmakers* (Jefferson, NC: McFarland, 2010), 154; "'The Golden Mistress' interdit," *Le Nouvelliste*, Oct. 23, 1954, 1; "Golden Mistress Does Not Glitter," and "Haitian N.Y. Consulate Calls 'Golden Mistress' Blow to National Prestige," both in *Haiti Sun*, Nov. 14, 1954, 9; [Bosley Crowther], "'Golden Mistress' New Feature at the Palace," *New York Times*, Oct. 30, 1954, 15 ("a more clumsily made, clumsily acted picture has not been seen in these parts for quite some time"). The film's credits indicate the "generous co-operation"

of Haiti's government, with Edouard Cassagnol as the picture's official "Haitian coordinator" (thanks to Chelsea Stieber for helping identify him). Though *The Golden Mistress* has been mostly forgotten, see Lois E. Wilcken on the authenticity of Narcisse's dance scenes, even if the film made them seem nefarious: "Spirit Unbound: New Approaches to the Performance of Haitian Folklore," in *Caribbean Dance from Abakuá to Zouk: How Movement Shapes Identity*, ed. Susanna Sloat (Gainesville: Univ. Press of Florida, 2002), 117–18. My appraisal of the film's weak box office is drawn from weekly reports in *Variety* (Nov. 1954–Feb. 1955) and the film's absence from works on the period; however, I have been unable to find official statistics for the film's budget and revenues.

92. On this increase between 1952 and 1957, see Alan Bruce Goldberg, "Commercial Folklore and Voodoo in Haiti: International Tourism and the Sale of Culture" (PhD diss., Anthropology, Indiana Univ., 1981), 144–45; and Hugues Séraphin, "Hispaniola: The Future Tourism Destination of the Caribbean?," *Journal of Tourism Consumption and Practice* 3, no. 2 (2011): 38–44.

93. Judith Smith notes that Marshall had been named in the anti-Communist publication *Counterattack* in Dec. 1953, leading to his forthcoming television show *Harlem Detective* being canceled ("What Happened to *Lydia Bailey*?," 8). See also her comment that *Lydia Bailey* showed "what seemed possible *before* Cold War anti-Communism shut down this kind of filmmaking" (10).

Chapter 4. No White Hero, No Funding? Unmade Revolution Epics

1. Donald Bogle, *Toms, Coons, Mulattoes, Mammies, and Bucks: An Interpretive History of Blacks in American Films*, 5th ed. (New York: Bloomsbury, 2016), 1; Cripps, *Slow Fade to Black*, 13; Valerie Smith, ed., *Representing Blackness: Issues in Film and Video* (New Brunswick, NJ: Rutgers Univ. Press, 1997), 1. See also Kimberly Fain, *Black Hollywood: From Butlers to Superheroes, the Changing Role of African American Men in the Movies* (Santa Barbara, CA: Praeger, 2015), ch. 1.

2. Ty Burr, "Did 'Green Book' Win the Oscar Just because It Makes White People Feel Good?," *Boston Globe*, Feb. 25, 2019, https://www.bostonglobe.com/arts/movies/2019/02/25/did-green-book-win-oscar-just-because-makes-white-people-feel-good/Z56N6H1cLThbYn2jqaGVDK/story.html. See also Monique Judge, "*Green Book* Has Great Acting, a Misleading Title and Palatable Racism for White People," *The Grapevine: The Root*, Nov. 20, 2018, https://thegrapevine.theroot.com/green-book-has-great-acting-a-misleading-title-and-pa-1830572839. *Green Book*'s white-hero plot inspired numerous parodies, including Late Night with Seth Meyers, "White Savior: The Movie Trailer," YouTube, posted Feb. 21, 2019, https://www.youtube.com/watch?v=T_RTnuJvg6U.

3. On the general imbalance in film capital between whites and Blacks, see also Jesse A. Rhines, *Black Film, White Money* (New Brunswick, NJ: Rutgers Univ. Press, 1996).

4. Forsdick and Høgsbjerg, "Sergei Eisenstein" (which notes that Eisenstein initially sought to make his epic about Christophe, but later decided on Louverture); Kaisary, *The Haitian Revolution*, 8; and Hazel Wright, *Richard Wright: The Life and Times* (Chicago: Univ. of Chicago Press, 2001), 387. On James's efforts, see Forsdick and Høgsbjerg, *The Black Jacobins Reader* (Durham, NC: Duke Univ. Press, 2017), 30, 49n136.

5. Gregory Peck to Darryl F. Zanuck, Nov. 30, 1948, Gregory Peck Papers, AMPAS, 66.f-649; and Carey Peck, email to author, Mar. 6, 2017.

6. G. Peck to Zanuck, Nov. 30, 1948, Gregory Peck Papers. Peck does not seem to have understood that Christophe's regime was a monarchy rather than a democracy. Still, his knowledge about the Revolution was deeper than one might expect from a white nonacademic of his era. After his visit in the 1940s, Peck long retained a love for Haiti, joining several activist groups on Haitian issues in the 1990s and 2000s; see for instance "Groups Join Haitian Policy Protest," UPI, Apr. 12, 1994, https://www.upi.com/Archives/1994/04/12/Groups-join-Haitian-policy-protest/8048766123200/. Peck's interest in the country was sustained by his friendship with Harry Belafonte (Cecilia Peck, email to author, Mar. 3, 2017).

7. "Hollywood Plans to Film Life of Haitian King," *Jet*, Nov. 25, 1954, 60; Michaëlle Lafontant-Médard, "Cinema in Haiti: 1899 to 1982," trans. Latif Ndiaye, in *Ex-Iles: Essays on Caribbean Cinema*, ed. Mbye B. Cham (Trenton, NJ: Africa World Press, 1992), 80–81.

8. "Hollywood Eyes New Filming of *Emperor Jones*," *Jet*, Mar. 10, 1955, 57; "Dual Honors for Author of 'The Emperor Jones': Belafonte's Pix Part of Big Program," *Chicago Defender*, Mar. 3, 1956, 14; Steven J. Ross, *Hollywood Left and Right: How Movie Stars Shaped American Politics* (New York: Oxford Univ. Press, 2011), 452n41; and John O. Killens, "Hollywood in Black and White [Sept. 20, 1965]," in *Cinema Nation: The Best Writing on Film from* The Nation, *1913–2000*, ed. Carl Bromley (New York: Thunder's Mouth/Nation, 2000), 153–55.

9. Killens, "Hollywood," 153–54; see also Judith E. Smith, *Becoming Belafonte: Black Artist, Public Radical* (Austin: Univ. of Texas Press, 2014), 158, 179.

10. "Dual Honors," 14; Killens, "Hollywood," 154–55; ANP, "Belafonte Bans 'Porgy 'n Bess,' 'Emperor Jones' Roles," *Philadelphia Tribune*, Aug. 17, 1957, 7; and "Herb Jeffries Seeks Poitier to Star in Independent Film," *Jet*, Nov. 5, 1959, 58. On the 1958 teleplay, see BFI Screenonline, http://www.screenonline.org.uk/tv/id/534606/, accessed Mar. 14, 2019.

11. "'Not White,' Protests Quinn—'Black Must Play King'—Marshall," *Jet*, Aug. 10, 1972, 58–60.

12. Ellen Holly, "Black History Does Not Need Tony Quinn," *New York Times*, June 11, 1972, sec. 2:1.

13. Holly, "Black History"; Holly, "'For Me, the Most Wildly Romantic Figure,'" *New York Times*, Aug. 8, 1971, sec. 2:1, 9.

14. Anthony Quinn, "Anthony Quinn Answers Ellen Holly: 'Can I Not Play a Black?,'" *New York Times*, June 11, 1972, sec. 2:1.

15. "Movie Mailbag: Is It Fair for Tony to Play a Black?," *New York Times*, July 9, 1972, sec 2:7, 12 (letters by R. J. Thompson, N. Morton Fybish, and others).

16. "Movie Mailbag" (letters by Louise Meriwether, Rick Haynes, Ossie Davis, and others).

17. "Movie Mailbag" (letter by Alix Mathieu and Pierre-Michel Fontaine); M. Cordell Thompson, "New York Beat," *Jet*, Sept. 28, 1972, 63.

18. Tariq Marshall, email to author, Mar. 8, 2017; and David Caute, *The Great Fear: The Anti-Communist Purge under Truman and Eisenhower* (New York: Simon and Schuster, 1978), 531. Marshall, Belafonte, and Poitier had worked closely together in the American Negro Theater in Harlem (T. Marshall, email to author, June 4, 2017; William Marshall to Sidney Poitier, July 11, 1975, in Julian Mayfield Papers, Sc MG 339, Manuscripts, Archives and Rare Books Division,

Schomburg Center for Research in Black Culture, New York Public Library [henceforth "JMP-Schomburg"], box 6, folder 8).

19. Simone M. Sebastian, "William Marshall, 78—Stage, Screen Actor Starred in 'Blacula,'" *Chicago Tribune*, June 19, 2003, https://www.chicagotribune.com/news/ct-xpm-2003-06-19-0306190206-story.html.

20. "'Not White,' Protests Quinn"; see also "Marshall to Go Ahead with Christophe Film," *Jet*, Apr. 26, 1973, 54.

21. "William 'De Lawd' Marshall Big Hit in His First Movie," *New York Amsterdam News*, July 28, 1951, 25, 36; "Bill Marshall Top Name for 'Emperor Jones' Role," *Los Angeles Sentinel*, Mar. 28, 1957, A10.

22. Marshall to Julian Mayfield, Nov. 15, 1972, and Sylvia Gussin to Mayfield, Mar. 16, 1973, both in JMP-Schomburg, box 6, folder 8; "'The Tragedy of King Christophe,' by Aimé Césaire, Adaptation by William Marshall and Sylvia Gussin, Presented at San Fernando Valley State College, May 1970," in JMP-Schomburg, box 19, folder 6. Gussin was often referred to as Sylvia Jarrico even after her divorce, but used her maiden name on the playscript.

23. Marshall to Julian Mayfield, Nov. 15, 1972, JMP-Schomburg, box 6, folder 8; "Research Materials" file, JMP-Schomburg, box 19, folder 5; and Mayfield to Marshall, Mar. 6, 1968, JMP-Schomburg, box 18, folder 8.

24. Marshall to Mayfield, Apr. 16, 1975, Marshall to Poitier, July 11, 1975, Marshall to Mayfield, July 7, 1973, and Army Acherd, "Just for Variety," *Variety*, Mar. 12, 1973, all in JMP-Schomburg, box 6, folder 8.

25. "William Marshall Haiti Guest," *Los Angeles Sentinel*, Dec. 11, 1975, B4A.

26. John Henrik Clarke to Mayfield, Mar. 5, 1974 (referring to Earl Leslie Griggs and Clifford H. Prator, eds., *Henry Christophe and Thomas Clarkson: A Correspondence* [New York: Greenwood, 1968]); and Mayfield to Clarke, Mar. 27, 1974, both in JMP-Schomburg, box 6, folder 8.

27. Marshall to Mayfield, July 7, 1973, 2–3, JMP-Schomburg, box 6, folder 8; Mayfield to Marshall, Aug. 14, 1973, JMP-Schomburg, box 18, folder 8; "Christophe of Haiti, First Draft," 126, 121, JMP-Schomburg, box 19, folder 1. This characterization ignores Christophe's Anglophile tendencies and his eager relationship with Clarkson.

28. "Christophe of Haiti, First Draft," 152–53, JMP-Schomburg, box 19, folder 1; and "Why a Motion Picture on Henri Christophe," JMP-Schomburg, box 18, folder 8.

29. "Proposal and Treatment," 37, JMP-Schomburg, box 19, folder 9.

30. Gussin to Julian and Joan Mayfield, Aug. 11, 1973, and Marshall to John Johnson, Dec. 15, 1973, both in JMP-Schomburg, box 6, folder 8; "Marshall Roams Country for Funds for *Christophe* Film," *Jet*, Dec. 4, 1975, 56; "William Marshall Haiti Guest," *Los Angeles Sentinel*, Dec. 11, 1975, B4A.

31. Mayfield to Marshall and Gussin, July 14, 1975, and Poitier to Marshall, July 17, 1975, both in JMP-Schomburg, box 6, folder 8; and "William Marshall Haiti Guest."

32. Patricia Turnier, "Exclusive Interview with the First African-American Star in Soap Operas' History: The Legendary Ellen Holly," *Mega Diversities*, Jan. 14, 2013, http://www.megadiversities.com/index.php?option=com_content&view=article&id=207:exclusive-interview-with-the-first-african-american-star-in-soap-operas-history-the-legendary-ellen-holly&catid=36:entrevues-&Itemid=55.

33. In 1977, a joint Haitian-American production company in Miami declared that it would make a Christophe film. News of this project, circulated by UPI, appeared in many newspapers,

including "Christophe Movie Is Planned," *Sarasota Herald Tribune*, Nov. 27, 1977, 9C, but it was never completed.

34. David Richards, "Anthony Quinn: Man without Doubt," *Washington Post*, Oct. 14, 1983, https://www.washingtonpost.com/archive/lifestyle/1983/10/14/anthony-quinn-man-without-doubt/989ab1de-8752–46e6-a66e-f7a99f3347af/.

35. "Interview with Danny Glover," DVD extra, on *Black Dawn* reedition (Burlington, VT: Green Valley Media, 2004); Glover, "'We're in This Together': An Interview with Danny Glover," *Race, Poverty & the Environment* 15, no. 2 (2008): 41; Stuart Jeffries, "Interview: Danny Glover: The Good Cop," *The Guardian*, May 18, 2012, https://www.theguardian.com/film/2012/may/18/danny-glover-good-cop; and "Mos Def," in *Hip Hop in America: A Regional Guide*, ed. Mickey Hess (Santa Barbara, CA: Greenwood, 2010), I: 97.

36. "Danny Glover's Slavery Film Lacked 'White Heroes,' Producers Said," AFP, July 25, 2008, http://afp.google.com/article/ALeqM5i_e3UYOiNEhWo3rcVTpcB2e15IMg (discontinued), reprinted at https://www.amren.com/news/2008/07/danny_glovers_s/.

37. Comments by Danny Glover to author at San Diego American Indian Film Festival, Temecula, CA, Nov. 23, 2013; Ariston Anderson, "'I Can Make This Happen': Danny Glover on Producing," *Filmmaker*, Jan. 5, 2015, https://filmmakermagazine.com/88801-i-can-make-this-happen-danny-glover-on-producing/#.XIrE-_lKiUm; Tim Padgett and Kathie Klarreich, "Hugo Chavez, Movie Mogul," *Time*, May 24, 2007, http://content.time.com/time/world/article/0,8599,1624992,00.html; and George Rush and Joanna Rush Molloy, "Venezuela Film Bucks Buy Trouble for Glover in Haiti," *New York Post*, May 23, 2007, https://www.nydailynews.com/entertainment/gossip/venezuela-film-bucks-buy-trouble-glover-haiti-article-1.253735.

38. Martine Jean, "You Likely Won't Find a More Candid & Comprehensive Interview with Euzhan Palcy than This One," *Indiewire*, May 27, 2015, https://www.indiewire.com/2015/05/you-likely-wont-find-a-more-candid-comprehensive-interview-with-euzhan-palcy-than-this-one-154118/ (discontinued); Falila Gbadamassi, "Le cinéma, la clé d'Euzhan Palcy," *Afrik.com*, Feb. 16, 2010, https://www.afrik.com/le-cinema-la-cle-d-euzhan-palcy; Antoine Blanc, "9778: Re: Movie project of the life of Toussaint L'Ouverture (fwd)" [post on *Corbett List* Re: Euzhan Palcy interview on Radio France International], *Corbett List*, Nov. 29, 2001, http://faculty.webster.edu/corbetre/haiti-archive/msg09624.html; Marian Douglas, "Re: Famous Caribbean Natives: Euzhan Palcy, Film Director," soc.genealogy.west-indies [Usenet], July 15, 2000, https://groups.google.com/forum/#!msg/soc.genealogy.west-indies/6yZkpsm4a54/eSbwK97F75IJ.

39. Obenson, "Forgotten Films that Need to Be Re-Released: Med Hondo's 1979 Colorful Musical Epic 'West Indies,'" *Indiewire*, Nov. 13, 2012, https://www.indiewire.com/2012/11/forgotten-films-that-need-to-be-re-released-med-hondos-1979-colorful-musical-epic-west-indies-140281/ (discontinued).

40. Michel Martin, "Hollywood, Bollywood, Make Way For Nollywood," NPR, Feb. 3, 2014, https://www.npr.org/2014/02/03/269512144/hollywood-bollywood-make-way-for-nollywood; "Le réalisateur nigérian Jeta Amata de bonne volonté de la République d'Haïti," *Radio Metropole Haïti*, Feb. 6, 2013, http://www.metropolehaiti.com/metropole/full_une_fr.php?id=21832&action=print; Obenson, "Nigerian Director Jeta Amata Currently Shooting $15mill Toussaint l'Ouverture Film in Haiti," *Indiewire*, Feb. 3, 2013, https://www.indiewire.com/2013/02/nigerian-director-jeta-amata-currently-shooting-15mill-toussaint-louverture-film-in-haiti-details-233814/ (discontinued); "Haïti-cinéma: 17 à 20 millions de dollars pour le nouveau film sur

Toussaint Louverture," *Haiti Press Network*, Feb. 11, 2013, http://hpnhaiti.com/site/index.php/art-a-spectacle/8664-haiti-cinema-17-a-20-millions-de-dollars-pour-le-nouveau-film-sur-toussaint-louverture; Oyebade Dosunmu, "Trying to Create Some Thing Different: Interview with Jeta Amata," *Courrier des Afriques*, Aug. 15, 2014, http://www.courrierdesafriques.net/2015/01/trying-to-create-some-thing-different; the film's IMDb Pro page, https://pro.imdb.com/title/tt2309957; and "Toussaint l'Ouverture Of Haiti. The Feature Film. A KZP Production. Triumphant Entertainment to Co-Produce the Epic Drama," *The Business of Film*, Cannes Daily Edition, May 15, 2013, http://www.thebusinessoffilmdaily.com/Dailyeditioncannes2013/D2_S9.html.

Chapter 5. Black Lives Mattered in the Haitian Revolution: Hollywood and Slavery in Chris Rock's *Top Five*

1. *Top Five*, dir. Rock (2004), DVD, 101 min. (New York: IAC Films/Paramount, 2015). Portions of this chapter were previously published as "Black Lives Matter in History Too: Slavery, Memory and the Haitian Revolution in Chris Rock's *Top Five*," *Journal of American Culture* 41, no. 1 (2018): 5–16.

2. See for instance Manohla Dargis, "One Man's Crisis of the Soul (It's a Comedy)," *New York Times*, Dec. 11, 2014, C17; Allison Willmore, "'Top Five' Is the Most Chris Rock Movie of All Time," *Buzzfeed*, Dec. 11, 2014, https://www.buzzfeed.com/alisonwillmore/top-five-review-chris-rock; Jon Caramanica, "'O.K., Let's Make Something Great': Chris Rock and Questlove Discuss 'Top Five,'" *New York Times*, Nov. 26, 2014, https://www.nytimes.com/2014/11/30/movies/chris-rock-and-questlove-discuss-top-five.html; and Jada Yuan, "The Top 5 Things You Need to Know about Chris Rock's Toronto Breakout Hit, *Top Five*," *Vulture*, Sept. 8, 2014, https://www.vulture.com/2014/09/top-5-things-you-need-to-know-about-top-five.html.

3. Chris Rock, "We both made less money than Boo," Twitter, Nov. 17, 2016, https://twitter.com/chrisrock/status/799347136957677568.

4. There is a small literature on the political content of Rock's humor; see especially Watkins, *On the Real Side*, 579–82; Christine Acham, *Revolution Televised: Prime Time and the Struggle for Black Power* (Minneapolis: Univ. of Minnesota Press, 2004), esp. 179–94; Bambi Haggins, *Laughing Mad: The Black Comic Persona in Post-Soul America* (New Brunswick, NJ: Rutgers Univ. Press, 2007), esp. chs. 2 and 3; and Glenda Carpio, *Laughing Fit to Kill: Black Humor in the Fictions of Slavery* (New York: Oxford Univ. Press, 2008), 104–9.

5. Like many Hollywood celebrities, Rock participated in the Hope for Haiti telethon in 2010. In 2012, he also attended Sean Penn's Haiti Carnival in Cannes fundraiser; see Jake Coyle (AP), "Cannes Guests Bid up to $255,656 at Haiti Auction," *San Diego Union-Tribune*, May 19, 2012, http://www.sandiegouniontribune.com/sdut-cannes-guests-bid-up-to-255656-at-haiti-auction-2012may19-story.html.

6. Rock, "The Ugly (African-)American," *Vanity Fair*, July 2, 2007, https://www.vanityfair.com/news/2007/07/rock200707; Rock, "Such a good documentary. Where's James Baldwin when you need him. *I Am Not Your Negro*, a film by Raoul Peck," Twitter, Nov. 10, 2016, https://twitter.com/chrisrock/status/796733215490932736; Rock's webpage calling the Haitian American artist Jean-Michel Basquiat his favorite artist, http://www.chrisrock.com/story/favorite-artist-basquiat (discontinued; accessed Aug. 1, 2016); and *Head of State*, dir. Chris Rock (2003; 3 Arts Entertainment/Dreamworks, via Amazon Prime), 1:16:15.

7. Carpio, *Laughing Fit to Kill*, 4–5. See also Watkins, *On the Real Side*; and Sarah Wolk, "Moms Mabley and the Civil Rights Movement" (MA thesis, California State Univ.–San Marcos, 2012). For Black comedians' explanations of their work, see Darryl Littleton, *Black Comedians on Black Comedy: How African-Americans Taught Us to Laugh* (New York: Applause Theatre & Cinema, 2006); and *Why We Laugh: Black Comedians on Black Comedy*, dir. Robert Townsend, DVD, 86 min. (n.p.: Code Black Productions, 2009). On analogous traditions in the Caribbean, see Patrick Chamoiseau, *Creole Folktales*, trans. Linda Coverdale (New York: W.W. Norton, 1994). Gretchen Martin briefly alludes to Rock's signifying in *Dancing on the Color Line: African-American Tricksters in Nineteenth-Century American Literature* (Jackson: Univ. Press of Mississippi, 2015), 3–4; see also Michael Eric Dyson, *Debating Race with Michael Eric Dyson* (New York: Basic Civitas, 2007), 378.

8. On traditions of signifying or doubling in African American humor and their origins in slave culture, see Henry Louis Gates Jr., *The Signifying Monkey: A Theory of Afro-American Literary Criticism* (New York: Oxford Univ. Press, 1988).

9. Oscars, "Chris Rock's Opening Monologue," YouTube, posted Mar. 23, 2016, https://www.youtube.com/watch?v=kqhVNZgZGqQ; Frank Rich, "In Conversation: Chris Rock," *Vulture*, Nov. 30, 2014, https://www.vulture.com/2014/11/chris-rock-frank-rich-in-conversation.html; and *Hollywood Shuffle*, dir. Robert Townsend (1987), 121 min, via Amazon Prime(13:45–18:40). See also Rock's bit "How to Get a Black Movie Made," in *Rock This!* (New York: Hyperion, 1997), 189–93; and Nelson George's account of the difficulties he and Rock had making their gangsta-rap parody *CB4* (*Blackface: Reflections on African Americans and the Movies* [New York: Harper Collins, 1994], 136–90, esp. 155).

10. Malcolm X, "To Mississippi Youth," in *Malcolm X Speaks: Selected Speeches and Statements*, ed. George Breitman (New York: Grove, 1965), 145.

11. See Rock's comments on Pryor in "Interview with Chris Rock," DVD extra, on *Why We Laugh*, dir. Townsend; and André Allen's admiration for Pryor in *Top Five*.

12. Rock often uses a Black/white binarism that omits the perspectives of Asians, Latinos, and others. See however his invocation of Native American perspectives in "Weekend Update Segment—Chris Rock," *Saturday Night Live*, season 16, episode 3, Oct. 20, 1990, https://www.nbc.com/saturday-night-live/video/weekend-update-segment---chris-rock/n9950 (1:45).

13. Rock interviewed in *Why We Laugh*, dir. Townsend (46:12); Racquel Gates, "Bringing the Black: Eddie Murphy and African American Humor on *Saturday Night Live*," in *Saturday Night Live and American TV*, ed. Ron Becker, Nick Marx, and Matt Sienkiewicz (Bloomington: Indiana Univ. Press, 2013), 151–72. The Nat X sketches seemed to whites to be a parody of African American militants, rather than something targeting themselves. But this character allowed Rock to make subversive points about topics like white indifference to police brutality committed against Blacks; see "The Dark Side," *Saturday Night Live*, season 17, ep. 19, May 9, 1992, https://www.nbc.com/saturday-night-live/video/the-dark-side/n10257. Rock also made explicit the different ways he thought whites and Blacks would view his character; he featured a "White Man's Cam" moment in each Nat X sketch for an alternate gaze.

14. *Chris Rock: Bigger and Blacker* (1999, 65 min., HBO on Demand), 47:12.

15. Though *Boo!* was a joke film within a film imagined by Rock, Tyler Perry made a real film with this title in 2016 following pleas from *Top Five* fans. See discussion below on how the real *Boo!* mimicked the fictional one in drawing audiences away from a much-anticipated slave revolt film.

16. Rock's comments parallel scholarship that has blasted depictions of the Revolution that emphasize enslaved people's violence while ignoring that of their enslavers; see especially Dubois, *Avengers*; and Ghachem, *The Old Regime*.

17. See for instance Willmore, "'Top Five'"; and Lisa Kennedy, "Review: Chris Rock's 'Top Five' Nails Bawdy and Nice Notes," *Denver Post*, Dec. 10, 2014, https://www.denverpost.com/2014/12/10/review-chris-rocks-top-five-nails-bawdy-and-nice-notes/.

18. @bblizak, "Shoutout to @chrisrock . . . #TopFiveMovie," Twitter, Dec. 14, 2014, https://twitter.com/bblizak/status/544263530556719105; @TheKavita, "Lettin' 'em know . . . ," Twitter, Dec. 29, 2014, https://twitter.com/TheKavita/status/549777077659271170 (discontinued); @GarethWareth, "In Top Five, Chris Rock jokes . . . ," Twitter, Dec. 22, 2015, https://twitter.com/GarethWareth/status/679374639861268482.

19. Michael Bodey, "Chris Rock: Best of Times for a Stand-Up Guy," *The Australian*, Mar. 11, 2015, http://www.theaustralian.com.au/arts/film/chris-rock-best-of-times-for-a-standup-guy/news-story/5847e11a05e40275c4a7407749434df2 (discontinued for nonsubscribers).

20. Jason Di Rosso, "Chris Rock on 'Top Five' and Being Taken Seriously," *Final Cut*, Australian Broadcasting Corp. Radio, Mar. 12, 2015, https://www.abc.net.au/radionational/programs/archived/finalcut/chris-rock-on-top-five-and-being-taken-seriously/6308556.

21. On white preferences for Black humor in a "Sambo" form, see Watkins, *On the Real Side*, 102–3; and Bogle, *Toms, Coons*, on other Black archetypes in Hollywood. The name Hammy recalls another classic stock character, the Mammy, though Hammy is hardly a Mammy character in a bear suit.

22. Box Office Mojo [an IMDb company], "Chris Rock," https://www.boxofficemojo.com/people/chart/?id=chrisrock.htm, accessed Mar. 9, 2019.

23. Rich, "In Conversation."

24. Stephen Whitty, "'Top Five' Review: Chris Rock Gets Back to His Roots," *Star Ledger*/NJ.com, Dec. 12, 2014, https://www.nj.com/entertainment/2014/12/top_five_review_chris_rock_gets_back_to_his_roots.html.

25. Josh Rottenberg, "Chris Rock Is Just Being His Biting, Brazen Self in 'Top Five,'" *Los Angeles Times*, Nov. 26, 2014, https://www.latimes.com/entertainment/movies/la-et-mn-ca-chris-rock-20141130-story.html; Rock, "The Breakfast Club Interview, Power 105.1 (New York)," YouTube, Dec. 11, 2014, https://www.youtube.com/watch?v=BshTdogJ_-E&feature=youtu.be (discontinued); and Rock, "We both." On that film's reception, see Sepinwall, "Why Audiences Must See Nate Parker's *Birth of a Nation*, Despite the Controversy," *History News Network*, Oct. 12, 2016, http://historynewsnetwork.org/article/164115.

26. For critiques of Rock on gender, see especially Haggins, *Laughing Mad*, 82, 91–93; Carpio, *Laughing Fit to Kill*, 248n66; David Gillota, *Ethnic Humor in Multiethnic America* (New Brunswick, NJ: Rutgers Univ. Press), 30; and Acham, *Revolution Televised*, 188–93. These critiques have been prompted by jokes such as those on domestic violence, *Chris Rock: Bring the Pain* (1996), DVD, 58 min. (Beverly Hills, CA: HBO Films/Dreamworks Records, 2002), 26:29. As Rock raised daughters, he toned down his gendered jokes to some extent. He began his film *Good Hair* with photographs of his girls, as he discussed the social pressures that keep Black girls from feeling beautiful (2009, DVD, 96 min. [Santa Monica, CA: HBO Films/Lionsgate, 2010], 1:31).

27. The principal exception for some critics has been Rock's infamous "N***as v. Black People" sketch, performed in *Bring the Pain*. Rock later retired this routine after others complained that it had empowered whites to start using the n*** word. On this controversy, see Acham,

Revolution Televised, 179–83; Kara Hunt, "Off the Record: A Critical Perspective on *Def Comedy Jam*," *Journal of Popular Culture* 48, no. 5 (2015): 849; and Haggins, *Laughing Mad*, 83–84.

28. Littleton, *Black Comedians*, 258; *Why We Laugh*, dir. Townsend, 47:52, 48:50, 48:59; and Hunt, "'Not a Funny Place to Live': An Interview with Chris Rock," *Comedy Studies* 5, no. 2 (2014): 190–97.

29. *Saturday Night Live*, "Weekend Update Segment—Martin Luther King Day—SNL," season 17, ep. 11, aired Jan. 18, 1992, YouTube, https://www.youtube.com/watch?v=C2UKSh6H_Eo (1:50); and "Weekend Update Segment—Chris Rock" (1:04).

30. Rock, *Rock This!*, 26–27, which is a clean version of the bit in *Bring the Pain* (40:05–41:20).

31. See also Carpio, *Laughing Fit to Kill*, 107–8.

32. "The Chris Rock Show [reparations clip from season 5, ep. 3, Sep. 2, 2000]," YouTube, posted by Alberto Fo Sho, June 10, 2012, https://www.youtube.com/watch?v=keF7Nb_oVBI. Rock also invoked slavery in routines such as *Rock This!*, 10, 15, 30; and *Chris Rock: Never Scared* (2004, 79 min., HBO on Demand), 49:00. On this point, see also Carpio, *Laughing Fit to Kill*, esp. 104–9.

33. *Rock This!*, 10–11, 9; Rock, "I'm not even driving stop by the cops again," Twitter, Feb. 27, 2015, https://twitter.com/chrisrock/status/571515073396649984; Rock, "Stopped by the cops again wish me luck," Twitter, Mar. 30, 2015, https://twitter.com/chrisrock/status/582767497272803328; and Rock, "I'm not even gonna complain," Twitter, Jan. 29, 2017, https://twitter.com/chrisrock/status/825854750197440512.

34. Rock, "A system . . . ," Twitter, Nov. 25, 2014, https://twitter.com/chrisrock/status/537231833789124608; Rock, "This one . . . ," Twitter, Dec. 3, 2014, https://twitter.com/chrisrock/status/540233855861813250; Rock, "This is how you arrest a white man . . . ," Twitter, June 19, 2015, https://twitter.com/chrisrock/status/612031938912780289; Rock, "If I were to die . . . ," Twitter, July 23, 2015, https://twitter.com/chrisrock/status/624339223659827201; Rock, "WTF. It's gotta stop. Korryn Gaines," Twitter, Aug. 2, 2016, https://twitter.com/chrisrock/status/760504803529285633; and Rock, "Happy white peoples . . . ," Twitter, July 4, 2012, https://twitter.com/chrisrock/status/220512157937315842/. In 2019, Rock sadly repurposed the Dylann Roof tweet when a white man was taken peacefully into custody after murdering 19 people in El Paso (@chrisrock, "Shot and killed 19 people / Accused of selling loose cigarettes," Instagram, Aug. 5, 2019, https://www.instagram.com/p/BozAYn5poIJ/?hl=en).

Chapter 6. Remembering Haiti's Revolution in France and North America: Documentaries, Dramatic Shorts, and Animation

1. The catalog of the Inathèque, the French national television archive, also lists short segments on Toussaint on news programs, or longer in-studio newsmagazines including panels on the Revolution, such as "La Révolution de 1804," http://inatheque.ina.fr/doc/TV-RADIO/RD_4438907.001/la-revolution-de-1804?rang=358, accessed Mar. 10, 2019. Such programs lie beyond the scope of this book, but it would be worthwhile for a scholar to study portrayals of Haiti in French news programs, before and after the Taubira Law.

2. The play's full title was *Toussaint Louverture, ou la révolution d'un esclave africain devenu Général de la République* (Toussaint Louverture, or the Revolution by an African Slave Who

Became a General of the Republic). Information on funders from Moreau's website, http://www.claudemoreau.com (discontinued; accessed Mar. 24, 2019). The Inathèque's website (accessed Mar. 10, 2019) indicates that the program aired in the metropole and Martinique. The film screened subsequently at some festivals, including in Gorée and Paris.

3. The film version shown on French television (58 min., dir. Moreau) was never released on DVD. I drew information on it from Moreau's website, which includes a two-minute excerpt; media coverage; and the six-minute excerpt at "Toussaint Louverture. De Claude Moreau," YouTube, posted by brettragerjoseph, Oct. 5, 2012, https://www.youtube.com/watch?v=ojM_BkzXvow. The full film seems to be available only at the Bibliothèque nationale de France, the University of KwaZulu-Natal in South Africa, and some libraries in Guadeloupe; other WorldCat listings for the film point instead to Niang's *Toussaint Louverture.*

4. The landmark volume *A Critical Dictionary of the French Revolution*, edited by François Furet and Mona Ozouf (Cambridge, MA: Belknap/Harvard Univ. Press, 1989), did not include a single entry on anything related to slavery, the colonies, or Saint-Domingue. The same was true for other important works published that year. The major exceptions were Yves Benot, *La Révolution française; Révolutions aux colonies* [reprint of *Annales historiques de la Révolution française*, nos. 293–4] (Paris: Société des Études Robespierristes, 1993); and Michel Hector, ed., *La Révolution française et Haïti: filiations, ruptures, nouvelles dimensions* [based on a 1989 conference in Port-au-Prince featuring Haitian, French, and other scholars] (Port-au-Prince: Société haïtienne d'histoire et de géographie/H. Deschamps, 1995).

5. See Steven Kaplan, *Farewell, Revolution: Disputed Legacies, France, 1789/1989* (Ithaca, NY: Cornell Univ. Press, 1995), 406, 463.

6. http://www.claudemoreau.com/toussaint_video.htm; and http://www.claudemoreau.com/toussaint.htm, accessed Mar. 24, 2019 (discontinued). See also Olivier Salvatori, "Spectacle: 'Je Suis Toussaint Louverture, mon nom vous est peut-être connu," *Le monde du bicentenaire* 8 (1989): 27–28; and Serge Barcellini, "Two Memories in the Present: Léger Félicité Sonthonax, Victor Schoelcher," in *The Abolitions of Slavery: From Léger Félcité Sonthonax to Victor Schoelcher, 1793, 1794, 1848*, ed. Marcel Dorigny (New York: Berghahn, 2003), 348.

7. For more on Grégoire and how he was invoked during the Bicentennial, see Sepinwall, *Abbé Grégoire.*

8. Barcellini, "Two Memories," 348, 351n22; "Toussaint Louverture. De Claude Moreau" (2:05, 4:04).

9. Frith and Hodgson, "Slavery and Its Legacies: Remembering Labour Exploitation in the Francophone World," and Chivallon, "Representing the Slave Past," both in Frith and Hodgson, *At the Limits*, 3, 38; Fleming, *Resurrecting Slavery*, 11; and also Myriam Cottias and Audra Diptee, "The Future of Slavery: Social History as Radical History," *Histoire sociale/Social History* 53, no. 107 (2020): 9–16.

10. Salvatori, "Spectacle: 'Je Suis Toussaint Louverture,'" 27. This perspective was the opposite of that in Hondo's *West Indies*, which emphasized that enslaved people's rebellions had won them freedom, not French ideals ("Don't listen to their books and statues!" [1:21:12]).

11. *Toussaint Louverture: Haïti et la France*, dir. Laurent Lutaud (2004), DVD, 85 min. (Paris: L'Harmattan, 2006) [54 min. film plus two extras]; and *Toussaint Louverture, Haiti, Destiny of a Nation*, dir. Lutaud, DVD, 54 min. ([Paris]: TV5 Monde and France Télévision, 2005), distributed by Monkey Bay and Lutaud via https://www.filmsdocumentaires.com/. The credits in the French version indicate support from France 3 Bourgogne, various agencies in Franche-Comté,

the Centre nationale de la cinématographie, the Ministry of Foreign Affairs, TV5 Monde, and municipalities near the fortress. The Inathèque's catalog indicates numerous airings of the film on France's History Channel and other stations. Timestamps below refer to the English version; the quotes I give combine those from the English version with my translations from the French version.

12. The Bois Caïman ceremony's location is debated; see Geggus, "Bois Caïman Ceremony," in *Haitian Revolutionary Studies.*

13. *Bonaparte, côté noir*, dir. Dominique Maestrati (2016), DVD, 52 min. (Paris: Injam Productions, 2017). Also posted by Roy Noel as "Bonaparte contre Toussaint Louverture, côté noir de France," YouTube, Apr. 7, 2018, https://www.youtube.com/watch?v=9P7EF1NapTo.

14. *L'impasse Toussaint-Louverture*, dir. Gaetano Ciarcia and Jean-Christophe Monferran, 42 min. (Paris: IIAC/IMAF/CNRS/EHESS, 2019), Canal-U, https://www.canal-u.tv/video/ehess/memoire_de_l_esclavage.51621.

15. *Égalité for All: Toussaint Louverture and the Haitian Revolution*, dir. Noland Walker, DVD, 60 min. (New York: PBS Home Video, 2009). Funding information from credits. A French version, *Toussaint Louverture, le libérateur d'Haïti*, was later shown on the French channel ARTE.

16. Dubois's book was advertised when *Égalité for All* aired on television; see version aired on WNED, YouTube, posted by Uptown Flava, Dec. 29, 2012, https://www.youtube.com/watch?v=IOGVgQYX6SU (54:05).

17. Zak Leonard, "'Egalite for All' Reflects on Haitian Revolution," *Watson Institute News, Brown University*, Jan. 15, 2010, https://watson.brown.edu/news/2010/egalite-all-reflects-haitian-revolution. *Égalité for All*'s IMDb page reports that Toussaint was played by Haitian American Jacques Derosena.

18. Martin Hafer, user review of *Égalité for All*, "Uplifting yet ultimately disastrous . . . ," IMDb.com, Sept. 6, 2013, https://www.imdb.com/title/tt1368166/.

19. Dubois, *Avengers*, 5, 113.

20. Series website, https://hiddencolorsfilm.com/, and Indiegogo site, https://www.indiegogo.com/projects/1804-the-hidden-history-of-haiti#/, both accessed Mar. 24, 2019; *1804: The Hidden History of Haiti*, dir. Tariq Nasheed, DVD, 110 min. ([Los Angeles]: King Flex Entertainment, 2017).

21. Admin C ["Hyppolite"], "1804: The Hidden History of Haiti," *Haitian History Blog: HHB-Tumblr*, Nov. 27, 2017, https://haitianhistory.tumblr.com/post/167951845053/1804-the-hidden-history-of-haiti-1804-the-hidden.

22. On Dessalines's diplomacy, which Nasheed seems to have been unaware of, see Maurice A. Lubin, "Les premiers rapports de la nation haïtienne avec l'étranger," *Journal of Inter-American Studies* 10, no. 2 (1968): 277–305; and Gaffield, *Haitian Connections.*

23. On the implications of this term and of caricatures of people of mixed race in the Revolution more generally, see Daut, *Tropics of Haiti*, 17–18, 33–34. *Égalité for All* refers to "mixed-race citizens" rather than use this word.

24. Hyppolite ("Admin C"), "1804: The Hidden History."

25. See IMDb.com pages for Derick Alexander (https://www.imdb.com/name/nm0018373/) and for *The Last Days of Toussaint L'Ouverture* (http://www.imdb.com/title/tt1478449/?ref_=nm_flmg_act_7), both accessed Mar. 24, 2019. Only excerpts of the film are publicly available; see Derick Alexander, "Part I Scene from: The Last Days of Toussaint L'Ouverture," YouTube,

posted Jul. 13, 2018, https://www.youtube.com/watch?v=WlB_QdZpkkc; Derick Alexander, "Part II: Scene from: The Last Days of Toussaint L'Ouverture," YouTube, posted Jul. 14, 2018, https://www.youtube.com/watch?v=qcfk32hsYeA; and Ade Adeyemo, "Joseph Ademola Adeyemo—The Last Days of Toussaint L'Ouverture—Scene [excerpt from *The Last Days*]," YouTube, posted Jan. 9, 2010, https://www.youtube.com/watch?v=iElUeKOjKdQ.

26. Facebook page for "The Last Days of Toussaint L'Ouverture," https://www.facebook.com/The-Last-Days-of-Toussaint-LOuverture-161292942956/; and "Director Derick Alexander Dedicated #LatinNegr@s film to Haiti (Jan. 25, 2010)," http://lati-negros.tumblr.com/post/387745205/director-derick-alexander-dedicated-latinnegrs, both accessed Mar. 24, 2019; Adeyemo, "Joseph Ademola Adeyemo . . . Scene."

27. The museum's "Family Programs" page formerly contained a description of the film, https://www.moadsf.org/learn/family-programs, accessed Oct. 13, 2017. Though MoAD ceased showing it onsite, the film remains available on Vimeo ("Haitian Revolution—Toussaint L'Overture [sic]," posted by Shiree Dyson, June 8, 2010, https://vimeo.com/12407210).

28. Edward Rothstein, "Museum Review: Anecdotal Evidence of Homesick Mankind," *New York Times*, July 20, 2006, E1; Katherine Corcoran, "Out of Africa: Museum of the African Diaspora," *Mercury News*, Apr. 19, 2007, https://www.mercurynews.com/2007/04/19/out-of-africa-museum-of-the-african-diaspora/; and Sasha Panaram, "Toussaint: The Heartbeat of Freedom," *The Black Atlantic* course blog, Mar. 6, 2014, https://sites.duke.edu/blackatlantic/2014/03/06/toussaint-the-heartbeat-of-freedom/, comment by Doug McHenry, Jan. 20, 2015 (accessed Aug. 7, 2015; the page remains online but without McHenry's comment).

29. *Black Dawn*, dir. Robin Lloyd and Doreen Kraft (1979), DVD, 18 min. (Burlington, VT: Green Valley Media, 2004), with DVD extras and accompanying study guide; Antonin, *Material para una pre-historia del cine haitiano/Matériel pour une pre-histoire du cinéma haïtien* (Caracas: n.p., 1983), 72–73. Another terrific foreign/Haitian collaboration was released while this book was in press, *Independence or Death: The Haitian Revolution*, dir. Mark Bowsher (2020).

30. Lloyd, interview with author, June 14, 2017 (henceforth Lloyd, interview).

31. "Interview with the Directors" special feature, *Black Dawn* DVD; Lloyd, interview. For more on Lloyd and the background to the film, see Susan Green, "Hyper Activist: With Radical Cred Dating Back before World War I, Robin Lloyd Lives Out a Leftist Legacy," *Seven Days*, Jan. 24, 2001, https://www.sevendaysvt.com/vermont/hyper-activist/Content?oid=2131371. Dominique was better known as a journalist than a filmmaker; however, in 1962, he codirected Haiti's first feature-length film, *Mais Moi Je Suis Belle*. Lafontant-Médard notes that Dominique also "occupied a towering position in Haitian cinema" as director of the Ciné-Club ("Cinema in Haiti," 81–82).

32. The fourth writer credited was Mary Lloyd, Robin Lloyd's mother. Robin Lloyd explains that her mother was an author who had contributed to magazines like *Ladies Home Journal* under a pseudonym. While Mary Lloyd did not travel to Haiti or write the original script, she helped with final edits (Lloyd, interview).

33. "Interview with the Directors," *Black Dawn* DVD; identification of Trouillot on the soundtrack courtesy of Nadève Ménard. For more on Tanbou Libète, see Yarimar Bonilla, "Burning Questions: The Life and Work of Michel-Rolph Trouillot, 1949–2012," *NACLA Report on the Americas* 46, no. 1 (2013): 82–84.

34. "Interview with the Directors," *Black Dawn* DVD.

35. Lloyd, interview; and "Interview with the Directors," *Black Dawn* DVD.

36. Lloyd, interview.

37. On this point, see also Kaisary, *The Haitian Revolution*, 49. On Dessalines as the most popular revolutionary within Haiti, see Edwidge Danticat, "[Interview with] Evelyne Trouillot," *Bomb*, Jan. 1, 2005, https://bombmagazine.org/articles/evelyne-trouillot/.

38. Nasheed's *1804* also seeks to portray Vodou (which it calls voodoo) positively. However, Admin C (Hyppolite) has remarked that, in that film, "Sadly, even the positive descriptions of Vodou are paired with caricatured video footage that does not resemble Vodou ceremonies in the least" ("1804: The Hidden History").

39. Lloyd, interview.

40. "BLM-TO Freedom School," http://freedomschool.ca/; "Aiyiti by BlackLivesMatter—Toronto Freedom School Amber Williams-King," YouTube, posted by Blacklivesmatter To[ronto], June 12, 2017, https://www.youtube.com/watch?v=lsK8Zwy4dEw. For information on the filmmakers, see "BLM-TO Freedom School—Our Team," http://freedomschool.ca/our-team/; and Toronto Arts Foundation, interview with Amber Williams-King, https://torontoartsfoundation.org/initiatives/awards/hidden-pages/2017-finalists/amber-williams-king. Sites accessed Mar. 24, 2019. One more animated short on the Revolution was released in 2019: "The first and last king of Haiti," made by Ted-ED and Cabong Studios in conjunction with Prof. Marlene Daut, YouTube, posted Oct. 7, 2019, https://www.youtube.com/watch?v=q7lfSjjMNU8.

41. The use of *often* suggests that education was withheld frequently, as a kind of discrimination; however, enslaved peoples were forbidden in the French colonies to attend school or learn how to read.

42. I am grateful to Nadève Ménard for telling me about this short and pointing to this omission.

Chapter 7. From the Duvalier Years through the 2004 Bicentennial: Haitian Reflections on the Revolution's Legacy

1. Feguenson Hermogène, "L'Université haïtienne face aux Études filmiques" (2019), unpublished paper, communicated to author.

2. Lafontant-Médard, "Cinema in Haiti: 1899 to 1982"; Bruce Paddington and Keith Q. Warner, "The Emergence of Caribbean Feature Films," *Black Camera* 1, no. 1 (2009): 91–108; and Meredith N. Robinson, "Ciné woulé, ciné en progrès: An Investigation of the Francophone Caribbean Film Circuit, 1968–2010," *Small Axe* 33 (2010): 58–60.

3. An accounting of post-occupation efforts to create customers for Hollywood in Haiti and Latin America would go beyond the scope of this book. Sources that might be used include Joseph Montllor, "Completed Questionnaire on CIAA Post-War Motion Picture 16mm Program [for Haiti]," July 25, 1945, in Motion Picture Society for the Americas [MPSA] Papers, AMPAS, 37.f-580; and CIAA Press Division, Special Feature Service, "Amazed Haitians See Their First Moving Pictures, July 00, 1943" [sic], in MPSA Papers, AMPAS, 24.f-437.

4. Arnold Antonin, "Haïti," in *Les Cinémas de l'Amérique latine: pays par pays, l'histoire, l'économie, les structures, les auteurs, les œuvres*, ed. Guy Hennebelle and Alfonso Gumucio Dagron (Paris: Lherminier, 1981), 341–45; Antonin, *Material para una pre-historia*; and Antonin, "Cinema in Haiti," *Small Axe* 12, no. 3 (2008): 87–93.

5. See Inter-American Commission on Human Rights, "Report on the Situation of Human Rights in Haiti (Sept. 7, 1988)," http://www.cidh.org/countryrep/Haiti88eng/chap.3a.htm. On

Dominique's assassination, see *The Agronomist*, dir. Jonathan Demme (2004), DVD, 90 min. ([Los Angeles]: New Line Home Entertainment, 2005); and Jeb Sprague, *Paramilitarism and the Assault on Democracy in Haiti* (New York: Monthly Review, 2012), 97–100.

6. Antonin, "Cinema in Haiti," 89, 91–92; and quoted in Katheline St. Fort, "New Generation of Haitian Filmmakers Are Making a Scene," *Miami Herald*, June 29, 2003, http://www.hartford-hwp.com/archives/43a/541.html.

7. Robinson, "Ciné woulé," 58–60; Hancy Pierre, "Le cinéma dans la tourmente et la misère des politiques de loisirs en Haïti," *Le Nouvelliste*, Oct. 13, 2017, https://lenouvelliste.com/article/176977/le-cinema-dans-la-tourmente-et-la-misere-des-politiques-de-loisirs-en-haiti; and description of Ciné Institute, http://cineinstitute.com/about/ (accessed Apr. 14, 2019). Doris Posch offers more information on the Ciné Institute in "The Jollywood Manifesto: Trans-Local Film Cultures in Haiti's Emerging Cinemas," *Култура/Culture* 12 (2015): 157–71; and "Emerging Film Cultures: Spotlight on Post-Disaster Haiti," *International Journal of Cultural Studies* 21, no. 1 (2018): 27–41. While Posch's work is helpful in many regards, it includes a few errors, such as misattributing the French miniseries on Toussaint Louverture to Danny Glover; see "Oral Storytelling, the Gaze and the Everyday: Documentary Filmmaking in Haiti," in *Dynamiques culturelles dans les cinémas africains du XXIe siècle/Cultural Dynamics in African Cinemas of the 21st Century*, ed. Ute Fendler and Christopher Vatter (Saarbrücken, Germany: Universitätsverlag des Saarlandes, 2018), 119n30.

8. Fondasyon Konesans Ak Libète, or the Foundation for Knowledge and Liberty.

9. Robinson, "Ciné woulé," 58; Posch, "Emerging Film Cultures," 31; Pierre, "Le cinéma dans la tourmente."

10. Facebook pages for the first three (https://www.facebook.com/versailleshaiti/; https://www.facebook.com/colombescine; https://www.facebook.com/revcinema/) all listed screenings in June 2018. On the Ciné Triomphe's ups and downs, see Will Speros, "Haiti Opens a Movie Theater for the First Time in over Five Years," *Architectural Digest*, June 30, 2015, https://www.architecturaldigest.com/story/haiti-cine-triomphe-movie-theater-reopens; and "Haiti Cinema—All the Haitian Movie Theaters Have Disappeared: What Happened?" *BelFìm*, July 31, 2017, http://belfim.fouye.com/news/haiti-cinema-haitian-movie-theaters-gone.html. In a Nov. 2018 visit, I could see a staff member inside the glass-walled Ciné Triomphe, but the doors were locked, no films were being shown, and the public was not permitted to enter. See also Amélie Baron, "No Theaters, No Money: Haiti Labors to Keep Cinema Alive," AFP, *Digital Journal*, Jan. 13, 2019, http://www.digitaljournal.com/news/world/no-theaters-no-money-haiti-labors-to-keep-cinema-alive/article/540847. Special events at the Triomphe since then have included the Festival Nouvelles Vues Haïti ; see Jennifer Stavenya Dorestant, "Festival 'Nouvelles vues Haïti,' nouvelle vie du cinéma haïtien," *Palmes Magazine*, May 2019, https://palmes-magazine.com/archives/1488.

11. Pierre Lucson Bellegarde, email to author, Mar. 11, 2019. Bellegarde noted that the Ciné Institute's partner institution, the Audio Institute, still had full-time students. The schools together form a larger body called the Artists Institute.

12. On differences in Haitian and foreign writing about the Revolution, see M.-R. Trouillot, *Silencing the Past*, 96–105; and Sepinwall, *Haitian History*, esp. 103–8.

13. *Ayiti, men chimen libète/Haïti, le chemin de la liberté*, dir. Antonin (1974), DVD, 92 min. (Pétionville, Haiti: Centre Pétion-Bolivar, 2009). For more on this film, see Virginie Hémar, *Arnold Antonin: Le cinéma de la liberté* (Port-au-Prince: Éditions de l'Université d'État d'Haïti,

2013), 90–91. Antonin's view here parallels that of M.-R. Trouillot in *Haiti, State against Nation: The Origins and Legacy of Duvalierism* (New York: Monthly Review, 1989).

14. *Simparele*, dir. Humberto Solás, VHS, 31 min. ([Havana]: El Instituto Cubano del Arte e Industria Cinematográficos, 1974), Amherst College Library.

15. See "Martha Jean-Claude, 82, Legendary Haitian Singer," *South Florida Sun-Sentinel*, Nov. 17, 2001, http://www.sun-sentinel.com/news/fl-xpm-2001-11-17-0111160886-story.html; and "Singer Martha Jean-Claude Dead at 82," *Haïti Progrès*, Nov. 21, 2001, reprinted at http://www.hartford-hwp.com/archives/43a/534.html.

16. Antonin, "Cinema in Haiti," 89.

17. Lafontant-Médard, "Cinema in Haiti," 89–90.

18. *Anita*, dir. Rassoul Labuchin, VHS, 47 min. ([Paris]: Médiathèque des trois mondes, 1980); Lafontant-Médard, "Cinema in Haiti," 89.

19. Lafontant-Médard, "A Thematic Analysis of Rassoul Labuchin's *Anita*," in Cham, *Ex-Iles: Essays on Caribbean Cinema*, 135, 151, 142.

20. Lafontant-Médard, "Thematic Analysis," 153.

21. Lafontant-Médard, "Cinema in Haiti," 91–92.

22. See Mylène Dorcé, "Rassoul Labuchin," *Île en île*, Nov. 25, 2015, http://ile-en-ile.org/labuchin/.

23. *GNB kont Attila/GNB contre Attila, ou une autre Haïti est possible*, dir. Antonin, DVD, 102 min. ([Port-au-Prince]: UAV/CPB, 2004). The film is in Kreyòl and French with English and Spanish subtitles. On the Centre Pétion Bolivar's audiovisual unit (UAV), see "Centre Pétion Bolivar (CPB)," *Africine.org*, http://www.africine.org/?menu=fichedist&no=2502, accessed Apr. 14, 2019.

24. *GNB*'s English subtitles use the term "balls up the wall." I am grateful to Claudy Delné for helping me render this more precisely in English. As the film indicates, women students complained that this slogan was gendered, but cheerfully agreed to march "ovaries up the ass" alongside men.

25. Haitian intellectuals living under Aristide were far more critical of him than were idealistic foreign intellectuals such as Peter Hallward. See forum in *Small Axe* 13, no. 3 [30] (2009): 128–75; as well as Martin Munro, "Whose and Which Haiti? Western Intellectuals and the Aristide Question," *Paragraph* 36, no. 3 (2013): 408–24; and Alex Dupuy, *The Prophet and Power: Jean-Bertrand Aristide, the International Community, and Haiti* (Lanham, MD: Rowman & Littlefield, 2007).

26. *Moloch Tropical*, dir. Raoul Peck, DVD, 107 min. (Paris: Velvet Film/ARTE France, 2009). For further analysis of this film, see Pressley-Sanon, "Up Through the Cracks: Raoul Peck's *Moloch Tropical* and the Ghosts of Haitian History," *Cultural Dynamics* 27, no. 3 (2015): 1–27; and Tama Hamilton-Wray, "Haitian National Identity and Gender in Raoul Peck's *Moloch Tropical*," in *Raoul Peck: Power, Politics and the Cinematic Imagination*, ed. Pressley-Sanon and Sophie Saint-Just (Lanham, MD: Lexington, 2015), 127–51. On Peck's other films, see also Sepinwall, "Who Is Raoul Peck? (And Why You Should Know if You Care about History)—The Filmmaker behind *I Am Not Your Negro*," *History News Network*, Feb. 19, 2017, http://historynewsnetwork.org/article/165190; and other essays in Pressley-Sanon and Saint-Just, *Raoul Peck*.

27. In addition to the film's opening credits and DVD, which state that *Moloch Tropical* was produced by Velvet Film with support from the CNC, the closing credits indicate "support" from Haitian agencies including the Ministry of Tourism, the Ministry of Culture and Communication, and the National Police (1:50:24). Presumably, this support was not financial, but

with the logistics needed for filming at the famously remote Citadelle. Peck discusses the difficulties of shooting there in the "Film Introduction" special feature, *Moloch Tropical* DVD.

28. See Robert Fatton Jr., "The Haitian Authoritarian *Habitus* and the Contradictory Legacy of 1804," *Journal of Haitian Studies* 10, no. 1 (2004): 22–43.

29. This ending parallels that of *Murder in Pacot*, dir. Peck (2014), DVD, 130 min. (Berlin: Velvet Film/Filmgalerie 451, 2016). In that film, a young Haitian woman hopes that her relationship with a foreign NGO worker will lift her from poverty. But he proves not to care about the country, and she ends up brutally murdered by a wealthy Haitian intellectual (the NGO worker's landlord) who had proclaimed his concern for the nation's youth. As she lies buried, never to be found again, the wealthy man, his elegant wife, and the NGO worker drive off in a BMW (1:59:09–2:05:43).

30. *Port-au-Prince, Dimanche 4 janvier*, dir. François Marthouret, 80 min. DVD screener for 2016 César Awards. A public release of the DVD, advertised for 2016, seems not to have happened.

31. Information communicated by N. Ménard; members of Trouillot's family are also thanked in the credits. Though Trouillot is not listed among the film's producers, the closing credits indicate his active participation by including his list of special thanks after those of the director and producers (1:19:53).

32. These included the CNC as well as the EU's Media Programme, Procirep, the Guadeloupe Region, France 3 Cinéma, and France Télévisions, as well as private companies such as Kasso Productions.

33. See Isabelle Regnier, "'Port-au-Prince, dimanche 4 janvier': frères ennemis en Haïti," *Le Monde*, July 28, 2015, https://www.lemonde.fr/cinema/article/2015/07/28/port-au-prince-dimanche-4-janvier-freres-ennemis-en-haiti_4701673_3476.html; Lyonel Trouillot, *Bicentenaire: Roman* (Arles, France: Actes sud, 2004); and Martin Munro's discussion of the novel's nuances ("Interdependence and Intertextuality in Lyonel Trouillot's *Bicentenaire*," *Small Axe* 12, no. 3 (27) [2008]: 42–52). Though most of the film was shot in Haiti, a few scenes were filmed in Point-à-Pitre, Guadeloupe (film credits).

34. Lyonel Trouillot and others have offered more nuanced analyses of Aristide's rule. But Marthouret seemed more interested in adding Haiti into the history of global student protest than in offering a complex treatment of Aristide's successes and failures. See the director's comments in Valérie Marin la Meslée, "'Port-au-Prince, dimanche 4 janvier': un autre regard sur Haïti," *Le Point*, July 28, 2015, https://www.lepoint.fr/cinema/port-au-prince-dimanche-4-janvier-un-autre-regard-sur-haiti-28-07-2015-1952904_35.php.

35. On these brothers embodying the conflict between Toussaint and Dessalines in Trouillot's original novel, see Munro, "Interdependence and Intertextuality," 46. For nonfiction analogues to Joe Joe (who are humanized more than he), see the *chimère* siblings 2Pac and Bily, *Ghosts of Cité Soleil*, dir. Asger Leth, DVD, 88 min. (n.p.: Imagine Entertainment, 2006).

36. On this speech, see Fatton, "The Rise, Fall, and Second Coming of Aristide," in Sepinwall, *Haitian History*, 308n27.

37. *Haïti, la fin des chimères*, dir. Charles Najman, 70 min., DVD [same disc as *Royal Bonbon*] (Paris: Malavida, 2004). The title has a double meaning in French. Literally it means, "Haiti: The End of Illusions?" but it also refers to the paramilitary *chimères*. So the title refers either to illusions ending or the *chimères*' demise. A few foreign directors made films about the conflict over Aristide but discuss the Revolution cursorily or not at all (for instance *Aristide*

and the Endless Revolution, dir. Nicolas Rossier [2005], 84 min., via Amazon Prime [discussion of Toussaint, 48:17–49:20]; and *Ghosts of Cité Soleil*).

38. Funders of *Haïti, la fin des chimères* included Arte France, the CNC, the Agence Nationale de Gestion des Œuvres Audiovisuelles, and Procirep. Munro offers a short analysis of this film in "The Apocalyptic Creole, from Dessalines to the Chimères," *Diaspora: A Journal of Transnational Studies* 17, no. 1 (2008): 115–16.

39. M.-R. Trouillot, *Haiti, State against Nation*; see also Hector and Hurbon, *Genèse de l'état Haïtien*.

40. For more on Dessables, see "Djalóki Jean-Luc Dessables," Georgetown University Berkley Center, https://berkleycenter.georgetown.edu/people/djaloki-jean-luc-dessables; on Boursiquot and his organization CODEHA, see Dr. Carolle [Jean-Murat], "TFT Relief in Haiti—La Vallee de Jacmel," https://www.tfttapping.com/tft-relief-in-haiti-la-vallee-de-jacmel/. Both accessed Sept. 29, 2020.

41. Wyclef Jean, "Baba ft. Kofi Black," YouTube, posted Feb. 22, 2019, https://www.youtube.com/watch?v=dA4R33fihkc; and Your Zouk TV, "T Micky Ft. Wyclef Jean—Nou Pare," YouTube, posted June 17, 2014, https://www.youtube.com/watch?v=_i9A1-SlP3I. Other Wyclef songs invoking revolutionary heroes include "Election Time," "Toussaint v. Bishop," "Marasa," and "Ghetto Racine."

42. Régine Jean-Charles, "The Myth of Diaspora Exceptionalism: Wyclef Jean Performs *Jaspora*," *American Quarterly* 66, no. 3 (2014): 848–49.

43. In addition to these other films by diaspora Haitians, Haitian American director Michelange Quay (one of the founding instructors at the Ciné Institute) has invoked the trauma of colonial slavery in works such as *Haïti Ground Zero* (version in progress, https://vimeo.com/78421665, password provided by Quay; more information at "Haïti Ground Zero," http://www.cinemadefacto.com/portfolio/haiti-ground-zero/, accessed Apr. 14, 2019).

44. *Liberty in a Soup*, dir. Dudley Alexis (2017), 66 min. Vimeo On Demand, https://vimeo.com/ondemand/libertyinasoup.

45. Dudley Alexis, interview with author, Aug. 17, 2019; *Liberty in a Soup* website, http://www.libertyinasoup.com/, accessed Aug. 15, 2019.

46. *Ayiti Toma*, dir. Joseph Hillel, 2013, 81 min. Vimeo On Demand, https://vimeo.com/ondemand/35875 (timestamps are from now-discontinued streaming venue, https://www.nfb.ca/film/ayiti_toma_en/); "Ayiti Toma" Press Kit, http://www.ijdh.org/wp-content/uploads/2014/04/dossierPresseAyitiTomaEN03.pdf, 1–4, 13.

47. G. Ulysse, *Why Haiti Needs New Narratives*, xxv. For criticisms of Penn and his J/P Haitian Relief Organization, see *Fatal Assistance* (Assistance mortelle), dir. Raoul Peck, DVD, 100 min. ([Paris]: Velvet Film, 2013); and J. Katz, *The Big Truck that Went By*, esp. 164–65.

48. *Haïti—La Route* (*Le Chemin Parcouru*), dir. Francine Saillant, Frantz Voltaire, and Ralph Maingrette, narration by Dany Laferrière, 2016, 33 min. (digital copy provided by Voltaire). The film has screened in Montreal several times but is not available for purchase. Though the digital version does not have English subtitles or full credits, Voltaire provided me with both in text form (email to author, June 19, 2017). All translations are my own, drawn from the film, but I refer to some details from this separate credit list.

49. For more on Maingrette, see his website, http://ralphmaingrette.com/Home.html, accessed Apr. 14, 2019.

50. Voltaire also served as chief of staff to Haitian prime minister Robert Malval (1993–94). His other films cover a range of topics in Haitian history and culture; see a partial list at https://www.africanfilmny.org/2013/frantz-voltaire/, accessed Apr. 14, 2019.

51. Francine Saillant's many works on Afro-Brazilians and African-descended people in the New World more generally include *Le mouvement noir au Brésil (2000–2010): Réparations, droits et citoyenneté* (Québec: Presses de l'Univ. Laval, 2014). She has also made a series of films about reparations and the legacy of slavery in Brazil. A longer discussion of the project can be found in Saillant, "Transmettre la mémoire de l'esclavage par la recherche collaborative" (unpublished essay, courtesy of the author).

52. The credits also note support from UNESCO's project La Route d'esclaves, as well as the Conseil de recherches en sciences humaines du Canada (CRSH).

53. Saillant, "Transmettre la mémoire."

54. Though Maingrette covered twelve themes in the camp (email to author, Aug. 4, 2018), an image on screen shows only the first eleven (5:02).

55. Camille Robitaille (Laferrière's PR agent), email to author, June 23, 2017; F. Voltaire, email to author, July 8, 2017; Saillant, email to author, June 20, 2018; and Maingrette, email to author, Aug. 4, 2018. Saillant notes that Laferrière "lent much more than his voice to this narration, which ultimately proved to be a creation unto itself" ("Transmettre la mémoire").

56. Maingrette, email to author, Aug. 4, 2018. Saillant has added that Désir was added to the film to feature a "strong feminine presence" alongside Maingrette and Laferrière ("Transmettre la mémoire").

57. *Haïti—La Route*'s inclusion of this detail offers more precision than other cinematic references to the Bois Caïman ceremony; as Geggus has noted, the meeting on the Lenormand estate is often conflated with the Bois Caïman ceremony (*Haitian Revolutionary Studies*, 85).

58. *Ayiti: The Awakening*, dir. Sage Love (2019), 26 min. On demand, via https://www.ayititheawakening.com/store.

Chapter 8. The Rising Generation, Toussaint Louverture, and the Problem of Funding

1. On Caribbean- or African diaspora–themed festivals providing an audience for young Haitian filmmakers, see Posch, "Emerging Film Cultures," 32.

2. Barbara Prézeau Stephenson, "Agression sur Maxence Denis," *Le Nouvelliste*, Feb. 10, 2009, https://lenouvelliste.com/article/67139/agression-sur-maxence-denis. See also Stephenson, "Contemporary Art as Cultural Product in the Context of Haiti," trans. Rachel Douglas, in *Small Axe* 12, no. 3 [27] (2008): 94–104; and Carlo Célius, "Quelques aspects de la nouvelle scène artistique d'Haïti," *Gradhiva* 2015/1 (no. 21): 107. Denis's video installation *Kwa Bawon* and his mixed-media sculpture *Joshua Tree* have been featured in *Small Axe* 9, no. 2 (2005), and 12, no. 3 (2008). Denis changed the spelling of his name to Maksaens in 2009.

3. Laurence d'Ist, "Maksaens Denis," https://www.maksaens-denis.com/about; "Maksaens Denis," *Kolektif509*, https://www.kolektif509.com/maksaens-denis; Chris Cozier, "Maksaens Denis," *BOMB Magazine*, Jan 1. 2005, https://bombmagazine.org/articles/maksaens-denis/; "E pluribus Unum de Maxence Denis," https://www.collectif2004images.org/shop/E-pluribus-Unum-de-Maxence-Denis_p5.html; Denis, "Marchons unis . . . ," YouTube, posted Aug. 3, 2017, https://www.youtube.com/watch?v=xbmKAD-t5Ak; and videos on Denis's Vimeo (https://vimeo.com/user3563092) and YouTube (https://www.youtube.com/user/Maksaens) channels.

4. *L'arbre de la liberté*, dir. Maxence Denis, DVD, 66 min. ([Paris]: Jakaranda Productions, 2004) (also as Denis, "L'arbre de la liberté," YouTube, posted Dec. 4, 2011, https://www.youtube.com/watch?v=Y5BTYLwoofo); and Denis, interview with author, Aug. 22, 2017. For the full text of my interviews with Denis, Kendy Vérilus, and Pierre Lucson Bellegarde, see "Films haïtiens sur la figure de Toussaint Louverture et la Révolution haïtienne: Entretiens avec Maksaens Denis, Kendy Vérilus et Pierre Lucson-Bellegarde," *Haitian History Journal/Revue d'Histoire Haïtienne* 1 (2019): 557–78.

5. Denis, interview.

6. Denis, interview.

7. Denis, interview.

8. Denis, interview; list of screenings at "l'Arbre de la liberté de Maxence Denis," *Collectif2004 Images Haïti*, https://www.collectif2004images.org/shop/l-Arbre-de-la-liberte-de-Maxence-Denis_p20.html, accessed Mar. 24, 2019.

9. *Toussaint Louverture, par devoir de mémoire*, dir. Kendy Vérilus (2003), 20 min., digital copy provided by Vérilus.

10. "Dominique Batraville et Kendy Vérilus au festival Cinamazonia," *Le Nouvelliste*, Nov. 4, 2005, https://lenouvelliste.com/article/22213/dominique-batraville-et-kendy-verilus-au-festival-cinamazonia; photo credits for Vérilus on different websites; "Court-métrage de Kendy Vérilus sur nos disparus du 12 janvier 2010," *Le Nouvelliste*, Jan. 10, 2018, https://lenouvelliste.com/article/181609/court-metrage-de-kendy-verilus-sur-nos-disparus-du-12-janvier-2010; "Agenda: Culture," *Le Nouvelliste*, Mar. 5, 2018, http://www.lenouvelliste.com/public/index.php/article/184054/agenda; and Michel DeGraff and Vérilus, "MIT-Haiti Initiative: Opening Up Education in Haiti," NSF Teaching and Learning Video Showcase, 2015, https://resourcecenters2015.videohall.com/presentations/519.

11. "Court-métrage de Kendy Vérilus"; Vérilus, interview with author, Sept. 11, 2017.

12. Vérilus, interview.

13. Vérilus, interview.

14. Vérilus, interview.

15. Vérilus shared the film with me as a digital file, noting "until I received your email, the film remained [only] in my archives" (Vérilus, interview).

16. Posch, "Emerging Film Cultures," 30; Posch, "The Jollywood Manifesto," 159, 162 (fig. 1); and Shirley Bruno, "Interview: Haiti's Ciné Institute Founder David Belle on Cultivating a Local Film Industry & More," *IndieWire*, Mar. 17, 2014, https://www.indiewire.com/2014/03/interview-haitis-cine-institute-founder-david-belle-on-cultivating-a-local-film-industry-more-161192/ (discontinued).

17. P. L. Bellegarde, interview with author, Aug. 15, 2017 (henceforth Bellegarde, interview).

18. "Pierre Lucson Bellegarde" biography, *Festival des 3 Continents*, Nov. 2013, http://www.3continents.com/en/individu/7188/; "Ciné Institute Graduates Attend Cannes Film Festival," *Ciné Institute* website, 2013, http://cineinstitute.com/project/cine-institute-graduates-attend-cannes-film-festival/ (discontinued); and Olivier Barlet, "Vers Jollywood? Entretien d'Olivier Barlet avec le cinéaste haïtien Pierre Lucson Bellegarde à propos de *Carmen*," *Africultures*, July 23, 2013, http://africultures.com/vers-jollywood-11710/.

19. Bellegarde, interview; Bellegarde, "ML Vosta [*Toussaint Louverture: Miroir d'une société* with English subtitles]," YouTube, posted Sept. 22, 2017, https://www.youtube.com/watch?v=Iu-yLB6ozX8&t=5s.

20. Bellegarde, interview. For an analysis of Bellegarde's film from a Cinema Studies perspective, see Posch, "Oral Storytelling" (116–19).

21. Bellegarde, interview. As this book was in press, Bellegarde released one more short centered on Toussaint. *Rasin* (shared with me by the director and screened virtually at the Haitian International Film Festival, 2020) showed Bellegarde's journey to Bénin to trace Toussaint's roots.

22. Bellegarde, interview; Bellegarde, email to author, Mar. 11, 2019.

23. Bellegarde, interview; Bellegarde, email to author, Aug. 17, 2017.

24. For foreign portrayals of the Haitian Revolution in graphic form, see *The Saga of Toussaint L'Ouverture and the Birth of Haiti* ([New York]: Fitzgerald Publishing, 1966); Forsdick, "Haiti and Comics: The Search for (New Graphic) Narratives," *Yale French Studies*, nos. 131/132 (2017): 189–214; and Rocky Cotard and L. Dubois, "The Slave Revolution that Gave Birth to Haiti," *The Nib*, Feb. 5, 2018, https://thenib.com/haitian-revolution. Forsdick notes that early graphic portrayals of Haitian history teemed with racist caricatures. Thorobred Books recently created a series of English-language graphic histories on the Revolution, with books by Frantz Derenoncourt Jr and by Bayinnah Bello.

25. *Haiti Open* (Spring 2015 issue), https://issuu.com/haitiopen/docs/haitiopen_spring2015, 68 - 80. I am grateful to Muriel Tramis for introducing me to Joseph's work.

26. Mp Mp, "full Noir&blanc de joseph kendy," YouTube, posted Dec. 13, 2014, https://www.youtube.com/watch?v=EFkkooBHmiM; and Kendy Joseph, "Noir et blanc Chevelin Illustration," YouTube, posted July 15, 2017, https://www.youtube.com/watch?v=CiTDDFAY_mE. Joseph confirmed that the earlier version was fan-made (email to author, July 14, 2017). Joseph had been circulating his own version privately, and then placed it on YouTube.

27. Lafontant-Médard, "Cinema in Haiti," 84–85.

28. "A Conversation with Paris-Based Filmmaker Elsie Haas," *CSMS Magazine*, Oct. 18, 2013, https://csmsmagazine.org/?p=6864; and Claire Andrade-Watkins, "Interview with Elsie Haas," in Cham, *Ex-Iles*, 310.

29. Gwen Douguet, "Raoul Peck pour Louverture," *Challenges*, Apr. 28, 2009, https://www.challenges.fr/cinema/raoul-peck-pour-louverture_529214; and [Jonel Juste], "Raoul Peck prépare un téléfilm sur Toussaint Louverture" [from Haitian Press Network], *Haïti en Marche* 23, no. 18 (May 27, 2009): 9 (reproduced at https://ufdcimages.uflib.ufl.edu/UF/00/09/88/09/00354/00005-27-2009.pdf).

30. Quoted in Claire Steinlen, "Toussaint Louverture, une icône," *Le Télégramme*, Feb. 12, 2012, LexisNexis.

31. I obtained this draft, which was not to have been the final shooting script, as well as information on Peck's scholarly collaborators, from a source close to the production who asked to remain unidentified.

32. M.-R. Trouillot, *Silencing the Past*, 96, 105–6.

33. Rosenstone, *Visions of the Past*, 68–76. On Peck's valorization of historical accuracy, see the essays in Pressley-Sanon and Saint-Just, *Raoul Peck*.

34. General Laveaux appears in the first episode of Peck's script, but to a far lesser extent than in the final miniseries. Peck's Laveaux seeks to persuade Toussaint to switch from the Spanish back to the French army, and Toussaint later seeks to press him into service on his behalf. But Peck's Laveaux is not a guide without whom Toussaint is lost, and he does not appear in episode 2. The fictional priest who teaches Toussaint to read in Niang's miniseries is absent in this earlier version.

35. Thornton, "African Soldiers."

36. M.-R. Trouillot, *Silencing the Past*, 105, 175n65.

37. On women in the Revolution, see for instance Judith Kafka, "Action, Reaction and Interaction: Slave Women in Resistance in the South of Saint-Domingue, 1793–94," *Slavery and Abolition* 18, no. 2 (1997): 48–72; and Sabine Manigat, "Les femmes au cours de la période révolutionnaire," in Hector and Hurbon, *Genèse de l'état haïtien*, 313–19.

38. It remains unclear whether Peck retains the rights to this script and could use it in the future, now that his Oscar nomination has raised his profile. In a 2017 interview, Peck hinted that he might someday try to do a similar project in the US (Rosny Ladouceur, "Un personnage historique au cœur d'un prochain film de Peck," *Loop*, June 16, 2017, http://www.loophaiti.com/content/un-personnage-historique-au-coeur-dun-prochain-film-de-peck [Soundcloud file, 5:37]). However, I have not found other indications that Peck is working on this plan, and, as Ladouceur noted, "the filmmaker refrained from giving any more details."

Chapter 9. North American and European Games: From MECC's *Freedom!* to *Assassin's Creed: Freedom Cry*

1. Video games on slavery have begun to receive attention from scholars in Literature and Communication Studies, if not from historians. Some of the games discussed here (but not the entire corpus analyzed here and in chapter 10) are treated in Souvik Mukherjee, "Video Games and Slavery," *Transactions of the Digital Games Research Association* 2, no. 3 (2016): 243–60; Emil Hammar, "Counter-Hegemonic Commemorative Play: Marginalized Pasts and the Politics of Memory in the Digital Game *Assassin's Creed: Freedom Cry*," *Rethinking History* 21, no. 3 (2017): 372–95; Sarah Juliet Lauro, "Digital Saint-Domingue: Playing Haiti in Videogames," in *SX Archipelagos*, no. 2 (2017), http://smallaxe.net/sxarchipelagos/issue02/playing-haiti.html; Kishonna L. Gray, "Power in the Visual: Examining Narratives of Controlling Black Bodies in Contemporary Gaming," *Velvet Light Trap* 81 (2018): 62–66; and Mukherjee, "Playing Subaltern: Video Games and Postcolonialism," *Games and Culture* 13, no. 5 (2018): 504–20. As this book was in press, Lauro's *Kill The Overseer! The Gamification of Slave Resistance* (Minneapolis: Univ. of Minnesota Press, 2020) appeared as part of that press's Forerunner series of short "digital works written between fresh ideas and finished books." Lauro's Forerunner discusses games such as *AC Liberation* and *AC Freedom Cry*, with an especially valuable focus on game form and ludology.

2. Marc Bernardin, "Gaming while Black: Has 'Red Dead Redemption 2' Shifted a Toxic Culture?," *Hollywood Reporter*, Dec. 6, 2018, https://www.hollywoodreporter.com/heat-vision/subversive-racial-commentary-red-dead-redemption-2-1165989.

3. Rizzo, Comment, on "Racist Video Game 'Playing History 2: Slave Trade' Pokes Fun at the Slave Trade," *Clutch*, Aug. 2015, http://www.clutchmagonline.com/2015/08/racist-video-game-playing-history-2-slave-trade-pokes-fun-at-the-slave-trade/ (discontinued); and Pazuzu, Comment, on Patrick Klepek, "Backlash over Supposedly Educational 'Slave Tetris' Video Game," *Kotaku*, Sept. 3, 2015, https://kotaku.com/this-is-a-screen-shot-from-slave-tetris-which-i-can-as-1728483373.

4. Joshua Holdenried with Nicholas Trépanier, "Dominance and the Aztec Empire: Representations in *Age of Empires II* and *Medieval II: Total War*," in Kapell and Elliott, *Playing with the Past*, 108.

5. See for instance William Uricchio, "Simulation, History and Computer Games," in *Handbook of Computer Game Studies*, ed. Joost Raessens and Jeffrey H. Goldstein (Cambridge, MA:

MIT Press, 2005), 327–38; Kapell and Elliott, *Playing with the Past*; Winnerling and Kerschbaumer, *Early Modernity and Video Games*; and Chapman, *Digital Games*.

6. Holdenried and Trépanier, "Dominance," 116; Michael D. Hattem, "American Revolution: The Game," *The Junto* blog, Jan. 4, 2013, https://earlyamericanists.com/2013/01/04/american-revolution-the-game/.

7. Trépanier, "The Assassin's Perspective"; Sarah Zaidan, review of *Playing with the Past*, by Kappell and Elliot, *Journal of Popular Culture* 48, no. 2 (2015): 428; and Whitaker, "Backward Compatible." On Disneyland and other sources of popular historical knowledge, see Mike Wallace, *Mickey Mouse History and Other Essays on American Memory* (Philadelphia: Temple Univ. Press, 1996).

8. Elie Wiesel, "Art and the Holocaust: Trivializing Memory," *New York Times*, June 11, 1989, sec. 2:1, and "TV View: The Trivializing of the Holocaust," *New York Times*, Apr. 16, 1978, sec. 2:29. Wiesel was not alone in expressing qualms about Holocaust dramas. On the initial controversies over now-iconic films such as *Schindler's List*, see Baron, *Projecting the Holocaust*, 1–2, 51–55; and Yosefa Loshitzky, ed., *Spielberg's Holocaust: Critical Perspectives on Schindler's List* (Bloomington: Indiana Univ. Press, 1997). Wiesel later softened his position; see his foreword to Annette Insdorf, *Indelible Shadows: Film and the Holocaust*, 3rd ed. (New York: Cambridge Univ. Press, 2003), xi–xii.

9. Sepinwall, "Elie Wiesel Interview, Carlsbad, California (Dove Lane Library), Apr. 19, 2007," YouTube, posted July 13, 2016, https://www.youtube.com/watch?v=sXhG7nXHdFc (8:48–9:30).

10. On applying Rosenstonian theories to video games, see also Chapman, "Privileging Form over Content: Analysing Historical Videogames," *Journal of Digital Humanities* 1, no. 2 (2012), http://journalofdigitalhumanities.org/1-2/privileging-form-over-content-by-adam-chapman/; Chapman, *Digital Games*, 7-15, 18-20; and Kapell and Elliott, *Playing with the Past*, 3, 6, 8. Though my mode of analysis is also inspired by Rosenstone, as a Haitian Revolution specialist I depart from Chapman in offering a content-focused approach, rather than Chapman's "form-focused" approach.

11. Kevin Schut, "Strategic Simulations and Our Past: The Bias of Computer Games in the Presentation of History," *Games and Culture* 2, no. 3 (2007): 220; Dom Ford, "'eXplore, eXpand, eXploit, eXterminate': Affective Writing of Postcolonial History and Education in Civilization V," *Game Studies* 16, no. 2 (2016), http://gamestudies.org/1602/articles/ford; and Rebecca Mir and Trevor Owens, "Modeling Indigenous Peoples: Unpacking Ideology in *Sid Meier's Colonization*," in Kapell and Elliott, *Playing with the Past*, 91–106.

12. Michel Marriott, "Blood, Gore, Sex and Now: Race," *New York Times*, Oct. 21, 1999, G1; Anna Everett, "Serious Play: Playing with Race in Contemporary Gaming Culture," in Raessens and Goldstein, *Handbook*, 312.

13. Marriott, "Blood, Gore"; Gonzalo Frasca, "Videogames of the Oppressed: Critical Thinking, Education, Tolerance and Other Trivial Issues," in Wardrip-Fruin and Harrigan, *First Person*, 90; and Kishonna L. Gray and David J. Leonard, eds., *Woke Gaming: Digital Challenges to Social Injustice* (Seattle: Univ. of Washington Press, 2018), 8. On Gamergate, see Caitlin Dewey, "The Only Guide to Gamergate You Will Ever Need to Read," *Washington Post*, Oct. 14, 2014, https://www.washingtonpost.com/news/the-intersect/wp/2014/10/14/the-only-guide-to-gamergate-you-will-ever-need-to-read/.

14. *Freedom!* (Apple II), Moby Games, https://www.mobygames.com/game/apple2/freedom; MECC, "MECC A-315 Freedom Manual" (1992), https://archive.org/stream/A2_MECC_A_315

_Freedom_manual/MECC%20A-315%20Freedom%20manual_djvu.txt, accessed Apr. 21, 2019; "Information. Version 1.0," Pixielation, "Freedom!" (walk-through), YouTube, posted June 3, 2016, https://www.youtube.com/watch?v=4HzKcG1SP6g (1:07), discontinued; *Freedom!* (Apple II), screenshot, Moby Games, posted by Alaka, Aug. 29, 2009, https://www.mobygames.com/game/apple2/freedom/screenshots/gameShotId,383640/.

15. MECC, "MECC A-315 Freedom Manual"; Pixielation, walk-through (19:28).

16. Pixielation, walk-through (esp. 2:40–2:47); Paul C. Schuytema, "What Cost Freedom?," *Compute!*, no. 156 (1993): 82.

17. Playing History website, http://www.playinghistory.eu/ (discontinued; accessed May 4, 2017); part of that text remains at Serious Games Portal, Slave Trade, https://school.seriousgames.net/slave-trade/, accessed June 10, 2019.

18. Wesley Yin-Poole, "'Slave Tetris' Pulled from Steam Game after Social Media Backlash," *Eurogamer*, Sept. 9, 2015, https://www.eurogamer.net/articles/2015-09-03-slave-tetris-pulled-from-steam-game-after-social-media-backlash; Andy Chalk, "'Slave Tetris' Cut from Playing History 2—Slave Trade after Backlash," *PC Gamer*, Sept. 3, 2015, https://www.pcgamer.com/slave-tetris-cut-from-playing-history-2slave-trade-after-backlash/; and also Wainwright, *Virtual History*, 196–98. The rest of the game remained available for purchase (https://store.steampowered.com/app/386870/Playing_History_2__Slave_Trade/, accessed Apr. 21, 2019).

19. Serious Games Interactive, "Playing History 2: Slave Trade," trailer, YouTube, posted Sept. 5, 2014, https://www.youtube.com/watch?v=o_Pfzv_71BY; and Serious Games Portal, Slave Trade.

20. Dexter Thomas, "I Played 'Slave Tetris' so Your Kids Don't Have to," *Los Angeles Times*, Sept. 7, 2015, https://www.latimes.com/entertainment/herocomplex/la-et-hc-played-slave-tetris-kids-20150904-htmlstory.html.

21. Serious Games Interactive, "Playing History 2" trailer.

22. *Mission 2, 'Flight to Freedom' Educator Guide*, https://assets.mission-us.org/wp-content/uploads/2019/12/26210532/complete_flight_to_freedom_classroom_guide_final.pdf, 5, accessed Sept. 30, 2020. Berlin, a former Organization of American Historians president who died in 2018, was white; Taylor (then associated with the National Underground Railroad Freedom Center and now at Howard University) and Moore (of NYPL's Schomburg Center for Research in Black Culture) are Black.

23. Statement from WNET Education, in Kellie Specter, "In Support of 'Flight to Freedom,' One of Many Ways to Teach History," *EdSurge*, Feb. 18, 2015, https://www.edsurge.com/news/2015-02-18-in-support-of-flight-to-freedom-one-of-many-ways-to-teach-history. *Flight to Freedom* parallels a recent board game called *Freedom—The Underground Railroad* in focusing on enslaved people's efforts to escape with help from abolitionists (AcademyGames, https://www.academygames.com/products/freedom-the-underground-railroad-1, accessed Apr. 21, 2019).

24. *Mission US: Flight to Freedom*, downloadable at http://www.mission-us.org/games/flight-to-freedom/, accessed Sept. 30, 2020. Analysis and dialogue are based on my own gameplay, unless otherwise indicated.

25. Christy Matte, Common Sense Media review of *Mission US: Flight to Freedom*, https://www.commonsensemedia.org/game-reviews/mission-us-flight-to-freedom, accessed Apr. 21, 2019; Kirk Hamilton, "They Made a Video Game about Slavery, and It's Actually Good," *Kotaku*, Feb. 14, 2012, https://kotaku.com/they-made-a-video-game-about-slavery-and-its-actually-5885194.

26. Rafranz Davis, "Is a Slave Simulation Game Appropriate for Classrooms?," *EdSurge*, Feb. 17, 2015, https://www.edsurge.com/news/2015-02-17-opinion-slave-simulation-an-edtech-game-for-classrooms; and Joseph Williams, "Teachers to Game Makers: Slavery's Not for Fun," *Takepart*, Feb. 18, 2015, http://www.takepart.com/article/2015/02/18/teachers-to-game-makers-slavery-not-for-fun/.

27. Cited in Dru Sefton, "Second School District Halts Use of WNET's 'Mission US' Games," *Current*, Nov. 3, 2017, https://current.org/2017/11/second-school-district-halts-use-of-wnets-mission-us-games/.

28. Specter, "In Support."

29. Cited in Sefton, "Second School District."

30. *Mission 2, 'Flight to Freedom' Educator Guide*, 79, 97, 99, 147, 121.

31. On this discrepancy, see also Alice Reid, Comment, in "Video Game Gets US Students to Role Play as Escaping Slave," *Al-Jazeera: The Stream*, Feb. 16, 2015, http://stream.aljazeera.com/story/201502162039-0024562.

32. Stewart King and Allison Shutt have been working on an in-class role-playing game on the Haitian Revolution, as part of the Reacting to the Past series. Because I saw only a partial version during a 2018 workshop, and the game is not yet released, I am not analyzing it here.

33. Forsdick, "Toussaint Louverture in a Globalized Frame: Reading the Revolutionary as Icon," *Contemporary French and Francophone Studies* 19, no. 3 (2015): 332. *Age of Empires III: The WarChiefs* (2006, Microsoft Game Studio) is available for download at Amazon.com. A description of the Toussaint character can be found at the Age of Empires Wiki, https://ageofempires.fandom.com/wiki/Toussaint_L%27Ouverture. Initial sales were two million copies ("'Age of Empires III' Expands into the Eastern World This Fall," http://www.agecommunity.com/press.aspx?PressReleaseID=161), with more sold since. Accessed Apr. 21, 2019.

34. Neil Smith, "An Island in Flames: The Revolution in Haiti, 1791–1804/Wargaming the Haitian Revolution," *Wargames Illustrated*, no. 277 (2010): 54, 58. The game *80 Days*, based on Jules Verne's *Around the World in 80 Days*, offers some positive representations of Haiti by presenting an alternative reality in which the country became rich after the Revolution and owns the Panama Canal. However, it also includes representations of Haiti as primitive. Whereas other countries have automatons made from steam and metal, "Haitian machines are made from bone and wood and seem to run on blood and Voodoo" in the game ("Video Games: 80 Days," https://tvtropes.org/pmwiki/pmwiki.php/VideoGame/EightyDays, accessed Apr. 21, 2019).

35. Graeme McMillan, "Titan to Bring 'Assassin's Creed' Back to Comics," *Hollywood Reporter*, June 24, 2015, https://www.hollywoodreporter.com/heat-vision/titan-bring-assassins-creed-back-804743; "Assassin's Creed," Box Office Mojo, https://www.boxofficemojo.com/movies/?id=assassinscreed.htm, accessed June 10, 2019. On Martin's collaboration with Ubisoft, see Jean-Clément Martin and Laurent Turcot, *Au cœur de la révolution: Les leçons d'histoire d'un jeu vidéo* (Paris: Vendémiaire, 2015). On other titles in the *AC* series, see Winnerling and Kerschbaumer, *Early Modernity and Video Games*, 151–211.

36. Chris Suellentrop, "Slavery as New Focus for a Game," *New York Times*, Jan. 27, 2014, C1; Writers Guild of America, News Release, Feb. 17, 2013, https://www.wgaeast.org/wp-content/uploads/typo3/user_upload/_temp_/2013_Writers_Guild_Awards_-_WINNERS_Announced_2-17-13_FINAL-js.pdf; Everett, "Race," in *The Routledge Companion to Video Game Studies*, ed. Mark J. P. Wolf and Bernard Perron (New York: Routledge, 2014), 400, 404.

See also Tobias Kraft, "Towards the Digital Atlantic? New Orleans's Open World in *Assassin's Creed III: Liberation HD*," in *New Orleans and the Global South: Caribbean, Creolization, Carnival*, ed. Ottmar Ette and Gesine Müller (Hildesheim, Germany: Georg Olms, 2017), 259–73. Soraya Murray offers a positive appraisal of *AC Liberation*, but notes how its mechanics (such as swashbuckling) "closely connect to the history of European imperial expansion" (*On Video Games*, 48–87, quote from 67). On race in games, see also Jennifer Malkowski and TreaAndrea M. Russworm, eds., *Gaming Representation: Race, Gender, and Sexuality in Video Games* (Bloomington: Indiana Univ. Press, 2017).

37. In 2020, many women developers began to speak publicly about their struggles to create female characters and about sexual abuse in the industry, including at Ubisoft. Those who shared such stories on Twitter included Jill Murray, the lead scriptwriter for *Freedom Cry* and co-writer of *Liberation*, and Kim Belair. See Belair, "We Need a Movement to Tackle Systemic Abuse, Not a Moment," *GamesIndustry.biz*, July 7, 2020, https://www.gamesindustry.biz/articles/2020-07-06-we-need-a-movement-to-tackle-systemic-abuse-not-a-moment-opinion; and Jill Murray, "The gentleman from editorial said 'the protagonist must be a STRAIGHT WHITE ALPHA MALE' . . . ," Twitter, July 21, 2020, https://twitter.com/disco_jill/status/1285590827830517761.

38. *Liberation* was designed for the Playstation Vita but later released on other platforms. For more on the characters Jeanne and Makandal, see the *Assassin's Creed Wiki* entries (https://assassinscreed.fandom.com/wiki/Jeanne and https://assassinscreed.fandom.com/wiki/Fran%C3%A7ois_Mackandal, accessed Apr. 21, 2019). On how *Liberation* was designed to showcase the Vita's capabilities rather than be *AC*'s most historically accurate game, see Sceablog, "Assassin's Creed III: Liberation—Developer Interview," YouTube, posted Oct. 26, 2012, https://www.youtube.com/watch?v=3kkLBgAlT_E.

39. Chivallon, "Representing the Slave Past," 31.

40. Iampanax, "Assassin's Creed Liberation HD All Cutscenes Movie," YouTube, posted Jan. 18, 2014, https://www.youtube.com/watch?v=fIPx3MiNWY4 (for instance 29:35). In contrast to *AC Liberation*, *AC Freedom Cry* offers no such portrayals of Vodou ceremonies, something that drew Evan Narcisse's praise: "I'm glad Ubi Quebec didn't go there because it's become a tired cliché to have some sort of voodoo/hoodoo mumbo jumbo in period-piece entertainments dealing with Haiti" ("A Game that Showed Me My Own Black History," *Kotaku*, Dec. 19, 2013, https://kotaku.com/a-game-that-showed-me-my-own-black-history-1486643518).

41. Lauro, "Digital Saint-Domingue." See, however, Lauro's discussion of the game's post-modern layer, whereby a twenty-first-century hacker explains that he has made the false Makandal look more evil than he was.

42. The game was called *Assassin's Creed IV: Black Flag—Freedom Cry* when released as bonus content for the main *AC IV* game; however, it was so successful that Ubisoft subsequently released it as a stand-alone game with a separate name.

43. Narcisse, "Come On, Video Games, Let's See Some Black People I'm Not Embarrassed by," *Kotaku*, Mar. 29, 2012, https://kotaku.com/come-on-video-games-let-s-see-some-black-people-i-m-n-5897227; Narcisse, "The Natural: The Trouble Portraying Blackness in Video Games," *Kotaku*, Feb. 23, 2017, https://kotaku.com/the-natural-the-trouble-portraying-blackness-in-video-1736504384; Narcisse, "A Game That Showed Me"; and Bernardin, "Gaming while Black."

44. The game developers had specific reasons for placing the game in the 1730s: they needed the timing to match what was happening in *AC IV: Black Flag*. In addition, they wanted to tie the game to an expedition by scientist Louis Godin in the mid-1730s.

45. See for instance Lauro's concern about whether "Haiti's legacy of slave resistance was being reduced to an entertainment commodity" ("Digital Saint-Domingue").

46. See also the game's trailer, Ubisoft, "Freedom Cry DLC Trailer Featuring Adewale|Assassin's Creed 4 Black Flag [UK]," YouTube, posted Oct. 8, 2013, https://www.youtube.com/watch?v=yoxNjLX4M-A, which gave further information on Adéwalé's painful childhood in slavery and the basis for his wanting revenge.

47. Because it is hard to transcribe dialogue while playing, all dialogue cited here comes from cutscene videos (unless otherwise noted, Gamer's Little Playground, "Assassin's Creed 4—Freedom Cry Game Movie w/Gameplay 1080p NEW DLC," YouTube, posted Dec. 18, 2013, https://www.youtube.com/watch?v=nA-Ht2gaN88) or the *Assassin's Creed Wiki*, beginning at https://assassinscreed.fandom.com/wiki/The_Calm_Before_the_Storm, accessed Apr. 21, 2019). Animus Database material is not accessible online, so all Animus information comes from gameplay of the PS4 version.

48. Lisa Nakamura has questioned whether having white gamers play as Black male bodies really represents progress; see *Digitizing Race: Visual Cultures of the Internet* (Minneapolis: Univ. of Minnesota Press, 2008), 18–19. Anna Everett and S. Craig Watkins have suggested that Black avatars can promote racism if coded with hyperaggressive "urban" characteristics; see "The Power of Play: The Portrayal and Performance of Race in Video Games," in *The Ecology of Games: Connecting Youth, Games, and Learning*, ed. Katie Salen (Cambridge, MA: MIT Press, 2008), 141–66. However, Everett has praised *AC Liberation*'s Aveline as different from other avatars of color ("Race"). Similarly, I would argue that Adéwalé is different from the avatars Nakamura points to in *Madden Football* or *Grand Theft Auto*; he is a thoughtful postcolonial hero who exposes the injustices of slavery.

49. Technically, gamers are not playing unmediated as Adéwalé but rather as Milton Jones (a twenty-first-century descendant of Adéwalé who works for the game's fictional Abstergo Industries) playing as Adéwalé. However, gamers who play the stand-alone version of *Freedom Cry* without looking at *Initiates* content may not know this postmodern angle.

50. My assessment of *Freedom Cry* differs from that of Mukherjee ("Playing Subaltern") and others who have criticized the game based on its mechanics, particularly given my comparison of the game to existing films. As Mukherjee notes, some of the game's subalterns (by whom he means the slaves whom Adéwalé frees) are silent. However, the game foregrounds other subalterns on the island to a much greater extent than do most existing films; several Haitians, including Bastienne and Augustin, speak to Adéwalé, and their perspectives shape his actions.

51. Moreau de Saint-Méry, *A Civilization that Perished*; Dominique Rogers and Stewart King, "Housekeepers, Merchants, Rentières: Free Women of Color in the Port Cities of Colonial Saint-Domingue, 1750–1790," in *Women in Port: Gendering Communities, Economies, and Social Networks in Atlantic Port Cities, 1500–1800*, ed. Douglas Catterall and Jodi Campbell (Leiden: Brill, 2012), 357–97.

52. On this tradition, see James P. Gee, *What Video Games Have to Teach Us about Learning and Literacy*, rev. ed. (New York: Palgrave Macmillan, 2007), 11.

53. I would argue that Bastienne departs from the "tropical temptress" stereotype described by Daut; she better fits the figure of a "female revolutionary hero" who enables "male bravery" (*Tropics of Haiti*, 286, 327).

54. Olivia Salazar, personal communication with author, May 9, 2017. Salazar plays and moderates as MsTron (https://twitter.com/iammstron).

55. The entry attributed the success of the Revolution to maroons, something debatable among scholars. Compare for instance Fouchard, *Les marrons de la liberté* (Paris: Éditions de l'École, 1972) and Geggus, "Marronage, Vodou, and the Slave Revolt of 1791," in *Haitian Revolutionary Studies*, 69–80.

56. See *Asssassin's Creed Wiki*: "Toussaint Louverture," https://assassinscreed.fandom.com/wiki/Toussaint_Louverture; "Dutty Boukman," https://assassinscreed.fandom.com/wiki/Dutty_Boukman; "Georges Biassou," https://assassinscreed.fandom.com/wiki/Georges_Biassou; "Saint-Domingue Brotherhood of Assassins," https://assassinscreed.fandom.com/wiki/Saint-Domingue_Brotherhood_of_Assassins; "Eseosa's Codex," https://assassinscreed.fandom.com/wiki/Eseosa%27s_Codex; and "François Mackandal," https://assassinscreed.fandom.com/wiki/Fran%C3%A7ois_Mackandal, all accessed May 13, 2019.

57. This content brought some *Initiates* material into the main games. On "Mackandal" as leader of the Saint-Domingue chapter of the Assassin's Brotherhood, see "Lessons and Revelations" section of *AC Rogue* (partial dialogue at *Assassin's Creed Wiki*, https://assassinscreed.fandom.com/wiki/Lessons_and_Revelations, accessed May 13, 2019).

58. Lois Wilcken, email to author, Apr. 1, 2017. On different types of Vodou songs, see Elizabeth McAlister, liner notes to *Rhythms of Rapture: Sacred Musics of Haitian Vodou* (Washington, DC: Smithsonian Folkways Recordings, 1995), https://media.smithsonianfolkways.org/liner_notes/smithsonian_folkways/SFW40464.pdf. Alexis's compositions include the song "1492," decrying what has happened to Haiti since Columbus's arrival (Bohio Music – Topic, YouTube, posted Sept. 2, 2015, https://www.youtube.com/watch?v=6CX2NRHC5Zk; translated lyrics at http://laughingmaze.blogspot.com/2014/08/bohio-music-band-1492-written-and.html).

59. James Southall, Review of *Assassin's Creed IV: Black Flag—Freedom Cry* soundtrack, *Movie Wave*, May 12, 2014, http://www.movie-wave.net/assassins-creed-iv-black-flag-freedom-cry/; also Gil Almogi, "Assassin's Creed IV: Black Flag—Freedom Cry Soundtrack Review," *GameRevolution*, May 20, 2014, http://www.gamerevolution.com/manifesto/assassins-creed-iv-black-flag-freedom-cry-soundtrack-review-25909 (discontinued).

60. Ubisoft is headquartered in France but its game studios are spread around the world. *Freedom Cry* began its development at Ubisoft Montreal as part of *Assassin's Creed IV: Black Flag*, but was released by Ubisoft Quebec when it became a stand-alone game. Jill Murray of Ubisoft Montreal had written all side missions for *AC IV: Black Flag* and became lead scriptwriter for *Freedom Cry*.

61. Jill Murray, email to author, Apr. 8, 2014.

62. Jean-Pierre Le Glaunec, *L'armée indigène: La défaite de Napoléon en Haïti* (Montreal: Lux, 2014); Le Glaunec, Comments in USherbrookeTV, "Histoire et jeux vidéo," and in Isabelle Pion, "Un historien derrière le jeu *Freedom Cry*," *La Tribune*, Feb. 4, 2014, http://www.lapresse.ca/la-tribune/affaires/201402/04/01-4735416-un-historien-derriere-le-jeu-freedom-cry-video.php (discontinued).

63. Soraya Murray, *On Video Games*, 69; J. Murray, "Diverse Game Characters: Write Them Now!" (Game Developers Conference, Mar. 29, 2013), audio at https://www.gdcvault.com/play/1019100/Diverse-Game-Characters-Write-Them (quote at 12:09); Le Glaunec and Léon Robichaud, "Marronnage in Saint-Domingue (Haïti)" Database, http://www.marronnage.info/en/, accessed May 13, 2019; J. Murray, email.

64. Evan Narcisse, "This *Assassin's Creed* Heroine Is a Great Black Game Character. Here's How It Happened" [interview with J. Murray], *Kotaku*, Feb. 27, 2013, https://kotaku.com/this-assassin-s-creed-heroine-is-a-great-black-game-cha-5987083; Josh Harmon, "AC: Freedom

Cry Writer Says Difficult Topics Deserve as Much Focus as Fun," *EGMNow*, Mar. 17, 2014, http://www.egmnow.com/articles/news/ac-freedom-cry-writer-says-difficult-topics-deserve-as-much-focus-as-fun/ (discontinued); J. Murray, email.

65. Mike Williams, "Assassin's Creed IV Freedom Cry: DLC that Digs Deeper," *USGamer*, Dec. 23, 2013, https://www.usgamer.net/articles/assassins-creed-iv-freedom-cry-the-dlc-; Lisa Gilbert, "'*Assassin's Creed* Reminds Us that History Is Human Experience': Students' Senses of Empathy While Playing a Narrative Video Game," *Theory and Research in Social Education* 47, no. 1 (2019): 122.

66. Dominick Rabrun, "My dream came true. In the new AC4 DLC, you get to play Adewale liberating slaves in Haiti. Fucking awesome," Twitter, Dec. 13, 2013, https://twitter.com/domrabrun/status/411694657282658305; Illi, "Freeing slaves in Haiti on assassins creed freedom cry. Why didn't anyone tell me about this!?" Twitter, Apr. 16, 2015, https://twitter.com/IlliDWilliams/status/588667070176460800; Yung Crescendo, "I really wanna try that freedom cry add on. You free slaves in Haiti for 10 hours," Twitter, Jan. 25, 2014, https://twitter.com/itsbenok/status/427315416420335616. For further analysis of Black gamers' enthusiastic and emotional reactions to *Freedom Cry*'s trailer and to the game itself, see Kishonna L. Gray, *Intersectional Tech: Black Users in Digital Gaming* (Baton Rouge: Louisiana State Univ. Press, 2020), 108–15.

67. See for instance Thierry Jethro, "Rise up against slavery with Assassin's Creed®Freedom Cry, Play as Adewale, an Assassin fighting for the freedom of slaves in modern day Haiti," Twitter, Feb. 18, 2014, https://twitter.com/Thitro_/status/435922479480307712; Vladimir, "I love Assassin's Creed and the next video game is based off Port-Au-Prince, Haiti. It's based off Haiti's independence. I'm so happy," Twitter, Dec. 17, 2013, https://twitter.com/greenvamt/status/413028568579710976; and Ill Nono, "The new Assassin's Creed has a storyline about freeing slaves in Haiti? And the hero is a black guy? Sign me up," Twitter, Jan. 25, 2014, https://twitter.com/_sugatits/status/427308938129080320.

68. Scott Murray, "Fiiiinally playing . . . ," Twitter, Apr. 29, 2016, https://twitter.com/strangewander/status/726251831295393793; and Amin Elchie, "Assassin's Creed IV . . . ," Twitter, Mar. 1, 2016, https://twitter.com/ViraniKenya/status/704749373570293760.

69. Narcisse, "A Closer Look at How Three *Assassin's Creed* Games Have Handled Slavery," *Kotaku*, Mar. 31, 2014, https://kotaku.com/why-assassins-creed-freedom-crys-use-of-slavery-was-1555358077; Scott Murray, "This is a lot . . . ," Twitter, Apr. 29, 2016, https://twitter.com/strangewander/status/726252522470559744; and Murray, email to author, May 16, 2017. Mukherjee, "Playing Subaltern"; and Mukherjee, "Video Games and Slavery," 253 (citing Narcisse).

70. Amanda Kerri, "How Historical Games Integrate or Ignore Slavery," *Rock Paper Shotgun*, Jan. 17, 2017, https://www.rockpapershotgun.com/2017/01/17/how-historical-games-integrate-or-ignore-slavery/; Errant Signal [Chris Franklin], "Assassin's Creed and Emotionally Resonant Mechanics," YouTube, posted Mar. 30, 2014, https://www.youtube.com/watch?v=2bsxQZ5JDec; Hammar, "Counter-Hegemonic Commemorative Play," 380–401; and Gray, "Power in the Visual," 64.

71. Monvelyno Alexis, interview with author, July 20, 2017.

72. M. Alexis, interview.

73. Kerri, "How Historical Games"; Narcisse, "A Closer Look"; Errant Signal, "Assassin's Creed"; and Hammar, "Counter-Hegemonic Commemorative Play," 387–88.

74. Schut, "Strategic Simulations," 229.

Chapter 10. French Caribbean Games: Honoring Rebel Ancestors in *Méwilo* and *Freedom: Rebels in the Darkness*

1. On twentieth-century Martinican identity, see Kristen Stromberg Childers, *Seeking Imperialism's Embrace: National Identity, Decolonization, and Assimilation in the French Caribbean* (New York: Oxford Univ. Press, 2016); Andrew Daily, "Race, Citizenship, and Antillean Student Activism in Postwar France, 1946–1968," *French Historical Studies* 37, no. 2 (2014): 331–57; and Fleming, *Resurrecting Slavery*. On Antillean ideas about Haiti, see Annette Joseph-Gabriel, "Beyond the Great Camouflage: Haiti in Suzanne Césaire's Politics and Poetics of Liberation," *Small Axe* 20, no. 2 (2016): 1–13; and Silyane Larcher, *L'autre citoyen: L'idéal républicain et les Antilles après l'esclavage* (Paris: Armand Colin, 2014). On appropriations of Toussaint and Christophe by Martinicans like Aimé Césaire and Édouard Glissant, see for instance Walsh, *Free and French*; and Past, "Reclaiming the Haitian Revolution," 160.

2. Patrick Chamoiseau, *Solibo Magnificent*, trans. Rose-Myriam Réjouis and Val Vinokur (New York: Pantheon, 1997); Chamoiseau, *Texaco*, trans. Réjouis and Vinokur (New York: Pantheon, 1997); Chamoiseau, *Creole Folktales*; and Jean Bernabé, Raphaël Confiant, and Chamoiseau, *Éloge de la Créolité* (Paris: Gallimard/Presses universitaires créoles, 1989).

3. Tony Delsham and Abel [Patrick Chamoiseau], *Le retour de Monsieur Coutcha* (Fort-de-France: Éditions MGG, 1984); Chamoiseau and Thierry Ségur, *Encyclomerveille d'un tueur* ([Paris]: Delcourt, 2009); and *Middle Passage* [Passage de milieu], dir. Guy Deslauriers, script by Claude Chonville and Patrick Chamoiseau (1999), DVD, 78 min. (English version, New York: HBO Video, 2003).

4. Miller, *French Atlantic Triangle*, 381.

5. I have not found any scholarship analyzing this game; it is not mentioned in studies on Chamoiseau such as Lorna Milne, *Patrick Chamoiseau: Espaces d'une écriture antillaise* (New York: Rodopi, 2006); Maeve McCusker, *Patrick Chamoiseau: Recovering Memory* (Liverpool: Liverpool Univ. Press, 2007); and Wendy Knepper, *Patrick Chamoiseau: A Critical Introduction* (Jackson: Univ. Press of Mississippi, 2012). Bloggers such as Phil Salvador, Ilmari Jauhiainen, and Oli have discussed it; however, they have been more interested in gaming pioneer Tramis than in Chamoiseau. The only books I have found that even refer to Chamoiseau's participation in passing are Tristan Donovan, *Replay: The History of Video Games* (East Sussex, UK: Yellow Ant, 2010), 127; and Alexis Blanchet, "France," in *Video Games around the World*, ed. Mark J. P. Wolf (Cambridge, MA: MIT Press, 2015), 181–82.

6. "Muriel Tramis, première créatrice de jeux vidéo décorée de la Légion d'honneur," *Le Monde*, July 19, 2018, https://www.lemonde.fr/pixels/article/2018/07/19/muriel-tramis-premiere-creatrice-de-jeux-video-decoree-de-la-legion-d-honneur_5333620_4408996.html.

7. I am grateful to Tramis for sharing information with me about her background and her authorial intentions. Information here is based on multiple personal communications (including interview, June 14, 2017 [henceforth Tramis, interview]), and Sierra Chest, "Lost in Time interview with Muriel Tramis (French) [1993]," YouTube, posted May 20, 2013, https://www.youtube.com/watch?v=D9otTnYRu-Y. As this book was going to press, Tramis told me of a new interview with her, conducted in 2019 by Alenda Y. Chang and published as "Une Vie Bien Jouée/A Life Well Played: The Cultural Legacy of Game Designer Muriel Tramis," *Feminist Media Histories* 6, no. l (2020): 147–62.

8. Tramis, interview.

9. Tramis, interview. On Évelyne Trouillot's novel *The Infamous Rosalie*, see conclusion. Tramis does not feel that it is always illegitimate for white artists to treat slavery; for her, Steven Spielberg's *Amistad* far surpassed *Django Unchained* and was of similar quality to Spielberg's *Schindler's List* (Tramis, interview).

10. Tramis, interview.

11. Tramis had also worked on a math game for Coktel in 1987, *La bosse des maths*, which French Wikipedia terms the first math video game and the first video game ever used in French schools ("*La Bosse des maths*," Wikipedia, https://fr.wikipedia.org/wiki/La_Bosse_des_maths, accessed July 5, 2017). However, while Tramis is credited as director (*réalisateur*) for that game, Philippe Truca was the game's official creator. *Méwilo* was thus the first game Tramis both created and directed for Coktel. She later created the hugely successful *Adibou*, an educational game aimed at ages four through seven.

12. Tramis, interview. The paper insert in the jewel case of the French-language Atari version suggested that the "original idea" was Chamoiseau's (back cover image at "Freedom—Les Guerriers de l'Ombre," AtariMania, http://www.atarimania.com/game-atari-st-freedom-les-guerriers-de-l-ombre_9384.html, accessed June 17, 2019), but Tramis recalls that they developed it collaboratively.

13. Tramis, interview.

14. Information on *Méwilo* is drawn from YouTube walk-throughs, screenshots, and blogs by vintage game aficionados. For walk-throughs, see petsasjim1, "ATARI ST Mewilo Coktel Vision France Muriel Tramis Philippe Truca Patrick Chamoiseau In 1988 st zip," YouTube, posted July 17, 2014, https://www.youtube.com/watch?v=SCbSbk1AT5Q; and petsasjim1, "AMIGA Mewilo OCS Coktel Vision Muriel Tramis Philippe Truca Patrick Chamoiseau 1988 France adf zip," YouTube, posted Feb. 5, 2015, https://www.youtube.com/watch?v=U8m_NAN8Ttk. For screenshots, see "Méwilo Screenshots (Amiga)," MobyGames, https://www.mobygames.com/game/amiga/mwilo/screenshots; and "Méwilo OCS," *Hall of Light: The Database of Amiga Games*, http://hol.abime.net/4767/screenshot (accessed June 16, 2019). On gameplay, see Ilmari [Jauhiainen], "Missed Classic 26: Mewilo (1987)—Introduction," *The Adventure Gamer*, Aug. 5, 2016, https://advgamer.blogspot.com/2016/08/missed-classic-26-mewilo-1987.html; Jauhiainen, "Missed Classic: Mewilo—End to slavery," *The Adventure Gamer*, Aug. 11, 2016, https://advgamer.blogspot.com/2016/08/missed-classic-mewilo-end-to-slavery.html; Jauhiainen, "Missed Classic: Mewilo—Won! (with Final Rating)," *The Adventure Gamer*, Aug. 19, 2016, https://advgamer.blogspot.com/2016/08/missed-classic-mewilo-won-with-final.html; Oli, "Méwilo (Atari ST, 1987)," *Jeux vidéo et des bas*, Jan. 21, 2015, https://jeux.dokokade.net/2015/01/21/mewilo-atari-st-1987/; and Oli, "Soluce rétrocompatible: Méwilo (Atari ST, Amiga, Amstrad)," *Jeux vidéo et des bas*, Feb. 12, 2015, https://jeux.dokokade.net/2015/02/12/soluce-retrocompatible-mewilo-atari-st-amiga-amstrad/. For shortcuts, see "Méwilo," *MicroNews*, no. 33, Apr. 15, 1990, https://www.amigaland.com/index.php?option=com_content&view=article&id=569:micro-news-033-04-1990&catid=16&Itemid=122.

15. At the time, Chamoiseau's story ("Les derniers jours") was available only in *Méwilo*'s manual. He later reprinted it in *La nouvelle revue française*, no. 421 (1988), 28–33.

16. Screenshots in Oli, "Méwilo." Tramis confirmed my spotting Chamoiseau, and noted her and Truca's cameos (email to author, June 25, 2017).

17. On this point, see Oli, "Soluce rétrocompatible."

18. Copies of *Méwilo*'s manual are available digitally, including at CPC-Power (Conservation du patrimoine culturel de notre jeunesse), http://www.cpc-power.com/extra_lire_fichier.php?extra=notice&fiche=1406&slot=1&part=A&type=.pdf, accessed Apr. 16, 2019. While her creative writing in the 1980s was limited to manuals, Tramis has turned more recently to longer-form works, including her autobiographical novel, *Au cœur du giraumon* (Paris: Dagan, 2011), and her collection of Creole folktales, *Contes créoles et cruels* (Paris: Dagan, 2013).

19. Since the first French abolition of 1794 was not implemented in Martinique, the game asks about 1848, the second French abolition of slavery.

20. Oli, "Soluce rétrocompatible"; and Ilmari [Jauhiainen], "Missed Classic 26." Jauhiainen is a Finnish scholar of Hegel who blogs about games using his first name.

21. Questions appeared randomly in each gameplay. A sampling can be seen in the walkthroughs by petsasjimi: "ATARI ST Mewilo Coktel Vision France Muriel Tramis Philippe Truca Patrick Chamoiseau In 1988 st zip," YouTube, posted July 17, 2014, https://www.youtube.com/watch?v=SCbSbk1AT5Q; and "AMIGA Mewilo OCS Coktel Vision Muriel Tramis Philippe Truca Patrick Chamoiseau 1988 France adf zip," YouTube, posted Feb. 5, 2015, https://www.youtube.com/watch?v=U8m_NAN8Ttk. Tramis has noted that in developing the game in Paris, she felt "a bit 'in exile,' far from my native island." Including Caribbean culture helped her "bring herself closer in spirit" to Martinique (Interview).

22. On the long legacy of slavery, see also *Sugar Cane Alley* (*Rue cases-nègres*, 1983), dir. Euzhan Palcy, DVD ([New York]: New Yorker Video, 2004). On the Saint-Pierre revolt, see Rebecca H. Schloss, "The February 1831 Slave Uprising in Martinique and the Policing of White Identity," *French Historical Studies* 30, no. 2 (2007): 203–36.

23. As Linda Cloverdale has noted, "Many Caribbean islands have stories about *béké* treasure buried at night in a hole that becomes the grave of the slave who dug it." She adds that Chamoiseau's *Chronicle des sept misères* includes a slave murdered in this way; See "Notes," in Chamoiseau, *Slave Old Man*, trans. Coverdale (New York: New Press, 2018), 144n54.

24. Screenshots from Oli, "Méwilo." Description of Makandal's relation to Condette from Tramis, email to author, July 12, 2017.

25. Jauhiainen, "Missed Classic 26."

26. Tramis, email to author, June 25, 2017. Tramis adds that, though *Méwilo*'s texts are in French, they are suffused with Creole proverbs. For instance, Chamoiseau drew from the adage "Rayi chyen mé di dan'y blan" to write Echevin's line of dialogue "il faut haïr les chiens mais reconnaître qu'ils ont les dents bien blanches—il faut haïr les colons mais reconnaître que leur rhum est bon" (one must hate dogs but realize that they have very white teeth—one must hate the colonists but realize that their rum is good).

27. E. C., review of *Méwilo*, *Tilt*, no. 51 (1988): 41, http://amigaland.com/dataz/press_magazine/tilt/PDF_TXT/TILT_Numero_051_fev_1988.pdf; review of *Méwilo*, *Génération4*, no. 3 (1988), via Amigaland.com.

28. Tramis, emails to author, June 25, 2017, and July 2, 2017; Tramis, interview. On this award, see "Qui peut obtenir la médaille de la Ville?," *Le Parisien*, May 16, 2007, http://www.leparisien.fr/paris/qui-peut-obtenir-la-medaille-de-la-ville-16-05-2007-2008035142.php.

29. Tramis, interview.

30. Donovan, *Replay*, 127–28.

31. Information from *Freedom* credits, and Tramis, email to author, July 12, 2017.

32. *Freedom: Rebels in the Darkness* page, MobyGames, https://www.mobygames.com/game/dos/freedom-rebels-in-the-darkness, accessed Apr. 16, 2019; Petsasjimi, "ATARI ST Freedom Les Guerriers de l'Ombre 2Coktel Visionfrcr Bladerunnersm Atariforce zip," YouTube, posted Aug. 8, 2014, https://www.youtube.com/watch?v=jQ_LgjDO4dQ; and Petsasjimi, "Freedom Rebels in the DarknessLosGuerrosdelaNocheDieKriegerdesSchattenAMIGACoktelVisionRandomAccess88," YouTube, posted Oct. 13, 2014, https://www.youtube.com/watch?v=XCYWWVNXPXA.

33. Phil Salvador, "Freedom: Rebels in the Darkness," *The Obscuritory*, July 30, 2015, https://obscuritory.com/strategy/freedom-rebels-in-the-darkness/; Anatoly Shashkin, "DOS version of a Coktel Vision game about slavery has been found. Now you can get it here: https://archive.org/details/freedom-dos . . . ," Twitter, May 2, 2016, https://twitter.com/dosnostalgic/status/727171986322018305; Phil Salvador, *The Obscuritory Tumblr*, May 2, 2016, http://obscuritory.tumblr.com/post/143751751509/the-dos-version-of-freedom-rebels-in-the, signaled by Maddi Chilton, "A Forgotten, Decades-Old Game about Slavery Has Returned," *Kill Screen*, May 31, 2016, https://killscreen.com/articles/can-now-play-decades-old-forgotten-game-slavery/. Game files in German, French, and Spanish were available in June 2017 at "Commodore Amiga Roms Download Section," *The Game Archives*, http://thegamearchives.net/?val=0_2_1_0_0_4_17_0_6_7_0.

34. Internet Archive page for *Freedom*, https://archive.org/details/freedom-dos; zip file including the game and code at https://archive.org/download/freedom-dos/freedom-dos.zip; both accessed Apr. 17, 2019. I am grateful to Phil Salvador for directing me to these files and helping me to play. I own an original Amiga UK version, but did my gameplay on a PC running Windows 10, using the DOS file.

35. French version of *Freedom*'s manual, downloadable for subscribers, at *EmuMovies* as part of the "Atari ST Game Manuals (Pack 1) 1.0" collection, https://emumovies.com/files/file/1250-atari-st-game-manuals-pack-1/, accessed Apr. 17, 2019. English version of *Freedom* manual, Coktel/Monkey Business Amiga edition (UK), author's personal collection.

36. Tramis, emails to author, June 8, 2017, and July 2, 2017; Leo Sun, "Will Assassin's Creed 4 Be the Last Yearly Update to the Franchise?" *Motley Fool*, Nov. 6, 2013, https://www.fool.com/investing/general/2013/11/06/will-assassins-creed-4-be-the-last-yearly-update-t.aspx; review of *Freedom: Rebels in the Darkness*, *Computer + Video Games* 88 (1989): 74–75; and Nev Astly, review of *Freedom: Rebels in the Darkness*, *Amiga Computing* 1, no. 9 (1989): 55, both at http://amr.abime.net/review_24095. See also Phil Campbell, "Freedom," *The Australian Commodore and Amiga Review* 6, no. 9 (1989): 55.

37. Where Makandal was from Haiti, *Freedom*'s other avatars come from elsewhere in the Antilles. Solitude was an enslaved Guadeloupian who fought alongside Louis Delgrès and was hanged. Chamoiseau wrote a play about her in his twenties, *Solitude la mulâtresse*, adapted from a novel by André Schwarz-Bart (see listing in Bibliothèque Nationale de France catalog, https://catalogue.bnf.fr/index.do, accessed Apr. 17, 2019). The other male option, Sechou, appeared as a legendary Martinican maroon in Chamoiseau's works *Chronicle of the Seven Sorrows*, trans. Coverdale (Lincoln: Univ. of Nebraska Press, 2003), 120, 138–39; and *Un dimanche au cachot* (Paris: Gallimard, 2007). Délia was a creation of the game, not linked to one island. However, Tramis has said that, given the rebellious spirit of enslaved women, she is certain that "there was [a Délia] among the *marronnes*" somewhere in the Antilles (Interview).

38. Tramis, interview. Tramis provided answers in English and French; my translation retains her English while incorporating some elements present only in her French responses. *Freedom*'s use of pan-Caribbean icons is not uncommon in the Antilles; it can also be seen in Hondo's *West Indies*, which celebrated Solitude and Makandal, along with Boukman, Toussaint, Dessalines, Delgrès, and slave rebels from elsewhere (1:24:00–1:24:17).

39. *Freedom* manual (English version), 1. I am using the English from this translation, with the exception of the phrase "head of your group." The English-language manual says "head of your band of men"; however, the French one did not use a gendered term and simply said that the leader was "à la tête de votre troupe" (*Freedom* manual [French version], 1).

40. From the game's English-language introduction, "Freedom: Rebels in the Darkness Screenshots (DOS)," MobyGames, posted by Karsa Orlong, https://www.mobygames.com/game/dos/freedom-rebels-in-the-darkness/screenshots/gameShotId,841400/. However, I have refined the translation in brackets based on the original French ("Freedom: Rebels in the Darkness Screenshots [Atari ST]," MobyGames, posted by POMAH, https://www.mobygames.com/game/atari-st/freedom-rebels-in-the-darkness/screenshots/gameShotId,264700/), as well as replacing the English translation's "row of the negroes' huts" with the more common translation of *rue cases-Nègres*.

41. Chamoiseau, *L'esclave vieil homme et le molosse* (Paris: Gallimard, 1997); translated as *Slave Old Man*, 17, 5, 24, 20–21. On slave-hunting dogs in Saint-Domingue and elsewhere, see Georges Lutz, "Un avatar de la domestication des animaux: les chiens à esclaves: 'Buscadores' de Cuba et de Saint Domingue," in *Haïti: première république noire*, ed. Marcel Dorigny (Paris: Société française d'histoire d'outre-mer, 2003), 61–81.

42. Screenshot at "Freedom: Rebels in the Darkness Screenshots (Amiga)," MobyGames, posted by Macs Black, https://www.mobygames.com/game/amiga/freedom-rebels-in-the-darkness/screenshots/gameShotId,222130/.

43. The first response appears in a screenshot on MobyGames, http://www.mobygames.com/game/dos/freedom-rebels-in-the-darkness/screenshots/gameShotId,841409/. I received the second response while playing.

44. This response and the others below can be seen in screenshots such as https://www.mobygames.com/game/amiga/freedom-rebels-in-the-darkness/screenshots/gameShotId,222118/, or by playing. Additional responses are contained in the code file ESSAI4.TOT, https://archive.org/download/freedom-dos/freedom-dos.zip, accessed Apr. 17, 2019.

45. Screenshot at MobyGames, https://www.mobygames.com/game/dos/freedom-rebels-in-the-darkness/screenshots/gameShotId,841422/.

46. From screenshot reproduced in Salvador, "Freedom." This line reappeared if I played as Makandal or Sechou, but with "brother" replacing "sister."

47. From screenshots at MobyGames, https://www.mobygames.com/game/amiga/freedom-rebels-in-the-darkness/screenshots/gameShotId,222120/; and in Salvador, "Freedom."

48. On the Manman-Dlo, see *Freedom* manual, 2 (English and French versions); and discussion and screenshot in Jauhiainen, "Missed Classic 28: Freedom: Rebels in the Darkness (1988)," *The Adventure Gamer*, Sept. 14, 2016, https://advgamer.blogspot.com/2016/09/missed-classic-28-freedom-rebels-in.html. *La sirène* is also associated in Haitian Vodou with the *lwa* Erzulie and Simbi. Both Chamoiseau and Tramis have created other works on the Manman-Dlo; see Chamoiseau's play *Manman Dlo contre la fée Carabosse* (Paris: Éditions caribéennes, 1982); and

the trailer from Tramis's animation studio Avantilles3d, "Fragile-Fatale, la jeune manmandlo: le Film," YouTube, posted Jan. 27, 2012, https://www.youtube.com/watch?v=U__4Slorhkc.

49. Voltgloss, comment on Jauhiainen, "Call for Questions for Muriel Tramis," *The Adventure Gamer*, Apr. 6, 2017, https://advgamer.blogspot.com/2017/04/call-for-questions-for-muriel-tramis.html. Similarly, in my gameplay, I never experienced winning the game.

50. From gamecode in ESSAI.TOT file from freedom-dos.zip (https://archive.org/download/freedom-dos).

51. *Freedom* manual (English version, 3; French version, 4).

52. *Freedom* manual (English version, 3; French version, 4). Tramis has explained that winning the game is not impossible, but she does not recall the inputs used (Interview). See also discussion about the game's seeming impossibility at Jauhiainen, "Call for Questions," comments section.

53. Text from gamecode, ESSAI.TOT file from freedom-dos.zip (https://archive.org/download/freedom-dos); sample screenshot at MobyGames, https://www.mobygames.com/game/dos/freedom-rebels-in-the-darkness/screenshots/gameShotId,841420/.

54. Salvador, *The Obscuritory Tumblr*; Salvador, "Freedom"; Jauhiainen, "Missed Classic 28"; Tramis, email to author, June 8, 2017; Sebastien Genvo, "Muriel Tramis, l'itinéraire d'une pionnière. Théories des jeux vidéo. Ep. 13," YouTube, posted Mar. 10, 2017, https://www.youtube.com/watch?v=LMq9X-WaB1k; Blanchet, "France."

55. *Case départ*, a dark comedy about two men of Antillean descent in modern France who time travel to the era of slavery, was a box office hit in France (dir. Lionel Steketee, Fabrice Eboué, and Thomas N'Gijol [2011], DVD, 90 min., [Paris]: TF1, 2014).

56. For a summary and screenshots, see "Lost in Time (DOS)," MobyGames, https://www.mobygames.com/game/lost-in-time_; Sierra Chest, "Lost in Time Interview"; Retrogamer.biz, "Lost in Time (1993, Coktel Vision)" walk-through, YouTube, posted Nov. 12, 2010, https://www.youtube.com/watch?v=HvvNDokuN6A; and *Lost in Time* manual, https://www.freegameempire.com/games/Lost-in-Time/manual (all accessed Apr. 17, 2019). CD-ROMs of the game are held at the Library of Congress and Bibliothèque nationale de France.

57. Tramis, interview.

58. Tramis, interview; Tramis, email to author, Aug. 4, 2019.

Conclusion

1. See Eric Greene, *Planet of the Apes as American Myth: Race, Politics, and Popular Culture*, 2nd ed. (Middletown, CT: Wesleyan Univ. Press, 1998), 5, 12, 18; and André's comments in *Top Five*: "It's staring you right in the face. Every *Planet of the Apes* movie is about race. . . . It's about the white man's fear of a Black planet. The darker apes are bigger and stronger, the lighter apes are smarter. That's racist bullshit. It's not a coincidence that a movie about n***s taking over the world comes out the day before the most powerful Black man on earth [Martin Luther King Jr.] is assassinated" (48:35). See also Anne Crémieux, "La représentation de l'esclavage dans *Planet of the Apes* et *The Brother from Another Planet*," in *Cinéma et histoire/Film and History*, ed. Melvyn Stokes and Gilles Menegaldo (Paris: M. Houdiard, 2008), 232–41.

2. Feagin, foreword to Vera and Gordon, *Screen Saviors*, xi.

3. Gregory Ellwood, "The Birth of a Nation Just Smashed Records at Sundance," *Vox*, Jan. 31, 2016, https://www.vox.com/2016/1/31/10871544/birth-of-a-nation-nate-parker-interview; Brent Lang and Ramin Setoodeh, "Sundance: 'Birth of a Nation' Lands at Fox Searchlight in Record $17.5 Million Deal," *Variety*, Jan. 25, 2016, https://variety.com/2016/film/festivals/sundance-birth-of-a-nation-1201688520/.

4. For a fuller discussion, see Sepinwall, "Why Audiences Must See Nate Parker's *Birth of a Nation*."

5. *The Birth of a Nation* page, Box Office Mojo, http://www.boxofficemojo.com/movies/?id=thebirthofanation.htm; Sepinwall, "Why Audiences"; and A. O. Scott, "Review: In Nate Parker's 'The Birth of a Nation,' Must-See and Won't-See Collide," *New York Times*, Oct. 6, 2016, https://www.nytimes.com/2016/10/07/movies/the-birth-of-a-nation-review-nate-parker.html.

6. *Black Panther* page, Box Office Mojo, https://www.boxofficemojo.com/movies/?id=marvel2017b.htm; Carvell Wallace, "Why 'Black Panther' Is a Defining Moment for Black America," *New York Times*, Feb. 12, 2018, https://www.nytimes.com/2018/02/12/magazine/why-black-panther-is-a-defining-moment-for-black-america.html.

7. I am grateful to my favorite comic book/action film fans, Steve Goldstein and Alan Sepinwall, for help on this point.

8. See for instance Fatton, "The Rise, Fall, and Second Coming," in Sepinwall, *Haitian History*, 294–311; and Sprague, *Paramilitarism*.

9. Robyn C. Spencer, "Black Feminist Meditations on the Women of Wakanda," *Medium*, Feb. 21, 2018, https://medium.com/@robyncspencer/black-feminist-meditations-on-the-women-of-wakanda-5cc79751d9cd. On the irony of the friendly CIA agent, see also Steven Thrasher, "There Is Much to Celebrate—and Much to Question—about Marvel's *Black Panther*," *Esquire*, Feb. 20, 2018, https://www.esquire.com/entertainment/movies/a18241993/black-panther-review-politics-killmonger/; and Lynn Stuart Paramore, "Why Does a White CIA Agent Play the Hero to Killmonger's Villain in 'Black Panther'?," *NBC News: Think*, Mar. 11, 2018, https://www.nbcnews.com/think/opinion/why-does-white-cia-agent-play-hero-killmonger-s-villain-ncna855401. On the CIA's working with studios, see Tricia Jenkins, *The CIA in Hollywood: How the Agency Shapes Film and Television* (Austin: Univ. of Texas Press, 2012). See however Marlene Daut, "Inside the Kingdom of Hayti, 'the Wakanda of the Western Hemisphere,'" *The Conversation*, Jan. 23, 2019, https://theconversation.com/amp/inside-the-kingdom-of-hayti-the-wakanda-of-the-western-hemisphere-108250, which draws parallels between the kingdoms of Christophe and T'Challa.

10. C. C. Saunders, "Black Panther, A Review," *Whispers of a Womanist* blog, Feb. 16, 2018, https://whispersofawomanist.com/2018/02/16/black-panther-a-review/; Russell Rickford, "I Have a Problem with 'Black Panther,'" *Africa Is a Country* blog, Feb. 22, 2018, http://africasacountry.com/2018/02/i-have-a-problem-with-black-panther/; Shannon Liao, "Chadwick Boseman Says T'Challa is the Enemy in *Black Panther*," *The Verge*, Feb. 28, 2018, https://www.theverge.com/2018/2/28/17063218/chadwick-boseman-tchalla-enemy-black-panther; and Pierrot, *The Black Avenger*, 202, 205.

11. For a fuller exploration of these factors, see Sepinwall, *Haitian History*. See also Dupuy, *Haiti, from Revolutionary Slaves to Powerless Citizens: Essays on the Politics and Economics of Underdevelopment, 1804–2013* (New York: Routledge, 2014), on how wealthier nations undermine Haitian sovereignty, treating the country as a "vassal state" (131).

12. Claire A. Payton, "Building Corruption in Haiti," *NACLA Report on the Americas* 51, no. 2 (2019): 182–87; Peck, *Fatal Assistance*; Katz, *The Big Truck*, 50–51, 130–31; Schuller, *Killing with Kindness*; and the articles by François Pierre-Louis and others in *The Journal of Black Studies* special issue (March 2011) on the earthquake.

13. Posch, "Emerging Film Cultures," 34.

14. FOKAL, discussed in chapter 8, is an unusual NGO, with foreign funding but in-country Haitian leadership. Though several filmmakers I discuss have benefited from its support, FOKAL's film program is not large enough to fund high-budget features.

15. Barlet, *African Cinemas: Decolonizing the Gaze* (New York: St. Martin's, 2000), esp. 5, 221–29, and 260–70; Ella Shohat and Robert Stam, *Unthinking Eurocentrism: Multiculturalism and the Media*, 2nd ed. (New York: Routledge, 2014), 395–96.

16. For an overview of such arguments, see Tryon, *Reinventing Cinema*, 7–8, 93.

17. Vera and Gordon, *Screen Saviors*, 9.

18. Ryan Parker, "'Red Dead Redemption 2' Breaks Records with $725 Million Opening Weekend," *Hollywood Reporter*, Oct. 30, 2018, https://www.hollywoodreporter.com/news/red-dead-redemption-2-breaks-records-725-million-opening-weekend-1156235.

19. On the resemblance, see @dwannb, "The Game red dead redemption 2 has a mission where they play on Haiti and its revolution," Twitter, Nov. 20, 2018, https://twitter.com/dwannb/status/1065051676569190400.

20. I am grateful to my former students David Johnson and Jordan Jefferson for first alerting me to *Red Dead Redemption 2*'s Haitian connection. My discussion of the game is based on initial information from them as well as the Guarma walk-through posted by GamersPrey: "Red Dead Redemption 2—Chapter 5: Guarma Walkthrough [HD 1080P]," YouTube, Oct. 26, 2018, https://www.youtube.com/watch?v=VDC8Oub3irY&t=3767s. In its portrayal of Haitians, *Red Dead Redemption 2* departs from the racial stereotypes that had been prevalent in *Red Dead Redemption* (2010); on that game, see Wainwright, *Virtual History*, 126–28.

21. Information on Overwatch communicated by John Ess; see also Brian Crecente, "Voice of 'Overwatch's' Latest Hero Says Role Changed His Life," *Variety*, Mar. 13, 2019, https://variety.com/2019/gaming/features/voice-of-overwatchs-latest-hero-says-role-changed-his-life-exclusive-1203162567/; PlayOverwatch, "Baptiste Origin Story/Overwatch," YouTube, posted Feb. 25, 2019, https://www.youtube.com/watch?v=ZfWgcjeG83E; and "Story" section at Baptiste's Overwatch page, https://playoverwatch.com/en-us/heroes/baptiste/, accessed Aug. 11, 2019.

22. Information and screenshots communicated by Anthony Martino; see also Jean La Fortune page, *Anno 1800* Wiki, Fandom, https://anno1800.fandom.com/wiki/Jean_La_Fortune, accessed Aug. 13, 2019. On the *Anno* series more generally, see Wainwright, *Virtual History*, 21.

23. On *Grand Theft Auto Vice City* and other early representations of Haiti in games, see Steve Mercil, "Haitian Representation through Video Games and Media," *The [8-Bit] Generation* blog, May 31, 2017, http://www.the8bg.com/2017/05/haitian-representation-through-video.html.

24. Vera and Gordon, *Screen Saviors*, 192–93.

25. See esp. Baron, *Projecting the Holocaust*, viii.

26. Rosenstone, *History on Film*, 34–35.

27. Évelyne Trouillot, *The Infamous Rosalie*, trans. M. A. Salvodon (first published in French, 2003; Lincoln: Univ. of Nebraska Press, 2013); Sepinwall, "If This Is a Woman: Évelyne Trouillot's *The Infamous Rosalie* and the Lost Stories of New World Slavery," *Fiction and Film for French Historians: A Cultural Bulletin* 5, no. 4 (2015), https://h-france.net/fffh/classics/if-this-is-a-woman-evelyne-trouillots-the-infamous-rosalie-and-the-lost-stories-of-new-world-slavery/;

Madison Smartt Bell, *All Souls' Rising* (New York: Pantheon, 1995) [followed by *Master of the Crossroads*, 2000, and *The Stone that the Builder Refused*, 2006]; Isabel Allende, *Island Beneath the Sea: A Novel*, trans. Margaret Sayers Peden (New York: Harper, 2010). On the reception of these novels, see Popkin, "Madison Smartt Bell's Haitian Revolution Trilogy," and Dubois, "Unwritten Stories," both in *Fiction and Film for French Historians* 1, no. 3 (2011), https://h-france.net/fffh/maybe-missed/madison-smartt-bells-haitian-revolution-trilogy/ and https://h-france.net/fffh/the-buzz/unwritten-stories/.

28. Guy Endore, *Babouk*, foreword by Jamaica Kincaid, afterword by David B. Gaspar and M.-R. Trouillot (originally published 1934; New York: Monthly Review Press, 1991), 79, 97, 101, 167, 191ff.; *Babouk* radio play, *Columbia Workshop*, WCBS, June 27, 1937, 23 min., at https://archive.org/details/ColumbiaWorkshop/370627_Babouk.mp3.

29. For information on *You Are There*, "The Betrayal Of Toussaint L'ouverture," aired Jan. 23, 1949, see the series' Paley Center page, https://www.paleycenter.org/collection/item/?q=You+Are+There&p=1&item=R78:0098, and recording of the episode at https://www.oldtimeradiodownloads.com/drama/you-are-there/you-are-there-48-05-30-32-toussaint-louverture-liberates-haiti. On this series, see Erik Christiansen, *Channeling the Past: Politicizing History in Postwar America* (Madison: Univ. of Wisconsin Press, 2013), 100–145.

30. Peter White, "Kwame Kwei-Armah to Adapt Haitian Revolution Story for TV with Foz Allan's Bryncoed," *Deadline*, Nov. 28, 2018, https://deadline.com/2018/11/kwame-kwei-armah-the-black-jacobins-1202508415/.

31. On *Underground* and both *Roots* versions, see Stevenson, "Finding Black Voices." On producers' skepticism that viewers would watch the original *Roots*, see Joe Adalian, "*Roots* Is Still One of the Biggest TV Success Stories Ever," *Vulture*, May 26, 2019, https://www.vulture.com/2016/05/roots-miniseries-ratings-were-off-the-charts.html. Given that *Underground* focused on the Underground Railroad rather than revolt, it (like *Book of Negroes*) included several friendly white characters; see Alan Sepinwall, "Review: WGN's 'Underground' is 'Roots' meets 'Prison Break,'" *Uproxx*, Mar. 8, 2016, https://uproxx.com/sepinwall/review-wgns-underground-is-roots-meets-prison-break/.

32. Kristel [Tracy] (@the_vajabond), "Finally reading The Black Jacobins by CLR James . . . ," Twitter, May 31, 2019, https://twitter.com/the_vajabond/status/1134368378267852806; and Ralph Leonard, "If I was a filmmaker . . . ," Twitter, Mar. 10, 2018, https://twitter.com/buffsoldier_96/status/972538601476100096.

33. The Public Archive, "Unless it can be cast . . . ," Twitter, Dec. 22, 2012, https://twitter.com/public_archive/status/282682505071562753; Greg Carr, "Danny Glover signs deal . . . ," Twitter, Apr. 1, 2015, https://twitter.com/AfricanaCarr/status/583250184588623872; Stevenson, "Filming Black Voices," 514.

Acknowledgments

1. Avant-garde hobbyists had played on consoles since the 1960s, but playing via a networked terminal, as we did, was rare. For an overview of pre-internet platforms, see Simon Egenfeldt-Nielsen, Jonas H. Smith, and Susana P. Tosca, *Understanding Video Games: The Essential Introduction*, 2nd ed. (New York: Routledge, 2008), 50–78.

SELECTED BIBLIOGRAPHY

The endnotes offer a full documentation of sources used in this study. This selected bibliography lists all manuscripts and most secondary sources cited, as well as all films and games analyzed on the Haitian Revolution. I also list interviewees as well as periodical titles, websites, and blogs used as primary or secondary sources.

Archival Sources

Academy of Motion Picture Arts and Sciences/Margaret Herrick Library, Beverly Hills, CA
  Michael Blankfort Papers
  William "Billy" Gordon Papers
  Milton Krims Papers
  Jean Negulesco Papers
  Gregory Peck Papers
  Motion Picture Association of America—Production Code Administration Papers
  Motion Picture Society for the Americas Papers
Howard Gotlieb Archival Research Center at Boston University, Boston, MA
  Michael Blankfort Collection
Library of Congress, Washington, DC
  National Association for the Advancement of Colored People Records (via ProQuest History Vault)
New York Public Library, Manuscripts and Archives Division, New York, NY
  V. F. Calverton Papers
New York Public Library, Schomburg Center for Research in Black Culture, Manuscripts, Archives and Rare Books Division, New York, NY
  Julian Mayfield Papers
University of Iowa, Special Collections, Iowa City, IA
  Twentieth Century Fox Film Scripts Collection
University of Southern California, Cinematic Arts Library, Los Angeles, CA
  Twentieth Century-Fox Collection
  Philip Dunne Papers

Films Related to the Revolution

1804: The Hidden History of Haiti, dir. Tariq Nasheed. DVD, 110 min. [Los Angeles]: King Flex Entertainment, 2017.

Aiyiti by BlackLivesMatter, dir. Toronto Freedom School/Amber Williams-King (2017). 6 min., YouTube.

Almacita di Desolato, dir. Felix De Rooy (1985). DVD, 112 min. New York: ArtMattan Productions, [200-?].

Anita, dir. Rassoul Labuchin. VHS, 47 min. [Paris]: Médiathèque des trois mondes, 1980.

L'arbre de la liberté, dir. Maxence Denis. DVD, 66 min. [Paris]: Jakaranda Productions, 2004.

Ayiti, men chimen libète/Haïti, le chemin de la liberté, dir. Arnold Antonin (1974). DVD, 92 min. Pétionville, Haiti: Centre Pétion-Bolivar, 2009.

Ayiti: The Awakening, dir. Sage Love (2019). 26 min. Streaming, via https://www.ayititheawakening.com/store.

Ayiti Toma, dir. Joseph Hillel (2013). 81 min. Streaming, Vimeo.

Black Dawn, dir. Robin Lloyd and Doreen Kraft (1979). DVD with new extras, 18 min. Burlington, VT: Green Valley Media, 2004.

Bonaparte, côté noir, dir. Dominique Maestrati (2016). DVD, 52 min. Paris: Injam Productions, 2017. Also on YouTube.

Burn! (Queimada), dir. Gillo Pontecorvo (1969). DVD, 112 min. Culver City, CA: MGM, 2005.

Égalité for All: Toussaint Louverture and the Haitian Revolution, dir. Noland Walker. DVD, 60 min. New York: PBS Home Video, 2009.

El siglo de las luces [*Le siècle des lumières*], dir. Humberto Solás. VHS, 258 min. [New York]: [Videoteca del Sur], 1992. 3 videocassettes.

The Emperor Jones, dir. Dudley Murphy (1933). 73 min. Streaming, Amazon Prime and public domain.

GNB kont Attila/GNB contre Attila, ou une autre Haïti est possible, dir. Arnold Antonin. DVD, 102 min. [Port-au-Prince]: UAV/CPB, 2004.

The Golden Mistress, dir. Joel Judge [Abner Biberman] (1954). 82 min. R.K. Productions/United Artists. Streaming, Amazon Prime.

Haïti, la fin des chimères, dir. Charles Najman. DVD, 70 min. [same disc as *Royal Bonbon*]. Paris: Malavida, 2004.

Haïti—La Route (*Le Chemin Parcouru*), dir. Francine Saillant, Frantz Voltaire, and Ralph Maingrette, narration by Dany Laferrière (2016). 33 min. Digital copy provided by F. Voltaire.

L'impasse Toussaint-Louverture, dir. Gaetano Ciarcia and Jean-Christophe Monferran (2019). 42 min. IIAC/IMAF/CNRS/EHESS. Streaming, Canal-U.

Independence or Death: The Haitian Revolution, dir. Mark Bowsher (2020). 33 min. Streaming, access.historyhit.com.

Kafe Negro, dir. Mario Delatour (2020). 52 min. Streaming, New York African Diaspora International Film Festival.

The Last Days of Toussaint L'Ouverture, dir. Derick Alexander (2009). 24 min. Excerpts on YouTube.

The Last Supper (*La Última Cena*), dir. Tomás Gutiérrez Alea (1976). DVD, 110 min. New York: New Yorker Video, 2008. Also on YouTube.

Liberty in a Soup, dir. Dudley Alexis (2017). 66 min. Streaming, Vimeo On Demand.

Lydia Bailey [as *Revuelta en Haití*], dir. Jean Negulesco (1952). DVD, 89 min. Madrid: Impulso Records, licensed from 20th Century Fox, 2010.
Moloch Tropical, dir. Raoul Peck. DVD, 107 min. Paris: Velvet Film/ARTE France, 2009.
Noir et blanc, dir. Kendy Joseph/Chevelin Illustration. 4 min. YouTube.
Port-au-Prince, Dimanche 4 janvier, dir. François Marthouret. 80 min. DVD screener for 2016 César Awards [not publicly available].
Rasin, dir. Pierre Lucson Bellegarde (2020). 22 min. Streaming, Haitian International Film Festival.
Royal Bonbon, dir. Charles Najman (2002). DVD, 85 min. Paris: Malavida Films, 2004.
Simparele, dir. Humberto Solás. VHS, 31 min. [Havana]: El Instituto Cubano del Arte e Industria Cinematográficos, 1974.
Top Five, dir. Chris Rock (2004). DVD, 101 min. New York: IAC Films/Paramount, 2015.
Toussaint Louverture, dir. Claude Moreau (1989). 58 min. Excerpts on YouTube.
Toussaint Louverture, dir. Philippe Niang. DVD, 180 min. [Paris]: France Télévision, 2012.
Toussaint Louverture: Haïti et la France, dir. Laurent Lutaud (2004). DVD, 85 min. Paris: L'Harmattan, 2006 (English version available as *Toussaint Louverture, Haiti, Destiny of a Nation*, dir. Lutaud. DVD, 54 min. [Paris]: TV5 Monde and France Télévision, 2005, Distributed by Monkey Bay and Lutaud).
Toussaint Louverture: Miroir d'une société, dir. Pierre Lucson Bellegarde (2016). 12 min. Streaming, YouTube.
Toussaint Louverture, par devoir de mémoire, dir. Kendy Vérilus (2003). 20 min. Digital copy provided by Vérilus.
Toussaint: The Heartbeat of Freedom, dir. Douglas McHenry (2005). 15 min. Streaming, Vimeo.
Tropiques Amers, dir. Claude Barny. DVD, 312 min. [Paris]: France télévisions, 2007. 2 discs.
Tula: The Revolt, dir. Jeroen Leinders. DVD, 98 min. [Amsterdam]: A-Film/Fisheye Feature Films, 2013; on Amazon Prime, under the title *The Revolt*.
West Indies: Les nègres marrons de la liberté, dir. Med Hondo (1979). 112 min. Streaming, YouTube.

Games

Age of Empires III: The WarChiefs. Ensemble/Microsoft Game Studio, 2006. Microsoft Windows, Mac OS X.
Assassin's Creed: Freedom Cry. Ubisoft Montreal/Ubisoft Quebec, 2013. Originally DLC (downloadable content) for *Assassin's Creed IV: Black Flag*, PlayStation 3, Xbox 360, Xbox One, Microsoft Windows; released in 2014 as a stand-alone game for PlayStation 3, PlayStation 4, Microsoft Windows.
Assassin's Creed: Liberation. Ubisoft Sofia, 2012. PlayStation Vita; released in 2014 for PlayStation 3, Xbox 360, Microsoft Windows; and in 2019 for PlayStation 4, Xbox One, Nintendo Switch.
Freedom! Minnesota Educational Computing Corporation, 1992. Apple II.
Freedom: Rebels in the Darkness [*Freedom: Les Guerriers de l'ombre*]. Coktel Vision, 1988. Amiga, Amstrad CPC, Atari ST, DOS.
Lost in Time. Coktel Vision, 1993. DOS.
Méwilo. Coktel Vision, 1987. Amiga, Amstrad CPC, Atari ST, DOS, Thomson TO7.
Mission US 2: Flight to Freedom. WNET Thirteen/PBS Learning, 2012. Microsoft Windows, Mac OS X.
Playing History 2—Slave Trade. Serious Games, 2013. Microsoft Windows, Mac OS X.

Interviews and Personal Communications

Dudley Alexis, phone, Aug. 17, 2019
Monvelyno Alexis, phone, July 20, 2017
Ellie Blankfort, email, Oct. 24, 2015
Susan Blankfort Camiel, in person, San Diego, CA, Nov. 15, 2015
Maksaens Denis, email, Aug. 22, 2017
Danny Glover, in person, Temecula, CA, Nov. 23, 2013
Kendy Joseph, email, July 14, 2017
Robin Lloyd, phone, June 14, 2017
Pierre Lucson Bellegarde, email (main interview), Aug. 15, 2017; in person, Port-au-Prince, Nov. 8, 2018; other emails, Aug. 2017–Mar. 2019
Ralph Maingrette, email, Aug. 4, 2018
Tariq Marshall, email, Mar. 8, 2017, and June 4, 2017
Jill Murray, email, Apr. 8, 2014
Carey Peck, email, Mar. 6, 2017
Cecilia Peck, email, Mar. 3, 2017
Francine Saillant, email, June 20, 2018
Muriel Tramis, email (main interview), June 14, 2017; other emails, June 2017–Aug. 2019
Kendy Vérilus, email, Sept. 11, 2017
Frantz Voltaire, email, June 19, 2017, and July 8, 2017
Lois Wilcken, email, Apr. 1, 2017

Selected Newspapers and Magazines

AFP
Afro-American
Amiga Computing
The Australian Commodore and Amiga Review
Baltimore Sun
Boston Globe
Box Office
Cahiers du cinéma
California Eagle
Cedar Rapids Gazette
Chicago Defender
Chicago Tribune
Clutch Magazine
Computer + Video Games
Courrier des Afriques
Daily Worker
Dallas Morning News
Denver Post

Film Bulletin (New York)
Film Daily
France-Antilles
Génération4
Haïti en Marche
Haïti Progrès
Haiti Sun
Hollywood Reporter
Jet
La Tribune
L'Est Républicain
Le Figaro
Le Monde
Le Nouvelliste
Le Parisien
Le Point
Le Télégramme
Libération
Los Angeles Sentinel
Los Angeles Times
Mercury News
Miami Herald
Modern Monthly
New York Amsterdam News
New York Herald Tribune
New York Post
New York Times
Palmes Magazine
PC Gamer
Philadelphia Tribune
Picturegoer
Pittsburgh Courier
Plaindealer (Kansas City)
Radio cinéma télévision
Richmond Times-Dispatch
San Diego Union (continued as the *San Diego Union-Tribune*)
Sarasota Herald Tribune
Saturday Review
South Florida Sun-Sentinel
Star Ledger/NJ.com
Variety
Vibe

Selected Websites and Blogs

The [8-Bit] Generation
The Adventure Gamer
Africa Is a Country
Africine.org
Afrik.com
Assassin's Creed Wiki
BelFim
BFI Screenonline
Box Office Mojo
CPC-Power
Collectif2004 Images Haïti
Corbett List
Digital Library of the Caribbean [dLoc]
EdSurge
EGMNow
EmuMovies
Eurogamer
The Game Archives
GameRevolution
Haiti Press Network
Hall of Light: The Database of Amiga Games
Île en île
Internet Archive
Internet Movie Database (IMDb)
IndieWire
Jeux vidéo et des bas
The Junto
Kill Screen
Kotaku
MobyGames
The Obscuritory
Radio Metropole Haïti
The Root
Twitter
USGamer
Vimeo
Vox
Vulture
YouTube

Other Sources

12 Years a Slave, dir. Steve McQueen (2013). DVD, 134 min. Beverly Hills, CA: 20th Century Fox Home Entertainment, 2014.

Aaron, Daniel. *Writers on the Left, Episodes in American Literary Communism*. New York: Octagon, 1974.

Acham, Christine. *Revolution Televised: Prime Time and the Struggle for Black Power*. Minneapolis: Univ. of Minnesota Press, 2004.

Admin C ["Hyppolite"]. "1804: The Hidden History of Haiti." *Haitian History Blog*, Nov. 27, 2017, https://haitianhistory.tumblr.com/post/167951845053/1804-the-hidden-history-of-haiti-1804-the-hidden.

Agronomist, dir. Jonathan Demme (2004). DVD, 90 min. [Los Angeles]: New Line Home Entertainment, 2005.

Alexis, Yveline. "Nationalism and the Politics of Historical Memory: Charlemagne Péralte's Rebellion against the U.S. Occupation of Haiti, 1915–1986." PhD diss., History, Univ. of Massachusetts, 2011.

Alcocer, Rudyard J., Kristen Block, and Dawn Duke, eds. *Celluloid Chains: Slavery in the Americas through Film*. Knoxville: Univ. of Tennessee Press, 2018.

Allison, Tanine. *Destructive Sublime: World War II in American Film and Media*. New Brunswick, NJ: Rutgers Univ. Press, 2018.

Amistad, dir. Steven Spielberg (1997). DVD, 155 min. Universal City, CA: DreamWorks, 1999.

Amazing Grace, dir. Michael Apted (2006), 118 min. Streaming, Amazon Prime.

Antoine-Dunne, Jean. "Sex, Spirit and the Artist in the Films of Felix De Rooy." *Caribbean Quarterly* 61, no. 2–3 (2015): 66–76.

Antonin, Arnold. "Cinema in Haiti." *Small Axe* 12, no. 3 (2008): 87–93.

Antonin, Arnold. "Haïti." In *Les Cinémas de l'Amérique latine: pays par pays, l'histoire, l'économie, les structures, les auteurs, les œuvres*, edited by Guy Hennebelle and Alfonso Gumucio Dagron, 341–45. Paris: Lherminier, 1981.

Antonin, Arnold. *Material para una pre-historia del cine haitiano/Matériel pour une pre-histoire du cinéma haïtien*. Caracas: n.p., 1983.

Araujo, Ana Lucia. *Shadows of the Slave Past: Memory, Heritage, and Slavery*. New York: Routledge, 2014.

Aristide and the Endless Revolution, dir. Nicolas Rossier (2005), 84 min. Streaming, Amazon Prime.

Barcellini, Serge. "Two Memories in the Present: Léger Félicité Sonthonax, Victor Schoelcher." In *The Abolitions of Slavery: From Léger Félicité Sonthonax to Victor Schoelcher, 1793, 1794, 1848*, edited by Marcel Dorigny, 340–52. New York: Berghahn, 2003.

Bales, Jack. *Kenneth Roberts*. New York: Twayne, 1993.

Barlet, Olivier. *African Cinemas: Decolonizing the Gaze*. New York: St. Martin's Press, 2000.

Barlet, Olivier. "The Ambivalence of French Funding." *Black Camera* 3, no. 2 (2012): 205–16.

Barlet, Olivier. "Vers Jollywood? Entretien d'Olivier Barlet avec le cinéaste haïtien Pierre Lucson Bellegarde à propos de Carmen." *Africultures*, July 23, 2013, http://africultures.com/vers-jollywood-11710/.

Baron, Lawrence. *Projecting the Holocaust into the Present: The Changing Focus of Contemporary Holocaust Cinema*. Lanham, MD: Rowman & Littlefield, 2005.

Battle of Algiers, dir. Gillo Pontecorvo (1966). DVD, 125 min. Irvington, NY: Criterion Collection, 2004.

Behlmer, Rudy, ed. *Memo from Darryl F. Zanuck: The Golden Years at Twentieth Century-Fox*. New York: Grove Press, 1993.

Bell, Madison Smartt. *Toussaint Louverture: A Biography*. New York: Pantheon, 2007.

Bellegarde-Smith, Patrick. *Haiti: The Breached Citadel*. Rev. ed. Toronto: Canadian Scholars' Press, 2004.

Bellegarde-Smith, Patrick, and Claudine Michel, eds. *Haitian Vodou: Spirit, Myth, and Reality*. Bloomington: Indiana Univ. Press, 2006.

Benedicty-Kokken, Alessandra, Kaiama L. Glover, Mark Schuller, and Jhon Picard Byron, eds. *The Haiti Exception: Anthropology and the Predicaments of Narrative*. Liverpool: Liverpool Univ. Press, 2016.

Benot, Yves. *La démence coloniale sous Napoléon*. Paris: La Découverte, 1991.

Benot, Yves. *La révolution française et la fin des colonies*. Paris: La Découverte, 1987.

Bernabé, Jean, Raphaël Confiant, and Patrick Chamoiseau. *Éloge de la Créolité*. Paris: Gallimard/Presses universitaires créoles, 1989.

Bernardin, Marc. "Gaming while Black: Has 'Red Dead Redemption 2' Shifted a Toxic Culture?" *Hollywood Reporter*, Dec. 6, 2018, https://www.hollywoodreporter.com/heat-vision/subversive-racial-commentary-red-dead-redemption-2-1165989.

The Birth of a Nation, dir. Nate Parker (2016). DVD, 120 min. Beverly Hills, CA: 20th Century Fox Home Entertainment, 2017.

Blanchet, Alexis. "France." In *Video Games around the World*, edited by Mark J. P. Wolf, 175–92. Cambridge, MA: MIT Press, 2015.

Blankfort, Michael. "Behind the Scenes of *Stevedore*." *Daily Worker*, April 27, 1934.

Blankfort, Michael. "The Education of a Jew." In *Mid-Century: An Anthology of Jewish Life and Culture in Our Times*, edited by Harold U. Ribalow, 45–51. New York: Beechhurst, 1955.

Blankfort, Michael. "Facing the New Audience: Sketches toward an Aesthetic for the Revolutionary Theatre [Pt. 1]." *New Theatre* 1 (June 1934): 11–12 [continued in *New Theatre* 1 (July/Aug. and Nov. 1934): 14–15 and 25–27].

Blankfort, Michael. *The Juggler*. Boston: Little, Brown, 1952.

Blasini, Gilberto M. "Caribbean Cinematic Créolité." *Black Camera* n.s. 1, no. 1 (2009): 70–90.

Bogle, Donald. "Lydia Bailey." In *Blacks in American Films and Television: An Encyclopedia*, 140–41. New York: Garland, 1988.

Bogle, Donald. *Toms, Coons, Mulattoes, Mammies, and Bucks: An Interpretive History of Blacks in American Films*. 5th ed. New York: Bloomsbury, 2016.

Bongie, Chris. *Friends and Enemies: The Scribal Politics of Post/Colonial Literature*. Liverpool: Liverpool Univ. Press, 2008.

Bongie, Chris. *Islands and Exiles: The Creole Identities of Post/Colonial Literature*. Stanford: Stanford Univ. Press, 1998.

Bonilla, Yarimar. "Burning Questions: The Life and Work of Michel-Rolph Trouillot, 1949–2012." *NACLA Report on the Americas* 46, no. 1 (2013): 82–84.

Bonilla, Yarimar. "History Unchained." *Transition* 112, no. 1 (2013): 68–77.

Brown, Vincent. *Tacky's Revolt: The Story of an Atlantic Slave War*. Cambridge, MA: Belknap Press/Harvard Univ. Press, 2020.

Buck-Morss, Susan. *Hegel, Haiti and Universal History*. Pittsburgh: Univ. of Pittsburgh Press, 2009.

Burgoyne, Robert. *The Epic Film in World Culture*. New York: Routledge, 2010.

Burgoyne, Robert. *The Hollywood Historical Film*. Malden, MA: Blackwell, 2008.

Burnard, Trevor G., and John D. Garrigus. *The Plantation Machine: Atlantic Capitalism in French Saint-Domingue and British Jamaica*. Philadelphia: Univ. of Pennsylvania Press, 2016.

Burton, Antoinette M. *Archive Stories: Facts, Fictions, and the Writing of History*. Durham, NC: Duke Univ. Press, 2005.

Cagle, Chris. *Sociology on Film: Postwar Hollywood's Prestige Commodity*. New Brunswick, NJ: Rutgers Univ. Press, 2017.

Camacho, Jorge. "The Falsification of History in Gutiérrez Alea's and Moreno Fraginals' *La última cena*." *Islas* 7, no. 21 (2012), http://www.angelfire.com/planet/islas/Islas21/English/58-67.pdf.

Carlsten, Jennie M., and Fearghal McGarry, eds. *Film, History and Memory*. New York: Palgrave Macmillan, 2015.

Carpentier, Alejo. *Explosion in a Cathedral* (1962). Translated by John Sturrock. Minneapolis: Univ. of Minnesota Press, 2001.

Carpio, Glenda. *Laughing Fit to Kill: Black Humor in the Fictions of Slavery*. New York: Oxford Univ. Press, 2008.

Case départ, dir. Lionel Steketee, Fabrice Eboué, and Thomas N'Gijol (2011). DVD, 90 min. [Paris]: TF1, 2014.

Casper, Drew. *Postwar Hollywood, 1946–1962*. Malden, MA: Blackwell, 2007.

Caute, David. *The Great Fear: The Anti-Communist Purge under Truman and Eisenhower*. New York: Simon and Schuster, 1978.

Célius, Carlo. "Quelques aspects de la nouvelle scène artistique d'Haïti." *Gradhiva* 2015/1 (no. 21): 104–29.

Ceplair, Larry, and Steven Englund. *The Inquisition in Hollywood: Politics in the Film Community, 1930–1960*. Berkeley: Univ. of California Press, 1983.

Cham, Mbye B., ed. *Ex-Iles: Essays on Caribbean Cinema*. Trenton, NJ: Africa World Press, 1992.

Chamoiseau, Patrick. *Chronicle of the Seven Sorrows* [*Chronique des sept misères*, 1986]. Translated by Linda Coverdale. Lincoln: Univ. of Nebraska Press, 2003.

Chamoiseau, Patrick. *Creole Folktales* [*Au temps de l'antan*, 1988]. Translated by Linda Coverdale. New York: W.W. Norton, 1994.

Chamoiseau, Patrick. *Un dimanche au cachot*. Paris: Gallimard, 2007.

Chamoiseau, Patrick. *Slave Old Man* [*L'esclave vieil homme et le molosse*, 1997]. Translated by Linda Coverdale. New York: New Press, 2018.

Chamoiseau, Patrick. *Texaco* [published in French 1992]. Translated by Rose-Myriam Réjouis and Val Vinokur. New York: Pantheon, 1997.

Chamoiseau, Patrick, and Thierry Ségur. *Encyclomerveille d'un tueur*. [Paris]: Delcourt, 2009.

Chanan, Michael. *Cuban Cinema*. Minneapolis: Univ. of Minnesota Press, 2003.

Chapman, Adam. *Digital Games as History: How Video Games Represent the Past and Offer Access to Historical Practice*. New York: Routledge, 2016.

Chapman, Adam. "Privileging Form over Content: Analysing Historical Videogames." *Journal of Digital Humanities* 1, no. 2 (2012): http://journalofdigitalhumanities.org/1-2/privileging-form-over-content-by-adam-chapman/.

Childers, Kristen Stromberg. *Seeking Imperialism's Embrace: National Identity, Decolonization, and Assimilation in the French Caribbean*. New York: Oxford Univ. Press, 2016.

Chivallon, Christine. "Representing the Slave Past: The Limits of Museographical and Patrimonial Discourses." In *At the Limits of Memory: Legacies of Slavery in the Francophone World*, edited by Nicola Frith and Kate Hodgson, 25–48. Liverpool: Liverpool Univ. Press, 2015.

Chris Rock: Bigger and Blacker (1999). 65 min., HBO on Demand.

Chris Rock: Bring the Pain (1996). DVD, 58 min. Beverly Hills, CA: HBO Films/Dreamworks Records, 2002.

Chris Rock: Never Scared (2004). 79 min., HBO on Demand.

Clark, VèVè A. "Haiti's Tragic Overture: (Mis)Representations of the Haitian Revolution in World Drama (1796–1975)." In *Representing the French Revolution: Literature, Historiography, and Art*, edited by James A. W. Heffernan, 237–60. Hanover, NH: Dartmouth College/Univ. Press of New England, 1992.

Clitandre, Nadège. "Haitian Exceptionalism in the Caribbean and the Project of Rebuilding Haiti." *Journal of Haitian Studies* 17, no. 2 (2011): 146–55.

Cottrell, Robert C. *Izzy: A Biography of I. F. Stone*. New Brunswick, NJ: Rutgers Univ. Press, 1992.

Cowans, Jon. *Empire Films and the Crisis of Colonialism, 1946–1959*. Baltimore: Johns Hopkins Univ. Press, 2015.

Crémieux, Anne. "La représentation de l'esclavage dans *Planet of the Apes* et *The Brother from Another Planet*." In *Cinéma et histoire/Film and History*, edited by Melvyn Stokes and Gilles Menegaldo, 232–41. Paris: M. Houdiard, 2008.

Cripps, Thomas. *Making Movies Black: The Hollywood Message Movie from World War II to the Civil Rights Era*. New York: Oxford Univ. Press, 1993.

Cripps, Thomas. *Slow Fade to Black: The Negro in American Film, 1900–1942*. New York: Oxford Univ. Press, 1993.

Custen, George Frederick. *Twentieth Century's Fox: Darryl F. Zanuck and the Culture of Hollywood*. New York: Basic Books, 1997.

Danticat, Edwidge. "[Interview with] Évelyne Trouillot," *Bomb*, Jan. 1, 2005, https://bombmagazine.org/articles/evelyne-trouillot/.

Daut, Marlene. *Tropics of Haiti: Race and the Literary History of the Haitian Revolution in the Atlantic World, 1789–1865*. Liverpool: Liverpool Univ. Press, 2015.

Davis, Chris. "Before They Were Haitians: Examining Evidence for Kongolese Influence on the Haitian Revolution." *Journal of Haitian Studies* 22, no. 2 (2016): 4–36.

Davis, Natalie Zemon. *Slaves on Screen: Film and Historical Vision*. Cambridge, MA: Harvard Univ. Press, 2000.

de Cauna, Jacques. *Toussaint-Louverture, le grand précurseur*. Bordeaux: Éditions Sud-Ouest, 2012.

Delné, Claudy. *La Révolution haïtienne dans l'imaginaire occidental: Occultation, banalisation, trivialisation*. Port-au-Prince: Éditions de l'Université d'État d'Haïti, 2017.

Delsham, Tony, and Abel [Patrick Chamoiseau]. *Le retour de Monsieur Coutcha*. Fort-de-France: Éditions MGG, 1984.

Desormeaux, Daniel. "The First of the (Black) Memorialists." *Yale French Studies*, no. 107 (2005): 131–45.

Dick, Bernard F. *The Screen Is Red: Hollywood, Communism, and the Cold War*. Jackson: Univ. Press of Mississippi, 2016.

Dinnerstein, Leonard. *Antisemitism in America*. New York: Oxford Univ. Press, 1994.

Doho, Gilbert. "Le Fou, le rebelle, l'enfant et la Révolution haïtienne," *Présence africaine* n.s., no. 169 (2004): 227–40.

Donovan, Tristan. *Replay: The History of Video Games*. East Sussex, UK: Yellow Ant, 2010.

Dubois, Laurent. *Avengers of the New World: The Story of the Haitian Revolution*. Cambridge, MA: Belknap Press/Harvard Univ. Press, 2004.

Dubois, Laurent. *Haiti: The Aftershocks of History*. New York: Metropolitan, 2012.

Dudziak, Mary L. *Cold War Civil Rights: Race and the Image of American Democracy*. Princeton, NJ: Princeton Univ. Press, 2000.

Dunne, Philip. *Take Two: A Life in Movies and Politics*. New York: McGraw-Hill, 1980.

Dupuy, Alex. *Haiti, from Revolutionary Slaves to Powerless Citizens: Essays on the Politics and Economics of Underdevelopment, 1804–2013*. New York: Routledge, 2014.

Dupuy, Alex. *The Prophet and Power: Jean-Bertrand Aristide, the International Community, and Haiti*. Lanham, MD: Rowman & Littlefield, 2007.

Dupuy, Alex. *Rethinking the Haitian Revolution: Slavery, Independence, and the Struggle for Recognition*. Lanham, MD: Rowman & Littlefield, 2019.

Dyson, Michael Eric. *Debating Race with Michael Eric Dyson*. New York: Basic Civitas, 2007.

Eddins, Crystal N. "Runaways, Repertoires, and Repression: Marronnage and the Haitian Revolution, 1766–1791." *Journal of Haitian Studies* 25, no. 1 (2019): 4–38.

Egenfeldt-Nielsen, Simon, Jonas H. Smith, and Susana P. Tosca. *Understanding Video Games: The Essential Introduction*. 2nd ed. New York: Routledge, 2008.

Eldridge, David. *Hollywood's History Films*. New York, Palgrave Macmillan, 2006.

Elliot, Andrew B. R. *The Return of the Epic Film: Genre, Aesthetics and History in the Twenty-First Century*. Edinburgh: Edinburgh Univ. Press, 2014.

Endore, Guy. *Babouk*. Foreword by Jamaica Kincaid. Afterword by David B. Gaspar and Michel-Rolph Trouillot. Originally published 1934; New York: Monthly Review, 1991.

Everett, Anna. "Race." In *The Routledge Companion to Video Game Studies*, edited by Mark J. P. Wolf and Bernard Perron, 396–406. New York: Routledge, 2014.

Everett, Anna. "Serious Play: Playing with Race in Contemporary Gaming Culture." In *Handbook of Computer Game Studies*, edited by Joost Raessens and Jeffrey H. Goldstein, 311–25. Cambridge, MA: MIT Press, 2005.

Everett, Anna, and S. Craig Watkins. "The Power of Play: The Portrayal and Performance of Race in Video Games." In *The Ecology of Games: Connecting Youth, Games, and Learning*, edited by Katie Salen, 141–66. Cambridge, MA: MIT Press, 2008.

Fain, Kimberly. *Black Hollywood: From Butlers to Superheroes, the Changing Role of African American Men in the Movies*. Santa Barbara, CA: Praeger, 2015.

Fatal Assistance (*Assistance mortelle*), dir. Raoul Peck. DVD, 100 min. [Paris]: Velvet Film, 2013.

Fatton Jr., Robert. "The Haitian Authoritarian *Habitus* and the Contradictory Legacy of 1804." *Journal of Haitian Studies* 10, no. 1 (2004): 22–43.

Ferrer, Ada. *Freedom's Mirror: Cuba and Haiti in the Age of Revolution*. New York: Cambridge Univ. Press, 2014.

Fick, Carolyn E. *The Making of Haiti: The Saint Domingue Revolution from Below*. Knoxville: Univ. of Tennessee Press, 1990.

Figueroa, Víctor. *Prophetic Visions of the Past: Pan-Caribbean Representations of the Haitian Revolution*. Columbus: Ohio State Univ. Press, 2015.

Fischer, Sibylle. "Unthinkable History? The Haitian Revolution, Historiography, and Modernity on the Periphery." In *A Companion to African-American Studies*, edited by Lewis R. Gordon and Jane Anna Gordon, 360–76. Malden, MA: Blackwell, 2006.

Fleming, Crystal M. *Resurrecting Slavery: Racial Legacies and White Supremacy in France*. Philadelphia: Temple Univ. Press, 2017.

Ford, Dom. "'eXplore, eXpand, eXploit, eXterminate': Affective Writing of Postcolonial History and Education in Civilization V." *Game Studies* 16, no. 2 (2016): http://gamestudies.org/1602/articles/ford.

Forsdick, Charles. "Haiti and Comics: The Search for (New Graphic) Narratives." *Yale French Studies*, nos. 131/132 (2017), 189–214.

Forsdick, Charles. "Toussaint Louverture in a Globalized Frame: Reading the Revolutionary as Icon." *Contemporary French and Francophone Studies* 19, no. 3 (2015): 325–34.

Forsdick, Charles, and Christian Høgsbjerg. "Sergei Eisenstein and the Haitian Revolution: 'The Confrontation between Black and White Explodes into Red.'" *History Workshop Journal* 78, no. 1 (2014): 157–85.

Forsdick, Charles, and Christian Høgsbjerg. *Toussaint Louverture: A Black Jacobin in the Age of Revolutions*. Chicago: Pluto/Univ. of Chicago Press, 2017.

Fouchard, Jean. *The Haitian Maroons: Liberty or Death*. New York: E.W. Blyden Press, 1981.

Francaviglia, Richard V., and Jerome L. Rodnitzky, eds. *Lights, Camera, History: Portraying the Past in Film*. College Station: Texas A&M Univ. Press, 2007.

Frasca, Gonzalo. "Videogames of the Oppressed: Critical Thinking, Education, Tolerance and Other Trivial Issues." In *First Person: New Media as Story, Performance, and Game*, edited by Noah Wardrip-Fruin and Pat Harrigan, 85–94. Cambridge, MA: MIT Press, 2004.

Free State of Jones, dir. Gary Ross. DVD, 140 min. Universal City, CA: Universal Pictures Home Entertainment, 2016.

Frith, Nicola, and Kate Hodgson, eds. *At the Limits of Memory: Legacies of Slavery in the Francophone World*. Liverpool: Liverpool Univ. Press, 2015.

Gaffield, Julia. *Haitian Connections in the Atlantic World: Recognition after Revolution*. Chapel Hill: Univ. of North Carolina Press, 2015.

Gainot, Bernard, Marcel Dorigny, Jean Ehrard, and Alyssa Sepinwall. "Lumières et esclavage." *Annales historiques de la Révolution française*, no. 380 (2015): 149–69.

Garraway, Doris L. *The Libertine Colony: Creolization in the Early French Caribbean*. Durham, NC: Duke Univ. Press, 2005.

Garrigus, John D. *Before Haiti: Race and Citizenship in French Saint-Domingue*. New York: Palgrave Macmillan, 2006.

Gates, Henry Louis. *The Signifying Monkey: A Theory of Afro-American Literary Criticism*. New York: Oxford Univ. Press, 1988.

Gates, Racquel. "Bringing the Black: Eddie Murphy and African American Humor on *Saturday Night Live*." In *Saturday Night Live and American TV*, edited by Nick Marx, Matt Sienkiewicz, and Ron Becker, 151–72. Bloomington: Indiana Univ. Press, 2013.

Geggus, David P. *Haitian Revolutionary Studies*. Bloomington: Indiana Univ. Press, 2002.

Gentleman's Agreement, dir. Elia Kazan (1947). DVD, 118 min. Beverly Hills, CA: 20th Century Fox, [2002].

George, Nelson. *Blackface: Reflections on African Americans and the Movies*. New York: HarperCollins, 1994.

Ghachem, Malick W. *The Old Regime and the Haitian Revolution*. New York: Cambridge Univ. Press, 2012.

Ghosts of Cité Soleil, dir. Asger Leth. DVD, 88 min. n.p.: Imagine Entertainment, 2006.

Gilbert, Lisa. "'*Assassin's Creed* Reminds Us that History Is Human Experience': Students' Senses of Empathy while Playing a Narrative Video Game." *Theory and Research in Social Education* 47, no. 1 (2019): 108–37.

Gillota, David. *Ethnic Humor in Multiethnic America*. New Brunswick, NJ: Rutgers Univ. Press, 2013.

Girard, Philippe R. *The Slaves Who Defeated Napoleon: Toussaint Louverture and the Haitian War of Independence, 1801–1804*. Tuscaloosa: Univ. of Alabama Press, 2011.

Goldberg, Alan Bruce. "Commercial Folklore and Voodoo in Haiti: International Tourism and the Sale of Culture." PhD diss., Anthropology, Indiana Univ., 1981.

Good Hair, dir. Jeff Stillson (cowritten by and starring Chris Rock), 2009. DVD, 96 min. Santa Monica, CA: HBO Films/Lionsgate, 2010.

Gray, Kishonna L. "Power in the Visual: Examining Narratives of Controlling Black Bodies in Contemporary Gaming." *Velvet Light Trap* 81 (2018): 62–66.

Gray, Kishonna L., and David J. Leonard, eds. *Woke Gaming: Digital Challenges to Social Injustice*. Seattle: Univ. of Washington Press, 2018.

Greene, Eric. *Planet of the Apes as American Myth: Race, Politics, and Popular Culture*. 2nd ed. Middletown, CT: Wesleyan Univ. Press, 1998.

Griggs, Earl Leslie, and Clifford H. Prator, eds. *Henry Christophe and Thomas Clarkson: A Correspondence*. New York: Greenwood Press, 1968.

Guttenplan, D. D. *American Radical: The Life and Times of I. F. Stone*. New York: Farrar, Straus and Giroux, 2009.

Haggins, Bambi. *Laughing Mad: The Black Comic Persona in Post-Soul America*. New Brunswick, NJ: Rutgers Univ. Press, 2007.

Halle, Randall. "Offering Tales They Want to Hear: Transnational European Film Funding as Neo-Orientalism." In *Global Art Cinema: New Theories and Histories*, edited by Rosalind Galt and Karl Schoonover, 303–19. New York: Oxford Univ. Press, 2010.

Hammar, Emil. "Counter-Hegemonic Commemorative Play: Marginalized Pasts and the Politics of Memory in the Digital Game *Assassin's Creed: Freedom Cry*." *Rethinking History* 21, no. 3 (2017): 372–95.

Hector, Michel, ed. *La Révolution française et Haïti: filiations, ruptures, nouvelles dimensions*. Port-au-Prince: Société haïtienne d'histoire et de géographie/H. Deschamps, 1995.

Hector, Michel, and Laënnec Hurbon, eds. *Genèse de l'état haïtien (1804–1859)*. Paris: Maison des sciences de l'homme, 2009.

Hémar, Virginie. *Arnold Antonin: Le cinéma de la liberté*. Port-au-Prince: Éditions de l'Université d'État d'Haïti, 2013.

Henrichs, Hendrik. "Review Essay: A Children's Book and a Soap Opera as Public History? Two Dutch Films on Slavery, *Tula, the Revolt, The Price of Sugar* (*Hoe duur was de suiker*)." *The Public Historian* 36, no. 2 (2014): 117–21.

Hermogène, Feguenson. "L'Université haïtienne face aux Études filmiques." 2018. Unpublished paper.

Heuman, Gad J. "Slave Rebellions." In *The Routledge History of Slavery*, edited by Gad J. Heuman and Trevor G. Burnard, 220–33. New York: Routledge, 2011.

Holden, Stacy E. "The Cold War in Barbary: Re-Casting the Tripolitan War in Kenneth Roberts's *Lydia Bailey*." Lecture presented at King Abdul Aziz Foundation, Casablanca, 2016 (copy provided by author).

Holdenried, Joshua, and Nicolas Trépanier. "Dominance and the Aztec Empire: Representations in *Age of Empires II* and *Medieval II: Total War*." In *Playing with the Past: Digital Games and the Simulation of History*, edited by Matthew Kapell and Andrew B. R. Elliott, 107–19. New York: Bloomsbury, 2013.

Hollywood Shuffle, dir. Robert Townsend (1987). 121 min. Streaming, via Amazon Prime.

Horne, Gerald. *Paul Robeson: The Artist as Revolutionary*. London: Pluto, 2016.

Hughes-Warrington, Marnie. *History Goes to the Movies: Studying History on Film*. New York: Routledge, 2007.

Hughey, Matthew W. *The White Savior Film: Content, Critics, and Consumption*. Philadelphia: Temple Univ. Press, 2014.

Humphries, Reynold. *Hollywood's Blacklists: A Political and Cultural History*. Edinburgh: Edinburgh Univ. Press, 2008.

Hunt, Kara. "'Not a Funny Place to Live': An Interview with Chris Rock." *Comedy Studies* 5, no. 2 (2014): 190–97.

Hunt, Kara. "Off the Record: A Critical Perspective on *Def Comedy Jam*." *Journal of Popular Culture* 48, no. 5 (2015): 836–58.

Jackson, Maurice, and Jacqueline Bacon, eds. *African Americans and the Haitian Revolution: Selected Essays and Historical Documents*. New York: Routledge, 2010.

James, C. L. R., *Toussaint Louverture: The Story of the Only Successful Slave Revolt in History: A Play in Three Acts*. Edited by Christian Høgsbjerg. Durham, NC: Duke Univ. Press, 2013.

[Jauhiainen], Ilmari. "Missed Classic 26: *Mewilo* (1987)—Introduction." *The Adventure Gamer*, Aug. 5, 2016, https://advgamer.blogspot.com/2016/08/missed-classic-26-mewilo-1987.html.

[Jauhiainen], Ilmari. "Call for Questions for Muriel Tramis." *The Adventure Gamer*, Apr. 6, 2017, https://advgamer.blogspot.com/2017/04/call-for-questions-for-muriel-tramis.html.

Jean-Charles, Régine. "The Myth of Diaspora Exceptionalism: Wyclef Jean Performs *Jaspora*." *American Quarterly* 66, no. 3 (2014): 835–52.

Jenkins, Henry. "Game Design as Narrative Architecture." In *First Person: New Media as Story, Performance, and Game*, edited by Noah Wardrip-Fruin and Pat Harrigan, 118–30. Cambridge, MA: MIT Press, 2004.

Jenkins, Tricia. *The CIA in Hollywood: How the Agency Shapes Film and Television*. Austin: Univ. of Texas Press, 2012.

Jenson, Deborah. *Beyond the Slave Narrative: Politics, Sex, and Manuscripts in the Haitian Revolution*. Liverpool: Liverpool Univ. Press, 2011.

Johnson, Erica R. *Philanthropy and Race in the Haitian Revolution*. n.p.: Palgrave Macmillan, 2018.

Joseph-Gabriel, Annette. "Beyond the Great Camouflage: Haiti in Suzanne Césaire's Politics and Poetics of Liberation." *Small Axe* 20, no. 2 (2016): 1–13.

Kahana, Jonathan. *The Documentary Film Reader: History, Theory, Criticism*. New York: Oxford Univ. Press, 2016.

Kaisary, Philip. *The Haitian Revolution in the Literary Imagination: Radical Horizons, Conservative Constraints.* Charlottesville: Univ. of Virginia Press, 2014.

Kaisary, Philip. "The Haitian Revolution and Tomás Gutiérrez Alea's *La última cena.*" In *Racialized Visions: Haiti and the Hispanic Caribbean*, edited by Vanessa K. Valdés. Albany: SUNY Press, 2020, 113–33.

Kaisary, Philip. "The Slave Narrative and Filmic Aesthetics: Steve McQueen, Solomon Northup, and Colonial Violence." *MELUS: Multi-Ethnic Literature of the United States* 42, no. 2 (2017): 94–114.

Kallay, Jasmina. *Gaming Film: How Games are Reshaping Contemporary Cinema.* Basingstoke, UK: Palgrave Macmillan, 2013.

Kapell, Matthew, and Andrew B. R. Elliott, eds. *Playing with the Past: Digital Games and the Simulation of History.* New York: Bloomsbury, 2013.

Katz, Jonathan. *The Big Truck that Went By: How the World Came to Save Haiti and Left Behind a Disaster.* New York: Palgrave Macmillan, 2013.

Keane, Stephen. *Cinetech: Film, Convergence and New Media.* New York: Palgrave Macmillan, 2007.

Kee, Kevin, ed. *Pastplay: Teaching and Learning History with Technology.* Ann Arbor: Univ. of Michigan Press, 2014.

Kempshall, Chris. *The First World War in Computer Games.* New York: Palgrave Macmillan, 2015.

Kerri, Amanda. "How Historical Games Integrate or Ignore Slavery." *Rock Paper Shotgun*, Jan. 17, 2017, https://www.rockpapershotgun.com/2017/01/17/how-historical-games-integrate-or-ignore-slavery/.

Killens, John Oliver. "Hollywood in Black and White (September 20, 1965)." In *Cinema Nation: The Best Writing on Film from* The Nation, *1913–2000*, edited by Carl Bromley, 150–57. New York: Thunder's Mouth/Nation, 2000.

King, Geoff, and Tanya Krzywinska, eds. *Screenplay: Cinema/Videogames/Interfaces.* London: Wallflower, 2002.

King, Stewart. "Toussaint L'Ouverture before 1791: Free Planter and Slave-Holder." *Journal of Haitian Studies* 3/4 (1997–1998): 66–71.

Knepper, Wendy. *Patrick Chamoiseau: A Critical Introduction.* Jackson: Univ. Press of Mississippi, 2012.

Kraft, Tobias. "Towards the Digital Atlantic? New Orleans's Open World in *Assassin's Creed III: Liberation HD.*" In *New Orleans and the Global South: Caribbean, Creolization, Carnival*, edited by Ottmar Ette and Gesine Müller, 259–73. Hildesheim, Germany: Georg Olms, 2017.

Kutulas, Judy. *The Long War: The Intellectual People's Front and Anti-Stalinism, 1930–1940.* Durham, NC: Duke Univ. Press, 1995.

Kwon, Yun Kyoung. "Ending Slavery, Narrating Emancipation: Revolutionary Legacies in the French Antislavery Debate and 'Silencing the Haitian Revolution,' 1814–48." PhD diss., History, Univ. of Chicago, 2012.

Ladouceur, Rosny. "Un personnage historique au cœur d'un prochain film de Peck." *Loop*, June 16, 2017, http://www.loophaiti.com/content/un-personnage-historique-au-coeur-dun-prochain-film-de-peck.

Lafontant-Médard, Michaëlle. "Cinema in Haiti: 1899 to 1982/A Thematic Analysis of Rassoul Labuchin's *Anita*." Translated by Latif Ndiaye. In *Ex-Iles: Essays on Caribbean Cinema*, edited by Mbye B. Cham, 59–97, 134–54. Trenton, NJ: Africa World Press, 1992.

Landsberg, Alison. "Politics and the Historical Film: *Hotel Rwanda* and the Form of Engagement." In *A Companion to the Historical Film*, edited by Robert A. Rosenstone and Constantin Parvulescu, 9–29. Malden, MA: Wiley-Blackwell, 2013.

Landy, Marcia. *The Historical Film: History and Memory in Media*. New Brunswick, NJ: Rutgers Univ. Press, 2001.

Lauro, Sarah Juliet. "Digital Saint-Domingue: Playing Haiti in Videogames." *SX Archipelagos*, no. 2 (2017): http://smallaxe.net/sxarchipelagos/issue02/playing-haiti.html.

Lauro, Sarah Juliet. "Specters of Slave Revolt." In *Jordan Peele's* Get Out*: Political Horror*, edited by Dawn Keetley, 147–59. Columbus: Ohio State Univ. Press, 2020.

Le Glaunec, Jean-Pierre. *L'armée indigène: La défaite de Napoléon en Haïti*. Montreal: Lux, 2014.

Leinders, Jeroen. *Tula: The Revolt*. Translated by Brian Doyle-Du Breuil. London: HopeRoad, 2013.

Lev, Peter. *Twentieth Century-Fox: The Zanuck-Skouras Years, 1935–1965*. Austin: Univ. of Texas Press, 2013.

Lipke, Alan Thomas. "The Strange Life and Stranger Afterlife of King Dick Including His Adventures in Haiti and Hollywood with Observations on the Construction of Race, Class, Nationality, Gender, Slang Etymology and Religion." MA thesis, Univ. of South Florida, 2013.

Littleton, Darryl. *Black Comedians on Black Comedy: How African-Americans Taught Us to Laugh*. New York: Applause Theatre & Cinema, 2006.

Logan, Rayford W. *The Diplomatic Relations of the United States with Haiti, 1778–1841*. Chapel Hill: Univ. of North Carolina Press, 1941.

Lubin, Maurice A. "Les premiers rapports de la nation haïtienne avec l'étranger." *Journal of Inter-American Studies* 10, no. 2 (1968): 277–305.

Lutz, Georges. "Un avatar de la domestication des animaux: les chiens à esclaves: 'Buscadores' de Cuba et de Saint Domingue." In *Haïti: Première République Noire*, edited by Marcel Dorigny, 61–81. Paris: Société française d'histoire d'outre-mer, 2003.

Malkowski, Jennifer, and TreaAndrea M. Russworm, eds. *Gaming Representation: Race, Gender, and Sexuality in Video Games*. Bloomington: Indiana Univ. Press, 2017.

Manigat, Sabine. "Les femmes au cours de la période révolutionnaire." In *Genèse de l'état haïtien (1804–1859)*, edited by Michel Hector and Laënnec Hurbon, 313–19. Paris: Maison des sciences de l'homme, 2009.

Martin, Gretchen. *Dancing on the Color Line: African American Tricksters in Nineteenth-Century American Literature*. Jackson: Univ. Press of Mississippi, 2015.

Martin, Jean-Clément, and Laurent Turcot. *Au cœur de la révolution: Les leçons d'histoire d'un jeu vidéo*. Paris: Vendémiaire, 2015.

Martin, Michael. "Podium for the Truth? Reading Slavery and the Neocolonial Project in the Historical Film: *Queimada!* (*Burn!*) and *Sankofa* in Counterpoint." *Third Text* 23, no. 6 (2009): 717–31.

Martin, Michael T., and David C. Wall. "The Politics of Cine-Memory: Signifying Slavery in the History Film." In *A Companion to the Historical Film*, edited by Robert A. Rosenstone and Constantin Parvulescu, 445–67. Malden, MA: Wiley-Blackwell, 2013.

McAlister, Elizabeth A. "From Slave Revolt to a Blood Pact with Satan: The Evangelical Rewriting of Haitian History." In *The Idea of Haiti: Rethinking Crisis and Development*, edited by Millery Polyné, 203–42. Minneapolis: Univ. of Minneapolis Press, 2013.

McCall, Jeremiah B. *Gaming the Past: Using Video Games to Teach Secondary History*. New York: Routledge, 2011.

McCusker, Maeve. *Patrick Chamoiseau: Recovering Memory*. Liverpool: Liverpool Univ. Press, 2007.

Ménard, Nadève. *Écrits d'Haïti: perspectives sur la littérature haïtienne contemporaine (1986–2006)*. Paris: Karthala, 2012.

Middle Passage [*Passage de milieu*], dir. Guy Deslauriers, script by Claude Chonville and Patrick Chamoiseau (1999). DVD, 78 min. English version, New York: HBO Video, 2003.

Miller, Christopher L. *The French Atlantic Triangle: Literature and Culture of the Slave Trade*. Durham, NC: Duke Univ. Press, 2008.

Miller, Marilyn G. "Truths, Lies and Telling Silences in Gutiérrez Alea's *The Last Supper* and Pontecorvo's *Burn!*" *Studies in Spanish & Latin American Cinemas* 10, no. 1 (2013): 59–74.

Metzger, Scott Alan, and Richard J. Paxton. "Gaming History: A Framework for What Video Games Teach about the Past." *Theory and Research in Social Education* 44, no. 4 (2016): 532–64.

Mir, Rebecca, and Trevor Owens. "Modeling Indigenous Peoples: Unpacking Ideology in *Sid Meier's Colonization*." In *Playing with the Past: Digital Games and the Simulation of History*, edited by Matthew Kapell and Andrew B. R. Elliott, 91–103. New York: Bloomsbury, 2013.

Mirzoeff, Nicholas, and Jack Halberstam. "Decolonize Media: Tactics, Manifestos, Histories." *Cinema Journal* 57, no. 4 (2018): 120–23.

Montfort, Nick. *Twisty Little Passages: An Approach to Interactive Fiction*. Cambridge, MA: MIT Press, 2003.

Moreau de Saint-Méry, Médéric-Louis-Elie. *A Civilization that Perished: The Last Years of White Colonial Rule in Haiti*. Translated, edited, and abridged by Ivor D. Spencer. Lanham, MD: Univ. Press of America, 1985.

Mukherjee, Souvik. "Playing Subaltern: Video Games and Postcolonialism." *Games and Culture* 13, no. 5 (2018): 504–20.

Mukherjee, Souvik. "Video Games and Slavery." *Transactions of the Digital Games Research Association* 2, no. 3 (2016): 243–60.

Munford, Clarence J. *Race and Reparations: A Black Perspective for the 21st Century*. Trenton, NJ: Africa World Press, 1996.

Munro, Martin. "The Apocalyptic Creole, from Dessalines to the Chimères." *Diaspora: A Journal of Transnational Studies* 17, no. 1 (2008): 105–20.

Munro, Martin. "Interdependence and Intertextuality in Lyonel Trouillot's *Bicentenaire*." *Small Axe* 12, no. 3 [27] (2008): 42–52.

Murder in Pacot, dir. Raoul Peck (2014). DVD, 130 min. Berlin: Velvet Film/Filmgalerie 451, 2016.

Murray, Soraya. *On Video Games: The Visual Politics of Race, Gender and Space*. London: I.B. Tauris, 2018.

Najman, Charlie. *Haïti, Dieu seul me voit: Récit*. Paris: Balland, 1995.

Nakamura, Lisa. *Digitizing Race: Visual Cultures of the Internet*. Minneapolis: Univ. of Minnesota Press, 2008.

Narcisse, Evan. "A Closer Look at How Three *Assassin's Creed* Games Have Handled Slavery." *Kotaku*, Mar. 31, 2014, https://kotaku.com/why-assassins-creed-freedom-crys-use-of-slavery-was-1555358077.

Narcisse, Evan. "Come On, Video Games, Let's See Some Black People I'm Not Embarrassed by." *Kotaku*, Mar. 29, 2012, https://kotaku.com/come-on-video-games-let-s-see-some-black-people-i-m-n-5897227.

Narcisse, Evan. "A Game that Showed Me My Own Black History." *Kotaku*, Dec. 19, 2013, https://kotaku.com/a-game-that-showed-me-my-own-black-history-1486643518.

Narcisse, Evan. "This *Assassin's Creed* Heroine Is a Great Black Game Character. Here's How It Happened [interview with J. Murray]." *Kotaku*, Feb. 27, 2013, https://kotaku.com/this-assassin-s-creed-heroine-is-a-great-black-game-cha-5987083.

Navasky, Victor S. *Naming Names*. New York: Viking, 1980.

Nesbitt, Nick. *Universal Emancipation: The Haitian Revolution and the Radical Enlightenment*. Charlottesville: Univ. of Virginia Press, 2008.

Nora, Pierre. *Les lieux de mémoire*. 3 vols. Paris: Éditions Gallimard, 1992.

Obenson, Tambay. "Forgotten Films that Need to Be Re-Released: Med Hondo's 1979 Colorful Musical Epic *West Indies*." *Indiewire*, Nov. 13, 2012.

Obenson, Tambay. "Nigerian Director Jeta Amata Currently Shooting $15mill Toussaint l'Ouverture Film in Haiti," *Indiewire*, Feb. 3, 2013.

Oli. "Soluce rétrocompatible: *Méwilo* (Atari ST, Amiga, Amstrad)." *Jeux vidéo et des bas*, Feb. 12, 2015, https://jeux.dokokade.net/2015/02/12/soluce-retrocompatible-mewilo-atari-st-amiga-amstrad/.

Oostindie, Gert. "Slave Resistance, Colour Lines, and the Impact of the French and Haitian Revolutions in Curaçao." In *Curaçao in the Age of Revolutions, 1795–1800*, edited by Wim Klooster and Gert Oostindie, 1–22. Leiden: KITLV Press, 2011.

Paddington, Bruce, and Keith Q. Warner. "The Emergence of Caribbean Feature Films." *Black Camera* 1, no. 1 (2009): 91–108.

Past, Mariana. "Reclaiming the Haitian Revolution: Race, Politics and History in Twentieth Century Caribbean Literature." PhD diss., Romance Languages, Duke Univ., 2006.

Past, Mariana. "What's in a Name? Reading Transformative Farce in Césaire's *La tragédie du Roi Christophe* and Najman's *Royal Bonbon*." In *Latin American Studies: Critiques of Cinema, Literatures, Politics and Revolution*, edited by David Gallagher, 183–99. Bethesda, MD: Academica, 2012.

Payton, Claire A. "Building Corruption in Haiti." *NACLA Report on the Americas* 51, no. 2 (2019): 182–87.

Peabody, Sue. *Madeleine's Children: Family, Freedom, Secrets, and Lies in France's Indian Ocean Colonies*. New York: Oxford Univ. Press, 2017.

Philogene, Jerry. "'Dead Citizen' and the Abject Nation: Social Death, Haiti, and the Strategic Power of the Image." *Journal of Haitian Studies* 21, no. 1 (2015): 100–126.

Pierre, Hancy. "Le cinéma dans la tourmente et la misère des politiques de loisirs en Haïti." *Le Nouvelliste*, Oct. 13, 2017, https://lenouvelliste.com/article/176977/le-cinema-dans-la-tourmente-et-la-misere-des-politiques-de-loisirs-en-haiti.

Pierrot, Grégory. *The Black Avenger in Atlantic Culture*. Athens: Univ. of Georgia Press, 2019.

Plummer, Brenda Gayle. *Haiti and the United States: The Psychological Moment*. Athens: Univ. of Georgia Press, 1992.

Polyné, Millery. *From Douglass to Duvalier: U.S. African Americans, Haiti, and Pan Americanism, 1870–1964*. Gainesville: Univ. Press of Florida, 2010.

Polyné, Millery. *The Idea of Haiti: Rethinking Crisis and Development*. Minneapolis: Univ. of Minneapolis Press, 2013.

Popkin, Jeremy D. *A Concise History of the Haitian Revolution*. Malden, MA: Wiley-Blackwell, 2012.

Popkin, Jeremy D. "Madison Smartt Bell's Haitian Revolution Trilogy." *Fiction and Film for French Historians* 1, no. 3 (2011): https://h-france.net/fffh/maybe-missed/madison-smartt-bells-haitian-revolution-trilogy/.

Posch, Doris. "Emerging Film Cultures: Spotlight on Post-Disaster Haiti." *International Journal of Cultural Studies* 21, no. 1 (2018): 27–41.

Posch, Doris. "The Jollywood Manifesto: Trans-Local Film Cultures in Haiti's Emerging Cinemas." *Култура/Culture* 12 (2015): 157–71.

Posch, Doris. "Oral Storytelling, the Gaze and the Everyday: Documentary Filmmaking in Haiti." In *Dynamiques culturelles dans les cinémas africains du XXè siècle/Cultural Dynamics in African Cinemas of the 21st Century*, edited by Ute Fendler and Christoph Vatter, 113–28. Saarbrücken, Germany: Universitätsverlag des Saarlandes, 2018.

Prézeau-Stephenson, Barbara. "Contemporary Art as Cultural Product in the Context of Haiti," translated by Rachel Douglas. *Small Axe* 12, no. 3 [27] (2008): 94–104.

Pressley-Sanon, Toni. *Zombifying a Nation: Race, Gender and the Haitian Loas on Screen*. Jefferson, NC: McFarland, 2016.

Pressley-Sanon, Toni, and Sophie Saint-Just. *Raoul Peck: Power, Politics, and the Cinematic Imagination*. Lanham, MD: Lexington, 2015.

Price of Sugar (*Hoe duur was de suiker*), dir. Jean van de Velde. DVD, 120 min. [Hilversum]: Entertainment One, 2013.

Raessens, Joost, and Jeffrey H. Goldstein, eds. *Handbook of Computer Game Studies*. Cambridge, MA: MIT Press, 2005.

Ramsey, Kate. *The Spirits and the Law: Vodou and Power in Haiti*. Chicago: Univ. of Chicago Press, 2011.

Réimpression de l'ancien Moniteur. 32 vols. Paris: H. Plon, 1853–63.

Renda, Mary A. *Taking Haiti: Military Occupation and the Culture of U.S. Imperialism, 1915–1940*. Chapel Hill: Univ. of North Carolina Press, 2001.

Rhines, Jesse Algernon. *Black Film, White Money*. New Brunswick, NJ: Rutgers Univ. Press, 1996.

Ribalow, Harold Uriel. "American Jewish Writers and Their Judaism." *Judaism* 3, no. 4 (1954): 418–26.

Roberts, Kenneth Lewis. *Lydia Bailey*. Garden City, NY: Doubleday, 1947.

Robeson, Paul. *The Undiscovered Paul Robeson: An Artist's Journey, 1898–1939*. New York: Wiley, 2001.

Robinson, Meredith N. "Ciné woulé, ciné en progrès: An Investigation of the Francophone Caribbean Film Circuit, 1968–2010." *Small Axe* 33 (2010): 58–60.

Rock, Chris. *Rock This!* New York: Hyperion, 1997.

Rodriguez, Junius P. "Tula (Rigaud) (d. 1795)." In *Encyclopedia of Slave Resistance and Rebellion*, edited by Junius P. Rodriguez, 2: 525–26. Westport, CT: Greenwood, 2006.

Roffman, Peter, and Jim Purdy. *The Hollywood Social Problem Film: Madness, Despair, and Politics from the Depression to the Fifties*. Bloomington: Indiana Univ. Press, 1981.

Rogers, Dominique, and Stewart King. "Housekeepers, Merchants, Rentières: Free Women of Color in the Port Cities of Colonial Saint-Domingue, 1750–1790." In *Women in Port: Gendering Communities, Economies, and Social Networks in Atlantic Port Cities, 1500–1800*, edited by Douglas Catterall and Jodi Campbell, 357–97. Leiden: Brill, 2012.

Roots, dir. Marvin J. Chomsky, John Erman, David Greene, and Gilbert Moses (1977). Originally aired, ABC. Streaming, Amazon Prime.

Roots, dir. Bruce Beresford, Thomas Carter, Phillip Noyce, and Mario Van Peebles (2016). Originally aired, History Channel. Streaming, Amazon Prime.

Rosenstone, Robert A. *History on Film/Film on History*. 3rd ed. New York: Routledge, 2017.

Rosenstone, Robert A. *Revisioning History: Film and the Construction of a New Past*. Princeton, NJ: Princeton Univ. Press, 1994.

Rosenstone, Robert A. *Visions of the Past: The Challenge of Film to Our Idea of History*. Cambridge, MA: Harvard Univ. Press, 1995.

Ross, Steven J. *Hollywood Left and Right: How Movie Stars Shaped American Politics*. New York: Oxford Univ. Press, 2011.

Saillant, Francine. *Le mouvement noir au Brésil (2000–2010): Réparations, droits et citoyenneté*. [Québec]: Presses de l'Université Laval, 2014.

Saillant, Francine. "Transmettre la mémoire de l'esclavage par la recherche collaborative." Unpublished essay.

Salvador, Phil. "Freedom: Rebels in the Darkness." *The Obscuritory*, July 30, 2015, https://obscuritory.com/strategy/freedom-rebels-in-the-darkness/.

Sankofa, dir. Haile Gerima (1993). DVD, 125 min. Ennetbaden, Switzerland: Trigon Film, 2017.

Schloss, Rebecca H. "The February 1831 Slave Uprising in Martinique and the Policing of White Identity." *French Historical Studies* 30, no. 2 (2007): 203–36.

Schuller, Mark. *Killing with Kindness: Haiti, International Aid, and NGOs*. New Brunswick, NJ: Rutgers Univ. Press, 2012.

Schut, Kevin. "Strategic Simulations and Our Past: The Bias of Computer Games in the Presentation of History." *Games and Culture* 2, no. 3 (2007): 213–35.

Scott, Ellen C. *Cinema Civil Rights: Regulation, Repression, and Race in the Classical Hollywood Era*. New Brunswick, NJ: Rutgers Univ. Press, 2015.

Sepinwall, Alyssa Goldstein. *The Abbé Grégoire and the French Revolution: The Making of Modern Universalism*. Berkeley: Univ. of California Press, 2005.

Sepinwall, Alyssa Goldstein. "Atlantic Amnesia? French Historians, the Haitian Revolution, and the 2004–2006 Capes Exam." *Proceedings of the Western Society for French History* 34 (2006): 300–314.

Sepinwall, Alyssa Goldstein. "*Burn!*" In *Encyclopedia of Slave Resistance and Rebellions*, edited by Junius P. Rodriguez, 1: 86–88. Westport CT: Greenwood, 2006.

Sepinwall, Alyssa Goldstein. *Haitian History: New Perspectives*. New York: Routledge, 2012.

Sepinwall, Alyssa Goldstein. "If This Is a Woman: Évelyne Trouillot's *The Infamous Rosalie* and the Lost Stories of New World Slavery." *Fiction and Film for French Historians: A Cultural Bulletin* 5, no. 4 (2015): https://h-france.net/fffh/classics/if-this-is-a-woman-evelyne-trouillots-the-infamous-rosalie-and-the-lost-stories-of-new-world-slavery/.

Sepinwall, Alyssa Goldstein. "The Specter of Saint-Domingue: American and French Reactions to the Haitian Revolution." In *The World of the Haitian Revolution*, edited by Norman Fiering and David Geggus, 317–38. Bloomington: Indiana Univ. Press, 2009.

Sepinwall, Alyssa Goldstein. "Still Unthinkable? The Haitian Revolution and the Reception of Michel-Rolph Trouillot's *Silencing the Past*." *Journal of Haitian Studies* 19, no. 2 (2013): 75–103.

Sepinwall, Alyssa Goldstein. "Why Audiences Must See Nate Parker's *Birth of a Nation*, Despite the Controversy." *History News Network*, Oct. 12, 2016, http://historynewsnetwork.org/article/164115.

Seraphin, Hugues. "Hispaniola: The Future Tourism Destination of the Caribbean?" *Journal of Tourism Consumption and Practice* 3, no. 2 (2011): 38–44.

Shohat, Ella, and Robert Stam. *Unthinking Eurocentrism: Multiculturalism and the Media*. 2nd ed. New York: Routledge, 2014.

Short, K. R. M. *Feature Films as History*. New York: Routledge, 2014.

Smith, Jeff. *Film Criticism, the Cold War, and the Blacklist: Reading the Hollywood Reds*. Berkeley: Univ. of California Press, 2014.

Smith, Judith E. *Becoming Belafonte: Black Artist, Public Radical*. Austin: Univ. of Texas Press, 2014.

Smith, Judith E. *Visions of Belonging: Family Stories, Popular Culture, and Postwar Democracy, 1940–1960*. New York: Columbia Univ. Press, 2004.

Smith, Valerie. *Representing Blackness: Issues in Film and Video*. New Brunswick, NJ: Rutgers Univ. Press, 1997.

Solomon, Aubrey. *Twentieth Century-Fox: A Corporate and Financial History*. Metuchen, NJ: Scarecrow Press, 1988.

Sommers, Jeffrey W. *Race, Reality, and Realpolitik: U.S.-Haiti Relations in the Lead Up to the 1915 Occupation*. Lanham, MD: Lexington, 2016.

Srivastava, Neelam. "Anti-Colonial Violence and the 'Dictatorship of Truth' in the Films of Gillo Pontecorvo/Interview with Pontecorvo." *Interventions: International Journal of Postcolonial Studies* 7, no. 1 (2005): 97–117.

Stam, Robert, and Louise Spence. "Colonialism, Racism and Representation." *Screen* 24, no. 2 (1983): 2–20.

Stevenson, Brenda E. "Filming Black Voices and Stories: Slavery on America's Screens." *Journal of the Civil War Era* 8, no. 3 (2018): 488–520.

Stoler, Ann Laura. *Along the Archival Grain: Epistemic Anxieties and Colonial Common Sense*. Princeton, NJ: Princeton Univ. Press, 2009.

Stone, Alan. "Last Battle: Gillo Pontecorvo's *Burn!*" *Boston Review* 29, no. 2 (2004): http://bostonreview.net/archives/BR29.2/stone.html.

Sugar Cane Alley (*Rue cases-nègres*), dir. Euzhan Palcy (1983). DVD, 103 min. [New York]: New Yorker Video, 2004.

Tamango, dir. John Berry (1958), 100 min. Streaming, Fandor (via Amazon Prime).

Thomas, Steven W. "Cinematic Slavery and the Importance of *Belle*." In *The Cinematic Eighteenth Century*, edited by Srividhya Swaminathan and Steven W. Thomas, 170–86. New York: Routledge, 2017.

Thornton, John K. "African Soldiers in the Haitian Revolution." *Journal of Caribbean History* 25, nos. 1 and 2 (1991): 59–80.

Thornton, John K. "'I Am the Subject of the King of Congo': African Political Ideology and the Haitian Revolution." *Journal of World History* 4, no. 2 (1993): 181–214.

Toplin, Robert Brent. *History by Hollywood: Screening the American Past*. 2nd ed. Urbana: Univ. of Illinois Press, 2010.

Toplin, Robert Brent. "In Defense of the Filmmakers." In *Lights, Camera, History: Portraying the Past in Film*, edited by Richard V. Francaviglia and Jerome L. Rodnitzky, 113–35. College Station: Texas A&M Univ. Press, 2007.

Tramis, Muriel. *Au cœur du giraumon*. Paris: Dagan, 2011.

Tramis, Muriel. *Contes créoles et cruels*. Paris: Dagan, 2013.

Trépanier, Nicolas. "The Assassin's Perspective: Teaching History with Video Games." *Perspectives on History* 52, no. 5 (2014): https://www.historians.org/publications-and-directories/perspectives-on-history/may-2014/the-assassins-perspective.

Trouillot, Évelyne. *The Infamous Rosalie* (*Rosalie l'infâme*, 2003). Translated by M. A. Salvodon. Lincoln: Univ. of Nebraska Press, 2013.

Trouillot, Lyonel. *Bicentenaire: Roman*. Arles, France: Actes sud, 2004.

Trouillot, Michel-Rolph. *Haiti, State against Nation: The Origins and Legacy of Duvalierism*. New York: Monthly Review, 1989.

Trouillot, Michel-Rolph. *Silencing the Past: Power and the Production of History*. Boston, MA: Beacon, 1995.

Tryon, Chuck. *Reinventing Cinema: Movies in the Age of Media Convergence*. New Brunswick, NJ: Rutgers Univ. Press, 2009.

Twa, Lindsay J. *Visualizing Haiti in U.S. Culture, 1910–1950*. Burlington, VT: Ashgate, 2014.

Ulysse, Gina Athena. *Why Haiti Needs New Narratives: A Post-Quake Chronicle*. Middletown, CT: Wesleyan Univ. Press, 2015.

Ulysse, Jude. "'I Wait for Me': Visualizing the Absence of the Haitian Revolution in Cinematic Text." PhD diss., Social Justice Education, Univ. of Toronto, 2017.

Uricchio, William. "Simulation, History and Computer Games." In *Handbook of Computer Game Studies*, edited by Joost Raessens and Jeffrey H. Goldstein, 327–38. Cambridge, MA: MIT Press, 2005.

Vera, Hernan, and Andrew Gordon. *Screen Saviors: Hollywood Fictions of Whiteness*. Lanham, MD: Rowman & Littlefield, 2003.

Vogel, Joseph. "The Confessions of Quentin Tarantino: Whitewashing Slave Rebellion in *Django Unchained*." *Journal of American Culture* 41, no. 1 (2018): 17–27.

von Lünen, Alexander, Katherine J. Lewis, Benjamin Litherland, and Pat Cullum, eds. *Historia Ludens: The Playing Historian*. New York: Routledge, 2019.

Wainwright, A. Martin. *Virtual History: How Videogames Portray the Past*. New York: Routledge, 2019.

Walsh, John Patrick. *Free and French in the Caribbean: Toussaint Louverture, Aimé Césaire, and Narratives of Loyal Opposition*. Bloomington: Indiana Univ. Press, 2013.

Wardrip-Fruin, Noah, and Pat Harrigan. *First Person: New Media as Story, Performance, and Game*. Cambridge, MA: MIT Press, 2004.

Watkins, Mel. *On the Real Side: A History of African American Comedy*. Chicago: Lawrence Hill, 1999.

Weems, Robert E. *Desegregating the Dollar: African American Consumerism in the Twentieth Century*. New York: New York Univ. Press, 1998.

West, Dennis. "Slavery and Cinema in Cuba: The Case of Gutiérrez Alea's *The Last Supper*." *The Western Journal of Black Studies* 3, no. 2 (1979): 128–33.

Whelchel, Aaron. "Using Civilization Simulation Video Games in the World History Classroom." *World History Connected* 4, no. 2 (2007): 1–14.

Whitaker, Robert. "Backward Compatible: Gamers as a Public History Audience." *Perspectives on History* 54, no. 1 (2016): https://www.historians.org/publications-and-directories/perspectives-on-history/january-2016/backward-compatible-gamers-as-a-public-history-audience.

White, Ashli. *Encountering Revolution: Haiti and the Making of the Early Republic.* Baltimore: Johns Hopkins Univ. Press, 2010.

Why We Laugh. Black Comedians on Black Comedy, dir. Robert Townsend, DVD, 86 min. [n.p.]: Code Black Productions, 2009.

Wiesel, Elie. "Art and the Holocaust: Trivializing Memory." *New York Times*, June 11, 1989, https://www.nytimes.com/1989/06/11/movies/art-and-the-holocaust-trivializing-memory.html.

Wiesel, Elie. "Interview with Alyssa Sepinwall" (Carlsbad, CA, Apr. 19, 2007). YouTube, https://www.youtube.com/watch?v=sXhG7nXHdFc.

Wilcken, Lois E. "Spirit Unbound: New Approaches to the Performance of Haitian Folklore." In *Caribbean Dance from Abakuá to Zouk: How Movement Shapes Identity*, edited by Susanna Sloat, 114–23. Gainesville: Univ. Press of Florida, 2002.

Williams Jr, Roland L. *Black Male Frames: African Americans in a Century of Hollywood Cinema.* Syracuse, NY: Syracuse Univ. Press, 2015.

Willis, Sharon. "Moving Pictures: Spectacles of Enslavement in American Cinema." In *The Cambridge Companion to Slavery in American Literature*, edited by Ezra F. Tawil, 219–35. Cambridge: Cambridge Univ. Press, 2016.

Winnerling, Tobias, and Florian Kerschbaumer, eds. *Early Modernity and Video Games.* Cambridge: Cambridge Scholars, 2014.

Wood, Marcus. *The Horrible Gift of Freedom: Atlantic Slavery and the Representation of Emancipation.* Athens: Univ. of Georgia Press, 2010.

Wolf, Mark J. P. *The Medium of the Video Game.* Austin: Univ. of Texas Press, 2002.

Wolk, Sarah. "Moms Mabley and the Civil Rights Movement." MA thesis, History, California State Univ.–San Marcos, 2012.

Wright, Meredith N. "Fugitive Filmmaking: Third Cinema and the Caribbean." In *Rethinking Third Cinema: The Role of Anti-Colonial Media and Aesthetics in Postmodernity*, edited by Frieda Ekotto and Adeline Koh, 173–94. Berlin: Lit, 2009.

X, Malcolm. *Malcolm X Speaks: Selected Speeches and Statements.* Edited by George Breitman. New York: Grove, 1965.

INDEX

Page numbers in italics refer to figures.

ABOUT THE AUTHOR

Courtesy of California State University San Marcos

ALYSSA GOLDSTEIN SEPINWALL is professor of history at California State University–San Marcos. Before coming to CSUSM, she earned a BA at the University of Pennsylvania and MA and PhD degrees in History from Stanford University, and held a postdoctoral fellowship at the University of Pennsylvania. Her research specialties include modern Haitian history, the French and Haitian Revolutions, History and Film, French colonialism, French-Jewish history, the Enlightenment, and the history of gender. She is the author of *The Abbé Grégoire and the French Revolution: The Making of Modern Universalism* (UC Press, 2005; published in French by Les Perséïdes, 2008), *Haitian History: New Perspectives* (Routledge, 2012), and numerous articles in edited volumes and in journals such as the *Journal of Modern History*, the *Journal of Haitian Studies*, the *Journal of American Culture*, the *Annales historiques de la Révolution française*, and *Outre-Mers. Revue d'histoire*. Sepinwall is a past winner of CSUSM's Harry E. Brakebill Distinguished Professor Award (the university's top honor for faculty). She is a past member of the editorial board for *French Historical Studies* and has served on committees of the Society for French Historical Studies, American Society for Eighteenth-Century Studies, French Colonial Historical Society, Haitian Studies Association, Western Society for French History, and the American Historical Association. She currently serves on the advisory boards for H-France's *Fiction and Film for Scholars of France* and the *Revue d'histoire haïtienne/Haitian History Journal*.

CPSIA information can be obtained
at www.ICGtesting.com
Printed in the USA
BVHW032255230421
605450BV00003B/4

9 781496 833112